Nationality Group Survival in Multi-Ethnic States

edited by
Edward Allworth

Published in cooperation with the Program on Soviet Nationality Problems, Columbia University

The Praeger Special Studies program—utilizing the most modern and efficient book production techniques and a selective worldwide distribution network—makes available to the academic, government, and business communities significant, timely research in U.S. and international economic, social, and political development.

Nationality Group Survival in Multi-Ethnic States

Shifting Support Patterns in the Soviet Baltic Region

PRAEGER SPECIAL STUDIES IN INTERNATIONAL POLITICS AND GOVERNMENT

Praeger Publishers New York London

Library of Congress Cataloging in Publication Data

Main entry under title:

Nationality group survival in multi-ethnic states.

(Praeger special studies in international politics and government)
Bibliography: p.
1. Minorities—Russia. 2. Nationalism—Baltic States. I. Allworth, Edward.
JN6520.M5N265 1977 301.45'1'0947 77-4952
ISBN 0-275-24040-1

PRAEGER PUBLISHERS
200 Park Avenue, New York, N.Y. 10017, U.S.A.

Published in the United States of America in 1977
by Praeger Publishers, Inc.

789 038 987654321

Printed in the United States of America

PREFACE

The lessons to be learned from this inquiry into nationality group survival and the internal mechanisms of group maintenance in one region can be applied to any part of the Soviet Union or comparable composite (multinational) states, with necessary adjustments. Those findings are offered here in the real hope that the approach used in the research and this analysis of supports will be taken up and developed further by others.

The chain of events leading up to publication of this book begins in early autumn 1975 in the (graduate) Seminar in Soviet Nationality Problems, Columbia University. The membership of that group, consisting of two cultural historians, a Uralic specialist, and three political scientists, was soon augmented by two additional highly competent younger scholars—a sociologist and a politics major—from other universities (Maryland and Yale). Frequent consultations, regular group discussions, and repeated exchanges of ideas and drafts among the authors preceded presentation of a preliminary version of most of these chapters in public forums. An early draft of Chapter 1 was read first to the Conference on Nationality and Population Change in the USSR, December 5, 1975, sponsored by the Program on Soviet Nationality Problems, Columbia University, and chaired by geography professor Robert A. Lewis. Useful comments regarding this chapter came on that occasion from Professors Walker Connor, State University of New York at Brockport, Alec Nove, Glasgow University, and Dr. Abram Jaffe, Bureau of Applied Social Research, Columbia University. On May 20, 1976, all eight of the present coauthors participated when short preliminary drafts of Chapters 3, 4, 5, 6, and 7 were presented before a lively session of the large international Fifth Conference on Baltic Studies, held in New York City (cosponsored by the Association for the Advancement of Baltic Studies and Program on Soviet Nationality Problems). At that time, systematic, helpful comments were offered by Professors Oleh Fedyshyn, Richmond College, City University of New York, and Andris Skreija, University of Nebraska (Omaha). The full-sized research chapters, completed late in summer 1976 on the basis of those drafts, were already sufficiently lengthy and encumbered with scholarly apparatus and the various authors far enough scattered to make further mutual exchange and criticism, though perhaps desirable, impossible. Among the authors, only the editor, therefore, read all of the book before publication, but the year of close cooperation among the authors undeniably affected the conception and writing of all eight chapters and drew them together.

Sources employed here include, besides those in non-Soviet languages, materials in the original Estonian, Hebrew, Lithuanian, Russian, and Yiddish, as well as in translations from those five languages and Latvian. All the authors use original Russian-language sources and several know some of the different nationality languages found in the Baltic region.

Certain chapters of this study (especially 6, 7, and 8) give considerable attention to those nationalities that have been denied adequate Soviet recognition or franchise to be termed "eponymous," or namesake, nationalities (groups whose names are applied to suitable ethnic territorial-administrative units assigned in the region studied). The "eponymous nationalities" prominent in this study are those situated mainly within, and labeling, three Soviet socialist republics—Estonians, Latvians, and Lithuanians. Russians and nationalities are referred to generically under the term "ethnic groups," but Russians are not considered to be one of the nationalities. Occasionally, the word "Balt" or "Balts" is inserted for convenient variety in designating one or more of these eponymous nationalities, without regard to the linguistic fact that Estonians belong in another category entirely.

Generosity of the kind that makes all cooperative academic enterprises work effectively has been shown in this one not only by those named above but by others. Professors Wesley Fisher, Columbia University, Walter Jaskiewicz, Fordham University, Tõnu Parming, University of Maryland, and Jānis Krésliņš, Council on Foreign Relations, kindly gave essential expert advice when it was needed. Pearl Spiro interrupted her own heavy research schedule to order and prepare the substantial bibliography.

The facilities, research materials, and support of the Program on Soviet Nationality Problems, funded by a grant from the Ford Foundation to aid in systematic nationality studies, which helped make the entire present effort possible, are gratefully acknowledged. The publishers of the journal *Soviet Jewish Affairs* and those of Universe Books (for *The Last Exodus*, by Leonard Schroeter; New York, 1974) have kindly authorized reproduction of the documents in Appendix C.

CONTENTS

LIST OF TABLES AND FIGURES

Table		Page

Nationality Group Survival in Multi-Ethnic States

CHAPTER

1

FLEXIBLE DEFENSES OF A NATIONALITY

Edward Allworth

Modern nationalities display extraordinary durability. Their resilience under pressure for change, and capacity for retaining identity even as they alter, appear nearly boundless.[1] That stability results from group reflexes activating a kind of internal system of adaptive defenses. It seems paradoxical that this is less true in democracies, perhaps, than under authoritarian regimes, like those in China, Iran, South Africa, and the USSR. There, certain ethnic groups take active, often methodical steps to repress or weaken others. Nevertheless, the intangibility of the contemporary idea of nationality, plus those natural defensive antibodies, make such a group virtually indestructible. Ethnic persistence remains a reality today despite the fact that, in recent decades, substantial fractions of certain nationalities have, at least temporarily, relinquished aspects of one corporate ethnic identity, such as group language, for another. Therefore, the primary concerns of this book become: What serves to regenerate each nationality's overall self-identity complex? How does that system mobilize itself for defending group integrity? Under what circumstances and at which times can such activation occur? Those expressions of group vitality or vulnerability refer directly to the workings of the nationality question in general, as well as in particular cases.

The nationality question in which ethnic groups comprising a multinational state are enmeshed is a complex, human mechanism consisting of the major problems or issues involved in group identity, intergroup relations and parity, or regulation, necessarily connected with the phenomenon of nationality.[2] In an ethnically composite state, such as the contemporary USSR, such cardinal problems (group deprivation, discriminatory treatment, dilution, and the like) during any specific period affect at least two ethnic groups, usually more, or hold serious implications for them. This sets the USSR apart from polities embracing but one or two groups. The nationality question is being regarded basically as a domestic matter. It is regional in scope and essence. The question persists in a given area so long as certain conditions prevail. Within one state if the combination of a nationality with a ruling ethnic group remains or when two or more nationalities coexist, the question lives on. This holds true whether or not those several nationalities are subject to a dominant ethnic group. A ruling group in the Soviet Union or in the People's Republic of China cannot appropriately be called one of "the nationalities," for "a nationality" in that context connotes equality with like groups or signifies subordination to a master group. Hereafter, the term "nationalities" in the USSR, therefore, excludes Russians, whereas "ethnic groups" includes them.

The nationality question, as such, concerns above all the basic group satisfaction or dissatisfaction of a nationality in its immediate and extended environment (that environment often reaches out to points beyond the nationality's core area, where threatening or nurturing groups exert significant influence specifically noticeable to the particular nationality). For that and other reasons, the nationality question exists primarily or entirely in the collective views held by members of a given nationality rather than in those of others. The interpretations of foreign observers or the opinions of policy-making authorities within the same state, but belonging to an ethnic group different from the nationality or nationalities under their jurisdiction and control, cannot comprise the question.

Attitudes and actions of political authorities from a dominant ethnic group (the outsiders), as well as those of other nationalities, can, of course, create some problems and influence the way in which the insiders—the given nationality—see their question. Regardless of the possibility that the greatest effect upon the satisfaction or dissatisfaction in some particular period may originate outside the given nationality, the heart of "the question" resides basically within the nationality concerned. Consequently, except perhaps under catastrophic natural or man-made conditions temporarily resulting in widespread famines, epidemics, massive deportations, or general warfare, the question itself cannot be regarded completely as a matter of influence generated solely outside that nationality. Ultimate responsibility for group satisfaction, and surely for survival, rests with the nationality itself. Dissatisfaction among modern nationalities does not arise merely because of their ethnic awareness. Until a background of corporate disability or discrimination has been well established and fastened upon that ethnic identity, simple consciousness of group identity alone should not provoke nationality dissatisfaction. Well-known paired antipathies, like those between Poles and Russians, Armenians and Georgians, Estonians and Azerbaijanians in the USSR, seem to be aroused by the slightest signals. Those stimuli belong more appropriately, in the support system of a nationality, to forces of regulation than to those of relationships, possibly because of the rigid, categorical, and, today, unreasoning nature of these very specific polarizations (see Table 1.1).

TABLE 1.1

Main Group Support Factors Functioning in the Nationality Question

Factors
Identifying and physical
Characteristic human group physiognomy and other common behavior or traits
Group language
Group cultural pattern
Group configuration, concentration, and size
Kindred concentrations outside the group's home area within or beyond external state boundaries
Geopolitical position of the region of concentration, if any
Relativity—actual or believed
Parity/imparity among nationalities, based upon the economy, technology, specialization, and the like
Dependence/autonomy (degree of participation in decision making) of different nationalities
Association and ties with, or isolation from, other nationalities
Contact and links between a nationality and the ruling ethnic group, if any
Solidarity among the leaders and the led within a nationality
Regulatory—catalyzing or pacifying
Tolerance/prejudice, trust/mistrust, liking/dislike, pride/inferiority, indifference/concern, and other discriminatory attitudes
Public recognition and opinion
Vigor/lethargy, solidarity/fragmentation, tenacity/weakness
Social stability/instability and organization or arrangements
Policies and measures of the authorities

Source: Compiled by the author.

THE SOVIET CASE

In the USSR, the fact that the nationality question is made up neither predominantly nor exclusively of ideas and actions of the ruling ethnic group can readily be seen in the foregoing definition of a "nationality," in the reminder about standing hostility between various Soviet pairs, and in two sorts of additional evidence. Notwithstanding decades of disclaimers, the question, to begin with, is acknowledged by current and recent Soviet leaders to be virile and active. Both Communist Party of the Soviet Union (CPSU) General Secretary Leonid I. Brezhnev and Anastas I. Mikoyan, formerly member of the CPSU Central Committee's Politburo and Chairman of the Supreme Soviet's Presidium, clarified this publicly in their statements commemorating the fiftieth anniversary of the USSR's founding, issued in December and June 1972.[3] At that time, General Secretary Brezhnev spoke of nationality problems still to be solved and accommodations yet to be made between the interests of the nationalities and the Soviet state. Former Supreme Soviet Chairman Mikoyan alluded to "relapses into dominant-nation chauvinism and local nationalism." Presumably, these high-level remarks condemning aloofness among Russians and other Soviet ethnic groups confirm that the old drive aimed at arbitrarily dividing Soviet nationalities ever further from each other has been slowed. That enforced separation leading sometimes to partition was meant to facilitate the ruling Russian group's easy management of the nationalities. Separateness rates a lower priority now among ideologists, as the present official preference for ethnic homogeneity replaces the previous emphasis. Nationality differences once kept alive by the Soviet government and Communist Party now are muted. The authorities would seemingly at last prefer to wipe the nationality question out of existence or show it to be resolved. This would require reuniting and denationalizing, at least, the many related groups now separately distinguished, but that has proved impossible under Soviet modernization. To a striking degree, the peculiar sort of modernization undertaken and partially accomplished in the USSR may be held accountable for the persistence of many Soviet nationality problems. "Soviet modernization" has provided advanced technology and means of mass communication to a ruling group and its leaders anachronistically backward and traditional in their human understanding and methods.

Access to those modern means and devices, under democracy available broadly, remain in the USSR the monopoly of an old-style coterie embodied in this rigid political system. Only the agents of force, power, violence, and dogma in the Soviet Union—the military, the police, state capitalists, large industry's managers, and the privileged small core of Communist Party leadership—are in a position to express their interests openly. This exclusiveness accounts for the wretched position falling to the most courageous, educated, or creative dissenters, for their legitimate criticisms or complaints, under Soviet Communism, are met with stony intolerance.[4] That outlook allows the leaders to substitute verbiage and slogans for reality, to accept, in the 1970s, a master-servant relationship in nationality affairs. This antiquated arrangement is lightly covered over with claims of an internationalism, which amounts in reality to ideologically camouflaged Russian Messianism and imperialism, scarcely updated.

Besides official confirmation that the Soviet nationality question continues to flourish comes a second variety of testimony from the widespread expressions of nationality discontent. These started to be heard persistently in the 1960s from Soviet Armenians, Crimean Tatars, Estonians, Germans, Jews, Latvians, Lithuanians, Meskhetian Turks, Turkmens, Ukrainians, and others, especially regarding "the question." They corroborate the spread of festering dissatisfaction in significant units forming the Soviet Union's varied ethnic structure with respect to nationality problems.[5]

What sort of effect does that dissatisfaction have in the authoritarian Soviet state? Can such satisfaction or dissatisfaction exert a greater impact in a multi-ethnic democracy than in a police-supported dictatorship like the USSR? To what extent do modernized smaller states inhabited by three or four coherent nationalities or by a nationality plus a ruling group differ from large, technologically advancing multinational states in this respect? Further analysis of the nationality question's workings may help to answer one side (the nationality's side in particular) of queries like these. In its composition, the nationality question, by definition, normally remains constant and basically unalterable. But, changes occur in the configuration of the question. They manifest themselves through shifts in emphasis affecting the scale of satisfaction/dissatisfaction characteristic of the question at a particular time and place. A nationality's position on this scale of satisfaction depends indirectly upon the major nationality problems comprising the question but directly on the attendant supporting factors closely connected with those problems at a certain time.

SUPPORT FACTORS

A "support factor" is one among a set of fairly lasting influences especially important throughout a nationality's milieu, during a certain period, in sustaining group integrity and stamina, while the dynamism of a set as a whole signals the degree of satisfaction/dissatisfaction very recently experienced by the group.

Although these supporting factors may exert a circular impact upon one another, they fall generally into three separate categories: identifying and physical factors, relativity factors (real or imagined), and regulatory (catalyzing and pacifying) factors (see Table 1.1).

Without the support of one or more of the identifying and physical factors listed in Table 1.1, no nationality can long survive. Moreover, identifying and physical factors are brought into close combination with relativity and regulatory ones. Relative population size may have a bearing on policies at a particular period, just as human group appearance often stimulates prejudice, one of the most active regulatory factors. Relativity factors function both at the levels of necessity (actual need experienced by a nationality) and believed imparity. Notwithstanding the fact that a group has achieved economic equality or better throughout its membership, a sense frequently exists that it deserves more than certain rival people (Baltic groups regularly express feelings of superiority when comparing themselves with Transcaucasians or Central Asians—see Chapter 8). A distinction of identifying-physical factors is their absolute nature, taken without reference to neighboring or competing facts, and their basis in human physiology and geography. Between identifying-physical and regulatory factors the differences are obvious, for regulation entails disposing of the human situation in some way through neglect or manipulation. The identifying and physical factor is a fundamental tangibility, a condition setter or placer receiving action upon itself rather than acting, usually from regulatory agencies reacting to genuine or supposed relativity factors.

Is not the regulatory factor, embodied in actual application or state policies, the opposite of a supporting factor for a nationality in the workings of the composite (multi-ethnic) society? When the rulers regulate, their act may call into play a supportive response within the nationality affected. But can the act of regulation be categorized as a supporting one unless it is seen as just such a provocation or stimulus for healthy defensive reaction? (Where must such an act be placed on this scale if the expected defensive response from a nationality is not forthcoming, for example?) In practice, a regulatory support factor can also emanate from measures taken by the authorities if the measures serve to facilitate group development rather than simply to replace group initiative. Certainly, some policies provide means for building group strength. Such tools as official native-language newspapers may comprise supporting rather than destroying factors for most nationality groups. Patently, certain governmental and party acts may indirectly or directly support, while others undermine, the solidity of a group. Insofar as obviously negative acts cause a group to mobilize and bolster itself, they qualify as supporting factors. Overprotection by authorities has served to debilitate a group's resolve to save itself by removing motivation for struggling to retain a collective existence. This occurs especially if that policy is paralleled by provision of all or most wants, resulting in a deadening of sensitivity (defensive dissatisfaction) to threats from the actor (the ruling group). Such destructive patronage has imperiled the ethnic vitality of some American Indian nationalities, many groups of northern Siberia, and others in whom self-reliance was insufficiently fostered or self-instilled.

Relativity support factors concern much besides matters of parity or dominance and subordination among ethnic groups of a state. The ongoing relationships between groups entail antipathies or attractions, friction or imagined injury, familial ties, and many other connections between adjacent or distant groups. Relations between ethnic groups are said by some to constitute the entire nationality question. Soviet ideologists have long equated one sort of relativity—material inequity—with the whole nationality question.[6] They argued at the Twelfth Congress of the Russian Communist Party in 1923 (and much later) that disappearance of economic discrepancy throughout nationality areas in a country such as the USSR meant the end of the nationality question and its problems. Though the economic status of different Soviet nationalities still varies widely in the 1970s, officials claim these differences to be negligible. In spite of the arrival of alleged economic equalization, the nationality question, especially in its tendency toward greater dissatisfaction, can be seen to lose stability rather quickly. Now, it should be accepted that relativity makes up but one of the three principal sides to this question, whether such relations link people merely in perception of disadvantage or superiority or in real disparity among comparable and relevant groups. Nor is that relativity limited to material matters.

In summary, emphasis placed upon certain supporting factors will shift within these three categories (identifying-physical, relativity, and regulatory), as well as between them. Those transfers from one category to another of the principal dependence affect the equilibrium between satisfaction and dissatisfaction to the most noticeable extent. Such shifting serves as a barometer of the pressures building or abating in the nationality question. Heavy pressure felt by a nationality in the regulatory factors, if negative, influences it to place special stress upon some identifying-physical supports—language, population, culture, and the like. At the same time that stimulus generates a strong countervailing thrust, by a vital nationality, also in the regulatory sphere, usually within the factors of group attitude and public opinion. Insecurity experienced by an ethnic group (nationality) from threats to the identifying-physical supports causes great apprehension over survival, and in vigorous groups results in a notable shift of emphasis to supports in the relativity category. Discontent specifically tied to relativity support factors stimulates mainly the mobilization of emphasis to be placed in the regulatory category upon factors of discrimination, social unrest, and public opinion.

When shifts of emphasis occur between either supporting factors or the major categories of them, the nationality concerned generally may be only passively aware of the change, or even the need for it. Opinion leaders and other elites within the group are more likely to become conscious of quite gradual changes in emphasis. Drastic, sudden movements come to the attention of larger numbers. In the Soviet situation, emphasis transfers are unlikely to be contrived or directed by an organized faction within the nationality, unless it is very small (like the Crimean Tatar group for example). Nevertheless, circulation of samizdat (self-published) material and other expressions of distress from church, synagogue, or nationality represent initiatives that undoubtedly focus attention within the group upon specific nationality problems. Those actions may sooner or later lead to movement, by the nationality as a whole, from dependence upon one set of group supports to another.

Barring extraordinary disruptions, the readiness and ability of each nationality both to recognize and adjust to the realities of the nationality question—shifting emphasis when necessary from one combination of supports to another—determine the tenacity, durability, even stamina, of a group faced with the multiple pressures constantly playing upon it. Almost any modern nationality, again in the absence of major calamities, can expect to avoid corporate obliteration indefinitely if it possesses sufficient vitality and realistic awareness to adapt to the immediate and extended environment affecting it. An opportune change of reliance upon various supports, therefore, constitutes a sign of vitality for the nationality involved when one combination of factors becomes more burdensome than supportive. These adaptations have direct ties to the satisfaction/dissatisfaction range characterizing the entire nationality question in the region.

What are the consequences when group adjustment slips too far out of synchronization with actual conditions in a region? Satisfaction in the nationality question apparently conservatizes a group with respect to change, lessening the likelihood of its freely altering the emphasis it places upon the functioning main support factors. Prolonged group satisfaction stabilizes the focus in the nationality question. But complacency makes adaptation to changing times more and more difficult, possibly traumatic, the longer the term of contentment lasts. Conversely, the group dissatisfaction leading to a deliberate transferring of emphasis within any operational complex of supports can contribute greatly to the nationality's flexibility in evolving circumstances. This, in turn, enhances its opportunities not only for survival but for gaining strength under adverse conditions.

The primary danger to a nationality's future apparently lies in an unjustified feeling that all is well, complicated by an accompanying onset of ethnic arteriosclerosis (inflexibility). Over recent decades, a Belorussian acquiescence in weakening several identifying features may offer an example. Paradoxically, far more healthful would be a ceaseless bout, albeit fairly uncomfortable, with some persistent virus of group dissatisfaction or outside threat to physical welfare. With its false sense of security, prolonged satisfaction nearly always undermines a group's set of supports or creates gaps among them. Conscious or unconscious awareness of this deterioration should stimulate anxiety, which reaches most of the group. Such complacency in this way creates as its own antibodies the pangs of dissatisfaction, but perhaps not always in time. If the group allows itself to move toward the extremes on the satisfaction/dissatisfaction scale, one of two forms of dangerous maladjustment can develop: lethargic, unhealthy complacency or desperate discontent. Extreme dissatisfaction converts itself into self-destructive rage or immobilizing apathy (as it did among Hungarians, Chechens, and others) and, possibly, ultimate disintegration. Like exaggerated satisfaction-complacency, uncontrolled discontent requires drastic remedial action if the group is to reverse a rapid slide toward dissolution. A point on the satisfaction/dissatisfaction scale close to exact balance, but slightly on the side of dissatisfaction, offers reasonable stability, with moderate but continuing change consistent with ordinary times.

These constant adjustments to conditions in the state are the "ethnic processes" that must be considered in approaching the nationality question. They emerge long before the setting in of terminal symptoms, such as the "assimilation" and "consolidation" afflicting a group in its declining years. Those latter stages are dogmatically designated in recent Soviet writings as the totality of "ethnic processes" (earlier referred to by other specialists as "cultural convergence" and "loss and retention of ethnic self-consciousness."[7] The adjustments best called "ethnic processes" refer to accommodations required in the recent modernizing phases of ethnic group life. They include, at times, adaptation to new forms and means of communication; shifts from reliance upon political autonomy to cultural emphasis or effective participation within a larger political system; slight or substantial moves between religious and folk-literary, spiritual supports; acceptance or retention of rural life and values (if rejection implies loss of identity); and numerous others of minor or major import.

In connection with those virtually unending moves of a vital group adjusting to its environment, stimulated by degrees of satisfaction or dissatisfaction, it seems plausible to conclude that supporting factors operate in combination, rather than individually, to effect changes of focus in the nationality question. Among the whole range of factors, certain types probably never make the greatest impact on the question. Nevertheless, a particular support within the operating set of factors undoubtedly receives greater emphasis and carries more of the burden in one period than another for sustaining a nationality and satisfying its group needs. Possibly no one major factor is always indispensable in a particular dimension or degree. Except during extreme crises, no single factor will ordinarily exert exclusive influence upon the nationality question. Nor does one sole factor appear to dominate the question, as it is manifested in Soviet regions, in all situations. Evidence favoring some of these contentions can be seen in contrasting patterns developing in two cases during recent decades among certain support factors functioning within the three major categories already outlined in Table 1.1 (identifying-physical, relativity, and regulatory).

SHIFTING EMPHASIS AMONG GROUP SUPPORTS: TWO ACTUAL EXAMPLES

In the first Soviet instance, certain support factors play prominent roles. The character, the array, and size of distinct ethnic groups, their location, peculiarities of the corporate ruling group (Russian) outlook, and the policies followed by the USSR leadership make the difference. To a noticeable extent, status often corresponds with group size or historical stability. Asian nationalities are openly discriminated against in cultural and economic development (major industrial centers seldom are sited specifically in the Soviet East for the benefit of non-Russians). This deprivation has long been felt by Central Asians, many of whom harbor the conviction that the authorities in Moscow mean to retard Asian industrialization, maintaining the East indefinitely as a raw materials source and agricultural colony for Russia. Under these circumstances, Kazakhs, Uzbeks, and related groups concentrate upon building up their population and local language base (identifying-physical factors), while maintaining a deep, controlled hostility in relations with the master group. That antipathy and accompanying bias (regulatory factor) neutralizes efforts intended to homogenize by Russifying these nationalties through standardized ideological schooling, propaganda, and similar means of persuasion. So long as these Central Asians feel threatened by official measures prescribing economic and political inequality, their continued emphasis upon identifying-physical support factors will constitute a natural constructive response.

In a second case, a triangular, partial set of supporting factors includes a relativity factor of cultural inequality, a physical factor of population change, and a regulatory factor, response to official policy, possibly related to a factor of prejudice. One aspect of the relativity (cultural inequality) factor invites explanation. Over the 30 years from 1940 to 1970, in nearly every instance throughout the Soviet Union, the Autonomous Soviet Socialist Republic (ASSR) eponymous nationalities (see Table 1.2) (not including the Karakalpak) started the period with the highest absolute number of published book copies appearing at any time in the eponymous languages throughout the three decades. Those numbers toppled into substantial decline from that early peak to at least around 1970. This downward trend becomes apparent from analysis of data about local-language publishing. The information covers three four-year cycles, 1937-40, 1958-61, and 1968-71, coincident with the latest Soviet census dates (1939, 1959, and 1970). By contrast, the union republic (SSR) (see Table 1.2) eponyms simultaneously stood lowest, on the average, for them, during that same thirty years, in the earliest, 1937-40 quadrennium. But they all rose substantially in average absolute numbers of book copies published yearly in local languages during 1958-61 and 1968-71.[8]

Now the physical factor of population size enters into consideration, for the cultural perquisites due nationalities in the USSR sometimes depend upon a group's bulk. During approximately the same three decades, 1939-70, the average size of 15 eponymous ASSR groups increased by almost 23 percent. (Abkhazia, Daghistan, and Tuva omitted for lack of data or namesake identity). Among 10 nationalities maintained in SSR status after 1939, the namesake populations grew an average of 71 percent over the 30 years. Between 1959 and 1970 alone, the eponymous population of the 14 nationality SSRs increased 20 percent on the average.[9] From these figures, the movement of the cultural inequality factor—ASSR general local-language book-publishing trends—against the population size trend is at once evident. Several possible explanations for this suggest themselves, and certainly population variables offer one of them.

The quantity of publications supplied for every person reveals a similar picture. Most eponymous ASSR nationalities (again excepting the Karakalpaks, plus the Maris) begin the 1939-70 decades at their highest point in book printing per capita and decline substantially by the 1970 period. Yet, in the SSR instance, almost precisely the reverse pattern prevails. Disregarding the three Baltic and one Moldavian group, all SSR nationalities but the Belorussian start the 30 years at their lowest yearly average rate of book copies issued for each person. Nine, including the four newly annexed, advance

TABLE 1.2

Autonomous Republics and Soviet Union Republics, 1939, 1959, 1970

ASSRs		
22 in 1939	19 in 1959	20 in 1970
Abkhaz	Abkhaz	Abkhaz
Ajar	Ajar	Ajar
Bashkir	Bashkir	Bashkir
Buriat Mongol	Buriat	Buriat
Chechen-Ingush	Chechen-Ingush	Chechen-Ingush
Chuvash	Chuvash	Chuvash
Crimean	Daghistan	Daghistan
Daghistan	Kabardin-Balkar	Kabardin-Balkar
Kabardin-Balkar	Kalmyk	Kalmyk
Kalmyk	Karakalpak	Karakalpak
Karakalpak	Karelian	Karelian
Karelian	Komi	Komi
Komi	Mari	Mari
Mari	Mordvin	Mordvin
Moldavian	Nakhichevan	Nakhichevan
Mordvin	North Osset	North Osset
Nakhichevan	Tatar	Tatar
North Osset	Udmurt	Tuvan
Tatar	Yakut	Udmurt
Udmurt		Yakut
Volga German		
Yakut		
SSRs		
11 in 1939	15 in 1959	15 in 1970
Armenian	Armenian	Armenian
Azerbaijanian	Azerbaijanian	Azerbaijanian
Belorussian	Belorussian	Belorussian
Georgian	Estonian	Estonian
Kazakh	Georgian	Georgian
Kirgiz	Kazakh	Kazakh
[Russian]	Kirgiz	Kirgiz
Tajik	Latvian	Latvian
Turkmen	Lithuanian	Lithuanian
Ukrainian	Moldavian	Moldavian
Uzbek	[Russian]	[Russian]
	Tajik	Tajik
	Turkmen	Turkmen
	Ukrainian	Ukrainian
	Uzbek	Uzbek

Sources: Frank Lorimer, The Population of the Soviet Union: History and Prospects (Geneva: League of Nations, 1946), pp. 241-43, map between 152-53; Itogi vsesoiuznoi perepisi naseleniia 1959 goda. SSSR. Sovodnyi tom (Moscow: Gosstatizdat. TsSU SSSR, 1962), pp. 202-08; Itogi vsesoiuznoi perepisi naseleniia 1970 goda. Natsional'nyi sostav na seleniia SSSR. (Moscow: Statistika, 1973), 4: 16-19; Edward Allworth, Soviet Asia—Bibliographies: A Compilation of Social Science and Humanities Sources on the Iranian, Mongolian, and Turkic Nationalities/With an Essay on the Soviet-Asian Controversy (New York: Praeger, 1975), p. xlvii.

to a higher proportion during 1968-71. For exactly those eponyms, like the Azerbaijanians, Tajiks, and Turkmens, whose rapid population increase seems to have outrun the printing presses during the last decade of the period, numbers of books per capita subside again after reaching a high in 1958-61.

To explain such contradictory behavior, contrasting ASSR and SSR eponyms in general, more than the physical factor of population change, must be considered. In this step is encountered a tenacious Marxist prejudice against either the eventual survival or present governmental encouragement of certain types of small nationalities ("the debris of nationalities," Engels often called them; "fictitious . . . republics," said self-styled Russian patriots around 1970; and "pocket handkerchief states," commented a Soviet intellectual around 1974).[10] Translated into policy making, that bias emphasizes the influence of a regulatory factor in the combination of supports. This application of policy is here reasoned by analogy, for no clear assertion in official sources stating that local-language book publishing by ASSR nationalities would be noticeably restricted at a certain recent date has yet been found. But it is very suggestive that the Union-wide Soviet education decrees announced for 1958-59 had the effect of specifically limiting or reducing to zero local-language schooling for nearly all ASSR nationalities.[11] An accompanying secret decree probably curtailed ASSR publishing as well.

That completes the triad of factors in this example by indicating that the regulatory factor has overruled the physical imperatives and influences of human reproduction, as well as expected administrative moves toward balancing nationality cultural inequality. But this development may not end here, because the same publishing record reveals that another change has begun to take place. While general book copies for the ASSR in the local language, both actual and per capita, on the average continue to decrease in number, a curious rise occurs in copies of certain key categories published for the ASSR eponyms. This striking countertrend involves, besides the group's namesake language, all languages in which the ASSR's eponymous nationality publishes its belles lettres. The amounts of literary books being issued in all languages every year on the average during 1958-61 by the 17 ASSRs for each person grew vigorously by 1968-71 (these figures for Kalmyks, then only recently returned from official nonexistence in forced exile, were still omitted from statistical yearbooks for 1958-61). An increase between the two periods of something like 41 percent has resulted.

Nationalities of the ASSRs (excluding the Ajar and Nakhichevan units for lack of distinct eponymous languages and Kalmyk for shortage of available data) enlarged their average annual output for copies of literary works printed in all languages for the 17 groups from .8 of one book for every member of the local nationality, during the quadrennium starting in 1958, to 1.03 copies each over the period 1968-71. Simultaneously, the 14 SSR eponyms as a whole decreased literary book publishing from an annual average for those same four-year cycles of 1.28 copies per person to 1.24. Addition of Russians to the union-republic assessment fails to stem the downturn.

BALTIC TRENDS AND THE ASSRs—A REGIONAL SUPPORT SYSTEM IN ACTION

Three nationalities most recently assigned SSRs—Estonians, Latvians, and Lithuanians—in both general and literary publishing uncharacteristically continue upward and therefore exert a considerable effect upon the overall SSR record. When Baltic literary publishing around the two census periods 1959 and 1970 is separated from that of the others—again minus the Russian Soviet Federated Socialist Republic (SFSR)—the SSR record for the remaining 11 eponymous nationalities turns out to be almost the exact reverse of that observed among most ASSR groups. During 1958-61, the 11 SSRs provided an average of 1.0 copy for each member of the respective eponymous nationality annually. By 1968-71, that yearly average supply had fallen to .84 of a copy per person. The Baltic eponyms exactly at the same time were enlarging literary printings for their three namesake nationalities in all languages, from 2.3 to 2.7 copies per capita annually on the average. In that respect, therefore, these relatively small, Baltic SSR groups (several ASSR eponyms—Tatars, Chuvash, Mordvins, Bashkirs—exceed one or more Baltic namesake nationalities in size) superficially resembled the ASSR model more closely than the SSR pattern.[12]

The shift among ASSR groups toward an enlarged literary output evidently represents a turn away from relying principally upon the cultural support of general, local-language publishing. For them, the needed compensating effort, emerging in increased publishing of literature, with its peculiar, strong connections to nationality identity, has special significance. These 17 ASSR groups avoid, by this maneuver, complete dependence upon the specific eponymous nationality language of each in publishing. Together, these groups slightly relinquished adherence to their spoken native tongues by 1970, compared with 1959, though five of them actually gained in percentage of adherents within the nationality's population.[13] That action of replacing a language of publication demonstrates the sort of adjustment among available supporting factors that every nationality must undertake to keep the nationality question in reasonable equilibrium for itself and maintain the group as a whole in good health. For the three Baltic eponyms, however, the rise in literary publishing against the general SSR trend between 1959 and 1970 (approximate period) must have significance in group survival, but for a purpose different than offsetting deterioration in general publishing. Overall local-language publishing per capita in those same periods was rising vigorously rather than declining in the Baltic union republics. Soviet Estonians, Latvians, and Lithuanians appear to be compensating in advance for anticipated weakening in other group identity support factors. All three have experienced small gains in spoken language adherence since 1959 and can scarcely fear serious erosion of precise correspondence between numbers of eponymous speakers and membership in the nationality.

Most of them are aware of the absolute and relative increase in outsiders among the inhabitants of each Baltic SSR. They observe the consequent dilution of local-language speakers and the exposure to some pressure from Russian.[14] However, such a direct corrective action away from total dependence upon eponymous language identification hardly sounds like a plausible response to threat of language loss when such a high rate of retention is recorded. Only circumstantial evidence suggests the transfer. Among modern literate nationalities sensing danger to group solidarity, a response may naturally resemble the remedy explicit in the cautionary academic slogan of recent decades: "publish or perish." Linguistic defensiveness in the province of Quebec, Canada, illustrates the reaction both to general and specific threats (to eponymous language) felt by a peripheral nationality.

These developments among the eponymous nationalities of Soviet Central Asia, the ASSRs Union-wide, and the three key Baltic groups broadly suggest the functioning of an organism diligently at work adjusting to its changeable surroundings and defending its own skin. Clear understanding of the way the nationality question operates requires us to proceed several steps beyond that suggestion to a better view of the process involved in each nationality's fluid support system. For various reasons, the Baltic region of the USSR offers a particularly promising opportunity and area in which to consider the processes of group support through a narrower focus of attention. A large quantity of information is accessible about these three recently independent nationalities. Their modernity is widely recognized, and they offer possibilities for fruitful comparisons both within a coherent zone and on a Soviet-wide scale. In their borderland location are combined features that undoubtedly affect defensive ethnic processes. They live in a multi-ethnic state where the highly centralized government of the USSR superimposes itself over political-geographical divisions of land and people into more or less accurate ethnic administrative units. There is an authoritarian political system advocating retention of selected cultural distinctions among nationalities, each of them emphatically aware of a separate identity. Economic centralism and fairly strong local management of industry and agriculture coexist. The compact settlement and concentration of the three nationalities unites with certain kinship to adjacent foreign groups (especially Finns and Poles) to enhance the ethnic leverage they can exert. That relationship and other links and channels of communication abroad enable them not only to convey attitudes and information but to absorb ideas and impressions from foreign countries and to relay them to the Soviet interior. Significantly high levels of modern education and other cultural attainments among these nationalities qualifies them to be classified as relatively advanced, and that not merely in a limited Soviet sense of the term "modern."

Whether responding either to genuine or imagined perils to nationality group survival, the Baltic region's eponymous nationalities, and perhaps certain noneponymous ones, appear in the process of shifting their reliance from combinations of group supports emphasized by them earlier. Before the Soviet takeover in the Baltic region (1940-44), the nationality support system there referred to many institutions and activities now missing. It depended upon the apparatus of existing national statehood, economic independence, acknowledgment in international affairs by the world of nations, religious and cultural self-determination, intellectual diversity, internal political competition, and the like. For a time after 1944, Baltic ethnic reliance rested considerably upon memories from the immediate past. By the 1960s, the nationalities had shown an inclination for change in this respect. Responding to more than external threats, a real or sensed need to transfer reliance from past supports soon developed among several Baltic nationalities. That new realism conceivably represents a movement away from nostalgia toward maturity in the local reading of current domestic affairs in the USSR. The shift allows for building up a suitable group maintenance system to replace the outdated one. Supports increasingly emphasized may include regulatory factors of pride or intolerance; a relativity factor of solidarity among different classes, including elites, constituting the Estonian, Jewish, or Lithuanian nationalities individually for example; and greater accent than before upon certain identifying and physical factors, such as outlets in literary and artistic expression of group life. Others may be a more lively appreciation for preserving local values in village and countryside; a stronger interest in facets of social, historical, or ethical legacies; an increased emphasis upon the suppleness and richness of each native language; and in addition, some others related to active mobility and the communication important in genuine or imagined parity/imparity between groups concerned with one another.

High material and cultural achievement in the Soviet Baltic region has been reported in recent years. That accomplishment has led almost directly to greater group awareness of the dilemmas, under Soviet Communism, of responsibility, initiative, and autonomy. In those spheres, limited flexibility by Soviet authorities in Moscow might satisfy growing numbers of Baltic technicians and administrators and, thus, lend greater stability to the nationality question there. This could perhaps safely have been accomplished, from the regime's standpoint, for selected segments of society, such as agricultural economists and managers, manufacturing executives, housing specialists, and other practical men. There is a risk that any concession to such well-prepared recipients could whet the desire for more operating leeway, though that wish might require a different impetus before it would be converted into an ethnic support. An unexpectedly swift, effective adjustment by a Baltic nationality's representatives to newly offered possibilities for strengthening group supports might well stimulate its wish for real parity in the yet unequal Soviet federation. This could work to dissipate Moscow's nearly total, high-level control over that nationality's affairs. Significant sharing of command with Baltic figures is evidently regarded still as intolerable by the central Soviet leaders. Nevertheless, the ruling ethnic group and its spokesmen may understand that sustaining the previous degree of hegemony probably cannot in practice be continued indefinitely—not in an area as advanced as the Baltic region, without reversion to the large-scale deportations, police terror, and other traditional Soviet methods of coercion. Resort to those techniques of governance could substantially diminish the Baltic area's respectable economic productivity. Worse yet, it would disturb some of the most enlightened visible societies in the USSR. This is probably an exorbitant price for the leading ethnic group to pay for predominance in the absence of outright, full-fledged rebellion.

In order to identify what accounts for the notable vigor and durability of the Baltic eponymous nationalities, why the particular sets of supporting factors functioning there now seem to be appropriate, and what degree and nature of satisfaction/dissatisfaction characterizes the Baltic nationality question of the 1970s, this multidisciplinary research effort makes a coordinated inquiry to substantiate a common hypothesis. It is proposed that, to a significant extent, technical, plus cultural and political modernization of a Soviet variety (Communist mobilization, using education, media, and other communications means focused around an urban-industrial economic base), and other forces have a special effect. Because of an enlarging group awareness, leading nationalities to ever more critical self-analysis and evaluation of the current situation (and because economic and cultural standards and facilities are satisfactory or better), the emphasis tends to change in the nationality question of the Baltic region in the 1970s. This alteration causes a basic reorientation in the attitudes and beliefs of several Baltic ethnic groups toward the potentials of nationality as a rallying point under new circumstances, and toward the nationality question in their own collective region. Thus, with the achievement and continuation of noticeably above-average material and cultural status among key Baltic nationalities in the late 1960s and early 1970s, the publicly articulated levels of group discontent, evidently connected with increasingly perceived intangible deprivation, appear to rise rather than fall. That trend reflects, it would seem, an intensified awareness of, and concern with, group identity. It is expressed through varying degrees or balance* of satisfaction/dissatisfaction within the region's nationality question. It evidently prompts crucial shifts in emphasis from certain combinations of group supports to sets of replacements available and needed under evolving conditions.

While testing that general hypothesis, in this study of how a nationality group survives through adjusting the accent placed upon various support factors in combination, the authors have had in mind a number of narrow approaches that offer promising intellectual rewards. Primary were the identifying of indispensable supporting factors, if any, and ranking them in order of importance for the nationality question. But balance and change within sets of factors came to seem more pointed than hierarchic location of individual factors in a single list. Catalysts for changing emphasis upon certain factors and results of those shifts were sought. The effect of the supporting factors, and their changing importance within each constellation of factors, constituted another crucial target of the study. The impact of one nationality upon the attitudes of others in the region and on the discontent or contentment expressed throughout such an area was considered interesting. Finally, patterns of use or disuse among supporting factors seemed of basic import.

Rather than addressing one or another of these topics directly, the authors of the various chapters have chosen in this first test of

---

*"Balance" in the satisfaction/dissatisfaction scale implies that greater amounts of satisfaction may outweigh dissatisfaction, but this is not always necessarily so. The more concentrated the attention a group turns to certain supporting factors, the greater the likelihood that focus may effect the equilibrium between satisfaction/dissatisfaction. But satisfaction, in fact, probably never replaces dissatisfaction entirely. They coexist—but the weight given one set of factors or another results in changed degrees of satisfaction/dissatisfaction and an altered "balance" in the nationality question.

the method and approach to prepare specific case studies. Guided by the considerations outlined above, along with the common hypothesis, the book endeavors to reach some (however preliminary) understanding of the workings of the nationality question through this structural analysis of its operation in an unusually promising period and region.

Without explicitly claiming to prove that nationalities are durable, all parts of this combined research effort give persuasive evidence for an ethnic body's resilience in its own self-defense. Again, rather by implication than design, the entire effort shows that the nationality support mechanism works effectively in mobilizing a viable group living under an authoritarian regime like that in the USSR. The system of group supports functions better there than it does in a state governing itself democratically, for several reasons. In each field examined here, conditions prevailing among Soviet nationalities, or official pressure applied to them by the ruling ethnic groups have recently stimulated development of concerted, constructive supports for nationality, though only a very restricted range of choices was open to them. The dilemmas analyzed here in connection with Soviet history teaching and interpretation, religious adherence and recognition, economic management, and political leadership, or group cultural expression, among the nationalities reflect themselves differently in democratic societies. Authoritarian rule, unlike democracy, seems to engender creative, ingenious construction of ethnic group support systems. But, when such nationalities under democracy are regionally concentrated and at the same time constrained by economic or other circumstances (isolation, limited education, and the like) from participating normally in general social benefits or in influencing decision making at the centers of state power, there is a certain similarity in expressions of satisfaction/dissatisfaction. Democratic nationalities often turn to open social protest, opposition party politics, and even violence, none a feasible, effective alternative at present for nationality groups in the authoritarian USSR. The democratic solution to such difficulties is not always likely to be couched in ethnic terms, for democracy, by its nature, customarily offers its people diverse routes to securing their own satisfaction. In effect, this weakens the factors supporting nationalities in democratic composite societies by reducing the need felt by their members to rely upon ethnicity in the way a Soviet Latvian or Baltic Jew may, who continues to seek security through such affiliation. In the USSR today, people do not so much turn to nationality for achieving social-cultural-economic goals as they use institutions or devices in those spheres with the express aim of preserving their nationality for the future—acting upon a stubborn group survival instinct.

THEORETICAL ORIENTATION OF FOLLOWING CHAPTERS

In the following chapters, contributions from Judith Fleming, Kenneth E. Nyirady, and Richard Shryock adopt the view that knowing the leading figures or minds in a society, understanding their preoccupations, their actions, and gestures, provides revealing insights into the life processes of the ethnic groups whom those figures truly represent. In that approach, such outstanding men reflect the ways a nationality senses, then employs or responds to, its own strengths and predicaments. Those reactions occur in practical politics, economics, and public education (respecting group history for example). These are fields not ordinarily expected in the USSR to sustain a group's ethnicity.

A "turning outward" to world history among historical topics shown in Chapter 3 for certain Baltic groups may verify the ways used by these Soviet nationalities to escape somewhat from the obligatory devotion to a stultifying form of fraternity expected of nationalities in the USSR.

Christopher Doersam and Eli M. Lederhendler have analyzed the current importance of traditional beliefs and cultural institutions. Nor are these factors customarily meant by Soviet authorities to support contemporary group ethnicity. Those two contributions to the present joint study hint strongly that, despite the risks, the Soviet regime has attempted to extract ethnicity from faith and employ nationality against religion in the Baltic area (and perhaps others). Party chiefs accurately regard Catholicism, Judaism, and Lutheranism (as well as ecumenism) to be competitive and antithetical both to their ideology and policies intended to heal ethnic divisiveness with a prescribed, class-oriented internationalism. The coincidence between religion and nationality identity in the Lithuanian and Baltic Jewish cases compounds the difficulty Soviet leaders face in trying to implement their plans.

Tõnu Parming's careful delineation of influences playing upon contemporary patterns of ethnic strength or weakness adds depth to the entire inquiry. He shows that today's situation stems directly or indirectly from social, historical, or political developments that occurred during the recent or more distant Baltic past. His findings make the present status of group support configurations seem both consistent and logical. Juozas A. Kazlas's essential investigation into the all-important biases and latent prejudices with which certain Baltic groups partially sustain themselves in relation to outsiders demonstrates the force of such seemingly trivial regulatory support factors. His chapter suggests, too, the wide application and strong effect of attitudes derived from often long-forgotten origins. The vital function of mutual or unilateral antipathy in helping secure group awareness and boundaries seems especially applicable to the Soviet Baltic nationalities today. Energetic state programs encourage immigration into the little Baltic SSRs by the three Soviet Slavic SSR groups, each so much larger than any Baltic nationality. At the same time, the depopulating outmigration to Central Russia or the Soviet East, urged notably upon the limited numbers of young Estonians, Latvians, and Lithuanians, has apparently helped prolong what turns out to be a salutory ethnic friction and corresponding complex of supportive antagonisms, inside and outside the Soviet Baltic region, for members of those nationalities.

NOTES

1. Walker Connor, "Self-Determination: The New Phase," World Politics 20 (October 1967): 30-53; Walker Connor, "The Politics of Ethnonationalism," Journal of International Affairs 27, no. 1 (1973): 1-21; Frederik Barth, ed., Ethnic Groups and Boundaries (Boston: Little, Brown, 1969); Cynthia Enloe, Ethnic Conflict and Political Development (Boston: Little, Brown, 1973); R. A. Schermerhorn, Comparative Ethnic Relations (New York: Random House, 1970).

2. Edward Allworth, "Restating the Nationality Question," Soviet Nationality Problems, ed. Edward Allworth (New York: Columbia University Press, 1971), p. 13.

3. Leonid I. Brezhnev, O piatidesiatiletii Soiuza Sovetskikh Sotsialisticheskikh Respublik. Doklad na sovmestnom torzhestvennom zasedanii tsentral'nogo komiteta KPSS, Verkhovnogo Soveta SSSR i Verkhovnogo Soveta RSFSR v kremlevskom Dvortse S''ezdov 21 dekabria 1972 goda (Moscow: Izdatel'stvo Politicheskoi Literatury, 1972), pp. 24-25; A. I. Mikoian, Sovetskomu Soiuzu. Piat'desiat let. (Moscow: Izdatel'stvo Politicheskoi Literatury, 1972), pp. 55-56.

4. Walter D. Connor, "Differentiation, Integration, and Political Dissent in the USSR," Dissent in the USSR, ed. Rudolf L. Tőkes (Baltimore: Johns Hopkins Press, 1976), pp. 140, 149.

5. A Chronicle of Current Events Nos. 28-31 (London: Amnesty International Publications, 1975); Peter Reddaway, Uncensored Russia (New York: American Heritage Press, 1972); George Saunders, ed., Samizdat: Voices of the Soviet Opposition (New York: Monad Press, 1975); Evrei i evreiskii narod: Evreiskii samizdat, nos. 1-9 (Jerusalem: Tsentr Dokumentatsii Vostochno-Evropeiskogo Evreistvo, 1974-76); Chronicle of the Catholic Church in Lithuania, nos. 9-12 (Maspeth, N.Y.: The Lithuanian Roman Catholic Priests' League of America, 1975-76), also earlier translated editions.

6. *Dvenadtsatyi s"ezd rossiiskoi kommunisticheskoi partii (Bol'shevikov). Stenograficheskii otchet. 17-25 aprelia 1923 g.* (Moscow: Izdatel'stvo "Krasnaia Nov'," Glavpolitprosvet, 1923) (republished in Moscow in 1968 by Izdatel'stvo Politicheskoi Literatury), see 1968 edition, pp. 691-97; Maxim Kim, *The Soviet People—A New Historical Community* (Moscow: Progress Publishers, 1974), pp. 168-69 and elsewhere.

7. A. I. Kholmogorov, *Internatsional'nye cherty sovetskikh natsii* (Moscow: Izdatel'stvo "Mysl'," 1970), p. 139; Stephen P. Dunn, *Cultural Processes in the Baltic Area under Soviet Rule* (Berkeley: Institute of International Studies, University of California, 1966), pp. 28-29.

8. Edward Allworth, "Mainstay or Mirror of Identity—The Printed Word in Central Asia and Other Soviet Regions Today," *Canadian Slavonic Papers* 17, nos. 2/3 (Summer and Fall 1975): 439-50.

9. *Itogi vsesoiuznoi perepisi naseleniia 1970 goda. Natsional'nyi sostav naseleniia SSSR* (Moscow: Statistika, 1973), 4: 9-19 (hereafter cited as *Itogi . . . 1970 goda*).

10. Friedrich Engels, *Neue Rheinische Zeitung* [The battle in Hungary], no. 194 (January 13, 1849), trans. as "Bor'ba v Vengrii," in K. Marks i F. Engel's, *Sochineniia* (Moscow: Gosudarstvennoe Izdatel'stvo Politicheskoi Literatury, 1957), 6: 183; Friedrich Engels, *Neue Rheinische Zeitung* [Democratic Panslavism], nos. 222-23 (February 15, 16, 1849), trans. as "Demokraticheskii Panslavism," in ibid., pp. 293-94; E. Bernstein, ed., *Die Briefe von Friedrich Engels an Eduard Bernstein* (Berlin, 1925); letter dated February 22, 1882, cited in Horace B. Davis, *Nationalism and Socialism: Marxist and Labor Theories of Nationalism to 1917* (New York and London: Monthly Review Press, 1967), p. 140; Igor Shafarevich, "Separation or Reconciliation," *From under the Rubble*, ed. Aleksandr Solzhenitsyn et al. (Boston: Little, Brown, 1975), pp. 99-100; "Slovo natsii" (signed "Russkie Patrioty"), *Sobranie dokumentov samizdata (Arkhiv samizdata)*, vol. 8, entry no. 590, (n.p., n.d.), p. 17, retyped from the periodical *Russkaia mysl'* (November 26, 1971).

11. "Ob ukreplenii sviazi shkoly s zhizn'iu i o dal'neishem razvitii sistemy narodnogo obrazovaniia v strane. Tezisy TsK KPSS i Soveta Ministrov SSSR," *Pravda*, November 16, 1958, pp. 1-3; Yaroslav Bilinsky, "The Soviet Education Laws of 1958-9 and Soviet Nationality Policy," *Soviet Studies* 14, no. 2 (October 1962): 138-57; Brian D. Silver, "The Status of National Minority Languages in Soviet Education: An Assessment of Recent Changes," *Soviet Studies* 26, no. 1 (January 1974): 28-40.

12. *Itogi . . . 1970 goda*, vol. 4 (1973), pp. 9-11; *Pechat' SSSR v 1958* (and 1959, 1960, 1961, 1968, 1969, 1970, 1971) *godu. Statis-*

ticheskie materialy (Moscow: Vsesoiuznoi Knizhnoi Palaty, 1959 1962), (Moscow: Izdatel'stvo "Kniga," 1969-1972), for 1958-1960, pp. 60-61, 119; for 1961, pp. 21, 52; for 1968-1971, pp. 10-11, 52.

13. Itogi . . . 1970 goda, vol. 4, pp. 9-11.

14. Ibid., vol. 4, pp. 14-15.

CHAPTER

2

ROOTS OF NATIONALITY DIFFERENCES

Tönu Parming

The most crucial element affecting social-political stability within industrialized composite (multi-ethnic) countries in the 1970s is probably ethnic harmony or disharmony. The present study focuses upon that component of societal processes and dissatisfaction—in the USSR, specifically upon the Estonian, Latvian, and Lithuanian Soviet Socialist Republics—that is related to the nationality issue. Until quite recently, the predominant tendency in the West was to perceive the three eponymous (namesake) nationalities in the Soviet Baltic area to be on a road to cultural if not physical annihilation. This orientation in scholarship characterized especially an older generation of emigrant activists. They did most of the research or otherwise mediated the interpretation of processes in the Soviet Baltic zone and emphasized largely issues of political, cultural, or other types of oppression in conjunction with demands for extreme solutions to the ethnic dilemma, including withdrawal of Soviet forces and their apparatus of government.

However, by the middle of the 1960s, a cultural renascence was evident in Estonia, Latvia, and Lithuania—clearly the indigenous cultures had not been Russified, and their obituary appeared quite premature. By the end of the decade, the Baltic union republics, especially Estonia and Latvia, achieved a higher standard of living than the Soviet Union as a whole, perhaps a somewhat peculiar situation for people described as the victims of Russian colonialism. But in spite of the cultural rebirth that began after Khrushchev's famous 1956 de-Stalinization speech, the undeniable leaps in the standard of living at the end of the 1960s and in the early 1970s, and the weakening of earlier Stalinist terror-based methods of political control, nationality dissent—largely dormant in the 1950s and first half of the 1960s—was soon to intensify.[1] Latvian Communists sent a letter of complaint about both overt and covert Russification policies of the Union-wide government to Western comrades, rioting in Lithuania became so intense it necessitated the unusual step of using Soviet paratroop units to restore civil order, and a number of memorandums complaining against Russification emanated from Estonia.[2] Clearly, all was not well.

The current state of affairs in regard to nationality dissatisfaction in the Baltic union republics is theoretically intriguing for two reasons. First, if modernization leads to a demise of ethnic identification, as both traditional Marxist and Western analysts have theorized, then the one region of the Soviet Union that should be witnessing a decrease in nationality discontent is the Soviet Baltic. By virtually any indicator of modernization, it would rank at the high end of the scale relative to other Soviet union republics.[3] However, group dissatisfaction has persisted, and even intensified, in spite of modernization.[4] And second, postwar resistance to Soviet authority in the form of organized guerrilla warfare could be easily comprehended as a response to the brutality of early Soviet rule, especially the huge deportations from the Baltic republics that occurred between 1940 and 1949, and to the generally repressive Stalinist policies toward culture and civil rights. Contemporary Soviet Baltic discontent cannot readily be understood in these terms. Cultural levels of the eponymous nationalities and material standards of living were better, methods of maintaining political control and stability during the late 1960s less brutal, than at any time during Soviet rule. And in spite of the harassment of cultural figures and general dissenters, conditions during the early 1970s continued to be better than in the first decades of Soviet rule.

An examination of contemporary patterns in nationality dissatisfaction throughout the Soviet Baltic must therefore proceed beyond regarding it as a simple response to Soviet repression or using theories of modernization as a point of departure. The present inquiry is based on historical, comparative analysis of selected aspects of "the nationality support factors" discussed in the opening chapter of this book. Emphasis will be given to the interrelationship between religion and an ethnic group's collective identity; demographic processes; the extent of nationality solidarity; and aspects of culture, especially the extent of contacts with Western Europe and the strength of the cultural infrastructure of the group.

Historically, certain major similarities exist in patterns of nationality dissatisfaction among the Baltic union republics. All three were characterized by intensive armed resistance to Soviet rule for about five years following the end of World War II. Afterward, the period of quiet in all three lasted for around 15 years. Subsequently, in Estonia, Latvia, and Lithuania, demands have been heard for restoring full sovereignty to the three peoples.[5] However, the frequent focus on these similarities obscures a number of crucial differences in regard to the ways nationality dissatisfaction is precipitated and channeled. A reexamination of the distinctions allows for greater insight into the general causes of nationality dissatisfaction in the Soviet Union.

Among the noteworthy differences between the three eponymous Baltic people in the generation and expression of dissatisfaction are the role played by religion in Lithuania and the role played by demographic shifts in Estonia and Latvia. In Lithuania, religious issues evoke strong nationality responses, and religion is often used as a channel for expressing what essentially amounts to nationality dissent. To the contrary, even though religious dissent is known to exist in Latvia and Estonia, there it has been largely devoid of nationality connotations. Indeed, there is no Estonian or Latvian equivalent to the Lithuanian Chronicle of the Catholic Church, an important samizdat informational source, or the protest memorandums of religious leaders and believers.[6] The nationality discontent in Estonia and Latvia has been expressed through lay channels instead. At the same time, the fear of Russification as a consequence of demographic changes is not apparently an important issue in Lithuania, but it is the primary source of fears about nationality survival in both Estonia and Latvia. This is evidenced by several memorandums sent from underground organizations to the West. In turn, an important difference between Latvia and Estonia has been the extent and duration of the cultural renascence that began to manifest itself slowly in the late 1950s. The current situation in Latvia in regard to the eponymous nationality is evidently so serious that one Western observer in late 1975 felt justified in judging the Latvians to be resigned and socially demoralized.[7] Latvians allegedly perceive further group resistance to pressures from the USSR leadership and their general Russification to be impossible.

While this chapter concentrates on aspects of the nationality support factors, political and ideological processes at a more general level should not be totally ignored as determinants of nationality satisfaction or dissatisfaction both in the Soviet Union and outside it. The world continues in an age of strong political nationalism, where the highest, idealized form of expressing collective nationality identity comes through separate statehood. So long as Third World people continue to achieve political sovereignty after colonialism, with the Soviet state and Communist Party championing this trend, it cannot be anticipated that the three Baltic peoples will expect less. The interwar sovereign republics of Estonia, Latvia, and Lithuania, moreover, are still recognized de jure by many Western states, and they preserve diplomatic missions in the West, without de facto governments or counties to represent—on the international scene, a peculiar situation.

Furthermore, any Soviet policy that is repressive, whether in terms of religion, culture, or civil rights, will evoke in the non-Russian people of the Soviet Union an anti-Russian response, thus channeling what in essence is religious, cultural, or civil discontent into nationality dissatisfaction. The Soviet Union in many respects is a state dominated by a political party in which the key decision-making elite is heavily ethnic Russian. Whereas the Russians in 1970 comprised 53.3 percent of the USSR population, Russians made up 60.9 percent of the Union-wide party membership, 57.2 percent of the Central Committee membership, and 56 percent of the Politburo and Party Secretariat membership.[8] They also supplied 72.5 percent of the membership in the USSR Council of Ministers and all Central Committee secretaries but one in December 1972. But even if these proportions were ethnically representative of the Union-wide population, there are numerically so many more Russians in the total population that their presence would still be overly visible to all non-Russians. Because of the reality of the Russian presence in the highest positions of the Party and the Union-wide government, both in relative and absolute terms, general dissatisfaction within the non-Russian population with Soviet life may be easily displaced perceptually from more ethnically neutral anti-Soviet attitudes to anti-Russian attitudes. In itself, this perceptual displacement to an ethnic plane may be seen as a force generating nationality dissatisfaction in Soviet society. And most significantly, this situation is aggravated by the increasing Russian presence in historically non-Russian territories, by the Russian visibility in the local territorial Party structures, and by the fact that when Party spokesmen discuss the emergence of a single new Soviet nation, its cultural core is seemingly defined in Russian ethnic terms.

In addition, nationality dissatisfaction within the Soviet Union is also fired by forces from without that society. Not only are there emigrant groups that are politically active,[9] but the ethnic cauldron has been stirred by both the Western powers and China. During the Cold War years, the Western powers had a much more active role in "dissent input" in the Soviet Baltic than generally had been known either to scholars or the public. Western infiltration of agents, radio broadcasting, and so forth may be interpreted as a Western response to nationality discontent that already existed. Such activities may equally well reflect Cold War policies designed to stimulate ethnic dissatisfaction in order to weaken the Soviet Union domestically. These two interpretations may both be true simultaneously. But in any case, because there are external influences, nationality dissatisfaction within the Soviet Union cannot be understood fully by merely studying the Soviet domestic scene.

A share of the nationality discontent in the Soviet Baltic region is possibly caused by circumstantial factors. The early postwar resistance to Soviet rule may be interpreted as an indicator of nationality dissatisfaction of the severest type.[10] The scope of the partisan resistance may also reflect the fact that tens of thousands of men in German-sponsored military units or in civil guard reserve units that were mobilized at the eleventh hour in 1944 (independently of the circumstances and motivation that brought them into these units) were armed and cut off from retreat by the advancing Red Army. These men had no option but to continue their resistance, for under the Soviet system they were doomed in any case. This is not to deny that nationalistic goals or ideals were present, even to a powerful degree, in the partisan movements. They also appear to have enjoyed great sympathy from rural people. Early postwar resistance could not be broken until coerced collectivization, in conjunction with sizable rural deportations, in 1949, wiped out the independent family farms.

But all dissent, dissatisfaction, disloyalty, and disobedience cannot and should not be interpreted automatically in nationality terms. Just as Marxist historians have a tendency to see the presence of the class struggle in almost every situation where a lower class/working class individual or group displays hostility or violent behavior toward those higher up in the class structure, so Western observers have not atypically seen nationality dissatisfaction in every form of disobedience and dissent in the Soviet Union.

Several aspects of the nationality issue have been largely ignored in the past. Also, this analysis, both methodologically and conceptually, was greatly facilitated by the development of the "nationality support factors" framework outlined in Chapter 1, because it forced a reexamination of previous thinking and approaches to the subject matter. But the comparative study of the Soviet Baltic remains difficult for three primary reasons. First, most researchers do not possess the multiple language skills necessary to use all Baltic sources written in the eponymous languages. This is not unimportant, for a great many key sources, both in the West and in the Soviet Baltic, are written in local languages. Second, while the amount of "mediated" materials written in the West in English has appreciably increased in quantity and quality between 1970 and 1975, there is a discrepancy in the extent of materials available for the three Soviet Baltic societies. Cultural coverage by Western scholars fluent in the three Baltic languages is most extensive, especially in regard to literature. But there appears to be more material available in the way of secondary sources concerning political and demographic processes about Estonia, for example, than about Latvia or Lithuania. And third, it is often difficult for a single scholar in the West to find all data or information required for detailed analysis because there is no adequate centralized collection of Soviet, and even Western, publications regarding the Baltic SSRs. Original Estonian and Russian, as well as Western, publications have supplied the basic information that follows.

The present discussion covers each eponymous nationality of the Estonian, Latvian, and Lithuanian SSRs. Nevertheless, there are ethnic groups in each Soviet republic that are neither eponymous nor Russian, and they too are subjected to all of the pressures and responses discussed here. In many respects, the position of such groups outside their own administrative Soviet territories is most precarious of all, for they have little opportunity to maintain or reinforce their own collective identities. Interethnic contacts and conflicts, other than along the eponymous nationality-Russian dimension are topics that need much greater specialized study.

RELIGION AND THE NATIONALITY ISSUE

The Soviet Union in theory is an areligious state, but in practice it has been strongly antireligious. The reason why oppression and harassment of religion evokes a nationality response in Lithuania but does not do so in either Estonia or Latvia cannot be understood by looking for differences in Soviet policies toward Catholicism and Protestantism (which have not been shown to exist in any case). Neither is it explained by the differences between the two religions as such, nor by the possible differentials in religiosity among the three eponymous nationalities. Rather, several other aspects of religion must be scrutinized. The degree to which the religion in question supplies a key element in the nationality's collective identity as a people is crucial. (The "collective identity" of the group refers here to those items—real, symbolic, or mythical—on the basis of which its members distinguish themselves from members of other groups.) To what degree has the predominant religion in its organizational form had an ethnic dimension, for example, in being an important sponsor of educational, cultural, political, or other societal institutions and activities historically? How far has religion as an organizational entity, as well as religious leaders, traditionally participated in the political processes of the society? Finally, is the religion in question localized to the given nationality group or does that group possess a religion that in its own identity and institutional structure transcends specific nationalities and thereby local territorial boundaries? The history and nature of religion in the three main Baltic societies of the USSR seems to be such that religious issues are much more likely to evoke nationality related responses in Lithuania than in the other two.

The Lithuanians accepted Christianity voluntarily, in the sense that their own ethnic leaders converted to the faith, beginning as early as the thirteenth century. In a way, this was a politically significant step, both because it deprived the German crusading orders of a religious justification for expanding their power into Lithuania and because it could ally the Lithuanian leadership with the authority and power of the Pope. Although the Church had a strong Polish presence in its hierarchy during the period of political union between Poland and Lithuania, representatives of the Lithuanians nevertheless were still found within it, and most important, at the level closest to the people, in the priesthood. The Catholic church played a key institutional role in education, this from the earliest years, in regard to the founding and maintaining of both primary schools and academies of higher learning.[11] From the earliest stages in the development of a Lithuanian nationality identity the Catholic church was closely intertwined with ethnic political and cultural institutions.

Both in Estonia and Latvia, by contrast, the religious conversion to Christianity, also in the thirteenth century and to Catholicism at the outset, was involuntary, the result of a rather brutal foreign conquest, with religious shifts afterward frequently reflecting changing rulers.[12] Whether the church in Estonia and Latvia was Catholic, Lutheran, or Orthodox, its hierarchy was essentially noneponymous. Local priests and pastors were predominantly foreigners as well. The Lutheran church, the majority church in both societies after the Reformation, remained a German institution until the twentieth century, and it appears to have been perceived as an alien one by the local people, both in its structure and religious content. In neither society was the church close to the eponymous nationality. Although the share of indigenous pastors had grown steadily from the end of the nineteenth century, in neither Latvia nor Estonia did the Lutheran church truly become "native" until after the founding of sovereign states in 1918. While the Lutheran church in both societies had been historically closely related to the institutions of political authority and culture/education, like the Catholic church in Lithuania, the important distinction was that in the first two societies the political and cultural, as well as the religious, institutions were all alien to the eponymous nationality.

Aside from these broad historical differences, an important breaking point occurred in the last half of the nineteenth century, during the era of Czarist Russification policies. Especially as a consequence of the events and ideologies of this period, the Roman Catholic religion is believed to have become an important component of the Lithuanian national identity, while no equivalent fusion of religion and nationality occurred in Estonia and Latvia. Whether in terms of religious, cultural, or political pressures, in Lithuania, Russification affected what essentially were ethnic Lithuanian institutions. An attack on the Catholic religion and its local structure was not only an assault on religion as such but also one against an organization whose influence spanned the institutional framework underlying the nationality identity of the Lithuanian people. Similarly, the Russification policies directed at culture and education at once inevitably affected organized religion, which was an important sponsor of the specialized institutions. Virtually any Russification policy in Lithuania was likely to affect religious identity as well as nationality identity simultaneously because of the interconnected institutional structure.

It should not be surprising that religious leaders and organizations in Lithuania played an important role in the resistance to Russification. They had already been significant in earlier ethnic rivalry, including the mid-nineteenth century national awakening, and the new activism further strengthened historical ties between religion and ethnic politics. The Catholic religion was already an element in Lithuanian collective identity before Russification policies were imposed by the Czars. The external pressures placed on the Lithuanians because of these policies unquestionably caused a further fusion of the religious and nationality identities, both emblematically and organizationally. Thus, organized religion played an important role in what was perceived from the Lithuanian viewpoint as a struggle for nationality survival.

In contrast, policies of Russification applied in Latvia and Estonia did not impact directly on the eponymous nationalities but, essentially, on what were Baltic German institutions, whether in the sphere of religion, culture, or political process. While local rule in Lithuania at the time was at least partially in the hands of Polish-assimilated Lithuanians, the Latvians and Estonians were ruled in their everyday lives neither by Russians nor their own ethnic kinsmen but rather by the Baltic Germans. Similarly, the most important aspects of cultural life, from the predominant language used in culture and education to the higher institutions of learning, were also German. Baltic Germans not only controlled religion in its organized form, they also held sway over the theological education of Lutheran pastors at the University of Tartu (then Dorpat).

Russification policies evoked political, cultural, and religious responses in the territorial area of Latvia and Estonia, but these were not so much an eponymous nationality response as a Baltic German reaction. Among Estonian and Latvian activists of the time, a debate of significant proportions developed over whether or not to become allied with the Russians against Baltic Germans. Unlike Lithuania, where Russification was perceived as an ethnic threat, in

Estonia and Latvia, Russification assisted the emergence of a stronger nationality identity among the indigenous people by weakening the stranglehold of the Baltic Germans on the political, cultural, and religious institutions that regulated local day-to-day life.

By the time the Lutheran church in Estonia and Latvia passed to indigenous control, after 1918, religion in its organized form could no longer attain the nationality significance that it had already historically enjoyed in Lithuania. First of all, the nativization of religious life occurred simultaneously with a political process that separated church and state. Furthermore, secularization by this time was quickening in tempo, in any case, making it unlikely that religion would be used as an element in the symbols of differentiation on which ethnic group identities are based. As it was, much of the energy of religious leaders went to the organizational aspects of creating a new locally controlled church instead of outward into political or societal processes. Political sovereignty in Estonia and Latvia had also been achieved without any significant activism on the part of an indigenous religious structure.

The greater political activism of the church in Lithuania continued during the period of the separate interwar Baltic republics. So did the significance of religious issues in the political process generally. Between 1918 and 1940, church-related organizations remained quite insignificant in Estonian politics. This is shown by the fact that, among other things, the local Christian Democratic Party, the only clerical party, never held more than 8 percent of the parliamentary seats, and during the last parliament of the democratic period (1929-32), it had received only 4 percent of the national vote.[13] In Latvia, clerical parties acquired a greater electoral significance, occupying 16 percent of the parliamentary seats as late as 1931-34, but their total impact was considerably negated by the fact that these delegates represented several different religious and territorial groups.[14]

Lithuania also had only about 16 percent of the parliament's delegates representing a clerical party, but they represented a single group, the Christian Democrats. This particular party was "the dominant partner in every Government during the parliamentary phase [of the independent interwar Lithuanian Republic], except for the short-lived Populist-Socialist Cabinet of June-December 1926."[15] The Christian Democrats were, furthermore, nationalistic in their politics. Religion-based issues crept into both Lithuanian domestic and foreign politics, seemingly always with nationalistic connotations. Thus, during the 1920s, there was friction with the Vatican because of the pontifical stand on the Vilnius question, which Lithuanians felt to be too favorable toward Poland. And in 1930, political problems arose because of the government's harassment of the Catholic youth movement.

TABLE 2.1

Pre-Soviet Religious Composition of the Population of Estonia, Latvia, and Lithuania
(percentage of total population)

Religion	Estonia[a]	Latvia[b]	Lithuania[c]
Lutheran	78	57	9
Roman Catholic	–	24	81
Orthodox	19	9	3
Old Believers	–	5	–
Jews	1	5	1
Others	2	1	7

[a]1934.
[b]1930.
[c]1923.
Source: Royal Institute of International Affairs, The Baltic States (London: Oxford University Press, 1938), p. 38.

Soviet antireligious policies are applied in all three Baltic union republics. However, religious harassment and oppression in Estonia and Latvia does not provoke a nationalistic response, because religion historically has not been a component of the collective nationality identity and because the local and now indigenous-controlled churches do not have a tradition of nationalistic political activism. Furthermore, the Estonian and Latvian Evangelical Lutheran churches are local religious entities, not subcomponents of a larger extraterritorial religious structure. As a consequence, in neither society did the advent of Soviet rule sever important foreign religious ties. But again, the opposite is the case in Lithuania, where the establishment of Soviet rule resulted in basic interference in religious life by virtually eliminating the maintenance of normal ties between Lithuanian Catholics and the parent church in Rome. Lithuania's population has maintained a greater degree of religious homogeneity than that of either Estonia or Latvia, as data in Table 2.1 show. (See also, Chapter 6 for discussion of attempts at Sovietization of religious identity in the Baltic region.)

DEMOGRAPHIC CHANGE AND NATIONALITY PROCESSES

"Restoration of Estonia and Latvia as independent and sovereign members of the European community would be their only chance for preservation and free development of their nationhood, culture and frame of mind," states a joint memorandum from representatives of the Estonian and Latvian Democrats, sent to the European Security and Cooperation Conference in June 1975.[16] The many documents that have emanated from Latvia and Estonia during the past few years display dogged persistence in the rationalization for demanding political sovereignty, for it is seen as the only warranty for nationality group survival. The threat perceived in the continuation of the political status quo is usually identified rather explicitly as the probability of cultural Russification resulting from demographic Russification.[17]

Among postwar demographic changes, two merit special attention—depopulation and immigration. The first involved largely the eponymous nationalities of Estonia, Latvia, and Lithuania, either through deportations in 1940-41, 1944-45, and 1949, or the politically motivated flight of refugees westward in the face of the readvancing Red Army, mostly in the fall of 1944. Immigration, however, has been mainly a postwar phenomenon, involving noneponymous people, mostly Russians. The two types of population change have combined to alter the ethnic composition of the local populations radically. In addition, depopulation, the influence of which on nationality processes is profound in the Soviet Baltic, has been largely ignored in systematic analysis.

The early Soviet deportations of 1940-41, the flight westward in 1944, and the postwar partisan warfare during the years just following the end of the war appear to have almost fully decimated the ranks of that generation of Baltic leaders who had overseen the creation and development of sovereign Estonia, Latvia, and Lithuania. Whether murdered in Siberia or in Western exile, the interwar elites in almost all areas of societal life were not to be found in the ancestral territory. Further purges in the early 1950s just prior to Stalin's death ensured that the "nationalistic element" was removed from the local Communist Party apparatus and hierarchy as well. Depopulation thus deprived the eponymous nationalities almost entirely of effective ethnic leadership in the late 1940s and throughout the 1950s. It was not until a new generation had grown up that the cultural renascence occurred and that a new rise in nationality related dissatisfaction became evident. Many of the current activists have grown to maturity during the Soviet period or were born during the postwar years.

Losses through depopulation between 1939 and 1959 were large not only in percentage terms, but implications are especially significant for the postwar labor force. The Estonian case is typical of the three societies, and the following data summarize depopulation changes. The general population loss in Estonia between 1939 and 1949 was approximately 358,000 people in a prewar (1939) total population of 1,133,900.[18] Of the total loss, about 2,000 represents

Soviet executions during 1940-41; 129,000 represents deportations in 1940-41, 1944-45, and 1949; 6,000 represents executions by the German authorities between 1941-44; 117,000 represents the politically motivated flight westward, mostly in 1944; 71,500 represents people residing in territory transferred in 1945 from the Estonian SSR to the Russian SFSR; and 33,000 represents men mobilized into the Red Army in mid-1941 who can fairly surely be shown to have become fatalities. The total war-time losses were even larger than this. It is unknown how many men died in German military units or were civilian war fatalities. The 1934 census had shown 215,600 ethnic Estonian males in the age group 20 through 49; in 1959, the comparable figure was only 158,500.[19]

Essentially, for the future, depopulation meant that if rapid industrialization was undertaken before a natural population recovery took place through births, immigration would be inevitable. Furthermore, industrialization launched where the prewar technical and managerial personnel, and white collar employees in general, had been lost through murder, deportation, or flight meant that a great opportunity for upward mobility would be created for those remaining in the country. If this occurred, in turn, an especially acute shortage of industrial workers would develop. In fact, all of these possibilities materialized.

Planned industrialization, an aspect of Soviet modernization, was undertaken with great vigor. The sudden need for industrial labor led to immigration. Postwar increases in the number of Russians were quite large, both in absolute and relative terms, especially in Estonia and Latvia (see Tables 2.2 and 2.3). Figures presented in Table 2.2 record that immigration was especially sizable between the time of the integration of the Baltic states into the Soviet Union in 1944 and the Soviet census of 1959. In the case of Estonia, the bulk of the immigration during this period may be further narrowed down to the five-year period 1944-49.[20] It appears that this is the case also for Latvia and Lithuania.

Both of the two interpretations offered for this early postwar immigration may be partially substantiated from available data. One argument is based on the concept of industrial labor force migration that followed classical patterns of human migration, that is, people who move about in quest of a better livelihood. The competing argument asserts that the postwar movement of Russians into the Baltic region reflects a purposeful Russification scheme of the Union-wide government. The first viewpoint is supported by the fact that, in rank order, the early postwar immigration in absolute terms was greatest into Latvia, then Estonia and Lithuania. It could be concluded that this reflects a Soviet effort to reconstruct quickly industries already existing before the war. There was a differential level of prewar industrial development reflecting this rank order. But the competing argument is, in turn, supported by the actual large movement of Russians into Lithuania, which had a very low level of prewar industrial development. Hence, it is plausible that the movement also reflected one method of achieving greater political control over the Baltic societies in a five-year period characterized by extensive guerrilla warfare against Soviet rule.

Immigration has slowed between 1959 and 1970, as data in Table 2.3 show. However, the rank order of which of the three Baltic union republics has received the most and least immigrants remains the same, and in Estonia and Latvia, the size of the influx, in relation to the total population of the respective SSRs, remains large. In general, the interpretive consensus is that the post-1950 immigration represents, in large part, a labor force movement of the classical type. However, this presumably voluntary movement is perceived differently in the nationalistic perspective. From that standpoint, the labor force shortage exists largely because of Soviet policies to begin with, especially the deportations. Moreover, Latvian Communists alleged, in a letter circulated among Western comrades, that the industrialization itself may have been undertaken in the Baltic union republics as a means of stimulating population change, by creating an attractive labor market for Russian workers. Finally, large industrial concerns of Estonia, for example, which are under the direct operational control of Moscow ministries, are known to recruit labor outside the Estonian SSR.[21]

TABLE 2.2

General Population Composition of Estonia, Latvia, and Lithuania, Pre-Soviet Period, 1970 (in thousands)

	Estonia			Latvia			Lithuania		
Nationality	1934	1959	1970	1935	1959	1970	1938	1959	1970
Eponymous nationality	977	893	925	1,473	1,298	1,342	2,075	2,151	2,507
Russians	42	240	335	207	556	705	59	231	268
All others	39	64	96	271	239	317	440	329	353
Total population	1,058	1,197	1,356	1,951	2,093	2,364	2,575	2,711	3,128

Note: The 1934 data for Estonia are for the territorial area of the Estonian SSR; the data for Latvia and Lithuania, respectively, in 1935 and 1938, are for the territorial areas of the interwar Republics.

Sources: Tõnu Parming, "Population Changes in Estonia, 1935-1970," Population Studies 26, no. 1 (March 1972): 61; V. Stanley Vardys, "Modernization and Baltic Nationalism," Problems of Communism 24, no. 5 (September-October 1975): 39; Gundar J. King and Juris Dreifelds, "Demographic Changes in Latvia," Problems of Mininations: Baltic Perspectives, ed. Arvids Ziedonis, Jr., et al. (San Jose, Calif.: Association for the Advancement of Baltic Studies, 1973), p. 135; NSV Liidu Ministrite Nõukogu juures asuv Statistika Keskvalitsus, NSV Liidu Rahvastik (Tallinn: Eesti Raamat, 1972), pp. 30-32.

TABLE 2.3

Absolute Increase of Russians in Estonia, Latvia, and Lithuania, Pre-Soviet Period, 1970

SSR	Absolute Increase of Russians	
	Pre-Soviet to 1959	1959 to 1970
Estonia	198,000	95,000
Latvia	349,000	149,000
Lithuania	172,000	37,000

Note: The pre-Soviet base year for Estonia is 1934; for Latvia, 1935; and for Lithuania, 1938. The base-year population for Estonia is for the territorial area of the Estonian SSR—for Lithuania and Latvia, the territorial area of the interwar sovereign Republics. If the territorial area of the interwar Republic of Estonia were used, the increase of Russians between 1934 and 1959 would be smaller, while if the present territorial area of the Latvian SSR were used, the increase in Russians would be larger than shown in the table. Territories of eastern Estonia and Latvia were administratively transferred from the respective SSRs to the Russian SFSR, and these contained a significant portion of the two countries' ethnic Russian population.

Sources: Tõnu Parming, "Population Changes in Estonia, 1935-1970," Population Studies 26, no. 1 (March 1972): 61; V. Stanley Vardys, "Modernization and Baltic Nationalism," Problems of Communism 24, no. 5 (September-October 1975): 39; Gundar J. King and Juris Dreifelds, "Demographic Changes in Latvia," Problems of Mininations: Baltic Perspectives, ed. Arvids Ziedonis, Jr., et al. (San Jose, Calif.: Association for the Advancement of Baltic Studies, 1973), p. 135; NSV Liidu Ministrite Nôukogu juures asuv Statistika Keskvalitsus, NSV Liidu Rahvastik (Tallinn: Eesti Raamat, 1972), pp. 30-32.

In the case of Lithuania, population processes (depopulation and immigration) have not radically altered the ethnic composition of the union republic, whereas they have done so in Estonia and Latvia. From the data in Table 2.2, it may be calculated that the Lithuanians were 81 percent of Lithuania's prewar population, 79 percent of the population of the Lithuanian SSR in 1959, and 80 percent in 1970. But in Latvia, the eponymous nationality's share of the population had decreased from 76 percent in 1935 to 62 percent in 1959 and further to 57 percent in 1970. Similarly, in Estonia, the ethnic Estonians' share of the population had decreased from 92 percent in 1934, to 75 percent in 1959, to 68 percent in 1970. Differences between Lithuania and Latvia/Estonia reflect variations in the eponymous nationalities' birth rates, both historically and contemporaneously, and the differential Russian influx during the postwar period. There is reason to believe that these factors are interrelated.

Data regarding crude birth rates for the three union republics are shown in Table 2.4. Lithuania's higher birth rate relative to the other two probably has little to do with the Catholicism of the population. Rather, the roots of these differences reach back to the demographic catastrophe wrought by the Great Northern War (1700-21) and experienced in Latvia and Estonia, as well as the greater levels of industrialization they reached as early as the nineteenth century. In both territories, population decreased up to 75 percent as a result of the killings, widespread famine, and pestilence wrought by the war.[22] This occurred just at a time when most of western and northern Europe had entered, or was entering, an era of population explosion, brought about by a declining death rate. Hence, as the three Baltic populations entered the rapid growth phase of the demographic transition, the absolute number of Estonians and Latvians was relatively much smaller than that of Lithuanians.

Furthermore, changing patterns of land ownership among the Estonian and Latvian peasantry apparently began to raise the age of marriage, while decreasing marriage rates, sometime in the mid-nineteenth century, thus dampening the rate of population recovery and growth. To cap it all, the territory inhabited by the Estonians and Latvians underwent industrialization earlier than most of the Czarist Russian Empire. Whatever the complex effect on the birth rate industrialization and urbanization have, Estonians and Latvians

TABLE 2.4

Crude Birth Rate in Estonia, Latvia, and Lithuania, 1926-70

SSR	1926-30	1934	1940	1950	1960	1970
Estonia	17.6	15.4	16.1	18.4	16.6	15.8
Latvia	20.7	17.1	19.3	17.0	16.7	14.5
Lithuania	28.1	24.7	23.0	23.6	22.5	17.6

Sources: 1926-34: Riigi Statistika Keskbüroo, Rahvastikuprobleeme Eestis, II. rahvaloenduse tulemusi (Tallinn: Riigi Statistika Keskbüroo, 1937), 4: 111; 1940-70: Eesti NSV Ministrite Nôukogu juures asuv Statistika Keskvalitsus, Eesti NSV rahvamajandus 1971. aastal. Statistiline aastaraamat (Tallinn: Kirjastus Statistika Eesti Osakond, 1972), pp. 42-43.

felt it appreciably earlier than the Lithuanians. Consequently, the decline of the Lithuanian birth rate has lagged about 40 years behind that of Estonia and Latvia.

Past birth rate is, of course, one of the important determinants of current labor force availability. The Lithuanians were thus in a position, independently of the causes of, or motivations for, postwar industrialization, to meet industrial labor needs from their own population resources much better than the Estonians and Latvians. A high birth rate currently helps offset the relative effects of immigration, and here, too, Lithuania has been in a stronger position than Estonia and Latvia between 1945 and 1949, the immigrant groups, concentrated in the fertile age brackets, had an exceedingly high rate of natural increase as well, because of high age-specific birth rates and low age-specific death rates. Indeed, persistent immigration and differential fertility among the eponymous nationality and the immigrants in Estonia and Latvia have led to a situation where, between 1959 and 1970 in the Estonian SSR, only 20 percent of the total population increase was attributable to ethnic Estonians (as calculated from data in Table 2.2). The equivalent figure in the Latvian SSR for ethnic Latvians was 16 percent. The bulk of the remainder of the substantial growth in both republics is attributable to ethnic Russians, whether through immigration or natural increase. For example, in the Estonian SSR, in 1959, the rate of natural increase for the ethnic Estonians was a mere 2.2, while for all non-Estonians together it was 15.2.[23] In both the Estonian and Latvian SSRs, immigration between 1950 and 1970 was numerically larger than natural increase.

The consequence of the demographic changes may be assessed in both objective and subjective terms. Subjectively, the important matter is the way the changes are perceived by the eponymous nationality. The authors of the underground memorandums already mentioned anticipate that demographic Russification may result in the full loss of the Estonian and Latvian nationality identity because of its impact on cultural maintenance and other societal processes. Fear of this, in any case, is currently real. Whether or not the demographic turnover, especially the Russian influx, in fact poses a direct threat to the indigenous culture has hardly been studied in objective or empirical terms. Some indicators, such as publication, show a decrease in the percentage of titles of books, magazines, and newspapers in Estonia officially issued in Estonian in proportion to the percentage of Estonians in the union republic's population.[24] There are also reports from tourists that in social situations in which a person is present who does not speak Estonian or Latvian, Russian inevitably becomes the language of communication. The changing population composition creates a statistically greater likelihood that Russian must be used in daily life, especially in urban areas, where the immigrants have clustered. Yet it should be noticed that among offspring from intermarriages involving a Russian and Estonian or Latvian, more children choose the Estonian and Latvian nationality than Russian upon reaching the age of majority.[25]

An appreciably greater amount of research must be conducted into the ethnic consequences of population changes, especially through the use of empirical indicators. Nevertheless, a key point in an analysis of nationality processes in the Soviet Baltic area is that demographic changes have been important in causing dissatisfaction in Estonia and Latvia. From the accounts rendered by Western journalists, especially their descriptions of booing of Russian teams at sports events and the frequent refusal of Estonians and Latvians to speak Russian unless it is known that the speaker is a Westerner and not a Russian, it would appear that this discontent reaches beyond the eponymous groups' intellectuals to the bulk of the people.[26] The essence of the discontent is an anxiety that the continuing influx of Russians will lead to the full loss of the nationality's collective identity. Although this anxiety, at present, cannot be fully substantiated with data, as a causal factor of dissatisfaction, the anxiety itself is also an empirical fact.

CULTURE AND GROUP IDENTITY

Cultural elements—whether in terms of artifacts, language, social organization, or other forms—are universally important components of ethnic collective identities, probably because they are the most obvious and utilitarian means, other than physical appearances, for group differentiation. Because of this, in situations of interethnic contact, the social forces that challenge the cultural heritage of a group are especially likely to evoke strong group-level responses from the nationality affected. To lose the basis on which group differentiation can be made is to lose collective identity itself. The analysis of cultural processes is thus, in many respects, central to the understanding of nationality assertiveness, whether in the Soviet Union or elsewhere.

Soviet policies of socialist realism inhibit the creativity of all cultures of the USSR, including the Russian. Nevertheless, these policies may provide one of the basic determinants of nationality dissatisfaction among the non-Russian people, by stimulating interpretative displacement of attitudes from anti-Soviet to anti-Russian ones. Such policies appear to evoke antiregime feelings, especially among the cultural-intellectual elites. The party's implication that a new Soviet nation will be defined essentially on the basis of a Russian cultural core further aggravates the general situation, for it does not appear that the non-Russian people are willing to abandon their different collective identities voluntarily. The Party's general control over the interpretation of the past of all ethnic groups in the USSR and the concomitant chauvinistic emphasis on the historical preeminence of the Russians[27] appear also to add tension to interethnic relations through the day-to-day political processes of the society.

Among many aspects of cultural life, for example, creative literature and ethnographic study both are mediums for expressing nationality identity as well as for discussing current political and social issues.[28] In this sense, culture not only underlies collective ethnic identity, it also reflects a continual manifestation of that identity. Soviet Baltic literature has been extensively scrutinized in the West. By now it is evident that the Estonian, Latvian, and Lithuanian cultures are neither dead nor dying. Indeed, in many areas of culture, the Baltic union republics are much more contemporary than the rest of the Soviet Union.

However, one of the greatest fears expressed by Estonians and Latvians, as well as Lithuanians, concerns the danger of cultural demise, with a total loss of ethnic collective identities, under pressure from socialist realism. Adding to the anxiety is the homage paid by the Party to notions of a new homogenized Soviet nation. Especially in Estonia and Latvia, as a consequence of the high rate of Russian influx, the ability of the eponymous culture to resist and persist is crucial. One of two vital areas should be the strength of the cultural infrastructure, primarily the institutions that underlie cultural communication and cultural inculcation. Communication includes, of course, language as well as the means of cultural expression, such as publications, theaters, and the like. And inculcation pertains to school systems (popular and scholarly activity in the areas of ethnographic and folklore study, Baltic-oriented aspects of the humanities, and so forth). The second matter of importance is the degree to which contact is possible with non-Russian culture, both in Western and Eastern Europe. Intellectually, Estonian, Latvian, and Lithuanian students of history and culture have persistently emphasized roots in Western and Northern Europe rather than Eastern Europe. Contact with non-Russian culture also provides a potential competitive vitality for the varieties of Baltic culture, thereby reducing the impact of Russian culture upon them. The stronger the eponymous nationality's cultural infrastructure and culture's competitive vitality, the less likely Russification will occur under currently existing circumstances.

The cultural infrastructure of the Estonians, Latvians, and Lithuanians in the Soviet Union is reasonably strong at present. Two major considerations point to this. During the brief interwar decades (1918-40) of sovereign republics, all three eponymous Baltic societies vastly expanded their educational structure, from the primary level through institutes of higher learning. Estonians and Latvians had already become almost fully literate by the turn of the twentieth century in Czarist days. Lithuanians caught up by the time their country was incorporated into the Soviet Union during World War II. Most important, all three languages had been radically modernized during the interwar period, allowing for the development of strong literary traditions, a contemporary cultural life, and even a contemporary science in the native tongues. Also in these societies, ethnographic and folklore study and Baltic-oriented humanistic inquiry blossomed during the interwar decades. Most other Soviet people, on the whole, were not in a position to modernize their cultural infrastructure prior to contact with the Soviet order.

Although the Soviet Union may be criticized, in many respects legitimately, for oppressing non-Russian ethnic groups in one way or another, it also perpetuates a striking structural pluralism connected with the culture of many ethnic groups. Most Western countries do not, either in domestic or colonial policies, maintain such an extensive cultural and educational apparatus, not to mention scientific activity, in languages other than that of the dominant group. Estonian, Latvian, and Lithuanian children may have to learn Russian, it is true, but their education from the earliest years through specialized higher institutions is offered primarily in the ancestral languages. So long as this pluralistic structure is maintained in the Soviet Union, ethnic assimilation is not likely.

Variations between Estonia and Latvia in respect to the cultural infrastructure help explain the relatively more precarious situation in which observers presently find the Latvians.[29] During the period of Swedish rule (1561-1721), and subsequently during Russian rule (1721-1918), the center of humanistic learning in the area that later made up Estonia and Latvia was the University of Tartu. This institution played a significant role in educating both Estonian and Latvian humanists, theologians, and pastors from the mid-nineteenth century onward. Tartu was, in addition, an important intellectual center for the emergence of the new nineteenth century brand of nationalism among both people. With the creation of separate Baltic states in 1918, Tartu, with its rich historical traditions, became an Estonian university. Latvia had to found a brand new university in Riga. Tartu possessed a strong humanistic tradition and rich intellectual life. It also maintained regular contacts with most important centers of learning in northern, western and central Europe, links that continued during the interwar period. The presence of the University of Tartu in Estonia instead of Latvia provided the Estonians with a relatively stronger cultural infrastructure and thereby, a stronger potential for resisting cultural encroachments than was to be the case with the Latvians.

Another important difference between Estonia and Latvia relates to the historical functions of their capital cities. In Latvia, Riga has simultaneously served as the major industrial center, the seat of political-administrative power, and from the late nineteenth century and especially after 1918, the preeminent center of ethnic Latvian cultural and intellectual life. In Estonia, no equivalent concentration of functions has existed for Tallinn. While it, too, was historically the seat of political-administrative power, the ethnic Estonian cultural and intellectual center has remained in Tartu instead. Furthermore, while Tallinn was traditionally the most important Estonian industrial locality, from the 1930s onward, there has been appreciable regional diversification, with the oil-shale basin east of Tallinn, near the Russian border, emerging as a major industrial center. Such differences in regard to urban functions could have great consequences for nationality processes. Because of Riga's and Tallinn's established political-administrative functions, both attracted the representatives of the new ruling order. But Riga's historical industrial role has resulted in the large-scale migration of labor to the city and its immediate environs. However, in Estonia much of the postwar immigration apparently never reached Tallinn. Rather, it stopped in the oil-shale region of northeast Estonia and in the border city of Narva. The impact of the greater Russian presence in Riga is, moreover, probably acutely felt on Latvian cultural identity, because it has been also the Latvians' main intellectual-cultural center, and because Riga was ethnically never as much a Latvian city as Tallinn was an Estonian city, even during the interwar years.

In contrast to Estonia and Latvia, Lithuania during the 1918–40 period stood at a great disadvantage because its historical cultural-intellectual center, Vilnius, was under Polish rule. Consequently, Lithuania was forced to develop a new national cultural-intellectual center at Kaunas. With the return of Vilnius to Lithuania after the German-Soviet conquest of Poland in 1939, Lithuania enjoyed two such centers, which turned out to work to its advantage considerably. Vilnius, the capital of the Lithuanian SSR, has a proportionately low Lithuanian population, 43 percent in 1970, but the opposite is the case with Kaunas, which remains preeminently a city inhabited by the eponymous nationality. Lithuania's low level of prewar industrial development, noted earlier, apparently buffered the cities against immigration, helping after World War II to preserve greater ethnic homogeneity in the republic's cities.

TABLE 2.5

Population of Kaunas (Lithuania), Vilnius (Lithuania), Riga (Latvia), and Tallinn (Estonia), 1959 and 1970 (in percent)

City	1959	1970
Kaunas	82	84
Vilnius	34	43
Riga	45	41
Tallinn	60	56

Sources: Frederic T. Harned, "Lithuania and the Lithuanians," in Handbook of Major Soviet Nationalities, ed. Zev Katz et al. (New York: Free Press, 1975), p. 124; Frederic T. Harned, "Latvia and the Latvians," ibid., p. 100; Tõnu Parming, "Population Changes in Estonia during the Soviet Period," in A Case Study of a Soviet Republic: The Estonian SSR, ed. Tõnu Parming and Elmar Järvesoo (Boulder, Colo.: Westview Press, forthcoming).

Tables 2.5 and 2.6 provide data regarding the demographic realities prevailing in the cities under discussion, except Tartu, for which the required information has not yet been obtained. Table 2.5 indicates that the share of the population of Kaunas and Vilnius which is Lithuanian increased between the intercensal period 1959 and 1970. Slight declines occurred in the Latvian share of Riga's population and the Estonian proportion in Tallinn. During the intercensal period, moreover, the Lithuanian population of Vilnius doubled and that of Kaunas increased by nearly one-half. But the Estonian population of Tallinn and the Latvian population of Riga grew much more slowly, only by 21 percent in the former case and 15 percent in the latter. Obviously, then, Lithuanians are gaining in significance in the cities that are the seats of the cultural-intellectual life of their nationality group. The Latvians' situation in Riga is worsening, as is the Estonians' position in Tallinn. Latvians, furthermore, suffer from not having a city equivalent to the Estonians' Tartu, which is reported by recent tourists to remain predominantly Estonian in population composition.

The degree to which the noneponymous groups in Soviet Estonia, Latvia, and Lithuania are concentrated in the key Baltic cities can be learned from data in Tables 2.5 and 2.6. Of the three union republics, a relatively greater share of all non-Latvians in the Latvian SSR are concentrated in Riga, 40 percent in 1959 and 42 percent in

TABLE 2.6

Increase of the Eponymous Nationality in the Cities of Tallinn, Riga, Kaunas, and Vilnius, 1959-70

	1959		1970		Increase of Eponymous Nationality	
City	Total City Population	Eponymous Population	Total City Population	Eponymous Population	Absolute Increase, 1959-70	Percentage Increase, 1959-70
Tallinn	282,700	169,600	365,000	204,400	34,800	20.5
Riga	580,400	261,200	732,500	300,300	39,100	15.0
Kaunas	214,300	175,700	312,000	262,100	86,400	49.2
Vilnius	236,100	80,300	378,000	162,500	82,200	102.4

Sources: Juris Dreifelds, "Characteristics and Trends of Two Demographic Variables in the Latvian S.S.R.," Bulletin of Baltic Studies, no. 8 (Winter 1971): 14, is the source for "total city population" in 1959 and 1970. Figures for the "eponymous population" are calculated from the former by way of the percentages given in Table 2.5. In turn, the figures in the "increase of eponymous nationality" columns are derived from the two sets of figures just noted.

1970, than is the case in Estonia or Lithuania. In Estonia, 37 percent of all non-Estonians in the republic in 1959 resided in Tallinn, with no change recorded by the 1970 census. In the Lithuanian SSR, 28 percent of all non-Lithuanians resided in Vilnius in 1959, which increased to 35 percent in 1970. However, in Kaunas, the respective figures were 7 percent in 1959 and 8 percent in 1970.

As with industrialization and immigration, the matter of established ethnic centers also has left the Latvians in a relatively disadvantageous situation in comparison with the Estonians and Lithuanians. And this also appears to be the case in regard to another parameter for gauging a nationality's cultural vitality, contacts with non-Russian European cultures. The channels of such contact need detailed study, but some major contrasts characterizing differences among the Baltic nationalities may nevertheless be sketched from existing information.[30] All three eponymous nationalities, of course, have sizable ethnic communities abroad. Although these have played primarily a political role since World War II, they have also provided competing ethnic cultures outside the ancestral homelands and have mediated transmission of Western culture to their societies of origin. Although the impact of this competition and mediation has hardly been studied, it is clear that there has been some influence. One major difference among the three groups in this respect has been the presence of a strong Estonian community in nearby Sweden, where there are few Latvians and even fewer Lithuanians. From the end of World War II, Sweden has been home for the largest exile Estonian community, which has so far been the major Estonian cultural center in the West as well. This has perhaps provided Estonians a somewhat better opportunity for gaining leverage in a potential mediation and competition role, in part by way of Finland.

The proximity of Finland provides Estonians with an advantage no other Soviet nationalities have. To a degree, Finland is a meeting ground for Estonians from the Soviet Union and the West, since both segments travel there as students, scholars, and tourists. Some of the historical and cultural ties between Estonia and Finland have continued in operation even during the postwar period, especially since the mid-1960s. Cultural groups, for example, are exchanged and professors from Soviet Estonia staff chairs in Estonian language and literature at all Finnish universities, where the study of the subjects is mandatory for many students. There is also a brisk tourist traffic from Finland to Estonia via a direct boat connection, and although many fewer Estonians visit Finland than the reverse, tourist groups nevertheless make the trip to Helsinki every summer. In addition, many Estonians in the Estonian SSR watch Finnish television, which is facilitated by the affinity of the two languages. Further, the publications of Finnish communists are often available in the Estonian SSR, and although these may not be impartial in their reporting of world events and cultural trends, they are richer sources of information than the Party-controlled media in either Soviet Estonia or the Soviet Union as a whole. Finland, in other words, to a large degree helps directly or indirectly to mediate Estonian contacts with non-Russian European culture.

Furthermore, Estonia's contacts with Hungary also follow channels of ethnic affinity. When the Soviet Union absorbed Estonia in 1944, it inherited one of the three major centers of Finno-Ugric studies in the world, the others being in Helsinki and Budapest. Programs of Finno-Ugric studies in the Estonian SSR keep in operation a sizable scholarly, cultural apparatus. These as a side benefit offer a channel for studying indigenous culture and history, thereby providing one additional prop for the group's cultural infrastructure.

For Lithuania, Poland appears to play a role equivalent to the one played for Estonia by Finland, albeit to a much lesser degree.[31] Latvia, however, has no comparable direct contacts with other Eastern or Western European societies. Thus, once again, for reasons that have no relation to a specific Soviet policy toward Latvia, the eponymous nationality is in a relatively weaker position than either the Estonians or Lithuanians. The difficulty of the Latvians' position could, of course, be ameliorated if there were intensive contacts between the three Baltic cultures, but no significant interchange has been identified during the postwar period by observers to date. The lack of intra-Baltic cultural contacts reflects their absence, even in the interwar period. On the other hand, the conditions of Soviet life seemingly are such that informal, unstructured contacts between intellectuals and cultural activists of various ethnic groups are not readily possible unless the individuals reside in a given city.

From the preceding, it is evident that demographically, the Estonians and Latvians both are in a relatively weaker position than Lithuanians. However, in the case of the Estonians, the situation is ameliorated by the fact that the cultural infrastructure appears to be somewhat stronger than that of the Latvians. However, nationality survival depends not only on demographic and cultural factors but also on the degree to which the group has a will to persist.

ETHNIC SOLIDARITY

Nationality solidarity is an important issue because it bears on the ability of the membership to act as a whole in response to real or perceived threats to the group's well-being or even existence. The greater the degree of within-group differentiation or fragmentation, the weaker the ability of the group to challenge and counteract effectively those social forces that the group perceives or feels to be detrimental. These principles relate to the following observation by a Baltic specialist:

> Some notable divergences are evident in the Estonian, Latvian and Lithuanian responses to the political contingencies of the 1900-1905 period, World War I, World War II, and the Soviet regime since 1945. Of the three response patterns, the Lithuanian exhibits the highest degree of political cohesiveness, capacity for internal compromise and disposition to rely on nationality generated political resources; the Latvian pattern shows the lowest degree of cohesiveness, internal compromise, and national self-reliance; while the Estonian occupies a middle position between the other two. . . . rather than being the products of random differences in contemporary political contingencies [such divergences] may be explainable in terms of the hitherto neglected formative influences of differential political developments in the Baltic territories prior to the 19th century.[32]

The populations of the three Baltic republics differed from each other in degree of religious and ethnic homogeneity long before Soviet times. Lithuanians stand at the high end of the scale of homogeneity and the Latvians on the low end (see Tables 2.1 and 2.2). The cognate population in the key centers of cultural and intellectual life for the three eponymous Baltic nationalities is also markedly differentiated (see Tables 2.5 and 2.6). All these data rank Lithuanians first, Estonians second, and Latvians third, the same order noted in the citation above.

Among the three nationalities, there are no major regional or subidentities in either Lithuania or Estonia that challenge the identity of the collective whole, but in Latvia the opposite is the case. Here the western, central, and eastern areas of the country have experienced appreciably different political histories. Courland, in the west, was a "major minor" feudal state in the Baltic area from 1561 to 1795, to the extent of having its own overseas colonies in Africa and the West Indies. While Courland was an independent state, parts of central Latvia, after the collapse of Old Livonia, shifted between Polish-Lithuanian, Swedish, and Czarist Russian rule. Latgale, in the east, was under Polish-Lithuanian domination until 1772, almost two generations longer than central Latvia, which had already passed to Russian control by 1721. Courland did not become part of

Czarist Russia until 1795, which is also the date when Lithuania was absorbed. Most Estonians, however, were administratively united under Swedish rule by the end of the seventeenth century and were taken all at once into the Russian Empire in 1721. Latgale's population was also separated from other Latvians by being largely Roman Catholic instead of Lutheran.

Relatively greater political fragmentation among Latvians, compared to Estonians and Lithuanians is evidenced, furthermore, during the years immediately preceding the formation of the sovereign Baltic states and during the interwar Republics as well. There was a great deal less unity in party politics and national political goals among the Latvians than Estonians and Lithuanians. Voting patterns reflected this during the 1917-18 years of turmoil in Russia.[33] Also, during the democratic years of the sovereign states, Latvian politics were characterized by parties that were regionally based, with Latgale especially manifesting a degree of separatism.[34] Estonia and Lithuania each had more distinctly national parties.

In terms of political perceptions, there is a significant difference among the three Baltic people that goes back to the era of Czarist rule. Lithuanians were attempting to reestablish political sovereignty, while both the Estonians and Latvians created it in 1918. The fact that Lithuania, alone and in union with Poland, was once a powerful, important state in Eastern Europe is evidenced continually in the eponymous nationality's political awareness. Latvia and Estonia were not, of course, sovereign states at all prior to 1918. Since the thirteenth century, they remained under foreign domination, and before this time, no political coalescence into nationhood had taken place. In Latvia, there was extensive fragmentation in the few years prior to 1918, in regard to both political goals and means, probably reflecting the presence of a sizable, radicalized industrial labor force in Riga and the presence of a large Baltic German minority. In Estonia, although the democratic political parties enjoyed the overwhelming majority of electoral support, the concept of sovereignty was not a goal until Russia itself collapsed in chaos as a result of the 1917 revolution. Until the Bolshevist seizure of power in Russia, Estonia's political leadership had favored an autonomous status in a democratic, federal Russia.

Historically, the type of national aspiration that has as its essential goal the establishment of statehood has obviously had a much stronger tradition in Lithuania than in either Estonia or Latvia. Yet even in the latter two, sovereignty as such appears to have become a very popular nationality concept during the interwar period. At present, this continues to be reflected in the many accounts of overt demonstrations and covert commemorations held at the graves of the leaders of the interwar republic, at statues having pre-Soviet nationality significance, and even at sites where statues used to stand before their removal or destruction by Soviet authorities. These occur especially in conjunction with dates pertinent either to the interwar leaders or the interwar sovereign states themselves.

Although the interwar era is deemphasized by current rulers, it is hardly ignored. In all three Baltic union republics, the tendency persists to compare all Soviet-era achievements and progress to the same home territory base year of 1940, rather than to the rest of Europe or the Third World at some other time. Furthermore, a great deal of official energy goes into denouncing the societal structure, the level of development, and the political leadership of the interwar republics. This particular type of Soviet policy itself reinforces the awareness in Estonians, Latvians, and Lithuanians of their own political past.

The role of the local Communist Party in nationality processes is also important with respect to group solidarity. The local party structure mediates, to a large degree, Moscow's rule and authority to the local inhabitants. There is an appreciably greater eponymous group presence in the Party in the Lithuanian SSR than there is in Estonia and Latvia. Pertinent data are summarized in Table 2.7. Why the Lithuanians overtook Estonians in percentage during the 1950s and 1960s and why the Latvians remain at a low level of Party membership are issues that deserve further study. (See Chapter 5.) Part of the difference may be explained by immigration, for the Russians have among the highest rates of Party membership of any ethnic group in the Soviet Union,[35] and immigration has been of minimal importance in Lithuania. However, this explains little, because Lithuanian membership in the Party appears to have outstripped Estonian and Latvian growth during the 1950s and 1960s in both absolute and relative terms.

The general percentage of the eponymous nationality present in the local party structure is overemphasized as an indicator of the nationality's influence in it. The eponymous nationality's weight in the Party elite and in key nonelite positions counts more. Who heads the Party structures are in those cities serving as the cultural-intellectual centers of the group? That is significant. Other crucial matters are the local Party elite's attitudes regarding the nationality issue and the degree to which the local leadership gets along with the central government and CPSU leaders in Moscow.

In 1971, 78 percent of the Central Committee members and candidates in the Party in Lithuania were ethnic Lithuanians; in the SSR's Politburo and Secretariat, this component reached 87 percent; and in the Council of Ministers still a higher 93 percent.[36] In the Estonian SSR, of those in the Central Committee, Estonians constituted 80 percent in 1971 and above 90 percent in the Council of Ministers

TABLE 2.7

Percentage of Eponymous Nationality in the Communist Party of Each Baltic SSR, 1945-73

Year	Lithuania	Estonia	Latvia
1945	31.8	–	–
1946	–	48.1	–
1952	–	41.5	–
1953	38.0	–	–
1959	55.7	–	–
1961	–	49.1	–
1966	–	–	≈33
1967	–	52.0	–
1970	67.1	52.3	–
1973	69.1	–	≈43*

*Maximum.

Sources: Jaan Pennar, "Soviet Nationality Policy and the Estonian Communist Elite," ed. Tõnu Parming and Elmar Järvesoo, A Case Study of a Soviet Republic: The Estonian SSR (Boulder, Colo.: Westview Press, forthcoming); V. Thomas Remeikis, "Nationalism in Lithuania Since 1964" (Paper presented at the Symposium on Nationalism in the USSR and Eastern Europe under Brezhnev and Kosygin, University of Detroit, October 1975); V. Stanley Vardys, "Modernization and Baltic Nationalism," Problems of Communism 24, no. 5 (September-October 1975): 40.

and among deputy ministers together.[37] Latvia's Party filled only 42 percent of the Central Committee's seats with Latvians. In Lithuania and Estonia, the eponymous nationality's presence in the Party elite is much higher than in the Party membership as a whole, while in the Latvian case, the share in the elite appears to be as low as in the membership. Little information is available regarding other key Party positions in the union republics, but data provided in Chapter 5 suggest pointedly that here, too, the position of Estonians is appreciably stronger than that of Latvians.

Attitudes of the eponymous party elites in Estonia, Latvia, and Lithuania toward the issue of nationalism, either factually or theoretically, remains largely veiled. However, issues of nationality dissatisfaction have occasionally, for example, toward the end of Stalin's rule, flared up within the party, leading to both leadership and membership purges. Latvians have been the least capable of dealing with this issue through the Party.

Another purge of the highest Latvian leadership, for exhibiting nationalistic tendencies, occurred toward the end of the 1950s under Khrushchev's direct pressure.[38] In Estonia, Johannes (Ivan) Käbin has maintained his extended tenure as Party first secretary, while currently a lively debate ensues in the republic, and even on the pages of party journals, about the nationality issue.[39] The eponymous Party elite in Estonia evidently does not look at ethnicity in negative terms theoretically, so long as its manifestations do not lead to active dissent in other areas of societal life.

The issue here is not one of whether Party leadership of the three groups is "communist" or "non-communist" in orientation. Rather, even within the CPSU, variations exist in regard to attitudes concerning the nationality issue. Ultraorthodox members favor homogenizing all the nationalities. Others are not theoretically disturbed by ethnicity. While both are dedicated to the Party and its expressed goals, one faction displays more tolerance of nationality expressiveness than another. Estonian Communists appear on the higher end of the "nationality tolerance scale," whereas Latvians seem to have trouble convincing Moscow that "Latvian identity" is not detrimental to the USSR politically, economically, or otherwise.

Many of the Baltic Party leaders are, in some respect, Russified, because they grew up in the Soviet Union during the interwar years. This was especially the case in regard to Estonians and Latvians. Nevertheless, these individuals are truly members of the eponymous nationality, and they identify themselves as such. Their interwar association with the membership of the Union-wide Party seems to enhance their ability to play a mediating role between their ancestral group and the central authorities. Among other things, this ability could reflect individual personality variations. Käbin, at least, seems very capable in this role, whereas most Latvians do not.

Thus, as with demographic, religious, and cultural factors, in politics, once more the Latvians are found in position of greatest relative group disadvantage among the three Baltic groups. In terms of nationality solidarity, the Latvians do not rate high either from a historical perspective or from a consideration of the current performance in the Party. Variations among the three Baltic nationality groups in regard to those aspects of the nationality support factors that have been considered, both historically and presently, help to explain the potential for, and the manifestation of, nationality discontent. The Lithuanians have a high degree of cohesion through almost any dimension and a high degree of nationality solidarity as well. It should not be surprising then that, in terms of overt resistance to Soviet rule, they have been the most active of the three Baltic nationality groups. The Latvians predictably display a great deal of nationality heterogeneity and a much lower level of solidarity than the Lithuanians or Estonians. This is reflected in the relative absence of direct confrontations with Soviet authority and in the currently reported social resignation. The Estonians, while lacking the uniform population found among Lithuanians, nevertheless display a high degree of nationality solidarity, which helps to explain both the low level of overt, confrontational type of resistance as well as the existence of a strong nationality assertiveness through culture.

CONCLUSIONS

Among those societal processes and forces within Soviet Baltic society that contribute to the persistence of ethnic or nationality assertiveness are the remarkable degree of cultural pluralism ensuing from the very administrative structure of the area; the generally repressive nature of the Soviet order in regard to civil, religious, and cultural rights; the disproportionately large role played by Russians in the Union-wide government and Party hierarchy; the dispersal of Russians to peripheral territories, which are the ancestral homelands of other groups; the Party's strong hold over the interpretation of history, whether Soviet, Russian, or non-Russian; and the continual emphasis that the new "Soviet nation" will have a Russian cultural core. Two important forces that operate from outside the Soviet Union are the influence of the age of nationalistic ideology, which champions the right of all people to create their own states, and outside agitation, whether by elements of Soviet nationality groups abroad or by other powers.

These competing forces provide a great deal of dynamism to the Soviet nationality issue. However, the manner in which nationality problems manifest themselves, in terms of catalysts of nationality satisfaction or dissatisfaction, the channels of their expression, the capacity of a given group to challenge and counteract perils it perceives, cannot be understood by focusing solely on the nature of present Soviet society, on modernization, or on outside pressures. Rather, the way in which these forces interact with the nationality support factors is fundamental. In the Soviet Baltic area, the uneven nature of nationality assertiveness reflects the differential nature of these support factors, today as well as historically. In some cases, a single Soviet policy affecting religious life, applied in three different localities simultaneously, leads to different results. In Lithuania, it may precipitate immediate nationality discontent, but little response in Latvia and Estonia. Early patterns of industrialization have appeared fateful in some respects, for Latvia's and Estonia's greater degree of economic development as early as the late nineteenth century depressed birth rates, while contributing, during the postwar period, to a larger immigration here than entered Lithuania. The urban functions of key cities and the availability of channels of contact with non-Russian Europe also have had a bearing on nationality issues. Also, historical factors have basically contributed to significant variation in the extent of nationality solidarity among the Soviet Baltic union republics.

NOTES

1. Rein Taagepera, "Estonia and the Estonians," and Frederic T. Harned, "Latvia and the Latvians" and "Lithuania and the Lithuanians," in Handbook of Major Soviet Nationalities, ed. Zev Katz et al. (New York: Free Press, 1975), pp. 75-93; Tõnu Parming, "Developments in Nationalism in Soviet Estonia Since 1964," Juris Dreifelds, "Developments in Nationalism in Soviet Latvia Since 1964," and Thomas Remeikis, "Developments in Nationalism in Soviet Lithuania Since 1964" (papers presented at the Symposium on Nationalism in the USSR and Eastern Europe under Brezhnev and Kosygin, at the University of Detroit, October 1975), to be published by the University of Detroit Press as a special volume edited by George Simmonds; V. Stanley Vardys, "Modernization and Baltic Nationalism," Problems of Communism 24, no. 5 (September-October 1975): 32-48.

2. George Saunders, ed., Samizdat, Voices of the Soviet Opposition (New York: Monad Press, 1974), pp. 427-40; Dimitry Pospielovsky, "The Kaunas Riots and the National and Religious Tensions in the USSR," Radio Liberty Research Bulletin (May 31, 1972), pp. 127-72; V. Stanley Vardys, "Protests in Lithuania Not Isolated," Lituanus 18, no. 2 (1972): 5-7; "A Declaration of the Lithuanian National People's Front," Lituanus 22, no. 1 (1976): 65-71; "Estonian and Latvian Memorandum to the Conference on Security and Cooperation," Lituanus 21, no. 3 (1975): 65-73; "Two Memoranda to the United Nations from Soviet Occupied Estonia," Lituanus 21, no. 2 (1975): 64-75.

3. Ellen Mickiewicz, ed., Handbook of Soviet Social Science Data (New York: Free Press, 1973); Teresa Rakowska-Harmstone, "The Dialectics of Nationalism in the USSR," Problems of Communism 23, no. 3 (May-June 1974): 4.

4. Vardys, "Modernization and Baltic Nationalism."

5. "A Declaration of the Lithuanian National People's Front," p. 70; "Estonian and Latvian Memorandum to the Conference on Security and Cooperation," pp. 69-70; "Two Memoranda to the United Nations from Soviet Occupied Estonia," pp. 65, 66, 75.

6. "National and Religious Protest in Lithuania. From the Underground Chronicle of the Catholic Church in Lithuania," pt. 1, Lituanus 20, no. 2 (1974): 68-75; pt. 2, ibid., 20, no. 3 (1974): 73-75; pt. 3, ibid., 20, no. 4 (1974): 62-68; "The Chronicles of the Lithuanian Catholic Church Continue Publication," Lituanus 21, no. 3 (1975): 64; "Declaration by the Priests of the Catholic Church in Lithuania Dated August 1969," Lituanus 19, no. 3 (1973): 46-53; Vardys, "Modernization and Baltic Nationalism," p. 47.

7. Dreifelds, "Developments in Nationalism in Soviet Latvia Since 1964."

8. Rakowska-Harmstone, p. 5.

9. Algirdas Budreckis, "Liberation Attempts from Abroad," ed. Albertas Gerutis, Lithuania 700 Years, 3d rev. ed. (New York: Manyland Books, 1969); Arvo Horm, Phases of the Baltic Political Activities (Stockholm: Baltic Humanitarian Association, 1973).

10. Algirdas Budreckis, "Lithuanian Resistance 1940-52," Gerutis, ed.; Zenonas Ivinskis, "Lithuania during the War: Resistance Against the Nazi and Soviet Occupants," and V. Stanley Vardys, "The Partisan Movement in Postwar Lithuania," in Lithuania Under the Soviets, ed. V. Stanley Vardys (New York: Praeger, 1965), pp. 61-84 and 85-108, respectively; Juozas Daumantas, Fighters for Freedom (New York: Manyland Books, 1975); Adolfs Silde, Resistance Movement in Latvia (Stockholm: Latvian National Foundation, 1972).

11. J. A. Rackauskas, "Education in Lithuania Prior to the Dissolution of the Jesuit Order (1773)," Lituanus 22, no. 1 (1976): 5-41; J. A. Rackauskas, "The Educational Commission of Poland and Lithuania 1773-1794," Lituanus 19, no. 4 (1973): 63-70.

12. Arthur Vööbus, Studies in the History of the Estonian People, 3 vols. (Stockholm: Estonian Theological Society in Exile, 1969-74).

13. Royal Institute of International Affairs, The Baltic States (London: Oxford University Press, 1938), p. 46.

14. Ibid., p. 52.

15. Ibid., pp. 40, 56-60.

16. "Estonian and Latvian Memorandum to the Conference on Security and Cooperation," pp. 69-70.

17. "Two Memoranda to the United Nations from Soviet Occupied Estonia," pp. 64-75.

18. Tõnu Parming, "The Impact of Demographic Changes on Ethnic Processes in Soviet Estonia" (Paper presented at the Conference on Population Change and the Soviet Nationality Question, Columbia University, December 6, 1975).

19. Tõnu Parming, "Population Processes in Estonia during the Soviet Period," ed. Tõnu Parming and Elmar Järvesoo, A Case Study of a Soviet Republic: The Estonian SSR (Boulder, Colo.: Westview Press, forthcoming).

20. Tõnu Parming, "Population Changes in Estonia, 1935-1970," *Population Studies* 26 (March 1972): 56-61.

21. Elmar Järvesoo, "The Economic Transformation of Postwar Estonia," ed. Parming and Järvesoo.

22. Parming, "Population Processes in Estonia during the Soviet Period," diagram 1.

23. Parming, "Population Changes in Estonia . . .," pp. 72-77.

24. Tõnu Parming, "Soziale Konsequenzen der Bevölkerungs-Veränderungen in Estland seit 1939," *Acta Baltica* 11 (1971): 31.

25. Ludmila Terentjeva, "How Do Youths from Bi-National Families Determine Their Nationality," *Bulletin of Baltic Studies* 6, no. 4 (December 1970): 5-11.

26. Andres Küng, *Estland zum Beispiel* (Stuttgart: Seewald, 1973); Andres Küng, *Saatusi ja saavutusi* (Lund: Eesti Kirjanike Kooperatiiv, 1973).

27. Lowell Tillett, *The Great Friendship: Soviet Historians on the Non-Russian Nationalities* (Chapel Hill: University of North Carolina Press, 1969).

28. Andres Jüriado, "Nationalism vs. Socialism in Soviet Estonian Drama," *Lituanus* 19, no. 2 (1973): 28-42; Valda Melngaile, "The Sense of History in Recent Soviet Latvian Poetry," *Journal of Baltic Studies* 6 (Summer/Fall 1975): 130-40; Gustav Ränk, "Scholarship in Ethnography in the Estonian SSR," in Parming and Järvesoo, eds.; Rein Taagepera, "The Problem of Political Collaboration in Soviet Estonian Literature," *Journal of Baltic Studies* no. 6 (Spring 1975): 30-40; Bronius Vaskelis, "The Assertion of Ethnic Identity via Myth and Folklore in Soviet Lithuanian Literature," *Lituanus* 19, no. 2 (1973): 16-27; Joan T. Weingard, "Language and Literature in Estonia: Kulturpolitik or Natural Evolution," ed. Ralph S. Clem, *The Soviet West* (New York: Praeger, 1975).

29. Vardys, "Modernization and Baltic Nationalism," p. 48.

30. Parming, "Developments in Nationalism in Soviet Estonia Since 1964."

31. Romuald Misiunas "History Revisited: Notes on a Sabbatical in Poland" (Talk given at the Fifth Conference on Baltic Studies, Columbia University, May 1976).

32. Janis J. Penikis, "Comparisons of Baltic Political Cultures" (Paper presented at the Third Conference on Baltic Studies, University of Toronto, May 1972), abstracted in Arvids Ziedonis, Jr., Rein Taagepera, and Mardi Valgamäe, eds., *Problems of Mininations: Baltic Perspectives* (San Jose, Calif.: Association for the Advancement of Baltic Studies, 1973), p. 65.

33. Stanley W. Page, *The Formation of the Baltic States* (Cambridge, Mass.: Harvard University Press, 1959), pp. 1-26, 62-85.

34. Royal Institute of International Affairs, pp. 41-62.

35. Rakowska-Harmstone, p. 5.

36. Remeikis, "Developments in Nationalism in Soviet Lithuania Since 1964."

37. Jaan Pennar, "Soviet Nationality Policy and the Estonian Communist Elite," in Parming and Järvesoo, eds.

38. Harned, "Latvia and the Latvians," pp. 94-117.

39. Pennar, "Soviet Nationality Policy . . ."

CHAPTER

3

HISTORIANS AND NATIONALITY DISSATISFACTION

Kenneth E. Nyirady

Soviet Estonian, Latvian, and Lithuanian historians are responding significantly to what they perceive is their nationalities' current status. This tendency seems evident both through their selection and, to a lesser extent, interpretation of historical topics. As Baltic society continues to modernize, changing emphasis occurs among the various factors that serve as nationality supports. This movement has given historians changing roles to play as active supporters of Baltic culture. Whereas earlier supports among Baltic nationalities, such as expectations of future political and economic independence or religious and cultural self-determination, could not be discussed by historians under Soviet conditions in a forthright manner, newer supports, such as the preservation of local culture and history, can be dealt with without their appearing to be politically unacceptable.

The nationality question in the Baltic region of the Soviet Union is not determined, at any given moment, solely by political or economic criteria but by three groups of factors that have a circular effect upon each other. These may be classified as (1) objective identity and physical factors, (2) relativity factors, and (3) regulatory factors. The relative weight of each component of this group is never static but always shifting in the face of new external circumstances. For example, the historical interests of a nationality could be considered part of the objective identity factor of cultural maintenance. An increase in emphasis upon this factor may result in the growth of a component of the regulatory factor of group pride. In turn, this pride could cause a Soviet government reaction against nationalistic tendencies in the nationality's culture, bringing into play another regulatory factor. As further ripples can be predicted in such a situation, it becomes clear that the relationship of these three groups of support factors is constantly in flux.

The major impetus for changing emphasis among these support factors comes from Soviet modernization. In the Baltic region of the USSR, this process is characterized under a demanding centralized power structure, and its ideology by rapid but recent economic development, industrialization, urbanization, massive non-Baltic immigration, and the attendant social pressures and tensions that occur when societies undergo such a change, especially within a short time. Whereas urbanization may appear to homogenize the various cultures comprising an urban setting, it may also bring ethnic differences into full view, thereby heightening awareness among certain groups. Dissatisfaction can arise when this heightened sense of common identity magnifies perceived differences between various groups, especially when one nationality believes itself to be materially or culturally deprived in relation to other ethnic groups.

The newly focused role of Baltic historians reflects the increase in group discontent publicly articulated by Baltic nationalities during the late 1960s and early 1970s. It indicates both the historians' awareness and concern with group identity and distinctiveness together with recognition of their possible role in altering the degree of group-oriented satisfaction/dissatisfaction within the region. Such a change could be accomplished, for example, through the stimulation of interest in local values, national historical legends, group pride and exclusiveness, and so on. Not every Baltic historian, perhaps, feels dissatisfied or nationalistic or is aware of taking a role in these processes. But when analyzed as a group, it becomes evident that Baltic historians are revealing certain areas of concern through their works.

Both the oral and recorded history of a people serve as a major transmission belt for cultural values, traditions, and many of the components that can be summarized in the term "nationality identity." The greatest stimulus for feelings of nationality, according to John Stuart Mill, "is identity of political antecedents; the possessing of a national history, and consequent community of recollections; collective pride and humiliation, pleasure and regret, connected with the same incidents in the past."[1] A present-day scholar also has noted that

> the historian informs his contemporaries of their historical development and in doing so provides them with a memory extending back before their own lives, a memory of their aspirations, difficulties, and achievements. Just as each individual's memory is essential for daily life so a collective memory is necessary for a community to maintain a sense of direction.[2]

Whether displaying past achievements or noting progress up to present feats, knowledge of the past can serve both as a source of nationality pride, by displaying past glories, and as a source of emotional security. It lends an aura of permanence to the group. Historical knowledge can help place contemporary hardships in their true perspective, suggesting that they are surmountable difficulties, not necessarily catastrophic events.

Precisely because of his intimacy with the group through his role as conveyor of knowledge about the past, the historian is profoundly affected by what has been called the "climate of opinion" of an age—the basic suppositions shared by the majority of a group at a given time.[3] Perhaps the attitudes of his society are diverse or, on the other hand, a definite consensus exists. In any event, exactly because the historian does not, and is expected not to, limit results of his scholarship to a small technical elite but to disperse part of it among the public, his own attitudes, reflected in his output, reflect this climate of opinion.

The historian is a product of the society in which he lives and cannot, so to speak, "jump out of his intellectual skin."[4] The relationship between the historian and society is reciprocal. Influence runs in both directions. Treatments of these interactions must be qualified somewhat when discussing Baltic historians who live and write within the Soviet Marxist environment. These qualifications will be discussed later.

History is vitally related to the emotional state of the nationality. It serves as a possible source of security, a framework for nationality self-examination. Group anxiety or doubt can stimulate an increase of nationality interest in its own history. Feelings of uncertainty about the present can trigger a preoccupation with the past or, at least, with particular periods that are perceived to have been "better" or simpler than the present. Extreme instances of this phenomenon occur especially after a traumatic national experience, such as a serious military defeat. It has been noticed that

> in such periods of total national degradation defeated peoples have frequently reacted by trimming their sails and turning inward in search of spiritual consolation. This agonized quest has often assumed the form of a heightened degree of historical consciousness, which impels the intellectual leaders of the chastened nation to dredge up past evidence of national glory to compensate for the present sentiment of national humiliation.[5]

One of the most notable examples of resort to such introspection was the reaction of French historians to their country's defeat in the Franco-Prussian War of 1870-71.

The relationship of present anxieties and historical preoccupation to the Soviet Baltic republics of Estonia, Latvia, and Lithuania is clear. Rising group discontent among these three eponymous nationalities during the past eight to ten years has been characterized by a desire for religious freedom in Lithuania, demands for home rule and a halt to Russian immigration in Latvia, and strivings toward democracy and independence in Estonia.[6] Both Latvia and Estonia have recently been subject to such a heavy influx of Russians that the original inhabitants could conceivably become numerical minorities within their own republics before the turn of the next century. Lithuania is being confronted by Soviet efforts to neutralize Catholicism there, posing a threat to the religious-cultural heritage. These developments could easily be perceived as portents of cultural disaster by the Baltic people. Such a threat of identity annihilation might easily have an effect on historians similar to a profound military defeat, causing them to reinforce nationality feelings through a re-emphasis on past glories. Again, the uncertainties about the future caused by Soviet modernization may also produce increased interest in a past that may be viewed as a simpler time if not necessarily a more prosperous one. Though Baltic historians experience this, they cannot be guided solely by their feelings. They are subject to the ideology of the Soviet state, which limits their range of historical expression.

Baltic historians may not openly express discontent with the effects of the Soviet system on their republics because such dissent is politically impermissible. In addition, discussing previous Soviet "errors" publicly admitted by the Communist Party, such as the Stalinist "cult of personality," is discouraged because, as the Party press has put it, it does not "facilitate the correct education of the population, especially young people."[7] Moreover, historians in the Soviet state are expected to participate actively in ideological warfare against the West. They must act as constant heralds for the "great friendship of peoples" slogan,[8] implying historically amicable ties between the Russians and the nationalities comprising the Soviet Union. The Party's position on these two themes was well stated, according to a 1973 review of the books <u>History of the Latvian Riflemen</u> and <u>And So I Went To War</u>:

> Books like these are up-to-date and timely. There is nothing paradoxical in this. The more acute the

> struggle between the two ideologies becomes, the oftener the friendship of the Soviet peoples becomes the object of ideological diversion of imperialists and their hangers on, the reactionary Latvian emigration. . . . Each new book of a writer on this theme becomes a genuine weapon in the unceasing ideological struggle.[9]

A comparison of these books, it was noted, "shows clearly how the historian and the literary man go hand-in-hand in the struggle against falsifiers of history."[10] It was said that such books smell of gunpowder "because they themselves are in the front ranks of the firing line."[11] A comparable Soviet analysis of the three-volume History of the Estonian Republic (1974) called that work "an effective weapon against falsification by the ideologists of anti-communism."[12] This thought was also reiterated by the first secretary of Lithuania's Communist Party's Central Committee, Petras Grishkavičus, who spoke in an address to Lithuania's Academy of Sciences in May 1974 about the role of social scientists and their duty to carry out tasks formulated by the Party. On that occasion, he instructed historians to devote more attention to "a scientific analysis of modern times."[13]

The Party's wishes are not always faithfully implemented. A March 1973 meeting of history institute directors stressed "the need to have the ideological and theoretical levels of works" raised, the necessity for strictly observing "a class-party approach to the evaluation of historical phenomena, and to intensify the offensive against anti-scientific bourgeois and nationalistic concepts."[14] Also noted was the fact that some publications are "largely descriptive in nature and do not contain profound conclusions and generalizations."[15]

A persuasive motive for conforming to Party directives is, of course, economic. Professional historians in the Soviet Union are members of the intellectual elite, who receive the material rewards of the system, including occasional high awards. The Red Banner of Labor prize was awarded to Estonian historian Joosep Saat and Latvian historian Janis Krastins on their respective seventieth and eightieth birthdays.[16]

PATTERNS IN SELECTION OF HISTORICAL TOPICS

Given this tension between nationality feelings and Party demands, Baltic historians may be revealing their attitudes in a more subtle way. The subjects about which they write may disclose their innermost feelings more than the interpretation of such topics. Interpretation does play a crucial role and cannot be ruled out altogether. But choosing to write about certain topics that may sublimate anxieties about the future is a more practical option for Baltic historians than attempting to interpret other historical topics in what might be an anti-Soviet manner. In such a situation, distinctively Baltic topics ought to be emphasized rather than those that are distinctively Soviet. Because the level of nationality discontent has increased during the past eight to ten years, Baltic historians could well be expected to write more about Baltic topics than before. Historians who write about the distant, distinctively Baltic past may not have to be as strenuously concerned with a class-conscious interpretation of their findings as scholars of more recent history. Writing about clearly Baltic topics would seem to provide an outlet for tensions produced by Soviet modernization and its accompanying nationality discontent among Soviet Baltic historians.

One test of this hypothesis comes in a survey taken (for this chapter) of the historical books published within the three Baltic republics from 1960-64 and 1970-74. These five-year cycles were chosen in order to determine if the increase of discontent evident in the region during the late 1960s and early 1970s would be evident in the second group of titles when compared to the first. Whereas journal publishing would appear to be directed toward other historians, a select group of readers, book publishing might embrace, in addition, those works intended for the general public. Moreover, all-inclusive lists of books published in the Baltic republics are easily accessible here, unlike such aids for journal publication. The 1960-64 cycle was chosen as a base period because it is located conveniently midway between the de-Stalinization campaign inaugurated in 1956 and the first persistent evidence of growing dissatisfaction in the Baltic region. Both five-year periods supply ample protection against distorting effects of year-to-year fluctuations in publications. The _Ezhegodnik knigi SSSR_ [USSR Yearbook of Books] provided the information for 1960-64 and 1970-72; the more recent statistics come from _Knizhnaia letopis'_ [Book chronicle]. The present survey includes works about ethnography and archaeology, because Soviet bibliographers classify both topics under "history" in the above-mentioned sources. Communist Party history is excluded not only because the same bibliographers list it independently but also because its subject matter may lie more in the realm of political science than history. The themes of listed works could usually be inferred from their titles or associated reviews. Those titles whose subjects could not be deciphered are so indicated. Foreign books translated into Baltic languages were excluded from the major classifications, but non-Baltic Soviet historical works republished in languages of the Baltic area could not be isolated.

For this analysis, fifteen subclassifications were created and divided into three major types of subjects: (1) local pre-Soviet history, (2) Soviet and socialist topics, and (3) world or foreign history. Books assigned to the first section—and considered to support Baltic culture that emphasizes its distinctiveness as opposed to Soviet internationalism—are Baltic history until 1917 (excluding the revolutionary movements), archaeology, ethnography, pre-1917 cultural history, regional history, and related museum and historical landmark topics. The second major classification of historical books, Soviet and socialist topics, encompasses Baltic history since 1917, including the revolutionary period leading up to that year; general Soviet history, the history of exiles and expatriates, and industrial history. The turbulent events of 1917-24 and "reincorporation" of 1940 are included here as they are used to legitimize Soviet rule in the three Baltic republics. The independence, or so-called bourgeois, period also falls here, because the approved ideological interpretation required by the Party still produces a distorted and derogatory account. Such a treatment cannot be seen to support Baltic culture or nationality. Industrial history is a topic that is purely socialistic in nature, given the almost simultaneous development claimed for the proletariat and socialism in Czarist Russia. The third major category, world and foreign history, perhaps nearly neutral in terms of nationality support, has possible implications worth exploring. Two other subcategories cover books whose subject obviously deals with both Baltic and Soviet topics, and also those titles whose subjects are unidentifiable. The languages of publications will also be noted, because the expected increase in Baltic topics may be accompanied by a greater use of the eponymous Baltic languages, adding a cultural support for nationality, in historical book publishing. The numerical results of this survey are summarized in Tables 3.1, 3.2, 3.3, 3.4, and 3.5.

Table 3.1 reveals that overall historical book publishing between 1960-64 and 1970-74 rose rather modestly from 286 to 307 works; an increase of 7.4 percent. Corresponding historical book publishing in the Soviet Union as a whole did not change significantly during the same time periods. Historical book publishing in the USSR averaged 983 books per year for the years 1960-64 and 986 per year for the period 1970-72.[17] However, the pattern varied noticeably among the three Baltic union republics. The Latvian SSR's output of historical books increased by 21.3 percent and the Estonian SSR's by 18.0 percent. At the same time, Lithuania's output of such books decreased by 13.2 percent.

Among the three Baltic republics, historical book publishing in Lithuania showed the most drastic changes between the two periods. Data in Table 3.3 show that books about local, Baltic topics increased

TABLE 3.1

Emphasis in Baltic Historical Book Publishing, 1960-64 and 1970-74
(absolute numbers of titles listed)

Topics	1960-64				1970-74			
	Estonia	Latvia	Lithuania	Total	Estonia	Latvia	Lithuania	Total
Local, Pre-Soviet Baltic Topics								
Archaeology, ethnography, pre-1917 cultural history, landmark and museum themes	16	7	5	28	29	11	26	66
Local regional and town history	4	0	0	4	4	1	0	5
General history to 1600	4	1	4	9	5	4	9	18
General history, 1600-1917 (socialist and revolutionary movements excluded)	13	4	6	23	0	6	6	12
General pre-Soviet history	2	0	1	3	4	0	0	4
Soviet, Socialist Topics								
General Soviet-Russian history	4	1	3	8	1	5	2	8
Socialist/revolutionary movement to 1917	4	4	1	9	1	4	1	6
Revolutionary era, 1917-24	11	14	6	31	7	10	1	18
Independence era, 1920-40	11	10	13	34	2	9	5	16
Incorporation into USSR	2	3	0	5	1	4	1	6
World War II	16	22	40	78	18	20	16	54
Soviet Baltic era, 1944-74	4	3	6	13	1	1	3	5
Works on exiles, expatriates	0	0	1	1	0	0	1	1
Local industrial history	0	1	0	1	5	1	0	6
World/Foreign History	5	5	10	20	22	9	9	40
Overlap (all categories)	0	1	3	4	8	5	5	18
Uncertain (all categories)	4	4	7	15	10	7	7	24
Total titles	100	80	106	286	118	97	92	307

Sources: Ezhegodnik knigi SSSR 1960 (Moscow: Vsesoiuznaia Knizhnaia Palata, 1962), 1: pp. 77-117; Ezhegodnik knigi SSSR 1961 (Moscow: Vsesoiuznaia Knizhnaia Palata, 1963), 1: pp. 72-108; Ezhegodnik knigi SSSR 1962 (Moscow: Vsesoiuznaia Knizhnaia Palata, 1963), 1: pp. 69-103. Ezhegodnik knigi SSSR 1963 (Moscow: Kniga, 1964), 1: pp. 56-103; Ezhegodnik knigi SSSR 1964 (Moscow: Kniga, 1965), 1: pp. 56-89; Ezhegodnik knigi SSSR 1965 (Moscow: Kniga, 1966), 1: pp. 49-84; Ezhegodnik knigi SSSR 1970 (Moscow: Kniga, 1972), 1: pp. 87-115; Ezhegodnik knigi SSSR 1971 (Moscow: Kniga, 1973), 1: pp. 87-131; Ezhegodnik knigi SSSR 1972 (Moscow: Kniga, 1974), 1: pp. 68-97; Knizhnaia letopis' 1973, nos. 1-52; Knizhnaia letopis' 1974, nos. 1-52; Knizhnaia letopis' 1975, nos. 1-52.

from 16.7 percent of Lithuania's total output to 51.3 percent, an absolute increase of 207.2 percent. A corresponding decrease in Soviet and socialist topics is also evident. They fell from 72.9 percent of total output to 37.5 percent, a decline of close to 49 percent. In the numerical canvass (Table 3.1), Lithuanian books about archaeology, ethnography, and related subjects were found to have increased more than five times, despite the general decrease noticed in historical book publishing by that union republic. Increases are evident in most sectors of Baltic topics for that SSR. Among Soviet and socialist topics, Lithuanian works about World War II decreased by three-fifths, roughly equal to the precipitous drop in topics published about the so-called bourgeois or independence era. Taking into account Lithuania's overall 13.2 percent decline in historical book publishing, the relative loss in these two sections of Soviet topics is reduced somewhat. Data for Lithuania show consistent sizable gains in distinctively Baltic topics, consistent substantial losses in clearly Soviet topics, and relatively little change in topics concerning foreign and world history.

Latvian historical book publishing resembles Lithuania's in the increase in Baltic topics and the decrease in Soviet topics, but here the differences are smaller. Overall historical publishing in local, Baltic topics for Latvia increased from 16.0 percent to 25.9 percent of all historical books published, an increase of 61.9 percent. Soviet topics decreased from an overwhelming 77.3 percent to 63.5 percent of all historical publications, reflecting a decline of about 18 percent. Topics in world and foreign history increased by an impressive 56.7 percent, but the increase raised this category's share of all historical book publishing to a mere 10.5 percent of the total. Latvian gains in Baltic topics and losses in Soviet topics matched Lithuania's, even among the Latvian subcategories, but again, the percentage changes were smaller for Lithuania's northern neighbor. Unlike the pattern in Estonia and Lithuania, in Latvia, Soviet and socialist topics still constituted the majority of historical book publishing during 1970-74.

The Estonian survey results are mixed and initially confusing. In this union republic, historical book publishing about local, Baltic topics increased slightly, from 40.6 percent to 42.0 percent, a 3.4 percent increase. The number of Soviet topics decreased from 54.2 percent to 36.0 percent, representing a decline of 36.6 percent. At the same time, world and foreign history coverage increased from 5.2 percent to 22.0 percent of the total, making a spectacular 323.1 percent increase. Trends in Estonian subcategories were mixed. While books about archaeology, ethnography, and related topics increased by over 80 percent, publications covering the 1600-1917 period decreased from 13 in 1960-64 to 0 in 1970-74. Among Soviet topics, books regarding the independence era decreased by more than four-fifths, those about the Soviet period in Estonia by 75 percent, and works treating the 1917-24 years declined by 36.4 percent. In contrast, separate volumes about World War II increased by 12.5 percent, Estonia being the only one of the three Baltic union republics to exhibit any increase in this sphere. Another significant change is the striking rise in the number of works published about world and foreign history, the implications of which will be discussed in the conclusion of this chapter.

The combined trends for the three union republics are less dramatic than those of the individual republics. The level of Baltic topics overall in the region went from 25.1 per 100 to 39.6 per 100, an increase of slightly less than 60 percent. Books concerning Soviet topics, on the other hand, decreased from a commanding 67.4 per 100 in 1960-64 to 45.3 in 1970-74, the latter figure being still higher than the corresponding one for Baltic topics but representing, nonetheless, a 32.8 percent decrease. Overall Baltic publishing on topics of world and foreign history doubled between the two periods, from a level of 7.5 per 100 in the earlier period to a respectable 15.1 per 100 in the second.

The trends noticed for historical titles in Tables 3.2 and 3.3 are basically reflected in Table 3.4, which shows copies of historical books printed according to category. This demonstrates that there is a definite, almost proportional relationship between the numbers of historical titles published and the amount of copies printed in the three Baltic union republics. It also shows that the population of this region was directly exposed to the newer concerns of their historians during the time periods studied.

The language data of Table 3.5 do not support the hypothesized correlation between an increase in Baltic historical topics and increased use of the eponymous languages in historical book publishing. In two of the three union republics, there was actually a decreased use of the eponymous language for such publishing. Of course, changes in the ethnic composition of these populations must be taken into consideration here. Other possible explanations may include factors such as an increased use of Russian in Baltic universities or a greater study of Baltic history by outsiders.

Briefly summarizing, between the two periods 1960-64 and 1970-74, historical book publishing in the Soviet Baltic region has been characterized by three distinct trends. Works about local, Baltic topics have increased by more than half, Soviet topics have decreased by about a third, and works concerning world and foreign history have doubled in number. These shifts are more decided in Lithuania and less so in Latvia. A variation of this movement emerges within Estonia, where the decrease in Soviet and socialist topics was not

TABLE 3.2

Summary of Baltic Historical Book Publishing Categories, 1960-64 and 1970-74
(absolute numbers of titles listed)

Area and Years	Total Titles	Total (less overlap and uncertain)	Local, Baltic Pre-Soviet Topics	Soviet Socialist Topics	World Foreign Topics
Estonia					
1960-64	100	96	39	52	5
1970-74	118	100	42	36	22
Latvia					
1960-64	80	75	12	58	5
1970-74	97	85	22	54	9
Lithuania					
1960-64	106	96	16	70	10
1970-74	92	80	41	30	9
Total					
1960-64	286	267	67	180	20
1970-74	307	265	105	120	40

<u>Sources</u>: <u>Ezhegodnik knigi SSSR 1960</u> (Moscow: Vsesoiuznaia Knizhnaia Palata, 1962), 1: pp. 77-117; <u>Ezhegodnik knigi SSSR 1961</u> (Moscow: Vsesoiuznaia Knizhnaia Palata, 1963), 1: pp. 72-108; <u>Ezhegodnik knigi SSSR 1962</u> (Moscow: Vsesoiuznaia Knizhnaia Palata, 1963), 1: pp. 69-103. <u>Ezhegodnik knigi SSSR 1963</u> (Moscow: Kniga, 1964), 1: pp. 66-103; <u>Ezhegodnik knigi SSSR 1964</u> (Moscow: Kniga, 1965), 1: pp. 56-89; <u>Ezhegodnik knigi SSSR 1965</u> (Moscow: Kniga, 1966), 1: pp. 49-84; <u>Ezhegodnik knigi SSSR 1970</u> (Moscow: Kniga, 1972), 1: pp. 87-115; <u>Ezhegodnik knigi SSSR 1971</u> (Moscow: Kniga, 1973), 1: pp. 87-131; <u>Ezhegodnik knigi SSSR 1972</u> (Moscow: Kniga, 1974), 1: pp. 68-97; <u>Knizhnaia letopis' 1973</u>, nos. 1-52; <u>Knizhnaia letopis' 1974</u>, nos. 1-52; <u>Knizhnaia letopis' 1975</u>, nos. 1-52.

TABLE 3.3

Number of Titles for Each Category per 100 Historical Titles in Each Soviet Baltic Republic, 1960-64 and 1970-74

Topics and Years	Estonia	Latvia	Lithuania	Baltic Average
Baltic Topics				
1960-64	40.6	16.0	16.7	25.1
1970-74	42.0	25.9	51.3	39.6
Soviet Topics				
1960-64	54.2	77.3	72.9	67.4
1970-74	36.0	63.5	37.5	45.3
World/Foreign History				
1960-64	5.2	6.7	10.4	7.5
1970-74	22.0	10.5	11.2	15.1
Percentage Change of 1970-74 to 1960-64				
Baltic topics	+3.4	+61.9	+207.2	+57.8
Soviet topics	-33.6	-17.9	-48.6	-32.8
World/foreign topics	+323.1	+56.7	+7.7	+101.3

Sources: *Ezhegodnik knigi SSSR 1960* (Moscow: Vsesoiuznaia Knizhnaia Palata, 1962), 1: pp. 77-117; *Ezhegodnik knigi SSSR 1961* (Moscow: Vsesoiuznaia Knizhnaia Palata, 1963), 1: pp. 72-108; *Ezhegodnik knigi SSSR 1962* (Moscow: Vsesoiuznaia Knizhnaia Palata, 1963), 1: pp. 69-103. *Ezhegodnik knigi SSSR 1963* (Moscow: Kniga, 1964), 1: pp. 66-103; *Ezhegodnik knigi SSSR 1964* (Moscow: Kniga, 1965), 1: pp. 56-89; *Ezhegodnik knigi SSSR 1965* (Moscow: Kniga, 1966), 1: pp. 49-84; *Ezhegodnik knigi SSSR 1970* (Moscow: Kniga, 1972), 1: pp. 87-115; *Ezhegodnik knigi SSSR 1971* (Moscow: Kniga, 1973), 1: pp. 87-131; *Ezhegodnik knigi SSSR 1972* (Moscow: Kniga, 1974), 1: pp. 68-97; *Knizhnaia letopis' 1973*, nos. 1-52; *Knizhnaia letopis' 1974*, nos. 1-52; *Knizhnaia letopis' 1975*, nos. 1-52.

TABLE 3.4

Number of Copies for Each Baltic Historical Book Publishing Category, 1960-64 and 1970-74*

Area and Years	Total Copies	Baltic	Soviet	Foreign/World
Estonia				
1960-64	347,600	132,400 (33.1)	200,000 (57.5)	15,200 (4.4)
1970-74	664,150	364,600 (54.9)	185,850 (28.0)	113,700 (17.1)
Latvia				
1960-64	453,320	47,600 (10.5)	389,520 (85.9)	16,200 (3.5)
1970-74	738,960	91,400 (12.4)	494,960 (67.0)	152,600 (20.6)
Lithuania				
1960-74	761,900	63,900 (8.4)	659,000 (86.5)	39,000 (5.1)
1970-74	764,100	526,700 (68.9)	205,900 (27.0)	31,500 (4.1)
Total				
1960-64	1,562,820	243,900 (15.6)	1,248,520 (79.9)	70,400 (4.5)
1970-74	2,167,210	982,700 (45.3)	886,710 (40.9)	297,800 (13.8)

*Number per 100 historical book copies in parentheses.

Sources: Ezhegodnik knigi SSSR 1960 (Moscow: Vsesoiuznaia Knizhnaia Palata, 1962), 1: pp. 77-107; Ezhegodnik knigi SSSR 1961 (Moscow: Vsesoiuznaia Knizhnaia Palata, 1963), 1: pp. 72-108; Ezhegodnik knigi SSSR 1962 (Moscow: Vsesoiuznaia Knizhnaia Palata, 1963), 1: pp. 69-103; Ezhegodnik knigi SSSR 1963 (Moscow: Kniga, 1964), 1: pp. 66-103; Ezhegodnik knigi SSSR 1964 (Moscow: Kniga, 1965), 1: pp. 56-89; Ezhegodnik knigi SSSR 1965 (Moscow: Kniga, 1966), 1: pp. 49-84; Ezhegodnik knigi SSSR 1970 (Moscow: Kniga, 1972), 1: pp. 87-115; Ezhegodnik knigi SSSR 1971 (Moscow: Kniga, 1973), 1: pp. 87-131; Ezhegodnik knigi SSSR 1972 (Moscow: Kniga, 1974), 1: pp. 68-97; Knizhnaia letopis' 1973 ("Istonia" sec.), nos. 1-52; Knizhnaia letopis' 1974, nos. 1-52; Knizhnaia letopis' 1975, nos. 1-52.

TABLE 3.5

Language of Publication per 100 Historical Titles in Each Soviet Baltic Republic, 1960-64 and 1970-74

Area and Years	Eponymous	Russian	Other/ Composite
Estonia			
1960-64	75.0	12.5	12.5
1970-74	60.0	21.0	19.0
Latvia			
1960-64	66.7	25.3	8.0
1970-74	71.8	24.7	3.5
Lithuania			
1960-64	83.3	4.2	12.5
1970-74	78.8	11.2	10.0
Baltic Average			
1960-64	75.7	13.1	11.2
1970-74	69.4	19.3	11.3

Sources: Ezhegodnik knigi SSSR 1960 (Moscow: Vsesoiuznaia Knizhnaia Palata, 1962), 1: pp. 77-107; Ezhegodnik knigi SSSR 1961 (Moscow: Vsesoiuznaia Knizhnaia Palata, 1963), 1: pp. 72-108; Ezhegodnik knigi SSSR 1962 (Moscow: Vsesoiuznaia Knizhnaia Palata, 1963), 1: pp. 69-103; Ezhegodnik knigi SSSR 1963 (Moscow: Kniga, 1964), 1: pp. 66-103; Ezhegodnik knigi SSSR 1964 (Moscow: Kniga, 1965), 1: pp. 56-89; Ezhegodnik knigi SSSR 1965 (Moscow: Kniga, 1966), 1: pp. 49-84; Ezhegodnik knigi SSSR 1970 (Moscow: Kniga, 1972), pp. 1: 87-115; Ezhegodnik knigi SSSR 1971 (Moscow: Kniga, 1973), 1: pp. 87-131; Ezhegodnik knigi SSSR 1972 (Moscow: Kniga, 1974), 1: pp. 68-97; Knizhnaia letopis' 1973 ("Istoriia" sec.), nos. 1-52; Knizhnaia letopis' 1974, nos. 1-52; Knizhnaia letopis' 1975, nos. 1-52.

balanced by a corresponding quantitative rise in local, Baltic topics but rather by a dramatic increase of publications dealing with world and foreign history.

SUBTLE INTERPRETATIONS BY BALTIC SCHOLARS

The interpretation by Baltic historians of their subjects, the way in which they handle the historical eras about which they write, under the circumstances, cannot be overtly anti-Marxist, anti-Soviet, or nationalistic. The remoteness of certain historical topics or a tangential treatment of them, however, tends to minimize official concern, thereby giving historians more flexibility in interpretation. The Party has not ceased demanding strictly Marxist interpretations of all history. The first secretary of the Communist Party of Lithuania, Antanas Sniečkus, in 1972, stressed the "necessity for the younger generation to comprehend correctly the process of the Lithuanian people's historical development and their cultural heritage, to rebuff any attempts to evaluate the latter uncritically, and even to idealize it."[18] This resembled a sentiment voiced by Alexandr Drizul, secretary of Latvia's Communist Party Central Committee. Speaking to his republic's Supreme Soviet in 1970, he warned that the "germs" of nationalism, nurtured by foreign propaganda, appear in the form of an "idealization of the former small-farm Latvia, . . . an uncritical attitude toward the cultural heritage, or . . . an exaggeration of national features."[19] Lithuania's Party press warned, in March 1973, that "it is essential to resist occasional tendencies to idealize antiquity."[20]

Not only the treatment of the distant past but its study in general was touched upon by First Secretary Sniečkus, this time in a March 1973 speech to a meeting of Party activists:

> Uneasiness (bespokoistvo) is caused because a certain idealization is not avoided, at times, in treating the historical past. . . . For example, some of those working in the ethnographical sector of the Institute of History began almost exclusively to analyze problems of the past instead of studying contemporary themes. . . . Also, publishing houses should appraise their own work critically. An obvious submission to the exaggerated has been noticed in their work at times [and] an artificial captivation of certain persons with the musty past.[21]

Investigating ethnography and archaeology in the Baltic region is imperative for this study, both because it is singled out for criticism by Sniečkus and because it represents an area of publication that expanded significantly between the 1960-64 and 1970-74 periods. Whereas Soviet analysis of the more recent topics of history must totally conform to the strictures of ideology, some flexibility of interpretation may exist for historians exactly in the areas of archaeology and ethnography, whose spheres cover the extreme past (in archaeology) or both the extreme and recent past (in ethnography). The role these two areas take as historical, cultural supports for nationality is quite obvious. They deal with the origins of people, the legacy of their physical existence, their culture, and so on. In fact, Baltic modernization plays an important role here, not only because it helps stimulate dissatisfaction but also because it creates the necessity to collect and preserve remnants of the fast-disappearing peasant culture of the region.[22]

Many Soviet Baltic ethnographic works, as a result of the tensions between Party and nationality, combine a curious patchwork of outstanding research and Marxist ideology. The ideology is not dissolved integrally into the works themselves but rather floats to the surface like oil on water, often appearing to be superficially applied as a concession to necessity. "Propagandistic phrases" may be found in the conclusion of a work that do not relate to the general objectivity of the text,[23] or the contents of a work may be "two-ply," as an emigrant Estonian ethnographer has succinctly put it. For example, the yearbooks of the Estonian Ethnographical Museum are characterized by a format originating in the initial 1947 volume, in which three articles possessed an "ideological bent which place[d] new contemporary requirements on research," but the other six essays "[did] not appear in the least influenced by these ideological declarations."[24] Another type of differentiation occurs in volume 10 (1972) of Latvia's Academy of Sciences journal, Arheoloģija un etnogrāfija. Most of the articles emphasized the nineteenth and twentieth centuries, but two essays about medieval archaeology reveal extensive new data.[25] The major obstacle preventing a workable synthesis of Soviet Marxism and ethnography, according to an observer of the Estonian experience, is that the ideology itself is "difficult to apply to research."[26]

Publications about museums, historical monuments, and local history also serve to support nationality distinctiveness, because the older landmarks and artifacts attest to the past physical existence of a nationality. In addition, ancient relics, which represent the deep historical roots of a people, aid as a cultural support. Soviet ideology can be incorporated in such topics and apparently has been, though it is difficult to determine the extent. One extreme viewpoint holds that the museums themselves "have been turned into propaganda tools," for this is considered to be their proper role, according to the Communist Party.[27] "The museums," said Valentina Lovyagina, deputy director of the agitation and propaganda branch of the Central Committee of Latvia's Communist Party, "propagate revolutionary and work-related traditions, the friendship of nations, the ideals of the Communist Party of the Soviet Union, [and] the achievements of the communist regime."[28] However, evidence persists that the Party is concerned with the apparent lack of ideological interpretations in museum-related fields. For example, at the March 1973 meeting of the Congress of Lithuanian Monument Protection and Regional Study Society, the chairman of the board of that Society warned his members that they were "to be guided in their work by Marxist-Leninist ideology and real scientific class criteria."[29] Continuing, he warned against idealization of the past, playing down the class struggle of the past, and "manifesting nationalism."[30] Also stressed at this same meeting was the need for giving major attention to the Soviet period. The publishing work of the society was criticized, according to the account appearing in the Party press of Lithuania, because

> the popular and pertinent collection of articles Regional Studies (Kraevedeniia) are not without serious shortcomings. Here one encounters theses which do not take into account the characteristic class antagonisms of the exploiting system, that focus attention primarily on the remote past, that study the economic and cultural accomplishments of the socialist period inadequately, and that poorly illuminate the remarkable traditions of the collaboration and friendship among the Soviet people.[31]

These shortcomings were stated more directly by the chairman of the Vilnius branch of the Society, a senior scholarly employee of the Party History Institute, who declared that "the primary task of the regional study workers is to determine everything by which the working man lives today and what Soviet power has given him."[32]

Despite these urgings for a class conscious approach to local studies, in reports from a conference about the preservation of old cities, also held in Vilnius about one-half year later, there was no mention whatsoever of ideology. That was a conference specifically organized for delegates from socialist countries. Much concern was voiced over the plight of cities in the face of what the conferees called "violent" growth, and plans were presented for the restoration of old Vilnius, block by block.[33] This is the apparent restoration of the distinctive and national, a return to the past that Party Secretary Sniečkus reminded his listeners should not be idealized.

Standing in contrast to the Lithuanian regional studies society is the Tallinn Regional Studies Circle, a semiprofessional society, with the publication Istoriia Tallina s 1860 g. (History of Tallinn from 1860) to its credit.[34] The society's members have engaged in research regarding archaeological excavations, architectural memorials, the history of photography in Estonia, and so on. In a May 1973 report about the society, no allusion was made to ideology in its role or its works. Aside from a reference to meetings with corresponding schools in "brother republics" and one member's research into workers who participated in the Estonian revolutionary movement, all of the projects mentioned embraced distinctively Estonian subjects.[35]

Progressing into topics dealing with the early modern period, there is evidence that the historical works of this era in the Baltic region also enjoy, though possibly to a smaller degree, much of the flexibility of interpretation allowed to the earlier periods. Of course, the "great friendship" between Soviet nationalities theme appears much more extensively here. An official view regarding this period can be seen in the words of Iuri V. Ruben, chairman of the Presidium of Latvia's Supreme Soviet. He declared that friendship between the Latvian and Russian people extends far back into the past. "During the most difficult periods of our history, beginning with the twelfth century when the Latvian people adamantly fought foreign aggressors and the German knights, we always found a loyal ally and a powerful protector in the great Russian people."[36] In Lithuania also, the "great friendship" slogan is invoked when the relations of the grand dukes of Lithuania and the princes of Muscovy are discussed. The role of the Lithuanian Grand Duchy in halting German eastward expansion is especially noted.[37] One recent book notable for its treatment of Lithuanian-Russian relations is Bronius Dundulis's Lietuvos uzsienio politica XVI a. [The Foreign Relations of Lithuania in the Sixteenth Century].[38] An emigrant scholar noted that the work had exercised "a great deal of restraint" in its discussion of these relations, blaming Lithuanian lords for wars with their Russian neighbor.[39] The same reviewer considered that this distortion of history was "an opportunistic gesture in view of Soviet historical censorship," and that "these statements, as in most Soviet controlled writings, can be discounted and do not minimize the extreme value of the historical work."[40]

Occasionally, works studying the more recent past that do not deal with historical events in a Marxist fashion can be published. Such a book is Marğers Stepermanis's Liclās liesmas atblāzma [The reflection of the great blaze], published posthumously in 1971.[41] This work is mentioned not because it necessarily demonstrates the function of history writing as a cultural support but because it shows that Soviet Baltic historians can occasionally produce relatively ideologically free interpretations about more recent events. Called "a minor masterpiece of Latvian historiography," it investigated the effects of the French Revolution on Latvia.[42] It is "virtually free" of the "meta-historical" suppositions of Soviet historiography and reportedly does not contain a single reference to Lenin, although a few brief quotations from Marx do appear.[43] Most of all, it discusses the lack of a class struggle in Latvia during the latter part of the eighteenth century.

Lithuania's Party leaders are especially concerned with the teaching of history in the republic's schools. Official attitudes are clearly stated in the journal Tarybine Mokukla [The Soviet school]:

> In history lessons about the Lituanian SSR we must resolutely abolish whatever gives expression to idealization of reactionary phenomena of the past. In explaining historical events in Lithuania, it must be stressed through concrete examples that the real creator of this history was the people, and not the princes.[44]

Such standards are apparently difficult to maintain in history teaching. Lithuanian historians whose books were being used in the republic's schools were charged with ideological carelessness in 1973. The principal of a secondary school, himself a history teacher, complained to the Party press that the history book intended for the seventh to ninth grades was found wanting by his teachers because "the class view of historical phenomena gets lost in secondary things."[45] Many books, he noted, tended to idealize the past, thereby overlooking the class antagonisms that existed at that time. Others possessed no depth or oversimplified the class struggle of the past. Asserting that the significance of each historical stage should be taken into account, the school principal implied that socialist topics were not receiving the attention that he felt were due them. In all of this, "the holy civic duty" of the teacher is "to treat Lithuania's remote past correctly, see it with the eyes of a communist, and reveal the manifestations of the class struggle."[46] (See Appendix A.)

This letter confirms that many earlier history books in Lithuania fail to emphasize class consciousness. The accusation of obscuring or oversimplifying the class position is similar to what was previously noted in the journals of ethnography. The "unnecessary sighing" over the simpler times may, in fact, be symptomatic of Baltic society at large and further evidence of rising dissatisfaction.[47]

Most earlier history would tend to support nationality culture, but all modern Soviet Baltic history would not. One means of creating the supranational patriotism that Moscow desires is through the weakening of nationality consciousness and the substitution of Soviet patriotism. Post-1917 Soviet history tends to emphasize the dependence of the various nationalities on either the Russians or the Soviet state. In Baltic history of recent times, this is also true. For that reason, the modern period cannot be seen to support Baltic culture. Strict class views are incorporated into modern works. The present era in history, according to Soviet reasoning, represents an acute stage in the struggle between capitalism and socialism. Historical works that examine this period, as mentioned earlier, are expected to provide ammunition in this ideological war. For example, Soviet Estonian historiography regarding the tumultuous 1917-18 events in that country and the "re-incorporation" of 1940 is crucial because it plays an important part in legitimatizing Soviet rule in that country.[48] The same is true for the other Baltic republics. The historical topic most widely published in the entire region—World War II—is also important, for it represents what are called heroic struggles of the unified "fraternal peoples" of the Soviet Union against the Nazis. The independence era of 1920-40 is regarded as a deviation from the historical unity of the Russian and Baltic people, brought about by something condemned as a collaboration of the Baltic bourgeoisie with foreign interventionists.

Declining numbers of books about Soviet and socialist topics apparently has caught the notice of the Party, because the authorities constantly prod historians to prepare such works. At a meeting of party activists in Vilnius in March 1973, B. Yu. Vaitkevičius, the director of the Institute of History of Lithuania's Academy of Sciences declared that "one of the important tasks of historical science is to create fundamental works that summarize the processes and characteristics of socialist development. Unfortunately," he noted, "there still are not enough of such works."[49] To remedy this, "the historians of the Soviet Union will . . . further expand [their] historical research into our times."[50] In 1974, the first secretary of Lithuania's Communist Party told the General Assembly of Lithuania's Academy of Sciences that "more attention should be devoted to a scientific analysis of modern times."[51] Meanwhile, the first secretary of Latvia's Communist Party, Alexandr Drizul, told his Party's activists that social scientists "are still not doing sufficient work" in the areas concerning the development of socialist society and that the republic's academy of sciences should take the appropriate measures.[52]

In the Estonian press, this type of direct Party pressure does not seem as evident. Instead, serious attempts have apparently been made to reevaluate the modern era, as suggested in the 1970 edition of the Eesti Nõukogude Entsüklopeedia (Soviet Estonian Encyclopedia).[53] In it, the 1934-37 Päts dictatorship is described as fascist, but not of the German type; the deportations of Estonians during the Collectivization (1949) in Estonia are admitted, and the "grave errors" of the 1950 antinationalist campaign recognized.[54] The so-called 1940 revolution, the Stalinist period, and other topics have been reevaluated also. One Western writer has claimed that "there is little difference in degree of cultural nationalism between the Soviet Estonian cultural establishment and the exiles."[55] While this statement may somewhat exaggerate the situation, Estonian historiography of the modern period does seem to be demonstrating more latitude of opinion than that of the two other Baltic republics.

An increase in world and foreign historical topics goes unexplained, because there seems to be no open discussion of this trend by Party officials. The numerical increase in these topics may suggest a "turning outward," away from nationality, or perhaps a move to circumvent official guidelines for domestic history. Many of these publications, in fact, dealt with such topics as foreign revolutionaries and leading foreign Communist figures.

Certain historical and institutional variations exist among the three Baltic union republics. They may explain somewhat the quantitative and qualitative differences among the published works about the history of the region. As a field of study, ethnography began much earlier in Estonia than in Latvia or Lithuania, developing through the 1920s and 1930s until the chair in ethnography at Tartu was raised to a professorial level in 1939. Latvian ethnography started developing very late in the interwar period. Formal Lithuanian progress in this sphere did not begin until after World War II.[56] This may explain the relative numerical superiority of Estonian publishing in this area during the 1960-64 period. Also, the major centers of learning in these three union republics may influence the historians who reside in or near them or who have attended such institutions. The historical Estonian center of learning is Tartu and not Tallinn, which is the administrative center. Riga is both the educational and administrative center of Latvia, and a greater percentage of its inhabitants are Russian than Lett. Lithuania's Vilnius was part of Poland during the independence era of 1920-40. The political atmosphere is also different among the three republics. The Estonian party journal is said to be the most liberal in the Soviet Union, but its Latvian counterpart is considered "a favorite forum for hard-core Stalinists."[57] Of the three, Estonia has traditional ties with Western Europe and Lithuania with Poland. Perhaps the Estonian surge in publishing in world history is a feature of its Western orientation.

When analyzed separately, the three Baltic republics reflect through their historians various levels of discontent and anxiety and express it differently. The relatively liberal situation in Estonia has seen a shift away from Soviet topics and a small increase in Baltic ones. Greater interest has been exhibited in foreign and world history, perhaps illustrating continuing Estonian desires to achieve again full-fledged membership in the world community of nations. The already high number of archaeological and ethnographic publications in the union republic during 1960-64 may suggest that the later shift toward foreign history represents a trend to a more mature, sophisticated channeling of discontent. Moreover, the apparent reevaluation of Estonian history would appear to weaken the relationship proposed here earlier between discontent and interest in earlier historical topics. More likely, this reclamation of the Soviet period by Estonian historians reflects the more liberal political situation there. The relative silence of Estonia's Communist Party concerning historical writings hints that its leaders might be sympathetic to the expression of their nationality's distinctiveness in historical publications. For the Baltic region, Estonia's tendency seems an exception to the rule.

Lithuania's profound shift in publishing topics, on the other hand, demonstrates the most drastic increase of nationality discontent in the Baltic region, confirmed by both the publishing data and the almost constant concern of that republic's Communist Party with its historians. In fact, Lithuania was the only one among the three Baltic eponymous groups to have its historians criticized in a 1974 Soviet article about Baltic historiography. That complaint alleged that some Lithuanian historians were guilty of "idealization of the historical past" and permitting "inconsistencies in building the principles of a class approach in the analysis of past phenomena."[58]

Publishing and interpretative data seem to reveal less drastic dissatisfaction in Latvia than in Lithuania, while demonstrating the same inclination toward earlier history as its southern Baltic neighbor.

This evidence shows that Baltic historians of the 1970s are more active supporters of Baltic culture than they were in the early 1960s, both reflecting and affecting their nationalities' increased reliance on the historical component of the cultural support factor. The substantial rise in number of works about distinctively Baltic topics, signaling a cultural support for the nationality, and the corresponding decline in Soviet and socialist topics, signaling a nonsupport, suggests that these historians recognize their own roles as supporters of their nationalities' cultures to a much greater degree in 1970-74 than they did in 1960-64. Their effect on Baltic society is apparently considered to be great enough to warrant persistent Party demands for more works about recent history and Marxist interpretations of past history. The tendency toward characteristically Baltic historical topics increases the role of history as a support factor for nationality culture. It represents the strengthening of Baltic culture. Most of all, this trend demonstrates the cultural vitality, tenacity, and durability of the three Baltic eponymous nationalities and, in that way, reflects regional change as a whole during the past decade.

NOTES

1. John Stuart Mill, "Nationality and Representative Government," reprinted in part in Modern Political Doctrines, ed. Alfred Zimmern (London: Oxford, 1939), p. 206.

2. Robert Allen Skotheim, The Historian and the Climate of Opinion (Reading, Mass.: Addison-Wesley Publishing Company, 1969), p. 3.

3. Skotheim, op. cit., p. 1.

4. Ibid., pp. 2-3.

5. E. N. Anderson, *Nationalism and the Cultural Crisis in Prussia, 1806-1815* (New York: Octagon Books, 1966), pp. 16-17.

6. For Latvia, see "Letter to Communist Party Leaders," *Congressional Record*, 92d Cong., 2nd sess., 1972, 118, pt. 4, 4820-23. For Lithuania, see *Lietuvos Katalikų Bažnyčios Kronika* [Chronicle of the Catholic Church in Lithuania] (Chicago: L. K. Religinės Šalpos Rėmėjai, 1974). For Estonia, see the multiple sources listed in Rein Taagepera, "Estonia and the Estonians," in *Handbook of Major Soviet Nationalities*," ed. Zev Katz et al. (New York: Free Press, 1975), pp. 135-36.

7. Antanas Sniečkus, "Vse sily—na vypolnenie reshenii XXIV S"ezda partii," *Sovetskaia Litva* (April 16, 1971), p. 3.

8. For a thorough study of this slogan, see Lowell Tillett, *The Great Friendship: Soviet Historians on the Non-Russian Nationalities* (Chapel Hill: University of North Carolina Press, 1969).

9. R. Trofimov, "Porokhovoi dym istorii," *Literaturnaia gazeta*, no. 46 (November 14, 1973), p. 5.

10. Ibid.

11. Ibid.

12. Arnold Koop, "Novye knigi Istoriia Estoniia," *Izvestiia*, January 11, 1972, p. 5.

13. "Dostizheniia nauki—stroitel'stvu kommunizma," *Sovetskaia Litva* (May 25, 1974), p. 2.

14. "Neotlozhnye zadachi istorikov," *Pravda*, March 29, 1973, p. 2.

15. Ibid.

16. "Nagrazhdeniia," *Izvestiia*, August 20, 1970, p. 5.

17. *Ezhegodnik knigi SSSR 1960* (Moscow: Vsesoiuznaia Knizhnaia Palata, 1962), vol. 1; *Ezhegodnik knigi SSSR 1961* (Moscow: Vsesoiuznaia Knizhnaia Palata, 1963), vol. 1; *Ezhegodnik knigi SSSR 1962* (Moscow: Kniga, 1963), vol. 1; *Ezhegodnik knigi SSSR 1963* (Moscow: Kniga, 1964), vol. 1; *Ezhegodnik knigi SSSR 1964* (Moscow: Kniga, 1965), vol. 1; *Ezhegodnik knigi SSSR 1965* (Moscow: Kniga, 1966), vol. 1; *Ezhegodnik knigi SSSR 1970* (Moscow: Kniga, 1972), vol. 1; *Ezhegodnik knigi SSSR 1971* (Moscow: Kniga, 1973), vol. 1; *Ezhegodnik knigi SSSR 1972* (Moscow: Kniga, 1974), vol. 1; *Knizhnaia letopis'* [Book chronicle] *1973*.

18. Antanas Sniečkus, "Narodnomu obrazovaniiu—partiinuiu, gosudarstvennuiu zabotu," *Sovetskaia Litva* (February 29, 1972), p. 2.

19. A. Drizul, "My—internatsionalisty," *Izvestiia*, September 10, 1970, p. 3.

20. "Denial and Down Grading of Lithuania's Past," in Chronicle of the Catholic Church in Lithuania, no. 6 (1974), p. 12.

21. "Vsilit' ideino-politicheskuiu rabotu, internatsional'noe vospitanie," Sovetskaia Litva (March 15, 1973), p. 2.

22. Gustav Ränk, "Soviet-Estonian Scholarship in Ethnography," in A Case Study of a Soviet Republic: The Estonian SSR, ed. Elmar Järvesoo and Tõnu Parming (Boulder, Colo.: Westview Press, forthcoming), p. 624.

23. Ränk, p. 637.

24. Ibid., p. 634.

25. Review of Arheoloģija un etnogrāfija, in Journal of Baltic Studies 5, no. 1 (1974): 71.

26. Ränk, p. 632.

27. Jonas Puzinas, "The Situation in Occupied Lithuania: Administration, Indoctrination and Russianization," Lituanus 19, no. 1 (Spring 1973): 66.

28. Ibid., p. 67.

29. V. Petrauskayte, "Kraevedenie—vazhnyi uchastok ideologicheskoi raboty," Sovetskaia Litva (March 27, 1973), p. 3.

30. Ibid.

31. Ibid.

32. Ibid.

33. "Na konferentsii IKOMOS," Sovetskaia Litva (September 5, 1973), p. 3.

34. E. Raydma, "Kravedy—entuziasty," Sovetskaia Estoniia (May 18, 1973), p. 4.

35. Ibid.

36. Iu. Ruben, "V bratskoi sem'e," Kommunist sovetskoi Latvii, no. 6 (June 1970), p. 9.

37. Harned, "Lithuania and the Lithuanians," in Katz et al., eds., p. 135.

38. Bronius Dundulis, Lietuvos uzsieno politica XVI a. (Vilnius, 1971), cited in Juozas Jakstas, Lituanus 19, no. 4 (Winter 1973): 74.

39. Ibid.

40. Ibid.

41. Marğers Stepermanis, Lielās liesmas atblāzma (1971), cited in A. Ezergailis, Journal of Baltic Studies 3, no. 1 (Spring 1972): 71-72.

42. Ibid.

43. Ibid.

44. Tarybine Mokykla, no. 3, cited in Chronicle of the Catholic Church in Lithuania, no. 6 (1974), p. 12.

45. Kantauskas, "Chto volnuet uchitelia istorii," Sovetskaia Litva (March 14, 1973), p. 2.

46. Ibid.

47. Ibid.

48. Olavi Arens, "Soviet Estonian Historiography with Special Reference to the Treatment of the 1918-1919 Revolutionary Period," in First Conference on Baltic Studies: A Summary of Proceedings, ed. Ivar Ivask (Tacoma, Wash.: Pacific Lutheran University, 1969), p. 51.

49. "Vospityvat' internatsionalistov patriotov sovetskoi rodiny," Sovetskaia Litva (March 16, 1973), p. 2.

50. Ibid.

51. "Dostizheniia nauki–stroitel'stvu kommunizma," Sovetskaia Litva (May 25, 1974), p. 2.

52. "Neustanno rastit' i vospityvat' ideologicheskie kadry," Sovetskaia Latvia (December 25, 1974), p. 2.

53. See Taagepera, pp. 88-89.

54. Ibid.

55. Ibid.

56. Ränk, pp. 618-19.

57. Rein Taagepera, "Dissimilarities Between the Northwestern Soviet Republics," in Problems of Mininations: Baltic Perspectives, ed. Arvids Ziedonis, Jr., Rein Taagepera, and Mardi Valgamäe (San Jose, Calif.: Association for the Advancement of Baltic Studies, 1973), p. 80.

58. V. Iu. Vaitkevichius, Iu. Iu. Kakhk, and V. A. Shteinberg, "Razvitie istoricheskoi nauki v pribaltike," Voprosy istorii, no. 2 (February 1974), pp. 3-20.

CHAPTER

4

INDIGENOUS ECONOMIC MANAGERS

Richard Shryock

Modernization is often seen as a complex process of social change unleashed by industrialization and profoundly affected by economic pressures. This process has important consequences for the nationality question because it profoundly alters the environment within which the nationality functions. As the environment of the nationality undergoes rapid transformation, many of the previous modes of group support are destroyed or seriously weakened. This necessitates a shift to new forms of support that can prove viable under changed conditions.

The Baltic region has shown an impressive degree of economic progress, judged in terms of industrial growth and standard of living. According to Soviet estimates used by Western scholars, Estonian and Latvian industrial production has increased 33-fold over 1940 levels, while Lithuanian production has increased almost 39-fold. These levels of economic growth have exceeded the Union-wide average in the postwar era. In addition, the share of industry (including construction) in gross social product has reached 73.1 percent for Estonia, 73.4 percent for Latvia, and 65.6 percent for Lithuania, while the corresponding share for agriculture has fallen to 17.3 percent, 16.9 percent, and 25.9 percent, respectively. Finally, the three republics have achieved the highest annual per capita income in the Soviet Union—1,587 rubles in Estonia, 1,574 rubles in Latvia, and 1,336 rubles in Lithuania (Union-wide average of 1,194 rubles in 1970).[1] A recalculation of Soviet economic figures confirms these indications of relative Baltic prosperity and growth.

Baltic authors, as well as non-Baltic Soviet writers, have called economic prosperity a principle support for Soviet nationality policies. This was most precisely articulated by a Soviet Lithuanian scholar in November 1971:

> It has long been known that a decisive indicator of the progressiveness of a social system is the scope that it creates for the development of productive forces. The more progressive a social system, the greater the opportunities for the development of productive forces and for increasing labor productivity. In the light of this premise, the development of the Baltic republics is a striking example of the strength and might of the socialist system and of the CPSU's national policy. . . .
>
> The growth of productive forces—an important element in the development of society—has guaranteed the development of all aspects of life. In the Baltic republics industry and agriculture have achieved an unprecedented upsurge, culture has flourished, the cadres of the working class and intelligentsia have increased, the cities have been renovated, and the well-being of the working peoples has risen.[2]

This interpretation would seem to be supported by Marxian theory and the socioeconomic reality of the Baltic region.

Economic prosperity does seem to offer some degree of satisfaction for the nationalities involved. Material well-being may, in part, compensate for the social disorientation that occurs during the modernization process. There appears to be a stage of development, however, during and after which the provision of material needs no longer acts as the fundamental criterion of nationality satisfaction. Not only does the group look for satisfaction in the noneconomic spheres of life but the measure of satisfaction in the economic sphere itself changes. The people of the group are no longer content with mere material well-being but seek to control the economic process through which this comes about.

The economic prosperity in the Baltic region has cultivated a sense of self-worth among the nationality groups. The Baltic people have demonstrated to date both in certain industrial sectors and in agriculture a qualitative superiority in productivity and efficiency over the other Soviet republics, which is due, in large measure, to skilled management and industrious labor in these sectors. Furthermore, the Baltic republics, unlike most other Soviet republics, enjoyed a period of independence in which to develop an ability to manage a modern economy. The successes achieved in this pre-1940 period, however limited, may lead the Baltic elite to believe that they have the capacity to manage their own economic affairs. This belief may conflict with the actuality of continued central Soviet hegemony and non-Baltic assistance in the economic sectors.

Furthermore, the industrial economy engenders a series of socioeconomic problems with which a people must deal. These include a rapid increase in the number of workers involved in industry, the ills of urbanization, and environmental pollution. The Baltic people feel an increasing concern that these problems be dealt with in a manner corresponding to the interests of the indigenous population.

The hypothesis that this study will seek to prove is the following: In the persons of economic elites, the Baltic nationalities today seek by various means to maintain some influence in, or gain greater control over, economic life. Success may, in turn, consciously or unconsciously foster increased confidence in each nationality's ability to manage its own affairs in the decision-making process and thus help to strengthen the viability of the nationality. If a contradiction between increased Baltic skill and continued central hegemony frustrates the attempts of the nationality to set and cope with what it perceives as the local economic priorities, then dissatisfaction may result, despite material prosperity.

This chapter will seek to examine two interrelated questions. The first is the nature of the measurement of economic success by the given nationality. This will help to clarify the Baltic sense of self-worth engendered through economic progress and the degree of satisfaction offered by material prosperity. The second is the nature of control sought by the three nationalities and the means utilized to achieve this.

The primary evidence in the present research is sought through a careful examination of the Baltic press. The period scrutinized is that of the Ninth Five-Year Plan (1971-76). The principal source material considered was the local Russian-language Party press. Articles by Baltic spokesmen appearing in central Party and government papers, as well as in certain specialized economic journals, have also been considered on a more selective basis.

POSITIVE SUPPORT FUNCTIONS OF ECONOMIC PROGRESS

Economic progress has been offered by Soviet spokesmen as a principal defense of the Communist Party's nationality policies in the Baltic region. It is thus necessary to examine first of all both the manner and effectiveness of economic progress as a support for the nationality group. This discussion will be divided into three sections: (1) Soviet Baltic perception of their economic progress, (2) the Soviet Baltic view of their present economic situation, and (3) ambivalence in the support functions of economic success.

The Soviet Baltic Perception of Their Economic Progress

In order to understand the manner in which the present economic status provides supports to nationality, the process by which this economic success has been achieved must be examined. Economic success is more likely to provide positive supports if the population believes that the nationality made a significant contribution to the achievement of this goal. A brief analysis of Baltic economic history, as seen through the eyes of high-level party and government spokesmen in the three republics, will provide insight into this question.

Baltic spokesmen in the Soviet Union commenting on economic history usually divide the modern era into five periods: the years under the Russian empire (mid-eighteenth century to 1917), the years of "bourgeois independence" (1917-40), the initial phase of Soviet rule (1940-44), the stage of economic recovery (1944-50), and the contemporary phase of "socialist construction" (1950 onward). Not all of these periods are mentioned in every discussion, and the interpretations often vary, but common themes are still to be found.

The years under the Russian empire are usually omitted in the popular presentations of Baltic economic history, probably because the colonial status with respect to the Russians would then have to be defined. The period is sometimes mentioned, however, to emphasize the importance of Baltic economic ties to Russia and the other areas of the present-day Soviet Union. The rise of Russian capitalism is described as having contributed to the growth of "productive forces" in the Baltic region;[3] Baltic scholars in the West themselves describe the area as the most progressive and economically developed part of the Russian empire.[4] Soviet Baltic spokesmen often state that a true colonial situation did not exist because the area, while "nationally oppressed" was an integral part of the Russian economy.[5] Stress is placed on the disruptive effect on the Baltic economy engendered by separation from the raw materials and markets of the Russian empire and subsequent Soviet state that occurred during the independence period.[6]

That interwar period is also a difficult topic for the official spokesmen to discuss. They do not want to belittle the economic abilities of their people, but for political reasons, they must stress the advantages of union with the other Soviet republics. The rhetorical device most frequently employed is to point out the economic stagnation allegedly brought on by the indigenous bourgeoisie and their "imperialist masters." While Western Baltic scholars praise the success of the Baltic states in reorienting their economies (especially in the agricultural and food-processing sectors),[7] Soviet spokesmen depict this process as one of "disindustrialization and agrarianization." The bourgeoisie, many of whom did not belong to the three eponymous nationalities, are described as weak and incapable of utilizing the capital inherited from Czarist Russia, especially as a result of their insistence on strict isolation from the resources and markets of socialist Russia.[8] The bourgeoisie, said to be unwilling to industrialize for fear of creating a strong indigenous proletariat, ostensibly entered into league with foreign capitalists in order to guarantee its political survival. The imperialist powers had no desire to modernize the region, according to this view, because they preferred to use it as a source of raw materials and as an outlet for the sale of their industrial goods, thus maintaining the area as a "raw material and agrarian appendage."[9] The result, it is claimed, was mass unemployment, both urban and rural.[10]

The initial phase of Soviet rule is used by Soviet commentators to demonstrate what the Baltic people could accomplish in alliance with the other "fraternal" republics of the Soviet Union. Those republics ostensibly provided aid in the form of materials, skilled personnel, and experience. The Baltic people utilized this assistance and their own efforts to create "favorable conditions" for rapid development of industrial production. Previously inactive facilities were reopened, new sectors were to be developed, and the beginnings of a planned economy were undertaken. The lower classes, according to this view, comprehended that rapid industrialization was the only means to overcome backwardness or retardation in the area's economies and initiate the process of "socialist construction."[11]

Both Western and Soviet scholars agree that the war caused serious damage to the Baltic economies. Western scholars usually stress that the Soviet central authorities rebuilt the Estonian and Latvian economies, the most developed area of the Soviet Union, in order to revitalize the Soviet economy in a short time.[12] Soviet Baltic spokesmen, on the other hand, prefer to stress that the economic dislocation engendered by the war would have taken decades for the Baltic people to overcome without "generous and selfless assistance" from other republics. The Baltic people had no choice but to rely heavily on raw materials, industrial equipment, consumer goods, and skilled personnel imported from the rest of the Soviet Union in the first years after the war. In the case of Estonia and Latvia, this assistance ostensibly enabled the two economies to recover by 1946 and quickly gain a prominent position in the economy of the Soviet Union as a whole.[13] In the Lithuanian case, commentators speak of the process of reconstruction through the mid-1950s.[14]

The official interpretations of Baltic economic history thus reflect on the evaluation of the nature of economic ties to the other Soviet nationalities and Russians and on the degree of dependence on others for economic success. Soviet Baltic spokesmen stress that the area's economies could not have achieved their present high level of industrialization without the materials and markets provided by the regions that comprise the Soviet Union. While Western scholars might argue that countries in the West could serve the same function, Soviet Baltic commentators attempt to portray the present situation as a geopolitical fact of life that must be accepted.

The question of dependence is another matter. While Soviet Baltic spokesmen are careful to stress the appreciation of their people for the "disinterested" assistance of the other republics, they imply that this aid is no longer so necessary, now that the material base for socialist development has been laid. They indicate that the Baltic economies, fully integrated into the USSR economy, have more than repaid the debt to the other republics through their contributions generally since the postwar years.[15]

Contributions made by eponymous nationalities to economic progress are implicit in this interpretation. The Baltic people are not said to lack productive capacity. Slow prewar, as compared to postwar, growth is attributed to external material factors (the isolation from raw materials and markets) and political factors (the supposed malevolence of the indigenous bourgeoisie and the foreign capitalists). The elimination of these two dampening factors in the period of Soviet rule, in combination with some assistance from the other Soviet republics, is portrayed as enabling the Baltic people to build a viable economy through their own diligent efforts. A feeling that the Baltic people can succeed through their own efforts provides a strong positive support for nationality. Baltic pride, however, may be offended at the repudiation of the efforts by the Baltic bourgeoisie and overemphasis on the assistance from the Russians and Soviet nationalities.

The Soviet Baltic View of the Present Economic Situation

For assessing nationality supports, the measurement of the economic status of the nationality is as important as the means by which economic progress was achieved. The published Baltic evaluation of the republics' economic position shows the criteria Baltic leaders believe important in this sphere. It also reflects how the people are taught to view themselves and so reveals sources of possible satisfaction or dissatisfaction.

Baltic spokesmen take pride in the rapid economic growth, which is claimed to have surpassed the pre-1940 level by more than 30-fold.[16] They view the most significant accomplishment of this process as the transformation of primarily agrarian societies into modern industrial units. The leaders stress that the share of industry in the Baltic economies' incomes has overtaken that of agriculture.[17] Their evaluations most often reflect the primary importance the Soviet central government has placed traditionally on the heavy industry indicators, which measure the "progressive sectors" of the economy. Thus, the accounts stress the rise under Soviet rule of the power, chemical, and construction industries. Heavy industrial sectors that more fully utilize Baltic specialized skills, such as electrical engineering, electronics, instrument manufacture, and metalworking, are also highly touted.[18]

Traditional sectors of the economy, such as light industry, the meat and milk industry, and the food-processing industry, are discussed in terms of their high level of mechanization and efficiency.[19] Agriculture is described as highly modernized and equipped with the most advanced technical and organizational devices. Production, "rationalized" through collective farming, results in high, stable yields of food crops and livestock products.[20]

Baltic spokesmen seem to have accepted the need for a heavy industrial base in their regional economies, which accords well with the beliefs of the central authorities. The Baltic elite, however, tends to stress the instrumental value of heavy industry. Reference is often made to the rise in the standard of living that this has engendered by providing the material base for an advanced consumer goods industry. They point out that the three economies specialize in the production of consumer goods, many of which go to satisfy the local population's desire for durable goods and other consumer items.[21] Baltic commentators also stress the rise in wages, the expansion of housing space, and the construction of schools, cultural institutions, and public service enterprises.[22] They frequently applaud the decision of the Twenty-Fourth CPSU Congress (1971) to make an improvement in the standard of living the highest goal of the Party.[23] The leaders probably realize the importance of this shift in priority, from heavy to light industry, in satisfying the rising expectations of their local populace.

The Baltic people take pride in the quality of their economic endeavors. Reports stress that the Baltic economies specialize in sectors requiring a high degree of technical skill, such as the production of electric motors, electronic equipment, and complex instruments.[24] They cite the high labor productivity of the industrial workers, which surpasses the Soviet average and has accounted in recent years for almost all of the increase in industrial production in Latvia and Estonia.[25] They also applaud the industriousness of Baltic farmers.[26] Furthermore, the press frequently comments on the contribution of regions, enterprises, or individual workers to "socialist competition."[27] Finally, Baltic commentators boast that, in many areas of production, the three economies provide goods to the Union-wide economy far in excess of their expected share.[28] Many products, such as Estonian petroleum apparatus or Latvian electric trains, are said to be of sufficiently high quality to earn these a reputation and market abroad.[29]

Baltic spokesmen admit that specialization of the regional economies in the advanced sectors of the overall economy could not occur without a rational Union-wide division of labor. They stress that the regional economies need the raw materials and manufactured goods produced in the other Soviet republics. The regional economies could not manufacture these goods on a sufficient scale to supply their primary sectors with needed materials at low cost.[30] Thus, they seem to have accepted a limited but still significant dependence on the other Soviet republics.

Finally, it is noteworthy to observe with whom the Baltic people compare their economic success. Although occasionally figures are given to show that the three republics have the highest standard of living in the Soviet Union,[31] the comparison more frequently made is with the countries of Western Europe. This probably stems from two factors: the Baltic people traditionally have considered themselves Western, and they may not want to point out the economic discrepancies separating Soviet republics. Thus, in 1972 the chairman of the Estonian SSR Council of Ministers, Valters Klauson, asserted that the aggregate income of Estonia, among the lowest in Europe in 1936 in per capita terms, had, by 1970, surpassed that of Norway, Denmark, Belgium, the Netherlands, and Finland, while the growth rate was almost double that of these countries. Klauson further noted that Estonia ranked among the highest of the north European countries in consumption of meat, dairy products, eggs, fish, sugar, potatoes, vegetables, and grain.[32] Similarly, in 1972, Latvia's Party head, Augusts Voss, stated that Latvia's growth rate had outstripped that of Britain, West Germany, and the Scandinavian countries.[33]

Most of these assertions are not accepted by scholars in the West. While they admit that the Baltic republics have made remarkable gains relative to the rest of the Soviet Union, they argue that many areas yet need substantial improvement. A study on Estonia, for example, pointed out that heavy industries still receive a high priority, resulting in shortages in many areas of consumer economics, such as housing.[34] It also stated that while Estonia may have a higher material standard of living than that of the third world, Eastern Europe, or even Mediterranean Europe, Soviet spokesmen were engaging in wishful thinking and statistical manipulation in ranking Estonia with the nations of Western Europe.[35]

The significant change is that these republics have made considerable gains in the postwar era. These advances place them somewhere between East and West in terms of material well-being. Such economic progress can provide a positive content to nationality supports. Economic progress can supply the material goods needed to satisfy rising demands during a period of social transformation. Owing to geopolitical considerations, this progress, in turn, can only be achieved through close association with the region's dominant neighbor, which provides the necessary markets and materials to keep the Baltic economy prospering. Nevertheless, the high economic level of the region, in both material and perceptual terms, allows links to be formed with the area's European neighbors, while it acts as a Soviet window to the West.

The economic success of the region fosters a sense of self-esteem within each nationality group. The population is made aware of the three republics' high standard of living, both with respect to the other Soviet union republics and to many European nations. The Baltic people are also praised, although along with the area's other inhabitants, for the industriousness that contributes to such progress. Despite the regime's attempt to discredit the independence period, the population may harbor memories of perceived achievements in the economic sphere during these years when they had to be more self-reliant. Such stimuli to self-esteem may, however, foster a sense of superiority with respect to other nationalities. A certain ambivalence may thus enter into the evaluation of economic success and engender dissatisfaction, despite relative material prosperity.

Ambivalence in Economic Progress

Baltic spokesmen have been shown to endorse the benefits of economic progress. This affirmative analysis exercises certain major supportive functions for the nationality concerned. In recent years, however, the Baltic elite have had to defend economic progress against charges made by the West, the central Soviet government, and their own people. This defensive posture injects a degree of ambivalence into the positive analysis of economic progress and may undermine any satisfaction created among the nationalities.

A Latvian scholar asserted that owing to the complexity of economic analyses, most bourgeois criticism did not speak of the material but rather of the nonmaterial concerns in the economic realm. This criticism, directed against Russification, economic integration, and the elimination of national peculiarities, is pictured in diametric opposition to the "Soviet reality" of the "flourishing and rapprochement of nations."[36]

Surprisingly, one of the most biting attacks on the Baltic economic situation reflecting such concerns came in the 1972 letter of 17 Latvian

Communists. They charged that industrial progress had been used and was still being used by the central government to exert greater control over the indigenous population. The letter voiced a complaint that the construction of large new industries and the expansion of existing plants was undertaken "disregarding any economic necessity."[37] Construction personnel, the labor force, and the needed specialists were brought in from outside, as were raw materials. The products of these industries, moreover, were exported from the republic. Existing resources, especially forests, were depleted. The extent of the problem was emphasized in one striking paragraph:

> In our republic there are already many large firms where almost no Latvians remain among the workers, technicians-engineers, or management (e.g., "REZ," Dizelestroitel'nyi zavod, Gidrometribor and many others) and there are other companies where the majority of workers are Latvian, but management does not understand the Latvian language (Popov radio factory, Wagon Car Mfg., Autoelektropribor, Rigasc Audums, etc.)[38]

Furthermore, this influx of Slavs has allegedly led to the Russification of existing political and cultural institutions.

The established elite of both Estonia and Latvia attempted to answer these charges, most directly in articles by SSR Party Secretary Voss and Council of Ministers Chairman Klauson published in Fall 1972 issues of a Moscow journal.[39] For the most part, the specific issues raised by the Latvian letter were not addressed. The two officials contented themselves with merely repeating the oft-cited argument for industrialization as a means to guarantee a high standard of living and an advanced cultural level. Klauson did attempt to refute the charge of environmental damage by pointing out the lack of any protection measures taken during the period of independence, although a critical reader might ask what countries in the world considered such matters during those early years.

The Russification charge was handled with caution. Economic ties with the other Soviet republics, in their view, are justified on the basis of a rational distribution of labor and the limited resources of the area. The ties and assistance are depicted as those of "fraternal and like-minded peoples" in stark contrast to the competitive relations found among capitalist countries.[40] The large influx of non-Baltic workers is attributed, for the most part, to the severe dislocations of World War II. These workers toiled under the same severe conditions as the indigenous populace and purportedly enjoyed no special privileges when they elected to settle in the region.[41] Soviet Baltic spokesmen charge that critics would prefer the area to remain underdeveloped if progress could be bought only through cooperation with other nationalities.[42]

They deny the charge of Russification in cultural life as well. Party Secretary Voss spoke of the expanded cultural and education facilities available to the Latvians and about the transmission of Latvian cultural accomplishments to other states of the world through the Russian language.[43] Estonia's Party chief, Johannes (Ivan) Käbin, stressed the use of the Estonian language in educational institutions, cultural institutions, and the press.[44] Finally, a Lithuanian spokesman pointed out that because prominent anti-Soviet scholars in the West equated Communism with Russian colonialism, complaints about Russification were in actuality anti-Communist attacks.[45]

The primary defense these leaders raised against charges of superindustrialization and Russification was the necessity for economic progress. They particularly emphasized the high standard of living enjoyed by the Baltic people. This defense, however, cannot be voiced too loudly in the Baltic republics because it emphasizes the vast differential in economic level between this region and other areas of the Soviet Union. This, in turn, might evoke measures on the part of the central government to redistribute the wealth of the Baltic region to the poorer areas of the USSR.

Some Baltic leaders seem to be sensitive to this danger to the privileged status, in economic terms, of these three republics. Instead of asserting the right to a higher economic status on the basis of the disproportionate contribution to the Union economy, Baltic spokesmen use the tactic of denying that any substantial difference exists. Thus, Party Secretary Käbin in a 1975 article listed two reasons why the high Estonian SSR income per capita was an unreliable measure of relative prosperity.[46] He stated that certain Estonian industries, especially the light and meat and dairy industries, use relatively expensive raw materials and, therefore, because an accounting method based on gross output is utilized, the income of the Estonian SSR is artificially raised. Furthermore, Käbin pointed out that gross income per capita fails to take into account the age and sex structure in different republics. Estonia has a higher percentage of able-bodied people or full consumers than the Union-wide average (54 percent as opposed to 50 percent); therefore, it is natural that the per capita production and consumption indicators stand somewhat higher.

The Baltic elite appear to be playing the difficult game of simultaneously asserting and denying the material prosperity of the Baltic republics. They apparently are attempting to use the dubious argument that Baltic economic indicators compare well with those of Western European countries but are difficult to measure with respect to the other Soviet republics. They simultaneously imply that the growth of "productive forces" in each republic insures the most rapid increase for the Union as a whole.

This precarious balance is endangered by the growth of nationalist currents among the lower-level officials and the population itself that stem from economic considerations. Käbin in 1975 described the "objective" and "subjective" problems that exist in nationality relations, closely paraphrasing Brezhnev's statements at the fiftieth anniversary celebrations in 1972 and the Twenty-Third CPSU Congress in 1971. Objective problems include the "determination of the most accurate ways for the development of the individual nations and nationalities and the most correct combination of the interests of each with the general interests of the Soviet people as a whole."[47] Specifically, in Käbin's interpretation, this means the development of republican productive forces and the position of the republic in the social division of labor based on its natural conditions, labor traditions, and historically developed lines of production. These considerations will be dealt with in the next section.

Subjective problems are of more immediate concern here. Käbin cited only the "manifestations of ethnic arrogance and disrespect for the nationality feelings of members of other peoples."[48] More specific instances of national pride and feelings of superiority have been reported. A Ukrainian living in Lithuania complained about officials who "forget modesty and exalt the successes of their collectives, cities, republics, and sometimes even counterpose them to successes attained by others, overevaluating their contribution to the national task."[49] The chairman of the Latvian SSR Council of Ministers, Yuri Ruben, cautioned that in articles which juxtaposed the production figures for certain items with the size of the Latvian populace to stress its contribution to the Union-wide economy, mention should also be made of items, used in Latvia, which are manufactured elsewhere.[50]

These "subjective problems" can also take other forms. A Soviet specialist on nationality problems pointed out the potential conflict of interest in the provision of resources:

> . . . as a result of definite differences existing among republics and nationality groups in customs and traditions, a tendency toward rigid, narrowly understood nationality interests as against general union-wide [interests], may manifest itself in the provision of material and labor resources. This would be fertile ground for the emergence of nationalist sentiments and manifestations of bourgeois nationalism.[51]

Another commentator in the Lithuanian press stressed the need for "disinterestedness" in this matter with no calculation of immediate advantage or consumer-oriented interests.[52] Articles have appeared in the press of all three Baltic union republics warning against the development of a consumer mentality. Many of these pieces have also disputed the "Maoist line," which is allegedly hostile to the provision of mass consumer goods.[53]

Finally, there is evidence that the population has not fully accepted the regime's official criteria for success. Baltic leaders warn that bourgeois propaganda is now aimed at cultivating an "apolitical attitude, nihilism, and indifference to social reality,"[54] or a "philistine passion for gain, the way of life under capitalism and its morality, nationalism and chauvinism."[55] The youth of the region, lacking "experience in the class struggle," are portrayed as particularly vulnerable targets.[56] Complaints about violations of work discipline, such as truancy, drunkenness, and theft, and about high personnel turnover reveal that such attitudes may be more widespread. Officials are criticized for tolerating such behavior and manifesting a purely formal attitude toward socialist competition.[57]

Economic progress, thus, does not automatically produce satisfaction among the nationalities. It may foster excess pride, bordering on a feeling of superiority, vis-a-vis other nationalities and the Russians. It can also engender a mistrust of the intentions of other groups, especially if a threat is perceived to the material well-being of the particular nationality. Pride, feelings of superiority, and mistrust of other groups, in combination, may promote a desire of of the members of the nationality for greater administrative autonomy. The fact that the official ideology endorses the right of self-determination and that people in the West of similar socioeconomic status are perceived to enjoy broad political rights may further this attitude. In this manner, a high degree of economic success may promote, rather than dampen, dissatisfaction.

SIGNIFICANCE OF CONTROL OVER THE ECONOMIC SECTOR

Economic progress has been shown to stimulate nationality self-assertiveness. The important question arising from this is: What effect does the conflict between central and local control of the union republic economic sector have on nationality satisfaction? The hypothesis guiding this chapter presumes that the Baltic people seek to gain a still greater degree of control over their economic fate. The type of control being sought and the means utilized to acquire it must be identified.

Existing Control

In order to understand the attempts to gain greater control in this area, it is first necessary to comprehend the nature of control exercised by union republic authorities that existed both prior to and during the period under examination (the Ninth Five-Year Plan). The following are a few of the most important considerations.

The administrative arrangement that exists today stemmed from the reforms of 1965 instituted by Premier Alexei Kosygin. The *sovnarkhoz* system, which had replaced the ministerial system from 1957 to 1965, granted greater powers to the union republic authorities. Almost all of the Union-wide ministries, which were organized along functional (branch) lines, were abolished and replaced by 105 (later 103) *sovnarkhozy* (regional economic councils). Enterprises were made subordinate to the sovnarkhozy, which were in turn responsible to the republican government (in actuality, the republic Gosplan—State Planning Office), and through these to the central bodies.[58]

The need for regional coordination was fundamental to the sovnarkhoz reform. Each SSR Council of Ministers was to approve plans prepared by the sovnarkhozy under it (one, except in the largest union republics) for the manufacture and distribution of goods, the specialization and cooperation of enterprises, and the allocation of raw materials and equipment.[59] The republic's Gosplan was to have the key role in planning and in the allocation of supplies. Such influential officials as those directing the sovnarkhoz were to be appointed by republic authorities.[60]

In practice, the system was characterized by a gradual recentralization of authority. The divisions of the USSR Gosplan responsible for overall planning and coordination constantly bypassed republic and sovnarkhoz officials to deal with the enterprise managers directly. Over the years, administrative changes further increased the powers of the central authorities.[61]

Nevertheless, local control, both on paper and to a lesser extent in practice, was greater under the sovnarkhoz system than under the ministerial system. Baltic officials occasionally voiced their concern at the steady erosion of republic control. A Latvian official in 1962 complained that only .2 of 1 percent of the republic production was allocated by republic authorities.[62] In 1964, the chairman of the Estonian SSR Council of Ministers argued that the republic sovnarkhoz did not control the republic's own Ministry of Communal Economy or the factories (making electric motors, clothing, and building materials) under the Ministry of Public Order (successor to the Ministerstvo Vnutrennykh Del [MVD] and Narodnyi Komissariat Vnutrennykh Del [NKVD].[63] The Baltic party elite vocally opposed abolition of the sovnarkhoz system in 1965.[64]

One of the stated reasons for the 1965 reinstatement of the ministerial arrangement was the need to combat localism (mestnichestvo). Premier Kosygin declared in a September 1965 speech that the reform entrusted the republics with new responsibilities in planning, investment, finance, employment, and wage policies.[65] Nevertheless, Western scholars generally agree that the reform reduced republic powers in the economic sphere.

The system established under the 1965 Kosygin reforms does attempt, however, to combine branch and territorial administration. There are three types of ministries: Union-wide, Union-republic, and republic. The Union-wide ministry directs the enterprises under its control from Moscow, and its enterprises are not responsible to republic authorities. The Union-republic ministry has offices both at the center and in the various SSRs, and its enterprises report to central and republic authorities. Finally, the republic ministry has offices only in the particular SSR, and its enterprises do not report directly to central authorities.[66] The ministries themselves are organized along functional lines (see Tables 4.1-4.3). Under this system, the republic Gosplan is formally limited to making suggestions about the plans of various Union-subordinate enterprises, which before 1965 were under its direct control.

The enterprises of Union subordination or joint subordination play a critical role in the republic's economy. Party Secretary Käbin, in 1975, asserted that 70 percent of Estonian industrial output is produced by enterprises under either Union-republic or republic ministries.[67] A Western scholar, however, pointed out that not merely was only 11 percent of industrial output produced under republic ministries but that most important products were made in enterprises under Union subordination, including the entire oil-shale industry, most of electric power generation, pulp and paper manufacturing, fisheries and fish processing, and some leading engineering and metal-working plants.[68] Many other important lines of production are under the dual Union-republic administration and, thus, subject primarily to central control.

The representation of the eponymous Baltic nationalities in the top economic bodies of their SSRs might also be considered important (see Tables B.3-B.5). Whereas the eponymous nationalities appear to be well represented, there are ministers with non-Baltic surnames in this group. Furthermore, many of the present ministers have spent a majority of the time before 1945 outside of the Baltic region (as the so-called Yestonians in the Estonian case).[69] While the loyalties of these people may have come closer to their own nationality during their tenure in the Baltic republics, the populace may still suspect them to be somewhat alien in their orientation. Finally, a top Baltic official may have an outsider (Russian, Ukrainian, Belo-

TABLE 4.1

Draft Directives for Five-Year Plans (Union Republics), Increase in Industrial Production, 1966-70, 1971-75, and 1976-80

Area	1966-70		1971-75		1976-80	
	Percent	Rank	Percent	Rank	Percent	Rank
USSR	47-50	–	42-46	–	35-39	–
RFSFR	50	12	44-47	9	35-39	8
Ukrainian SSR	50	12	38-41	12	30-34	12
Belorussian SSR	70	3	50-53	4	39-43	3
Uzbek SSR	60	7	46-49	6	35-39	8
Kazakh SSR	70	3	57-60	2	39-43	3
Georgian SSR	60	7	39-42	11	37-41	6
Azerbaijanian SSR	60	7	43-46	10	37-41	6
Lithuanian SSR	70	3	46-49	6	32-36	11
Moldavian SSR	70	3	56-59	3	45-49	1
Latvian SSR	50	12	35-38	15	26-30	14
Kirgiz SSR	60	7	45-48	8	33-37	10
Tajik SSR	80	1	37-40	13	38-42	5
Armenian SSR	80	1	60-63	1	43-47	2
Turkmen SSR	60	7	50-53	4	30-34	12
Estonian SSR	50	12	36-39	14	22-26	15

Sources: "Direktivy XXIII s"ezda KPSS po piatiletnemu planu razvitiia narodnogo khoziaistva SSSR na 1966-1970 goda," Pravda (February 20, 1966), pp. 1-6; "Direktivy XXIV s"ezda KPSS po piatiletnemu planu razvitiia narodnogo khoziaistva SSSR na 1971-1975 goda," Pravda (February 14, 1971), pp. 1-5; "Osnovnye napravleniia razvitiia narodnogo khoziaistva na 1976-1980 goda," Pravda (March 7, 1976), pp. 2-8.

russian, or another) as his deputy, who can report back to the center any inclinations toward localism. All of these considerations further reduce the potential influence exerted by officials of the eponymous nationality over republic economic policy. Many Soviet economists and political leaders have argued that republic powers in the economic realm are or should be increasing. One Russian economist, while pushing for less dependence on "obsolete" territorial divisions (see below), nevertheless described the broadening republic inputs in the following manner:

> At present, a consistent expansion of the union republics' rights in the field of economic management is taking place. Thus, with a view to ensuring the comprehensive planning of industry according to the branch principle of management, the republic agencies are now working out draft plans for the development of the national economy in all branches of industry of Union-republic and republic subordination and are also submitting proposals on draft plans for production (other than defense production) at enterprises of Union-wide ministries in the territory of the various republics.[70]

He went on to say that republic Gosplans had been instructed to study questions of interbranch production and distribution, the siting of industry, and the reconstruction and expansion of existing enterprises.[71] Proposals made at the Twenty-Fifth Party Congress of

TABLE 4.2

Level of Education of Population, by Union Republic, 1970

Area	Persons with Higher or Secondary Education (per 10,000 over age 10)	Rank in Educational Level by Republic
USSR	483	–
RSFSR	489	6
Ukrainian SSR	494	5
Belorussian SSR	440	12
Uzbek SSR	456	10
Kazakh SSR	470	9
Georgian SSR	554	1
Azerbaijanian SSR	471	8
Lithuanian SSR	382	15
Moldavian SSR	397	14
Latvian SSR	517	2
Kirgiz SSR	452	11
Tajik SSR	420	13
Armenian SSR	516	3
Turkmen SSR	475	7
Estonian SSR	506	4

Source: "Ethnographic Processes in the USSR," Soviet Sociology 10, no. 4 (Spring 1972): 353.

TABLE 4.3

Educational Level of Nationalities in the Three Baltic Union Republics, 1970 (per 1,000 people age 10 and over)

Nationalities	Higher	Partial Higher	Middle Special-ist	Middle General	Partial Middle
Estonian SSR					
Estonians	44	16	74	107	221
Russians	54	13	94	153	284
Ukrainians	69	15	133	216	328
Belorussians	33	9	90	163	318
Finns	17	7	55	76	240
Latvian SSR					
Latvians	38	19	80	103	250
Russians	56	23	94	141	244
Belorussians	28	12	71	106	256
Poles	21	12	57	113	231
Ukrainians	89	28	143	192	277
Lithuanians	12	6	30	51	195
Jews	209	72	119	214	159
Lithuanian SSR					
Lithuanians	33	13	55	66	189
Russians	56	18	95	161	248
Poles	9	6	23	59	196
Belorussians	40	14	90	142	289
Ukrainians	83	23	155	225	282

Source: Itogi vsesoiuznoi perepisi naseleniia 1970 goda. Natsional'nyi sostav naseleniia SSSR (Moscow: Statistika, 1973), 4: 544-49, 518-23, 509-13.

the CPSU (1976) called for increased responsibility of the republics in "resolving questions of industrial and sociocultural construction, increasing the output of consumer goods, and expanding trade and services for the population with a consideration for local and national features and the fullest utilization of natural, labor and other resources."[72]

It remains to be seen what reforms will be instituted by the central authorities either to increase or decrease the powers of republic bodies. Meanwhile, Baltic economists and some members of the top governmental and party bodies have been attempting to establish a closer harmony between central priorities and local needs. They have proposed various structural revisions that would grant more authority to republic officials. They have also tried to utilize the existing framework to achieve goals important to the eponymous nationalities.

PROPOSALS FOR STRUCTURAL REFORM

The Baltic elite have occasionally had to defend the existing administrative system against reforms advocated elsewhere that might reduce further the authority of republic bodies. The most dramatic exchange in recent years occurred between a Russian and a Lithuanian economist. An article appeared in the Moscow journal _Voprosy ekonomiki_ [Problems of economics], in which the Russian economist discussed the necessity for better regional economic planning. He criticized the lack of planning bodies at the level of the economic region (of which the three Baltic republics form one) when such bodies existed in republics that differed so greatly in natural resources and manpower. He even suggested that many of the reasons for divisions into republics had become outmoded, by pointing out such things as the equalization of social structures and the growth of a multinational work force.[73] He therefore proposed that

> nationality boundaries within the USSR are increasingly losing their former significance. This has already made it necessary in certain instances not only to create interrepublic economic agencies but also, through legislation, to institute certain changes in boundaries between union republics. Evidently there are no obstacles to this with respect to the autonomous republics and oblasts involved. It is apparent that some forms of associations including several nationalities may be economically expedient in certain cases. Those nationality regions that have greater productive capacity and homogeneity than others will undoubtedly develop their economies far more successfully, and this will lead to even greater flourishing of socialist _natsii_ (nations) and small nationalities.[74]

He warned that the approach to this question should be "cautious," because it affected a broad range of political and economic relationships.

Baltic officials could not be expected to applaud this suggestion to create still another level of economic decision making to overrule the republic bodies. A Lithuanian scholar employed in a Moscow institute responded to this proposal shortly thereafter in an issue of the Lithuanian Party journal, Kommunist. While he neglected to address directly the question of regional rather than republic planning, he tried to justify the existing arrangement in terms of its socio-economic significance. He argues that the strength of the Soviet economic system rests on the fact that it combines both functional and territorial planning, to yield a "qualitatively new internatsional'naia (integrated) productive force that markedly exceeds the simple sum of the nationality productive forces which comprise it."[75] He summarized the nature of the economic organization of the USSR in the following way:

> The organization of socio-economic life in the USSR not only rules out any infringement on the rights of natsii (nations) comprising it but also is constructed in such a way that all republics can, to the fullest extent possible, realize all the basic goals of their national development, which consist of rapid, effective economic growth and scientific-technical, and socio-cultural development. Under these conditions, the independence, equality, and sovereignty of each republic are utilized to make the maximum contribution to the Union-wide economy.[76]

He thus asserted that the political structure designed to protect the "national sovereignty" of an SSR also serves the economic interests of each nationality. The Soviet Union's economy, in turn, is said to develop at a faster rate than that of each of its components. This is almost the inverse of the Russian's implicit argument that the development of the Union economy benefits each of the constituent republics.

The Lithuanian economist also attempted to refute the charge that regional and central interests were not accorded sufficient weight under the existing system. He asserted that the territorial aspect allowed specialization of production on the basis of comparative advantage, which, in turn, contributed to a rise in production effectiveness and a reduction in cost. Central control was ensured through the formulation of the USSR economic plan and the diverse economic links between enterprises in different regions.[77] While he admitted the need for greater interrepublic cooperation, he argued that economic equality was best secured through the diligent efforts of each republic rather than through an artificial leveling carried out from above.[78]

Such a heated exchange over the feasibility of restructuring the territorial system of planning erupts rarely, owing to the extreme sensitivity of the issue. There is an ongoing discussion in the USSR, however, about the best means to harmonize the interests of the Union-wide bodies with local needs. One problem is that the Union-subordinate enterprises, located within the republics, and, to a lesser extent, the enterprises under the Union-republic administration, owe their primary allegiance to departmental interests. When production plans are formulated or shortages occur during actual production, the material requirements of the republic are accorded second priority to the needs of the industrial branch. Thus, local industries are often faced with a shortage of critical inputs for their industrial production despite the fact that goods may be exported by nearby Union-wide enterprises to other areas of the USSR.

Baltic economists have put forward various proposals to increase the horizontal links between enterprises found in the respective republics. The first deputy chairman of the Lithuanian SSR Council of Ministers proposed that Gosplan USSR and Gossnab USSR (State Committee for Material and Technical Supply) examine the problems involved in manufacture of goods for use between branches of the economy. He cited an example in which castings were made by one enterprise and shipped outside the republic while another local enterprise was forced to import the same product.[79] The party first secretary, Antanas Sniečkus, at the Twenty-Fourth CPSU Congress (1971) complained that branch ministries often assign a low priority to the production of items that are necessary to enterprises of other ministries and departments.[80]

Connected with this problem is that of centralizing the plants producing items used on a mass scale, such as forgings, welded components, packaging materials, spare parts, and repair implements. These goods are usually produced separately within each enterprise, resulting in a waste of materials and manpower. Suggestions have been made to establish plants, under republic authority, to produce such items for use within the SSR. There has been resistance to the allocation of funds for these plants on the part of Union-subordinate enterprises,[81] which probably do not want to be dependent on outside sources. The Lithuanian first deputy mentioned above and a chief specialist of the Latvian Gosplan have suggested that an intersectoral planning branch be established to coordinate the production of such items. This potentially powerful branch, according to the proponents of the plan, should be made subject to the authority of the republic bodies, because only these would have the fullest possible information about the development of the local economy as a whole and the needs of enterprises in their territory for such items.[82]

Enterprise associations (ob"edinenie) have often been promoted that would combine plants involved in a particular line of manufacture, regardless of administrative affiliations (such as the Lithuanian Sigma association for the manufacture of calculators and small computers). Some Baltic economists may hope that such associations would give local enterprises greater direct access to goods essential for their process of production and, thus, would reduce the "departmentalism" of the sectoral hierarchy. Baltic commentators have noted some resistance to this idea on the part of Union-wide enterprise officials out of the fear that it would constitute a return to a sovnarkhoz-type of arrangement.[83]

A distinct possibility exists, however, that such large groupings might reduce local control over the formerly Union-republic and republic-subordinate plants participating in them. Associations combining enterprises across branch lines seem to be directly responsible to ministry offices in Moscow. This chain of command may bypass republic officials this way. Such a danger apparently has been recognized by local specialists. Several Baltic economists have stated that the feasibility of such large associations should be reviewed continuously by republic authorities. Associations should be abolished if they do not contribute to local interests (for example, if an increase in the number of workers is required).[84]

The Baltic elite have also been concerned with acquiring a greater republic input to the planning process. The same Lithuanian first deputy suggested that annual and five-year plans be formulated at the republic and USSR levels simultaneously (instead of at the USSR level first) to provide the central authorities with a better idea of local needs and resources. He also proposed that the republic officials be required to approve rather than merely review the most important indicators for the Union-wide enterprises located within the republic.[85] An Estonian economist has argued that a means should be found to integrate the production forecasts of Union-wide enterprises into the automated planning system being developed for the republic's economy.[86] Another Estonian economist suggested that indicators be established like those used in the West or Eastern Europe, such as net output [value added], which would facilitate evaluation of the efficiency of Union-wide enterprises located within a constituent republic.[87] Although the argument here is that adoption of these indicators would enable the republic planning agencies to draw up a more realizable plan, the implication is that such a measure would allow a judgment to be made about whether a particular enterprise should fall under branch or territorial control.[88]

These samples of the administrative reforms advocated to give republic bodies greater control over each SSR's economy are rationalized in various ways. Reasons for such changes are put in terms of economic efficiency, but the primary concern seems to focus upon the hierarchal loyalty of Union-wide enterprises located in the republic, which leads to a neglect of local needs. These reform proposals, however, seem to have encountered both the resistance of Union-subordinate managers who do not want to tackle the complex coordination tasks and, surprisingly, the opposition of some republic-subordinate managers, who fear a loss of their limited autonomy.

Realization of Local Priorities within Existing Structures

The Baltic elite have not relied solely on proposals for administrative reforms to gain a greater amount of control over each SSR economy. They have also attempted to modify economic priorities in order to gear their unit's economy to the best utilization of local resources (both physical and manpower) and the highest possible satisfaction of local needs. Now that the material base for an advanced economy has been laid, the Baltic people wish to establish a system that would subordinate USSR demands to local priorities.

Many of the Baltic elite have been lobbying for a new approach to economic growth in the region. They have pushed for reduced growth rates and a shift in emphasis away from primary industries and either to traditional sectors, like instrument manufacture, food processing, and light industry, or to innovative sectors, such as automation systems. Thus, the draft five-year plans for both Latvia and Estonia have shown increasingly modest production increases, which are lower than the USSR average and the lowest of all the union republics (see Table 4.1 above). Lithuania has not yet completely established the material base that exists in the other two Baltic SSRs. Consequently, its forecast growth rate is somewhat higher, although still comparatively modest among all 15 Soviet republics. The nationality import of such moves is illustrated by Party Secretary Käbin's defense in 1975 of the lower growth rate, which he characterized not as a sign of lagging but as an indication of equalization in levels of development among the different economic regions in the USSR.[89] The time may come, however, when Baltic mistrust of the central authorities leads the eponymous nationalities to believe that central acceptance of modest growth rates for the area is designed to limit the rise in Baltic living standards.

Baltic spokesmen are especially concerned about the growing scarcity of manpower and raw material reserves. Käbin asserted recently that future growth must be based upon these considerations:

> Manpower shortages, the need for efficient utilization of limited natural resources, and the regard for the

> socialist state's ever stricter requirements for environmental protection create certain complications. We can maintain our high growth rates provided that there is maximum utilization of technical achievements, improvements in the structure of industry and organization of labor, and that moral and material incentives are perfected to promote further growth of labor productivity, while meeting the basic requirements of the modern production process: upgrading quality and effectiveness.[90]

The most critical problem facing the Baltic elite is the shortage of manpower. The increase in the workforce brought on by rapid industrialization in the postwar era has far outpaced the natural population increase of the eponymous nationalities, especially in Latvia and Estonia. This has resulted in drawing substantial immigration of non-Baltic people into the area. SSR population increase in the 1960s stemmed primarily from immigration in the Estonian and Latvian case—the 92,100 immigrants into Estonia between 1959 and 1969 accounted for 58 percent of the republic's population increase.[91] The percentage constituted by the eponymous nationality in the total population of the SSR has fallen sharply for both Estonia and Latvia. According to the 1959 and 1970 censuses, Estonians have declined from 74.6 percent to 68.2 percent of their SSR's total population, while the corresponding figures for Latvians in their SSR have fallen from 62.0 percent to 56.8 percent. The Lithuanians have been able thus far to maintain their position, and even gain slightly, rising from 79.3 percent to 80.1 percent.[92] Nevertheless, a Lithuanian scholar has pointed out that the natural population increase of the Lithuanians is on the decline due to the pressures of modernization. This has been combined with a shrinkage in the available nonworking population, such as housewives, and may, he implied, lead Lithuania into a situation similar to that of its Baltic neighbors.[93]

The Baltic elite have sought to alleviate this problem by taking measures that would reduce the need of the three economies for manpower in excess of already existing labor pools. In recent years, various elites have stressed that the economies must switch from an extensive to an intensive path of development. The head of Lithuania's Gosplan thus related that the manpower reserve in Lithuania had been "virtually exhausted" by 1972. Consequently, output had to be increased "to a decisive degree by the more effective use of manpower and by the steady growth of labor productivity in all branches of the material production sphere."[94]

Similarly, Latvia's Gosplan chief stated that, until 1965, Latvia had been following an extensive course of development, because not all the working-age population was engaged in "social production" (the public sphere). The population reserves (notably those people in housework and on private farms) had been utilized, with a resulting decline in free labor sources to 6.2 percent. Thus, Latvia in 1969 had switched to an intensive course of development. Growth was not to be achieved through multiplying the number of workers but through a better use of existing capacities by following measures such as the introduction of scientific and technical achievements, modernizing and reconstructing enterprises, mechanizing and automating production processes, and improving management on all levels. According to this official, the percentage increase in output achieved through raising labor productivity in Latvia jumped from 65 percent in 1968 to 91 percent in 1969.[95] Estonia's party chief, Käbin, in 1975 maintained that "labor productivity alone could be the basis for increasing industrial output."[96] Although Lithuanian productivity rates have lagged behind the other two Baltic republics, the stress placed on them by the leadership has increased in the past few years. The call by the Estonian and Latvian elite for increasing industrial output through labor productivity alone goes considerably higher than the goal of 87 to 90 percent through this means set in the Ninth Five-Year Plan.[97]

Various plans have been forwarded to cope with this dilemma, especially by Latvian officials. Two demographers, for example, suggested:

> The need for labor can be satisfied only if there is a large mechanical population increase [immigration]. . . . A rational way to utilize local and imported labor would be to encourage immigrants to fill jobs in industry, construction, and farming, whereas those freed from the above areas, as well as local youth, could work in the services sector.[98]

This proposal reveals a crucial aspect of the manpower dilemma: the diversification of the economy to meet consumer needs requires the opening up of sectors, such as the service sector, which utilize large numbers of workers. Thus, manpower must be freed from other sectors of the economy rather than merely frozen at existing levels. Furthermore, this is complicated by the high labor requirements of the Baltic economic specialities, such as machine manufacture and metal working. Finally, many of the immigrant workers are attracted to the area by its high living standard rather than through a recruitment policy. This may have led a Latvian Gosplan official to put forward the brazen idea that the number of workers be limited "on a territorial basis."[99] A Western scholar has concluded that the Latvian farm recruitment policy initiated in November 1973 demonstrated the hopelessness of efforts to limit immigration.[100]

A conflict seems to have developed here between the top level SSR Party/governmental elite and economists, on the one hand, and the USSR branch officials and lower-level SSR industrial managers, on the other. A member of Latvia's Gosplan complained that ministries, departments, and plants based their industrial output increase on an increase in the work force: a 10 percent decrease in productivity and a 33,000 increase in the work force had been projected by these groups in their draft plans for 1971 to 1976.[101] Lower-level managers have been charged with believing that their production needs can be solved most easily through a labor increase. The Baltic press criticized those people who "publicly agree with the notion of productivity increase [but] immediately run to the planning commission for permission to increase the number of workers."[102]

The lower-level managers may not be any less loyal to the needs of their nationality—in fact, a Western scholar suggested that precisely this group in Latvia opposed the introduction of new large-scale enterprises.[103] They may be merely suffering under pressure to increase production by whatever means available. A Western scholar outlined the problems faced by members of this category:

> Some of the workers are undisciplined and unproductive and, under conditions of a labor shortage, they have to be included in the overall plan of required staff. A surplus of labor, moreover, is insurance against the time [when] additional assignments for new and different output are required and, in some firms, for the so-called "storming" of production at the end of each month. Another headache for management is the extreme turnover of labor and the changing of specialities, with the resultant loss of experience and productivity.[104]

Some Soviet Baltic economists understand the lack of incentives for industrial managers to reduce their dependence on labor. An Estonian representative to a 1970 discussion in the USSR Supreme Soviet's Council of Nationalities on the plan and budget complained that central planning bodies had not acted on plans submitted by Baltic economists that might help resolve this dilemma.[105]

This problem relates to the question of education. Although the Baltic union republics rank high among all 15 Soviet constituent republics in educational standards, the eponymous nationalities within their own SSR rank relatively low (see Table 4.3 above). This illustrates that many immigrants to the Baltic area have been skilled workers, engineers, or technicians. These people have not only taken many of the better jobs but, through their positions in responsible posts, have exercised a disproportionate say in the future direction of the local economy. The Baltic leadership has thus sought to train workers of the eponymous nationalities to fill jobs requiring a high degree of skill. This is especially important in light of the emphasis on innovative fields in industry and many traditional sectors, which require specially trained workers. The leaders have thus requested that as its highest priority, the educational system be geared to provide for the needs of the economy. Great emphasis is put on vocational training, and students are told that all jobs are equally "romantic," in order to halt the trend toward high labor turnover.[106] Party chief Sniečkus posed the problem in concrete terms before a February 1972 meeting of Lithuania's Central Committee:

> Great attention should be devoted to the training of young people in the professions which are particularly needed by the national [SSR] economy when the training of worker cadres is being planned. . . . The Gosplan, the State Committee for the Utilization of Labor Resources, and the ministries, departments, and economic organizations must insure that the requirements help to eliminate the well-known disproportions which occur.[107]

It remains to be seen how effective the push for increased training of the work force will be. Here again, there appears to be less concern with this matter at the enterprise level. Numerous criticisms have been voiced that the enterprises do not provide necessary incentives for those workers already having jobs to take part-time vocational and correspondence courses.[108] One indication that some progress has been made (or, at least, the line held) is offered by the Estonian case. In 1970, 85,000 (76 percent) of the 114,200 specialists with higher or specialized secondary education working in the economy were ethnic Estonians.[109]

Entrance quotas set for the Riga Polytechnical Institute in 1972 (775 new students in Russian language groups and 700 in Latvian language groups) does not bode well for the Latvian case.[110]

The problem of natural resource reserves is another element in the fulfillment of industrial plans. Baltic economists have been calling with increasing frequency for more rational use of raw materials in order to avoid resource depletion. In 1972, the chief of the Estonian SSR Economic Institute stated that growth will be increasingly limited by water scarcity and pollution. He was particularly concerned with depletion of forested areas, although he seemed to believe at that time that oil shale reserves were not in danger.[111] By 1975, Party Secretary Käbin took the bold step of advocating that oil shale production (Estonia's major industry) be phased out and reserved for future emergencies in order to avoid the depletion of this key resource.[112] Moreover, the Baltic elite do not trust the central authorities to safeguard Baltic resources. This can be seen by a Latvian economist's rejection of the proposal to transfer control over timber resources to a regional authority.[113]

One way to slow down economic growth that does not accord with local interests is to block the introduction of new large-scale plants. Such plants cause a severe strain on already overtaxed manpower and natural resource reserves. In a 1975 statement, Käbin revealed that Estonia had utilized this technique:

> Manpower shortage was the main factor which determined the shifting of the center of gravity to the reconstruction of existing enterprises. At the present time, the growth of labor productivity alone can be the basis for increasing industrial output. Construction of new large-scale enterprises may proceed only on an exceptional basis, if dictated by general state interests.[114]

Members of the Latvian leadership have aired similar arguments. The dispute was sufficiently serious to warrant a denunciation in Pravda by Party First Secretary Voss:

> We cannot overlook the localistic tendencies and national narrowmindedness that can still be encountered in the views and attitudes of some people. Such people . . . think, for example, that it would not be worthwhile to build certain major industrial, power-engineering and other facilities in our republic. Why? Because, so they say, the numbers of the non-Latvian population in the Latvian Republic would increase in this connection, and the republic's nationalities composition would become mixed. The republic's party organization . . . has always resolutely opposed such sentiments and continues to do so.[115]

Several other means have been employed to block such enterprises. The priority of environmental protection is one such method. Still another argument made is that no new enterprises of a large-scale should be constructed without prior guarantees that adequate services, housing, school construction, protection of resources, and similar social planning measures be instituted beforehand.[116]

While many of these measures are important in their own right, the hope may be that the central authorities will decide to locate the planned enterprise at a site presenting fewer obstacles.

There have also been efforts to force the Union-subordinate enterprises located in the republic to be more responsive to local needs. Increases have been sought in the production of consumer goods, especially from enterprises in heavy industry. The Estonian Gosplan chief actually called on enterprises to utilize resources better in order to produce units of goods beyond the number planned to satisfy effective demand:

> Considering the further growth of the population's monetary income, which will probably increase at a higher rate than provided for in the plan, it is necessary that ministries and enterprises seek out possibilities for increasing the production of consumer goods beyond the plan through better utilizing existing raw material resources and productive capacities.[117]

The complaint voiced by the secretary of Latvia's Communist Party, A. Voss, that enterprises subordinate to Union jurisdiction neglected the production of many scheduled consumer items because "the managers simply did not want to be bothered with 'trifles' (for example, radio tubes, ironing boards, spare parts for washing machines, and nails) which are a lot of trouble and of very little use," is another one often voiced in the Baltic press.[118] In addition, Baltic officials have attempted to pressure Union-subordinate enterprises into allocating more funds for health and education services, housing, and the like for their employees and the populace of the town in which they are located. Leadership in all three Baltic SSRs has tried to promote the local Soviets as the primary instrument for applying this type of pressure.

The Baltic elite have also become concerned with remedying the ills of an advanced industrial society. Pollution has thus become a more crucial issue. The Baltic republics have to some degree been brought closer to their European neighbors by this common problem. A conference held in Rostock in 1973 on the problem of Baltic Sea pollution was attended by all the states bordering the Sea (except West Germany).[119] A Lithuanian delegate represented the Soviet Union. Baltic representatives at USSR conferences on pollution have advocated strong measures to ensure that Union-subordinate enterprises concern themselves with environmental protection. At a 1972 Supreme Soviet session, a Latvian delegate stated that the republic's administration was instituting measures to guarantee that enterprises of Union subordination located in Latvia allocated necessary funds for carrying out water protection measures.[120] Similarly, the Estonian delegate argued that natural resources be given an economic valuation so their utilization could be coordinated closely with cost accounting.[121] The Baltic elite have also used this issue to block the construction of new enterprises. A water code adopted by the Estonian SSR Supreme Soviet in July 1972 called for tougher measures against polluters and prohibited the construction of new plants without pollution control devices.[122]

Finally, there has been an attempt to meet the problems connected with urbanization. An Estonian economist discussed the problems of the city's work force, the adequacy of water resources, the burden on transportation networks, the provision of services for the population, the need for adequate housing, and the requirement of sanitary-hygienic conditions and environmental protection. He proposed such measures as the relocation of enterprises in overburdened cities to outlying areas and the development of long-range urban planning.[123] Another Estonian economist has criticized the lack of concern for urban planning on the part of central authorities and Union-subordinate enterprise managers.[124]

CONCLUSION

The Baltic elite involved in economic work have thus not been content with a mere implementation of orders from the central government. They have sought to gain greater administrative autonomy and to deal with the problems that economic progress engenders for the local population. Nationality satisfaction or dissatisfaction depends in large measure on the success or failure of the elite to achieve these goals.

While it appears that Baltic economists have been allowed some leeway in voicing their concerns, this is no guarantee that any significant action will be taken by bodies responsible to the central government to implement the measures proposed. An Estonian economist has complained that well-reasoned proposals submitted by the staff at the Economics Institute of the Estonian SSR Academy of Sciences have gone without reply from Gosplan USSR. He asserted that this has led to increased frustration among the Institute group.[125]

It is also of considerable importance whether or not the demands voiced by economic specialists are supported by top Party and governmental leaders in the three republics. There seems to be some variation among the union three republics in this respect. Estonia's top leadership has become increasingly outspoken about the need to adjust economic priorities of the republic to local resources and requirements and to tackle some problems of an advanced industrial society. Latvia's leadership appears to be divided on these questions. Party leader Voss takes a cautious approach. This may be both the result and the cause of some complaints voiced by the 17 Latvian Communists in 1971. The Lithuanian elite have echoed these concerns to a lesser degree, probably as a result of their perception that Lithuania has yet to establish the advanced material base of the Estonian and Latvian economies. Both Lithuanian leaders and economists, however, appear to have learned from the experience the other two union republics have acquired during industrialization.

Their ability to voice such concerns depends, in part, on the tolerance of Moscow. The "nationalist" disturbances of the 1970s in Latvia and Lithuania may have made the central government authorities more wary of allowing leaders from these republics to voice the concerns of their nationalities aloud. The relatively stable Estonian scene, on the other hand, may encourage Soviet leaders to permit Estonian elites to speak out against the ills of an advanced industrial society. The Twenty-Fifth CPSU Congress of 1976 in its economic pronouncements echoed many Estonian concerns, for example, about limiting growth of large cities; training local, skilled cadres; and siting labor-intensive enterprises in regions with a favorable manpower balance.[126] It remains to be seen what effect this official acknowledgment will have on the satisfaction of these nationality demands.

The setting of nationality priorities by the highest elite must take into account the attitudes at lower levels. A tension appears to have developed between the top SSR elite and middle-level personnel, particularly the industrial managers. Economic specialists and many of the foremost leaders have blamed the failure to implement reforms on the narrow outlook of the middle-level managers. These practical men, whose occupational fate is closely tied to the fulfillment of centrally determined production goals, may, in fact, be less concerned with the broader economic issues affecting the particular nationality. This disinterest would hinder the implementation of measures advocated by the upper-level elite. It is possible that they are used to some extent by the economists and top leadership as scapegoats for the slow implementation of far-reaching proposals in order to dampen popular demand for rapid change.

The Baltic populace cannot often openly voice its concerns about the economic life of their republic. Admonitions of the SSR leadership against a rise in "bourgeois nationalist" attitudes stemming from economic considerations reveal that the general public desires a reorientation in values in the economic sector and is less than content with official measurements of economic success.

The economic sphere is thus becoming a significant source of dissatisfaction in the Baltic region. Though some degree of satisfaction is provided by material rewards provided the Baltic people by economic progress, this is subject to change in the future. First, the ever higher demands for goods and services on the part of Baltic nationalities may prove difficult for the government to satisfy, owing to a lack of resources and the political problems inherent in countenancing a large discrepancy in the standard of living among Soviet nationalities as a whole. Second, the higher the material satisfaction of the Baltic people, the greater the degree of self-assertiveness and the desire for increased responsibility.

Baltic nationalities are in the process of reevaluating the effect of economic progress on nationality supports. Economic progress has destroyed many previous supports and, so, requires new ones. The complex problem of redefinition has already been explicitly recognized by some Baltic spokesmen in these republics:

> The anticommunists place still another false dilemma before the peoples of our country: either continued social and technical progress, and in such an event, loss of national peculiarities and culture, or preservation of national traditions together with renunciation of further progress toward building communism. The unsoundness of such a view of the matter consists in incorrectly equating that which is "national" with that which is "patriarchal," and of national customs with something rudimentary, related only to underdeveloped methods of production with intercourse between people. That which is "national" is not only what has been inherited from epochs past, but also that which has been transformed under new conditions and created by the present.
>
> In the course of socialist development customs and morals connected with antiquated living conditions in the past are dying out. They are replaced by progressive traditions, national as well as international. . . . For the flourishing of truly progressive national traditions, of socialist culture and education, socialism has given all the peoples the greatest possible opportunities.[127]

The aspirations of the Baltic nationalities for more responsibility in deciding their economic fate have produced a potential conflict. Proposals for greater administrative autonomy run counter to a system of total central control. Attempts to manage economic problems within the existing administrative structure are frustrated by the indifference of officials loyal to the hierarchical interests of central bodies.

The regeneration of older nationality supports or shifts among present ones may produce a sense of confusion among people in the short run. It is also frustrated by structural obstacles. This may generate a sense of dissatisfaction in the region despite attainment of material prosperity. Nevertheless, the process reflects a sense of nationality self-awareness, especially important in a sphere of life that so determines the environment in which the nationality acts, and which can give the eponymous groups the necessary vitality to maintain their ethnic individuality in a changing world. It remains to be seen whether this assertion in the economic realm is a prelude to similar endeavors in other areas, perhaps the cultural or political, or even a stimulant to such developments.

NOTES

1. V. S. Vardys, "Modernization and Baltic Nationalism," Problems of Communism 24, no. 5 (September-October 1975): 37; I. S. Koropeckyj, "National Income of the Baltic Republics in 1970," Journal of Baltic Studies 1 (Spring 1976): 61-73.

2. G. Zimanas, "Sila bratsva," Sovetskaia Litva (November 4, 1971), p. 2.

3. N. Khrabrova, "A korabli plyvut" (interview with Valter Klauson), Ogonek, no. 41 (October 1972): p. 6; A. Voss, Lenin's Behests and the Making of Soviet Latvia (Moscow: Progress Publishers, 1970), p. 58; A. Drizul and V. Maamiagi, "V soglasnom i moguchem khore," Kommunist (Vilnius), no. 8 (August 1972), p. 11.

4. Vardys, p. 35.

5. Khrabrova, p. 6; Voss, p. 59; Drizul and Maamiagi, pp. 14-15.

6. I. Keben (Käbin), "Uspekhi promyshlennosti respubliki," Kommunist Estonii, no. 7 (July 1975), p. 27; A. Voss, "Okrylennye druzhboi velikoi," Ogonek, no. 24 (June 1972), p. 5; Drizul and Maamiagi, p. 11.

7. V. S. Vardys, "The Baltic Peoples," Problems of Communism 16, no. 5 (September-October 1967): 56.

8. Khrabrova, p. 7; A. Sniečkus, Soviet Lithuania on the Road of Prosperity (Moscow: Progress Publishers, 1974), p. 58.

9. I. Kebin (Käbin), "Organizator i politicheskii rukovoditel' sovetskogo soiuznogo gosudarstva," Kommunist Estonii, no. 11 (November 1972), p. 10; Voss, Lenin's Behests and the Making of Soviet Latvia, p. 49; Iu. Maniushis, "Stanovlenie industrii Sovetskoi Litvy," Kommunist (Vilnius), no. 7 (July 1972), p. 3.

10. Khrabrova, p. 7; Voss, Lenin's Behests and the Making of Soviet Latvia, p. 50; Sniečkus, p. 59.

11. I. Kebin (Käbin), "V edinoi sem'e sovetskikh narodov," Kommunist Estonii, no. 7 (July 1975), pp. 15-16; A. Drobnis, "Sila sotsialisticheskoi planovoi ėkonomiki," Kommunist (Vilnius), no. 2 (February 1971), p. 15.

12. Vardys, "Modernization and Baltic Nationalism," op. cit., p. 37.

13. I. Kebin (Käbin), "Plechom k plechu," Krasnaia Zvezda, August 12, 1972, p. 1; Voss, "Okrylennye druzhboi velikoi," p. 5.

14. Maniushis, p. 4.

15. Kebin (Käbin), "Plechom k plechu," p. 1.

16. Kebin (Käbin), "V edinoi sem'e sovetskikh narodov," p. 16; Voss, "Okrylennye druzhboi velikoi," p. 5; Maniushis, "Stanovlenie industrii Litvy," p. 2.

17. Kebin (Käbin), "Uspekhi promyshlennosti respubliki," p. 27; Voss, Lenin's Behests and the Making of Soviet Latvia, p. 74; Drobnis, "Sila sotsialisticheskoi planovoi ėkonomiki," p. 20.

18. Kebin (Käbin), "V edinoi sem'e sovetskikh narodov," p. 18; Voss, Lenin's Behests and the Making of Soviet Latvia, p. 76; Maniushis, pp. 5-6.

19. Kebin (Käbin), "V edinoi sem'e sovetskikh narodov," p. 18; Voss, Lenin's Behests and the Making of Soviet Latvia, pp. 77; Drobnis, "Sila sotsialisticheskoi planovoi ėkonomiki," p. 18.

20. Kebin (Käbin), "V edinoi sem'e sovetskikh narodov," p. 18; Voss, Lenin's Behests and the Making of Soviet Latvia, p. 74; Sniečkus, Soviet Lithuania . . . , p. 92.

21. V. Paul'man, "Rost material'nogo blagosostoianie trudiashchikhsia-ob'ektivnaia zakonomernost' sotsializma," Kommunist Estonii, no. 11 (November 1972), pp. 63-64; Voss, "Okrylennye druzhboi velikoi," p. 5; Sniečkus, Soviet Lithuania . . . , p. 67.

22. Kebin (Käbin), "V edinoi sem'e sovetskikh narodov," pp. 19-20; Voss, Lenin's Behests and the Making of Soviet Latvia, pp. 81-82; Maniushis, p. 6.

23. Kebin (Käbin), "Organizator i politicheskii rukovoditel' sovetskogo soiuznogo gosudarstva," p. 15.

24. V. Klauson, "Tridstat' sovetskikh let," Kommunist Estoniia, no. 6 (June 1970), p. 6; A. Drobnis, "Ėkonomika Sovetskoi Litvy," Planovoe khoziaistvo, no. 9 (September 1972), p. 27.

25. Kebin (Käbin), "Plechom k plechu," p. 1; M. Raman, "Reshaiushchii god," Kommunist Sovetskoi Latvii, no. 2 (February 1973), p. 21; Sniečkus, p. 70.

26. Kebin (Käbin), "V edinoi sem'e sovetskikh narodov," p. 19; Voss, Lenin's Behests and the Making of Soviet Latvia, p. 81; Sniečkus, p. 82.

27. K. Vaino, "Uspeshno zavershit' reshaiushchii god piatiletki," *Kommunist Estonii*, no. 10 (October 1973), pp. 3-10; Sniečkus, "Grazhdanin velikogo sovetskogo soiuza," *Pravda*, September 8, 1972, pp. 2-3.

28. Voss, *Lenin's Behests and the Making of Soviet Latvia*, p. 76; Drobnis, "Ėkonomika Sovetskoi Litvy," p. 27.

29. Kebin (Käbin), "Plechom k plechu," p. 1; Voss, *Lenin's Behests and the Making of Soviet Latvia*, p. 75; Sniečkus, *Soviet Lithuania on the Road of Prosperity*, p. 66.

30. Khrabrova, p. 9; Iu. Ruben, "Toward the Highest Productivity," *Sotsialisticheskaia industriia*, October 6, 1970, p. 2, English trans. in Joint Publications Research Service, no. 51754, *Translations on USSR Economic Affairs*, no. 179 (November 10, 1970), p. 40.

31. V. Shteinberg, "Pod maskoi uchenosti," *Izvestiia*, April 6, 1974, p. 5; A. Drobnis, "Vziaty pervye rubezhi," *Sovetskaia Litva* (November 5, 1971), p. 2.

32. Khrabrova, p. 8.

33. Voss, "Okrylennye druzhboi velikoi," p. 6.

34. Elmar Järvesoo, "From an Agrarian to an Industrial State—Economic Change in Soviet Estonia," in *A Case Study of a Soviet Republic: The Estonian SSR*, ed. Tõnu Parming and Elmar Järvesoo (Boulder, Colo.: Westview Press, forthcoming).

35. Ibid. For a contrary view, see Koropeckyj, "National Income . . . ," p. 72.

36. K. Sondor, "Natsional'nyi vopros i antikommunizm," *Kommunist Sovetskoi Latvii*, no. 11 (November 1972), p. 75.

37. "Letter of Seventeen Latvian Communists," *Congressional Record*, 92d Cong., February 15-22, 1972, 118, pt. 4: 4821-22.

38. Ibid.

39. Khrabrova, p. 8; Voss, "Okrylennye druzhboi velikoi," pp. 5-6.

40. Voss, "Okrylennye druzhboi velikoi," p. 6.

41. Käbin, "Organizator i politicheskii rukovoditel' sovetskogo soiuznogo gosudarstva," pp. 13-14.

42. Sondor, "Natsional'nyi vopros i antikommunizm," pp. 77-78.

43. Voss, "Okrylennye druzhboi velikoi," p. 6.

44. Kebin (Käbin), "Organizator i politicheski rukovoditel' sovetskogo soiuznogo gosudarstva," pp. 12-13.

45. V. Lazutka, "Ideologicheskaia bor'ba i natsionalisticheskaia ėmigratsiia," *Kommunist* (Vilnius), no. 9 (September 1972), pp. 81-86.

46. Kebin (Käbin), "Uspekhi promyshlennosti respubliki," p. 29.

47. Kebin (Käbin), "V edinoi sem'e sovetskikh narodov," pp. 23-24.

48. Ibid., p. 24.

49. P. Gel'bak, "Po zakonam druzhby," Kommunist (Vilnius), no. 9 (September 1972), p. 32.

50. Ruben, "Toward the Highest Productivity," pp. 40-44.

51. Lazutka, "Ideologicheskaia bor'ba i natsionalisticheskaia ėmigratsiia," p. 86.

52. A. Smirnov, "Leninskaia druzhba narodov," Sovetskaia Litva (April 17, 1974), pp. 2, 3.

53. V. Rianzhin, "Lichnost'i obshestvo," Sovetskaia Estoniia (August 12, 1975), p. 2; Iu. Boriaev. "Potrebnosti i potreblenie pri sotsializme," Sovetskaia Latviia, January 30, 1975, p. 2.

54. A. Sniečkus, "Vechno zhivaia sila," Zhurnalist, no. 12 (December 1972), p. 12, in Joint Publications Research Service, no. 58066, Translations on USSR Political and Sociological Affairs, no. 323 (January 26, 1973), p. 36.

55. "Vyshe uroven' ideino-politicheskoi raboty!" Sovetskaia Estoniia (March 20, 1973), p. 2.

56. A. Sniečkus, "Usilit' ideino-politicheskuiu rabotu–internatsional'noe vospitanie," Sovetskaia Litva (March 15, 1973), p. 2.

57. L. Lentsman, "Otchet ėstonskogo respublikanskogo soveta profsoiuzov," Sovetskaia Estoniia (January 28, 1972), p. 2; V. Blium, "Shkoly kommunizma, khoziaistvovaniia, upravleniia," Sovetskaia Latviia (January 28, 1972), p. 2; Iu. Maniushis, "Bol'shoe i otvetstvennye zadachi sovetov," Sovetskaia Litva (February 16, 1972), p. 3.

58. Paul Gregory and Robert Stuart, Soviet Economic Structure and Performance (New York: Harper and Row, 1974), p. 122.

59. Eugene Zaleski, Planning Reforms in the Soviet Union 1962–1966, trans Marie-Christine MacAndrew and G. Warren Nutter (Chapel Hill: University of North Carolina Press, 1967), p. 46.

60. Alec Nove, The Soviet Economy, 2d rev. ed. (New York: Praeger, 1968), p. 85.

61. Ibid., p. 86.

62. Ekonomicheskaia Gazeta, January 5, 1962, p. 12, cited in Nove, p. 81.

63. V. Klauson, "Ministr respubliki," Izvestiia, August 25, 1964, p. 5, also cited in Nove, p. 87.

64. Vardys, "Modernization and Baltic Nationalism," p. 45.

65. Zaleski, p. 46.

66. Gregory and Stuart, p. 119.

67. Kebin (Käbin), "Uspekhi promyshlennosti respubliki," p. 29.

68. Järvesoo, "From an Agrarian to an Industrial State–Economic Change in Soviet Estonia," p. 267.

69. "Letter of Seventeen Latvian Communists," p. 4823.

70. V. Kistanov, "Leninskaia natsional'naia politika i ėkonomicheskoe raionirovanie v SSSR," Voprosy ėkonomiki, no. 12 (December 1972), pp. 62-63.

71. Ibid., p. 63.

72. "Osnovnye napravleniia razvitiia narodnogo khoziaistva SSSR na 1976-1980 goda," Pravda, March 7, 1976, p. 7.

73. Kistanov, pp. 61-63.

74. Ibid., p. 65.

75. A. Lebedinskas, "Edinyi mnogonatsional'nyi narodnokhoziaistvennyi kompleks," Kommunist (Vilnius), no. 12 (December 1972), p. 9.

76. Ibid., p. 10.

77. Ibid., pp. 11-12.

78. Ibid., p. 13.

79. K. Kayris, "A dynamic Process," Sotsialisticheskaia industriia, August 23, 1972, p. 2, English trans. in Joint Publications Research Service, no. 57346, Translations on USSR Economic Affairs, no. 411 (October 26, 1972), p. 19.

80. A. Sniečkus, "Rech'," (Speech at Twenty-Fourth Congress of the CPSU), Pravda, April 3, 1971, p. 5.

81. Iu. Proshkovich, "Joint Efforts," Sotsialisticheskaia industriia, February 12, 1972, p. 2, English trans. in Joint Publications Research Service, no. 52574, Translations on USSR Economic Affairs, no. 219 (March 10, 1971), p. 86.

82. Kayris, p. 20; I. Morev, "Problemy mezhotraslevoi spetsializatsii," Kommunist Sovetskoi Latvii, no. 6 (June 1973), p. 22.

83. I. Chernikov and E. Stanikas, "The Fate of Small Enterprises," Sotsialisticheskaia industriia, October 6, 1971, p. 2, English trans. in Joint Publications Research Service, no. 54573, Translations on USSR Economic Affairs, no. 307 (November 29, 1971), p. 25.

84. R. Butel', "Kurs—ob"edineniia," Sovetskaia Estoniia (August 31, 1973), pp. 1-2; I. Akulich, "Proizvodstvennye ob"edineniia: razvitie i problemy," Kommunist Sovetskoi Latvii, no. 2 (February 1973), p. 33.

85. Kayris, p. 19.

86. A. Vendelin, "Navehnye metody v rukovodstve ekonomikoi sovetskoi Estonii," Ekonomika i matematicheskie metody, no. 6 (1972), pp. 824-26, English trans. in Joint Publications Research Service, no. 58054, Translations on USSR Economic Affairs, no. 444 (January 23, 1973), p. 58.

87. I. Kiuttis, "Ėkonomicheskaia ėffektivnost' proizvodstva v vysshikh even'iakh narodnogo khoziaistva," Kommunist Estonii, no. 3 (March 1973), p. 69.

88. Baltic Events, no. 39 (August 1973), p. 5.

89. Kebin (Käbin), "Uspekhi promyshlennosti respubliki," p. 28.

90. Ibid., p. 32.

91. "O vozrastnoi strukture, urovne obrazovaniia, natsional'nom sostave, iazykakh i istochnikakh sredstv sushchectvovaniia naseleniia Ėstonskoi SSR po dannym vsesoiuznoi perepisi naseleniia na 15 Ianvaria 1970 goda," Sovetskaia Estoniia (May 18, 1971), p. 2.

92. Vardys, "Modernization and Baltic Nationalism," p. 39.

93. P. Adlis, "Zerkalo obshchestva," Kommunist (Vilnius), no. 6 (June 1971), pp. 55-59.

94. Drobnis, "Ėkonomika Sovetskoi Litvy," p. 30.

95. Raman, "Reshaiushchii god," pp. 21-22.

96. Kebin (Käbin), "Uspekhi promyshlennosti respubliki," p. 28.

97. "Postanovlenie XXIV s"ezda kommunisticheskoi partii sovetskogo soiuza po proektu TsK KPSS 'Direktivy XXIV s"ezda KPSS po piatiletnemu planu razvitiia narodnogo khoziaistva SSSR na 1971-1976 goda," Pravda, April 11, 1971, p. 2.

98. B. Mezgailis and P. Zvidrins, Padomju Latvijas Iedzivotaji (Riga, 1973), p. 376, quoted in Baltic Events, no. 41 (December 1973), p. 4.

99. E. Abolins (title not given), Cina, June 13, 1974, quoted in Baltic Events, no. 44 (June 1974), p. 8.

100. Juris Dreifelds, "Latvian National Demands and Group Consciousness in the Post-Berklay and Post-Khrushchev Periods" (Paper presented at the Symposium on Nationalism in the USSR and Eastern Europe under Brezhnev and Kosygin, University of Detroit, October 4, 1975), p. 17.

101. Vera Sulce, "Darbs—Bagatibas Avuts," Zvaigznc (Riga), no. 5 (March 1971), p. 25, cited in Dreifelds, p. 16.

102. Cina, December 5, 1972, cited in Baltic Events, no. 37 (April 1973), p. 3.

103. Mary Ann Grossman, "Soviet Efforts at the Socio-economic Integration of Latvians," in The Soviet West, ed. Ralph Clem (New York: Praeger, 1975), p. 76.

104. Juris Dreifelds, "Characteristics and Threads of Two Demographic Variables in the Latvian SSR," Bulletin of Baltic Studies, no. 8 (Winter 1971), p. 11.

105. "Preniia po dokladam o gosudarstvennom plane razvitiia narodnogo khoziaistva SSSR na 1971 god, o gosudarstvennom biudzhete SSSR na 1971 god i ob ispolnenii gosudarstvennogo biudzheta za 1969," (speech by A. Keerna in USSR Supreme Soviet Council of Nationalities, December 11, 1970), Izvestiia, December 12, 1970, p. 4.

106. A. Sniečkus, "Sluzhenie narodu, delu kommunizma—pochetnyi dolg Komsomola," Sovetskaia Litva, (March 19, 1972), pp. 1-2.

107. "Rabochemu klassu–dostoinoe popolnenie," Sovetskaia Litva (February 4, 1972), p. 2.

108. A. Barkauskas, "Grani bol'shoi problemy," Pravda, April 18, 1972, p. 3.

109. Noukogude Opetaja, July 22, 1972, cited in Baltic Events, no. 37 (April 1973), p. 8.

110. Padomju Jaunatne, April 26, 1972, cited in Estonian Events, no. 33 (August 1972), p. 3.

111. Rahva Haal (Tallinn), December 1, 1972, cited in Baltic Events, no. 36 (February 1973), p. 1.

112. Kebin (Käbin), "Uspekhi promyshlennosti respubliki," p. 30.

113. I. Penikis, "Ob organizatsii leshogo khoziaistva v Latvii," Ekonomika i organizatsiia promyslennogo proizvodstva, no. 3 (July 1973), pp. 178-82, trans. in Joint Publications Research Service, no. 59861, Translations on USSR Resources, no. 407 (August 21, 1973), p. 14.

114. Kebin (Käbin), "Uspekhi promyshlennosti respubliki," p. 28.

115. A. Voss, "V edinom stroiu," Pravda, March 20, 1971, p. 2.

116. A. Drobnis, "Vertikal' i gorizontal': nauka upravliat'," Pravda, July 14, 1975, p. 2.

117. Kh. Allik, "O gosudarstvennom plane razvitiia narodnogo khoziaistva Ėstonskoi SSR na 1971 god," Sovetskaia Estoniia (December 23, 1970), p. 2.

118. A. Voss, "Stil' nashego vremeni," Izvestiia, February 12, 1971, p. 3.

119. Iu. Sabaliauskas and I. Liantsbergas, "Baltiiskoe more i eeokhrana," Gidrotekhnika i melioratisiia, no. 8 (1973), pp. 84-89, trans. in Joint Publications Research Service, no. 60260, Translations on USSR Resources, no. 425 (October 11, 1973), pp. 3-8.

120. "Premiia po dokladu 'O merakh po dal'neishemu uluchsheniiu okhrany prirody i ratsional'nomu ispol'zovaniiu prirodnykh resursov'," Izvestiia, September 22, 1972, p. 2.

121. Ibid., p. 3.

122. Rahva Haal, July 7, 1972, cited in Estonian Events, no. 33 (September 1972), p. 8.

123. Kh. Paalberg, "Urbanizatsiia v estonskoi SSR i puti ee regulirovaniia," Izvestiia Akademii Nauk estonskoi SSR, vol. 23, Obshchestvennye nauki, no. 3 (1974): 237-48, trans. in Joint Publications Research Service, no. 62842, Translations on USSR Resources, no. 530 (August 28, 1974), pp. 21-34.

124. Kh. Tonsiver, "Planirovanie sotsial'nogo razvitiia goroda," Kommunist Estoniia, no. 10 (October 1972), pp. 70-76.

125. R. Otsoson, "Pravo na ėksperiment," Literaturnaia gazeta (January 12, 1972), p. 10.

126. "Osnovnye napravleniia razvitiia narodnogo khoziaistva SSR na 1976-1980 goda," p. 7.

127. Sondor, "Natsional'nyi vopros i antikommunizm," p. 78.

CHAPTER

5

POLITICAL LEADERS

Judith Fleming

The quality of the political leadership of various groups composing a multi-ethnic state like the Soviet Union can have an important effect on the way in which each nationality attempts to retain a sense of distinctness. There is increasing pressure from the central authorities to fuse Soviet nationalities and Russians to form a single Soviet people. Nevertheless, if a nationality's political elite can and will act to help maintain the group's sense of identity, the political elite can offer very important support for the traditional values, which have served to make the nationality coherent.

Examination of the function performed by a nationality's political leadership in ethnic-group maintenance reveals that the regulatory (catalyzing or pacifying) category of support factors sometimes overlaps with the relativity category.* A nationality's political leadership can serve as a regulatory factor by influencing governmental and party policies. Leadership will also function as a nationality support by working as a relativity factor to equalize status or protect nationality identity. A nationality's political leadership provides a regulatory support function when it has a chance to work for governmental and party policies favorable to the survival of nationality identity. This leadership operates as one relativity support factor when it implements these policies in a way that helps eliminate inequality between the various nationalities. These leaders can attempt to put governmental and party policies into practice in a way most favorable to

---

*Regulatory factors include official policies, public opinion, group vitality, and the like; relativity factors concern mainly the relations or different status among ethnic groups in one country.

the integrity of the group they "represent." This is probably the situation that exists in most countries. However, at other times, this leadership can act to undermine nationality interest.

In the Soviet Baltic republics, the leadership frequently finds itself under pressure from central authorities to enact policies intended to weaken nationality identity. If highly placed men are more interested in advancing their own careers or possibly in retaining important positions rather than in defending nationality culture, such leaders may not provide support for the group's identity. In the Baltic republics, where several nationalities and the Russians are involved, some of the ethnic Baltic leaders appear to have been coopted to act as agents for the ruling Russians. These men perhaps support Russian culture and traditions more than the nationality identity of indigenous groups. Thus, they may possibly encourage at least a partial Russification of the Baltic nationalities themselves.

Several important questions therefore emerge concerning the Soviet Baltic political leadership today. To what extent does this leadership function as a support for its own nationality's identity? To what degree, if any, does it undermine the nationality identity of the different Baltic people? How far does the leadership go in pressing for or against nationality interests of the noneponymous population of the Baltic republics? The amount and quality of influence exerted by the Baltic leaders relative to that of the Slavic chiefs in the republics' Party and government organizations also raises an important question at present.

In the three Baltic Soviet socialist republics of Estonia, Latvia, and Lithuania, the political leadership includes a significant number of persons who are Russians or members of non-Baltic nationalities (all the Soviet nationalities, with the exception of the Estonians, Latvians, and Lithuanians). Moreover, many Baltic leaders are individuals who have spent much of their lives outside their own territory. For these reasons, the present leaders of these republics may not meet the expectations for leadership that have been expressed, for example, in Baltic literature. There, the image of leaders who are not only indigenous to this area but who have also struggled selflessly and tirelessly for the freedom and independence of these nations appears repeatedly.[1]

Several considerations, including the fact that the present Baltic political elites fail to live up to the historical expectations of the Baltic people, suggest that this leadership supplies a major cause for dissatisfaction at present among the Baltic nationalities. It is the hypothesis of this chapter that the long, gradual rise of Estonians, Latvians, and Lithuanians as distinct nationalities and their recent experience (1918-40) as independent nations has led the relatively sophisticated Baltic nationalities, like nearly all nationally conscious groups today, to expect to receive support from leaders who are members of their own group. In spite of these expectations, it appears that in the three areas, key positions of power in the decisive Party organizations, as well as in the governments, are held by men who do not necessarily meet the requirements of the indigenous nationality. Wherever there is a leader who wishes to speak primarily for the interests of the Baltic people, he evidently falls under the scrutiny, and even dominance, of someone less representative of these people. This persistent deprivation of representative leadership, to which the Baltic people feel entitled, increasingly becomes a cause for dissatisfaction.

That feeling of leaderlessness connects strongly with the memory of the independence period, which remains vivid in the minds of the Baltic people. They are quite aware that they were then able to govern themselves and to maintain a relatively high standard of living without foreign supervision. Lithuanians, unlike Estonians and Latvians, can also look to the period of the thirteenth century to the sixteenth century, when Lithuania constituted one of the great empires of Europe.[2]

The socioeconomic level of these union republics may enter into the disapproving attitude that the Baltic people have taken toward the fact that Russians and members of non-Baltic nationalities occupy important political positions in the region. Each of the three Baltic union republics enjoys a higher living standard than either the Russian SFSR or the USSR as a whole. This material standing has apparently contributed to a feeling of superiority on the part of the Baltic people when they compare themselves either to other Soviet nationalities or to Russians. Both Latvia and Estonia started with well-developed industrial bases at the time of their annexation by the Soviet Union. These industries were being operated efficiently under Baltic control. This fact does not support retrospective claims that the economic development of Latvia and Estonia has been dependent on the assistance of other Soviet ethnic groups, especially Russians. This feeling of Baltic superiority, combined with the knowledge that Baltic nationalities have successfully governed themselves in the recent past, can enhance the belief among these groups that they are best qualified to make the important decisions that will affect the further development of the three union republics and the future of their inhabitants.

Modernization may contribute an important element helping to acquaint the Baltic people more closely with their political elite. Under Soviet rule modernization and industrialization have continued to advance in these union republics. By 1970, the population of each Baltic republic had become over 50 percent urban, and in Estonia and Latvia, over half of each eponymous nationality itself was urban.[3] Often, increasing urbanization and modernization is accompanied by a greater political awareness. With more access to press, radio, and television, not only people in the cities but also a larger proportion of the rural population are exposed to top officials of the republic. While the population as a whole may still identify more closely with municipal or raion (county) government and Party officials, as the mass communication network penetrates the society, the population can hardly escape a growing awareness of who controls higher political power in their union republic and how the SSR is governed. With modernization also comes an increase in the educational level of the population. A more highly educated population has greater potential for political awareness. This increased awareness seems likely to include a deeper understanding of the peculiarly close relationship between the Communist Party and the governmental structure of the republic.

Certain Western political writers have argued that with modernization comes a loss of ethnic identity;[4] however, this appears to be the case neither in the Baltic SSRs nor in the Soviet Union as a whole. Baltic nationalities remain strongly aware of their nationality identity. One evidence of the reluctance of the Baltic people to give up their nationality identity can be seen in the retention of their native languages. In 1970, a considerable number of these people claimed to know Russian fluently (Lithuanians 35.9 percent, Latvians 45.2 percent, Estonians 29 percent). Nearly all of them (Lithuanians 97.9 percent, Latvians 95.2 percent, Estonians 95.5 percent) continued simultaneously to consider the language of their nationality their native language.[5]

As the Baltic nationalities, or any ethnic groups, experience the effects of modernization, they see traditional values and ideas or objects that have always been closely associated with each group destroyed or drastically altered. In the case of the Baltic nationalities, this process has been complicated by incorporation into the Soviet Union, with its peculiar style of ideologically colored modernization. When rural societies are transformed into urban societies, the strong family ties, which predominate in agrarian societies, are broken down. Traditional ties to a given locality, as well as local identification and loyalty, are weakened. In the Soviet Union the official policies of the Communist Party of the Soviet Union and the Soviet government have made it more difficult for the numerous nationalities to retain their accepted values and hold to the security and identification that accompanies them in the face of pressure for creating a new Soviet society.

When this happens, the Baltic people, like others, can react in several ways. They can fail to adjust to these changes, thereby giving up their sense of nationality, they can find new means by which to maintain their distinctness, or modify the old means to make them serve traditional functions under new circumstances. Such changes usually produce a sense of insecurity within the nationality. The very fact that a group is forced to undergo such changes often leads to concern over whether the nationality will continue to exist in the future. This sense of insecurity can create fear that the group's identity will be subordinated to the official Soviet ideology to such an extent that it will be fused, as Soviet policy predicts, with the other Soviet nationalities and the Russians to form one new Soviet narod (people).

An important role in a group's retention of nationality identity is often played by members of its elite who hold decision-making positions within the government, and, in the USSR, within the Party, the real political force. Nationalist movements existed in both Latvia and Estonia before the Russian Revolution of 1917. Although these movements were small in size, they were significant in creating the independent nations of Estonia and Latvia. In that case, the political elite supported nationality feelings and aspirations.[6] Through such movements as this or, in the later Soviet case, via such actions as establishing the uncommon 11-year school in the Baltic republics, the political leadership can itself act to help sustain nationality identity.

If political leadership is to become an instrument for maintaining nationality identity, the leaders themselves must usually be aware of this sense of group consciousness. In the Baltic union republics, the political leaders on the local level seem more likely to be uniformly members of the eponymous nationality than the political leadership at the highest union republic reaches. This lower-echelon elite is also customarily in closer touch with its constituency than are the SSR's supreme leaders. Because the local chiefs are assigned the task of carrying out decisions made on the union republic level, they are responsible to their superiors for success or failure in implementing these policies.

Normally, men who have aspired to high leadership wish to retain their posts. In order to do this they have to be able to carry out the policies of the central authorities. Some of these policies, affecting the economy, culture, administration, and so on, run counter to many of the traditional values held by the nationalities. However, these leaders cannot afford to ignore the wishes of the members of an alert, educated nationality completely. The leaders of primary Party organizations and local government are confronted with the same problem. Primary Party organizations form the basic units of the party structure. They are formed wherever at least three Party members are similarly employed.[7]

COMPOSITION OF THE LEADERSHIP

The ethnic composition of Party and governmental leadership can be an important factor in determining how the general population of these republics relates to the leadership. Because of what they can perceive as a common background or shared experiences, the population is likely to identify more closely with leaders who are members of their own group than with outsiders. The population can feel that these leaders are more likely to support policies that are in the best interest of the ethnic group. Because the general public believes that members of their own group better understand their needs and are more representative of their interest than others, there is likely to be a preference for leaders from among their own group. For these reasons, patterns in ethnic composition of both the Party and governmental positions in the three Baltic union republics can be very important.

In January 1970, there were 36,729 Estonian members in the Communist Party of Estonia (CPE). (See Table 5.1.) This figure was equivalent to 52.3 percent of the total membership of the party in Estonia. Of the remaining members, 25,895 (36.9 percent) were Russian, whereas 7,571 (10.8 percent) were non-Baltic nationalities.[8] These figures show a significant underrepresentation of Estonians in the CPE, because in 1970, they made up 68.2 percent of Estonia's population. (See Table 5.2.) Russians then comprised only 24.7 percent of the SSR's population.[9] According to these figures, 7.73 percent of the Russians in Estonia were Party members, whereas only 3.97 percent of ethnic Estonians belonged to the party (see also, Table 2.7).[10]

TABLE 5.1

Membership in the Communist Party of Estonia, 1970

Membership	Number	Percent
Estonians	36,729	52.3
Russians	25,895	36.9
Others	7,571	10.8
Total	70,195	100

Source: A. Pankseev, in Nekotorye voprosy organizatsionno-partiinoi raboty (Tallinn: Eesti Raamet, 1971), p. 74, cited in Baltic Events 37, no. 2 (April 1973): 8.

TABLE 5.2

Communist Party Membership (estimated 1973) and Population in the Estonian SSR, 1970

	Number	Percent
Membership		
Estonians	46,424	59.0
Russians and others	31,006	41.0
Total	77,430	100.0
Population		
Estonians	925,000	68.2
Russians	335,000	24.7
Others	96,000	7.1
Total	1,356,000	100.0

Sources: "KPSS v tsifrakh (k 70-letiiu IIs" ezda RSDRP)," Partiinaia zhizn' 25, no. 50 (July 14, 1973): 11, 18; Itogi vsesoiuznoi perepisi naseleniia 1970 goda. Natsional'nyi sostav naseleniia SSSR (Moscow: Statistika, 1973), 4:15.

By 1973, although Russians continued to be overrepresented in the CPE, the number of Estonian Party members had notably increased. At least this is true if all Estonian members of the CPSU are assumed to be members of the CPE. At this time, there were 46,424 Estonian members altogether in the CPSU. This figure still represented only .3 of 1 percent of the CPSU's total membership, a figure registering the lowest percentage of any eponymous SSR nationality, but which was shared with the Soviet Kirgiz and Turkmens.[11] This overrepresentation of Russians may give rise to dissatisfaction among the Estonians with the CPE, which seems to be a disproportionally Russian institution.

Almost 21 percent, a significant number, of the Central Committee of the CPE elected in January 1976 consists of Russians or members of non-Baltic nationalities.[12] (See Table 5.3.) The membership of this present Central Committee seems comparable, ethnically, to the Central Committee elected in 1971, which was 80 percent Estonian. However, the 1971 Central Committee showed a 10 percent increase in the Estonian membership over the 1960 figures.[13] In 1976, only 15.3 percent of the alternate members on the central committee were not from one of the Baltic nationalities. The auditing commission elected at the same time was 16.6 percent non-Baltic. A larger proportion, 26 percent, of the delegates from the region elected to the

TABLE 5.3

Central Committee, Communist Party of Estonia, Ethnic Composition, 1966, 1971, and 1976 (in percent)

Membership	1966	1971	1976
Baltic (Estonian, Latvian, Lithuanian)	75	79	79
Non-Baltic	25	21	21

Sources: "Sostav TsK kompartii Estonii izbrannogo na XV s"ezde kp Estonii," Sovetskaia Estoniia (March 4, 1966), p. 1; "Sostav TsK kompartii Estonii izbrannogo na XVI s"ezde kp Estonii," Sovetskaia Estoniia (February 20, 1971), p. 1; "Sostav TsK kompartii Estonii, izbrannogo na XVII s"ezde kompartii Estonii," Sovetskaia Estoniia (January 31, 1976), p. 1.

Twenty-fifth CPSU Congress (1976) were members of non-Baltic nationalities.[14]

The CPE's Bureau of the Central Committee, elected in January 1976, consists of 11 members, 5 of whom also serve as party secretaries.[15] Of these 11, 2 are Russians. Both these Russians serve as secretaries and 1, Konstantin Lebedev, is the party's second secretary. This is a very important office, whose significance must not be overlooked. Another member of the present Bureau is Leonid Lentsmen, whose ethnic identity cannot be definitely determined from the published sources. He was born in the RSFSR. He majored in Finno-Ugric languages at Leningrad University and served in the Estonian Rifle Corps during World War II.[16] From his background it can be assumed that if he is not of Estonian ancestry, he is at least fluent in Estonian and acquainted with Estonian culture.

The ethnic composition of leadership on the raion (district level) and gorod (municipal) levels of CP organization can also be important. The raion might be compared to a small rural county or an urban ward. The raikom is the raion's Party committee. The Party committee of a gorod is referred to as a gorkom.[17] In 1971, there were 15 raions in Estonia, two of which had non-Baltic secretaries. In Pärnu the first secretary was a Russian, while Tartu had a non-Baltic second secretary. Of six cities in Estonia directly subordinate to the republic level of the Party rather than raion jurisdiction, five had non-Baltic secretaries. Four of these men held the post of second secretary. One was the first secretary of Sillamäe.[18] In 1975-76, out of a total of 22 gorkoms and raikoms for which secretaries' names could be found in this research, there were two first secretaries, four second secretaries, and three secretaries of non-Baltic origin.[19]

Personnel manning the Estonian governmental structure may be contrasted with that of the CPE. The republic Supreme Soviets are unicameral legislative bodies that serve a largely ceremonial function by concurring in the acts and policies of the republic's government.[20] Unlike the situation in the CPE, in the Supreme Soviet of Estonia, which was elected in June 1975, Russians and other persons of non-Baltic background seem to be underrepresented. Though participation has but symbolic meaning at this time, only 16 percent of the membership of the Supreme Soviet was of non-Baltic origin.[21] This figure again must be contrasted with the 24.7 percent of the republic's population that is Russian.[22]

Evidence that the SSR Supreme Soviets have little influence can be seen in the discovery that none of the non-Baltic members of the Estonian Supreme Soviet seemed to hold particularly important positions in the republic's government or in the Communist Party organization. The most significant political positions held by non-Baltic members of the Supreme Soviet of Estonia were the following: head of administrative agencies, chief of the department of organizational party work, deputy chairman, executive committee of the Tallinn city Soviet, second secretary of the CPE, and second secretary of the Tallinn gorkom of the CPE.[23]

The republic Council of Ministers acts as the executive body of the republic. Its chairman can be defined as the republic's premier or prime minister.[24] In Estonia in 1971, 90 percent of the ministers and their deputies were ethnic Estonians.[25] (See also Table B.3.) Ministers or deputy ministers who were not members of one of the Baltic nationalities did not occupy very important positions in the union republic's council of ministers. On the local governmental level in 1966-67, the makeup of city, town, and rural district Soviets was 89 percent Estonian, 8.7 percent Russian, and the remaining 2.3 percent consisted of other nationalities within the republic.[26]

If it is true that most people favor leaders who are members of their own ethnic group, Latvians have more reasons for dissatisfaction than do Estonians. In Latvia, on January 1, 1973, there were 61,755 Latvian members of the CPSU. (See Table 5.4.) This figure represented .4 of 1 percent of the CPSU total.[27] If the USSR average is considered to be 100 percent, the Party membership rate for Latvia is 72 percent. This figure can be compared with 60 percent for Lithuania and 72 percent for Estonia. It contrasts with 127 percent for Georgians, 117 percent for Russians, and 105 percent for Armenians,[28] the three groups that are overrepresented, on the basis of population, in the CPSU. The total membership of the Communist

Party of Latvia (CPLa) in 1973 was 134,000.[29] Without specific figures by nationality for the Latvian party, it may be assumed that the large majority of Latvians in the CPSU belong to the CPLa. If this is true, 72,245 members of the Latvian party are not Latvian, compared to 61,755 Latvians, and this figure assumes that all the Latvian members of the CPSU are to be found in Latvia.

Thirty-one percent of the Central Committee of the CPLa elected in June 1976 is composed of non-Baltic members. (See Table 5.5.) Non-Baltic politicians also comprised 30 percent of the alternate members in the Central Committee and 30 percent of the auditing commission. Of the delegates elected from Latvia to attend the Twenty-fifth Congress of the CPSU, February-March 1976, non-Baltic individuals composed slightly over half of the total (26 out of 51). Two of the five secretaries of the CPLa's Central Committee are of non-Baltic nationality. One of these two, N. A. Belukha, a Ukrainian, holds the important post of second secretary. The Bureau of the Central Committee consists of 11 full members, 5 of whom are secretaries, and 3 alternate members. Four of the full and 1 of the alternate members of the Bureau come from non-Baltic origins. In addition to the second secretary, one other secretary is of non-Baltic stock.[30]

In 1971, Latvia was divided into 26 raions, each of which had three party secretaries. Ten of these 26 raions each had a non-Baltic

TABLE 5.4

Communist Party Membership (estimated 1973) and Population in the Latvian SSR, 1970

	Number	Percent
Membership		
Latvians	61,755	46.0
Russians and others	72,245	54.0
Total	134,000	100.0
Ethnic Group		
Latvians	1,342,000	56.8
Russians	705,000	29.8
Others	317,000	13.4
Total	2,364,000	100.0

Sources: "KPSS v tsifrakh (k 70-letiiu II s"ezda RSDPP)," Partiinaia zhizn' 25, no. 50 (July 14, 1973): 11, 18; Itogi vsesoiuznoi perepisi naseleniia 1970 goda. Natsional'nyi sostav naseleniia SSSR (Moscow: Statistika, 1973), 4: 14.

TABLE 5.5

Central Committee, Communist Party of Latvia, Ethnic Composition, 1966, 1971, and 1976 (percent)

Membership	1966	1971	1976
Baltic members	65	58	69
Non-Baltic members	35	42	31

Sources: "Sostav TsK kompartii Latvii, izbrannogo na XX s"ezde KP Latvii," Sovetskaia Latviia (March 4, 1966), p. 1; "Sostav TsK kompartii Latvii, izbrannogo na XXI s"ezde KP Latvii," Sovetskaia Latviia (February 27, 1971), p. 1; "Sostav TsK kompartii Latvii, izbrannogo XXII s"ezdom partii," Sovetskaia Latviia, p. 1.

secretary. In one district, both the first and second secretaries were Russians or members of non-Baltic nationalities.[31] Also in 1971, six Latvian cities were under direct republic jurisdiction; four of them had non-Baltic party secretaries. Of these secretaries, one was a first secretary, and one was a second secretary.[32]

For 1975-76, secretaries could be identified in this research for seven raikoms and two gorkoms. These committees involved a total of 25 secretaries. Of these twenty-five, 10, 4 of whom were first secretaries, were members of non-Baltic nationalities.[33] The fact that Latvians make up less than half of the membership of the CPLa seems to indicate a disenchantment with the Party or, at least, some lack of desire for Party membership among Latvians. This situation could also indicate an absence of Latvians who are politically acceptable to the Party. Probably both of these elements play a role.[34] Though membership is advantageous in many ways, because of the demands that the Party places on a member, it seeks a certain type of individual. A person is required to make personal sacrifices or compromises in order to perform the duties that the Party places on him. A person ordinarily must want to belong to the Party in order to make these sacrifices. The Party expects to benefit from a person's membership. Often members are coopted by the Party because of their skills. In either case, elements of both desire or at least acceptance of the legitimacy of Party membership and cooptation are usually present. In Latvia, there seems to have been a problem for some time in attracting suitable Latvian members for the Party, in spite of the Party's attempts to solicit their membership. In 1958, it was reported that few Latvians were becoming Party members. This fact was blamed on inadequate political work among ethnic Latvians.[35]

In the Latvian government, members of non-Baltic nationalities are represented on a much smaller scale than in the Party. Only 20 percent of the Supreme Soviet of Latvia, elected in June 1975, was composed of Russians and non-Baltic nationalities.[36] Russians alone made up 29.8 percent of the population of Latvia in 1970.[37] These figures seem to show that Russians and members of non-Baltic nationalities are underrepresented in the Supreme Soviet of Latvia. In spite of this underrepresentation, the positions held by non-Baltic members in Latvia's Supreme Soviet appear to be of more significance than are the positions held by non-Baltic members in the Supreme Soviet of Estonia. Russians and members of non-Baltic nationalities who hold positions of importance in Latvia and who are members of the Supreme Soviet of Latvia include four first secretaries of raion committees, one first secretary of a city committee, a deputy chairman of the Latvian Council of Ministers, the procurator of Latvia, who is the union republic's chief legal officer,[38] the head of the frontier guard unit of the Committee of State Security (KGB) in Latvia, and, perhaps of special interest, the chairman of the theater society of Latvia and the chairman of the state committee of the Council of Ministers of Latvia on affairs of editing, printing, and book trade.[39]

TABLE 5.6

Communist Party Membership (estimated 1973) and Population in the Lithuanian SSR, 1970

	Number	Percent
Membership		
Lithuanians	97,000	73.0
Russians and others	35,000	27.0
Total	132,000	100.0
Population		
Lithuanians	2,507,000	80.1
Russians	268,000	8.6
Others	353,000	11.3
Total	3,128,000	100.0

Sources: "KPSS v tsifrakh (k 70-letiiu II s"ezda RSDRP)," Partiinaia zhizn' 25, no. 50 (July 14, 1973): 11, 18; Itogi vsesoiuznoi perepisi naseleniia 1970 goda. Natsional'nyi sostav naseleniia SSSR (Moscow: Statistika, 1973), 4: 14; "Sostav tsentral'nogo komiteta kp Litvy, izbrannogo XVII s"ezdom kommunisticheskoi partii Litvy," Sovetskaia Litva (January 23, 1976), p. 1.

TABLE 5.7

Central Committee, Communist Party of Lithuania, Ethnic Composition, 1966, 1971, and 1976 (in percent)

Membership	1966	1971	1976
Baltic	76	78	77
Non-Baltic	24	22	23

Sources: "Sostav tsentral'nogo komiteta kommunisticheskoi partii Litvy, izbrannogo XV s"ezdom kommunisticheskoi partii Litvy," Sovetskaia Litva (March 6, 1966), p. 1; "Sostav tsentral'nogo komiteta KP Litvy, izbrannogo XVI s"ezdom kommunisticheskoi partii Litvy," Sovetskaia Litva (March 6, 1971), p. 1; "Sostav tsentral'nogo komiteta KP Litvy, izbrannogo XVII s"ezdom kommunisticheskoi partii Litvy," Sovetskaia Litva (January 23, 1976), p. 1.

As far as ethnic composition is concerned, Lithuanians should feel that their political leaders are more representative than are the leaders of the other Baltic republics. In 1973, there were reported to be 97,000 Lithuanian members in the entire CPSU,[40] a figure that represented 73 percent of the total membership of the Communist Party of Lithuania (CPLi) of 132,000.[41] (See Table 5.6.) If all the Lithuanians in the CPSU belong to the CPLi, 35,000 members, or 27 percent of Lithuania's branch of the Communist Party, are of non-Baltic nationalities. The population of the Lithuanian SSR in 1970 was only 19.9 percent non-Lithuanian.[42]

The Central Committee of the CPLi elected in January 1976 is composed of 145 members. Of this membership, 23 percent consists of persons who are Russian or members of non-Baltic nationalities. Of the 67 alternate members elected at this time, 28 percent are non-Baltic. The auditing commission of the Central Committee is 24 percent non-Baltic. Of the delegates elected to the Twenty-fifth Congress of the CPSU in 1976, 26 percent were Russians or persons of non-Baltic nationality. The Secretariat of Lithuania's Communist Party elected at this time consisted of five secretaries, only one of whom did not come from a Baltic eponymous nationality.[43] The one outside member of the Secretariat is the second secretary, Valery Innokentevich Kharazov, a Russian.[44]

On the lower echelons of Soviet Lithuania's Party organization, secretaries can be identified in this research for twelve raikom committees. Names were found for 39 secretaries. Of these 39, only 6 names are Russian or those of non-Baltic nationalities.[45]

Russians and members of non-Baltic nationalities are not to be found in any large numbers within the governmental organization of Lithuania. In the Lithuanian SSR Supreme Soviet, elected in June 1975, only 10 percent of the total membership is non-Baltic.[46] This proportion does not significantly differ from the percentage of Russians in the population of Lithuania (8.6 percent in 1970).[47]

Offices within the Party and governmental structure that are held by non-Baltic deputies to the Lithuanian SSR Supreme Soviet are, on the whole, not of any great influence. The most significant of these positions is that of deputy chairman of the Committee for State Security. Other rather important positions held by non-Baltic members of the Lithuanian SSR Supreme Soviet are those of deputy chairman of the Council of Ministers of Lithuania and one first secretary of a raikom.[48]

Judging from the numerical composition of the Communist Party organizations in these union republics, Estonians and Latvians may have reason to be dissatisfied with the excessive number of Russians in the SSR Party organizations. While it appears that outsiders are underrepresented in the governmental structure of both these union republics, it is possible that these two eponymous nationalities feel that they are entitled to even greater numerical representation in their "own" governments. In Lithuania, members of the indigenous nationality seem to have a significant numerical advantage in Party membership. However, Lithuanians are not as well represented in their government as Estonians and Latvians are in their union republics' governments. Lithuanians may be more unhappy with the composition of the republic's government than with its branch of the Party. Dissatisfaction may persist among the three Baltic nationalities because of the character of the men who hold the most important offices in the republics and from the importance of offices that are held by Russians and other outsiders more than from the ethnic composition of the Party and government agencies.

HOW REPRESENTATIVE IS THE LEADERSHIP?

These brief sketches of the Party and governmental hierarchy demonstrate that in ethnic terms the political leadership in each of the Baltic republics differs significantly from that of the others. The question posed by these figures is: What do these differences and similarities mean in terms of satisfaction or dissatisfaction among the Baltic population of each republic with its political leaders? In Latvia, although Russians and members of non-Baltic nationalities are proportionally underrepresented in the SSR's Supreme Soviet, the importance of the offices that are held by outsiders may provide a reason for dissatisfaction with the republic's governmental, as well as Party, leadership.

The actions of some of the indigenous Baltic leaders raises the question of whether or not they have been coopted and now act more as representatives of the interests of the central authorities than as children of their own nationality. In Estonia, one reason for dissatisfaction with the first secretary of the CPE, as well as with a considerable number of other ethnic Estonian Party and government leaders, may be the charge that they are "Yestonians," a sarcastic term heard in the West that refers to ethnic Estonians who either were born in the Soviet Union or at least lived there during the years of Estonian independence, returning, or else coming to Estonia for the first time, along with Soviet rule.

The first secretary of the CPE, Johannes (Ivan) Käbin, was born in Estonia but educated at the Leningrad Soviet Party School. He graduated from the Institute of Red Professors in Moscow and joined the Communist Party in 1927, while Estonia was an independent country. From 1938-41, Käbin served as a senior instructor in the principles of Marxism-Leninism at the Moscow Petroleum Institute. In 1941, he returned to Estonia as head of the Department of Propaganda and Agitation of the CPE. He became a CPE secretary in 1948, and in 1950 became first secretary of it.[49] Käbin has headed Estonia's branch of the Party so long that his residence in the USSR, rather than the Baltic region, during the interwar period has diminished in importance both to himself and to the population for at least two reasons. First, the new generation of Estonians who grew up after the war is not as likely to be aware of Käbin's presence in the Soviet Union during Estonia's independence as are the members of the older generation. Second, in his own mind, he now probably identifies more closely with Estonia than he did when he first returned to the republic after his long absence. The fact remains that he is ethnically Estonian. Estonian is his native language, and he is knowledgeable about Estonian culture. His own success is tied to the effectiveness of Estonia's Party. In order to see the policies of the Party successfully implemented, he must be able to find some degree of support for them among the population. He will doubtless be able to do this more readily if he appears as a fellow Estonian rather than a 'Russified' representative of Moscow.

The background of the Estonian leaders obviously is a sensitive issue. Recently, Meta Jangolenko was appointed deputy chairman for the Supreme Soviet of Estonia. In Käbin's nominating speech for her, he stressed that Jangolenko is Estonian both by nationality and birthplace. Soon after this, Jangolenko's name appeared in the press as M. Vannas (Jangolenko), emphasizing her more Estonian-sounding name. Judging from that name change and the importance which Käbin gave to Jangolenko's origins, the first secretary seems very aware of the criticism aimed at "Yestonian" Party and government leaders.[50] But this objection against "Yestonian" leaders seems limited by time. Within the not too distant future, most of these people are sure to be retired by natural aging processes.

Another source of discontent among the public with the political elite, not only in Estonia, but in Latvia and Lithuania as well, may be the fact that a person who is not a member of the namesake nationality holds the very important position of Communist Party second secretary. In Estonia, this is a fairly recent phenomenon. In 1970, when Konstantin Lebedev was appointed to this position, he took a place which as far back as 1955 had regularly been held by an Estonian.[51] For the Estonians, even a "Yestonian" is probably preferable to an official who has no ethnic, and therefore to some degree cultural, ties to Estonia. Whoever holds the position of second secretary now has a great deal of power, for the second secretary is in charge of "cadres." By virtue of this position, he has considerable control over the entire union republic Party organization,[52] and through it the governmental organization of the republic. This position also gives its occupant the important role of representative, in the republic, of the CPSU Secretariat in Moscow.[53] In Estonia, presently, this position places a great deal of power in the hands of a Belorussian.

At the same time, Lebedev was appointed Estonian second secretary, another significant change in the Party Secretariat occurred. This was the appointment of Vayno Valjas as a Party secretary. Valjas is the first Estonian not a "Yestonian" to be appointed to the post of secretary since 1950.[54] His appointment may counter to some degree any dissatisfaction on the part of the Estonian population of the republic caused by Lebedev's appointment as second secretary. These changes also make Estonia's Party organization more like that of the majority of SSR's throughout the USSR, most of which have Russian, or other Slavic, second secretaries.

In some instances popular support, at least among the Party rank and file, may be important to the political elites of the union republics. Consider the case of Artur Vader in Estonia. Vader was born in Belorussia. Arriving in Estonia for the first time as a Party official at the age of 28, he served as the first secretary of the Tallinn Party organization from 1952 to 1959, after which he returned to Moscow. But in 1964, he was appointed second secretary of the CPE.[55] In October 1970, he was appointed chairman of the Supreme Soviet of Estonia.[56] This appointment was a definite demotion for Vader, who had been expected to become first secretary of the CPE when Käbin stepped down. One member of Estonia's Party commented that "Vader's election to the post of our supreme soviet chairman came as a surprise to us. We thought he aimed at the Party 1st secretary position. But all the people I know accepted the present solution with satisfaction."[57] This unofficial statement seems to imply that Vader did not enjoy wide support from the Party membership. This lack of enthusiasm for him may have extended to the population in general.

As long as Vader held a high Party position and appeared to be on his way up, he apparently did not try to cultivate the support of the general population. However, soon after his demotion, Vader undertook a visit abroad to the Cameroons. The trip received extensive media coverage in Estonia. In the past, Vader had shunned opportunities to gain publicity by speaking to university Party organizations, for example. Apparently, he did not feel at ease with these audiences. However, he now seems to realize that broader support can be important in retaining or perhaps regaining his high status in the Party.[58]

Not until the mid-sixties did the Estonians become a numerical majority in their SSR's branch of the Party. The fact that membership in Estonia's Communist Party became more attractive after the mid-fifties probably reflects not only self-interest but, possibly, a realization among Estonians that the Party can serve them as a source of influence, which, at least to some degree, can be used to support Estonian national interests.[59] The Party seems to have attracted educated Estonian white-collar workers. By 1970, 22.4 percent of the Party members had received some higher education and 59.84 percent had at least partially completed their secondary education, a proportion above the CPSU average.[60] However, with the exception of Valjas, Edgar Tonurist, first deputy chairman of the Estonian Council of Ministers, and possibly Nikolai Johanson, the first secretary of the Tallinn city Party committee, none of the ethnic Estonians joining the Party in significant numbers since 1956 has attained an important position. This pattern may reflect a reluctance on the part of Moscow CPSU headquarters, and the older, more Russian-oriented Estonian Communists to allow these better-educated, but purely Estonian, Communists too much power.[61] Such discrimination contributes to dissatisfaction among these Estonian Party members and their following within the population of the union republic. The concentration of Estonians at the Party's lower echelons seems to imply that most discontent with the political leadership of the republic stemming from its non-Estonian composition is directed toward the union republic-level leadership.

Latvian political leadership seems to be quite different from that of Estonia and probably provides Latvians more of a reason for dissatisfaction than the leadership of Estonia offers among Estonians.

In Latvia, there is a great deal of disenchantment with Communist Party membership, for Latvians, unlike Estonians in their SSR, have not joined the Party in sufficient numbers to make them a majority in the CPLa. The ethnic Latvian leadership is subject to the same charge as the ethnic Estonian leaders. Many of them spent the interwar years of Latvian independence in the Soviet Union. The party's first secretary of Latvia, Augusts Voss, has been referred to as "a Russian born Latvian: [who] as a rule . . . doesn't speak Latvian in public."[62] Nationality language is a major issue in the Baltic republics. A first secretary who does not use the local language can hardly be very popular among the eponymous nationality of the republic. Voss joined the Communist Party in 1942, while serving in the Soviet Army. He graduated from the Higher Party School in 1948. From 1948 to 1950, he headed the Party's section for Higher Education Establishments and Sciences in Latvia. He then served as secretary to Party agencies of Latvia from 1954 to to 1960. Under the Central Committee of the CPLa from 1960 to 1966, he worked as a Central Committee secretary. In 1966, he was made first secretary of the CPLa.[63] As in Estonia, the Latvian second secretary is of Slavic origin. Since 1963, this post has been held by N. A. Belukha. Belukha is a Ukrainian who reportedly does not know the Latvian language.[64]

An example of open and direct dissatisfaction with the leadership of the Latvian Party is to be found in the widely circulated letter of protest from 17 Latvian Communists.[65] These Latvian Communists, each of whom claims to have belonged to the Party for 25 to 35 years, are critical of the leadership for its non-Latvian and "Russified" character. They condemn the fact that many Party leaders do not speak Latvian. They are also disturbed by the large number of non-Latvians being brought into the union republic and by what they term "Great Russian chauvinism."[66] At least some of these concerns seem to be shared with a larger portion of the population.

Latvians may have an advantage over both Lithuanians and Estonians by virtue of having Arvid Pelshe as a spokesman for their interests on the Politburo of the CPSU. However, Pelshe provides an excellent example of a nationality leader who has been coopted by the regime. From his background, it appears that he is much more concerned about advancing his own career than defending any Latvian nationality interests. Pelshe seems to have been a victor in the purge conducted in the late 1950s, when many Latvian communists were charged with "having attempted to create a nationally exclusive economy, packing party and government agencies with Latvian personnel, and instituting cultural policies that smacked of bourgeois nationalism."[67] Following these removals, Pelshe became the first secretary of Latvia's Party. Pelshe's career seems to have been built on "the necessity to eradicate the various and sundry manifestations of national consciousness in Latvia."[68] The aged Pelshe has since been promoted to full membership in the Politburo of the CPSU Central Committee. The 17 protesting Latvian Communists referred to Pelshe as "a sycophant of power politics."[69]

The purges of the late 1950s, in which Pelshe was so active, may have played an important role in bringing an awareness of differences within the Party to the attention of the population as a whole and arousing sympathy for the Latvian leaders. Latvia's Party press commented that

> at the end of the purge many individuals "did not draw the proper conclusions" from the shakeup. . . . concerning the nationalist group, which was exposed and discredited in our republic in 1959. The members of this group to this time have not publicly condemned their activity and views, have taken the attitude of being offended, and have remained silent.[70]

Owing to the large concentration of non-Baltic personnel on the lower echelons of Latvia's Party leadership, the Latvian people must be aware that outsiders serve in leadership positions. Less-educated and less politically conscious members of society, too, are likely to know who such local political leaders are.

In Latvia, more than Estonia, governmental leadership provides reason for concern to Latvians who care about retaining their nationality culture. The fact that several very significant positions in the Latvian SSR government are held by non-Latvians is public knowledge. Neither the chairman of Latvia's theater society nor the chairman of the state committee for affairs of editing, printing, and book trade is Latvian.[71] That should be enough to worry Latvians concerned about retention of their nationality culture. These are positions in which the right person could do much to promote nationality culture. People who occupy these offices can exert great influence over Latvian literature and theater. If the occupants of these offices wish to see the traditional Latvian literary and dramatic heritage abandoned in favor of socialist realism, they can have a powerful effect in bringing this about.

In Lithuania, the ethnic composition of the Party and the population varies considerably from that of either Estonia's or Latvia's Party and population. Lithuania's Party (CPLi) includes a much larger percentage of the eponymous nationality than the Communist parties of the other two Baltic union republics. Nor does Lithuania's Party branch seem to have many members who resided outside independent Lithuania during the interwar years. Antanas Sniečkus, first secretary of the CPLi until his death in 1974, was born in Lithuania. Although he was a 1935 graduate of the International Lenin courses given in Moscow between 1925 and 1940, he was simultaneously engaged in illegal Communist activity in Lithuania, behavior that on several occasions led to his arrest.[72]

The present first secretary of the CPLi, Petras Griskevicius is a native-born Lithuanian. He joined the Communist Party in 1945 and attended Party schools. Before becoming Party secretary in 1974 he served as first secretary of the Vilnius Party committee.[73]

As in the higher echelons of the CPLi, the leadership of the SSR government and the raion level of the branch Party remains almost entirely Lithuanian. Judging from its ethnic composition, the political leadership of Lithuania should be able to serve as a support for Lithuanian culture and traditions. Here, Party decisions are carried out largely by Lithuanians and are, therefore, subject to application by members of the eponymous nationality.

Notwithstanding the large number of Lithuanians who hold important positions in the CPLi, Second Secretary Kharazov, the one Russian holding a top Party position in Lithuania, recently attacked "shortcomings" within the republic. He criticized numerous primary Party organizations for "corruption" and "shortcomings" in their work. In one rather revealing statement, Kharazov reported that

> even after these facts were uncovered and the guilty parties had received administrative penalities, thc assembly line's Party organization (S. Khrantsov, secretary) could not muster enough devotion to principle to give the incident a Party appraisal.[74]

The accused secretary who could not gain the support of his primary Party organization has a Russian name. Most of the members of the primary Party organization are likely to be Lithuanians. It is probable that the members of the organization identify more closely with a person of their own nationality than with an outsider. For this reason, a Lithuanian first secretary would seem more likely to have the support of the members than this Russian secretary.

Such political criticisms would be more credible to the Lithuanian population if a Lithuanian made them. Kharazov was also chosen to voice the difficulties that Soviet authorities are encountering in persuading Lithuanians to abandon their nationality traditions and fuse with the other ethnic groups of the USSR. He condemned members of the public who

> are trying to weaken the friendship of peoples, rekindle nationalistic feelings among backward sections of the

population, and sow distrust between citizens of different nationalities, using political demagoguery and all sorts of fabrications for this purpose.[75]

A leader who has the population's trust and respect may persuade the general public to accept Party policies and also his position. The Party's policies can no longer be implemented simply by coercion. Because of the effects of modernization, the population must be at least partially willing to accept these policies as correct. Yet the leadership of the Baltic republics has not made any sustained efforts to obtain the general public's support.

The composition and role of the political elite differs in each of the three Baltic union republics. In Lithuania, the political elite is capable of quite actively supporting Lithuanian nationality values and culture, but the political elite of Latvia, composed to a large extent of outsiders, is not as interested in the Latvian cultural heritage as are the Latvians themselves. The political elite of Estonia falls somewhere between these two extremes. The elite of Estonia is gaining additional Estonian members, and therefore is gaining potential for becoming a factor in supporting Estonian traditions. In the meantime, the increasing number of Estonians in the republic Party organization can, if these younger Estonians are not allowed in the near future to occupy the top positions of leadership, become an important source of dissatisfaction within the union republic.

From this research, it is evident that the three eponymous Baltic nationalities appear justified in feeling deprived of leadership. The small number of indigenous members in the Latvian SSR's Party organization suggests disillusionment with belonging to it. The Party branches in Estonia and Lithuania are numerically more representative of these nationalities, but Slavic second secretaries in these union republics each hold the key position, which allows them to choose personnel to fill the most important offices. Therefore, they can assign positions to their own people or at least to those loyal to the CPSU and its Russian leaders.

Unless the political leadership changes and becomes more representative and free from the control of outsiders, dissatisfaction is likely to spread in the Soviet Baltic area. The theory of modernization discussed earlier suggests that this feeling of deprivation becomes more widespread in the Baltic region as these people gain awareness of who their leaders are. If the Baltic political leadership becomes more representative of the general public, this leadership will, once again, become a major nationality support in the region.

As Soviet rule proves durable in the Baltic republics, the Baltic nationalities are becoming aware that Party membership can provide a new support factor for nationality interests. While many traditional cultural values still function, with some modification, as nationality support factors, Party membership can give these nationalities access to political decision making. By joining the Party, members of the Baltic nationalities gain a chance to contribute to political decisions and to be in a position to help put these decisions into effect. People who have become Party members have an opportunity to voice the nationality's interest in the Party, at least on the local level and eventually, perhaps, this chance will extend to the highest echelons of the party. Because the newest generation of Baltic leaders has not been "Russified" to the extent that their predecessors were, they are more inclined to work for the equalization of ethnic groups and for policies favorable to the eponymous nationalities than are the older members of the leadership. As this new generation looks for ways to maintain its sense of nationality identity, Party membership is becoming an additional and acceptable way in which this may be attempted. Baltic eponymous nationalities have come to realize that the Party has firmly entrenched itself in these republics. Through Party membership, the leaders gain the right to work within the most powerful, and only legal, political organization in the USSR. They can suggest or support policies that favor equal status among Soviet ethnic groups and the survival of nationality identity.

NOTES

1. Endel Nirk, Estonian Literature (Tallinn: Eesti Raamat, 1970), pp. 43, 61, 66-67, 71, 73, 91, 209; and Janis Andrups and Vitauts Kalve, Latvian Literature (Stockholm: M. Goppers, 1954), pp. 13-15, 18-20, 41-43, 97-98, 102-05.

2. Eugen Weber, A Modern History of Europe, Men, Cultures, and Societies from the Renaissance to the Present, (New York: W. W. Norton & Company, 1971), p. 313.

3. Itogi vsesoiuznoi perepisi naseleniia 1970 goda. Natsional'nyi sostav naselniia SSSR (Moscow: Statistika, 1973), 4: 274 (hereafter cited as Itogi . . . 1970 goda).

4. Cynthia R. Enloe, Ethnic Conflict and Political Development (Boston: Little, Brown, 1973), see chap. X, pp. 261-74, for a discussion of such works.

5. Itogi . . . 1970 goda, vol. 4, pp. 273, 280, 317.

6. E. H. Carr, The Bolshevik Revolution (1917-1923) (Middlesex, England: Penguin Books, 1971), 1: 316-18.

7. John S. Reshetar, Jr., The Soviet Polity, Government and Politics in the U.S.S.R. (New York: Dodd Mead, 1971), p. 149.

8. A. Pankseev, in Nekotorye voprosy organizatsionno partiinoi raboty (Tallinn: Eesti Raamat, 1971), p. 74, cited in Baltic Events 37, no. 2 (April 1973): 8.

9. Itogi . . . 1970 goda, vol. 4, p. 15.
10. Pankseev, p. 74.
11. "KPSS v tsifrakh (k 70-letiiu II s"ezda RSDRP)," Partiinaia zhizn' 25, no. 50 (July 14, 1973): 11.
12. "Sostav TsK kompartii Estonii, izbrannogo na XVII s"ezde kompartii Estonii," Sovetskaia Estoniia (January 31, 1976), p. 1.
13. Jaan Pennar, "Soviet Nationality Policy and the Estonian Communist Elite," in A Case Study of a Soviet Republic: The Estonian SSSR, ed. Tõnu Parming and Elmar Järvesoo (Boulder, Colo.: Westview Press, forthcoming).
14. "Sostav TsK kompartii Estonii, izbrannogo na XVII s"ezde kompartii Estonii," p. 1.
15. Ibid., p. 1.
16. Eesti Noukogude Entsüklopeedia (Tallinn, 1972), 4: 417.
17. Reshetar, p. 149.
18. Estonian Events, no. 24 (February 1971), p. 7.
19. See accounts of Party conferences in Sovetskaia Estoniia (December 1975 and January 1976).
20. Reshetar, p. 255.
21. "Soobshchenie tsentral'noi izbiratel'noi komissii ob itogakh vyborov v verkhovnyi sovet Estonskoi SSR deviatogo sozyva, sostoiavshikhsia 15 iiunia 1975 goda," Sovetskaia Estoniia (June 19, 1975), p. 3 (hereafter cited as "Soobshchenie tsentral'noi izbiratel'noi komissii . . .").
22. Itogi . . . 1970 goda, vol. 4, p. 15.
23. "Soobshchenie tsentral'noi izbiratel'noi komissii . . .," p. 3.
24. Reshetar, pp. 212-13.
25. Pennar, p. 15.
26. Ibid., Table 2, p. 143.
27. "KPSS v tsifrakh (k 70-letiiu II s"ezda RSDRP)," p. 11.
28. Baltic Events no. 6 (47), (December 1974): 5.
29. "KPSS v tsifrakh (k 70-letiiu II s"ezda RSDRP)," p. 11.
30. "Sostav tsentral'nogo kommiteta kommunisticheskoi partii Latvii, izbrannogo XXII s'ezdom partii," Sovetskaia Latviia (January 24, 1976), p. 1.
31. Estonian Events, no. 26 (June 1971), p. 6.
32. Ibid., p. 6.
33. See accounts of Party conferences in Sovetskaia Latviia (December 1975 and January 1976).
34. T. H. Rigby, Communist Party Membership in the U.S.S.R. 1917-1967 (Princeton, N.J.: Princeton University Press, 1968), p. 46.
35. Ibid., p. 393.
36. "Deputaty verkhovnogo soveta Latviiskoi SSR," Sovetskaia Latviia (June 19, 1976), pp. 2-3.

37. Itogi . . . 1970 goda, vol. 4, p. 14.
38. Reshetar, p. 206.
39. "Deputaty verkhovnogo soveta Latviiskoi SSR," pp. 2-3.
40. "KPSS v tsifrakh (k 70-letiiu II s"ezda RSDRP)," p. 18.
41. Ibid., p. 11.
42. Itogi . . . 1970 goda, vol. 4, p. 14.
43. "Narod izbral ikh deputatami verkhovnogo soveta Litovskoi SSR," Sovetskaia Litva (June 23, 1975), p. 1.
44. "Toeing the Line in Lithuania," Soviet Analyst 3, no. 15 (July 18, 1974): 4.
45. See accounts of Party conferences in Sovetskaia Litva (December 1975 and January 1976).
46. "Narod izbral ikh deputatami verkhovnogo soveta Litovskoi SSR," p. 1.
47. Itogi . . . 1970 goda, vol. 4, p. 14.
48. Accounts of Party conferences in Sovetskaia Litva (December 1975 and January 1976).
49. Prominent Personalities in the U.S.S.R., ed. Edward L. Crowley, et al. (Metuchen, N.J.: Scarecrow Press, 1970), pp. 252-53.
50. Rahva Raal, March 29, 1975, p. 1, and April 9, 1975, p. 1, cited in Baltic Events 50/51, nos. 3/4 (June-August 1975): 13.
51. Grey Hodnett and Val Ogareff, Leaders of the Soviet Republics, 1955-1972 (Canberra: Dept. of Political Science Research School of Social Sciences, Australian National University, 1973), p. 95.
52. Yaroslav Bilinsky, "The Rulers and the Ruled," Problems of Communism 16, no. 5 (September-October 1967): 21.
53. Pennar, op. cit., pp. 23-24.
54. Rahva Haal (December 23, 1970), cited in Estonian Events, no. 24 (February 1971), p. 7.
55. Ibid., p. 1.
56. Estonian Events, no. 25 (April 1971), p. 2.
57. Ibid., p. 2.
58. Estonian Events, no. 26 (June 1971), p. 5.
59. Pennar, p. 130.
60. Ibid., p. 21.
61. Ibid., p. 25.
62. "Letter to Communist Party Leaders," Congressional Record, 92nd Cong. 2nd sess., February 15-22, 1972, 118, pt. 4: 4823.
63. Prominent Personalities in the U.S.S.R., p. 683.
64. "Letter to Communist Party Leaders," p. 4823.
65. Ibid., p. 4823.
66. Ibid., p. 4823.

67. "Arvid Ianovich Pelshe: Political Profile," The Baltic Review, no. 27 (June 1964), p. 46.

68. Ibid., p. 46.

69. "Letter to Communist Party Leaders," p. 4823.

70. "Trudom kovat' pobedu kommunizma," Sovetskaia Latvia (November 24, 1961), p. 2, also cited in "Arvid Ianovich Pelshe: Political Profile," pp. 43-46.

71. "Deputaty verkhovnogo soveta Latviiskoi SSR," pp. 2-3.

72. Prominent Personalities in the U.S.S.R., p. 590.

73. "Toeing the Line in Lithuania," Soviet Analyst 3, no. 15 (July 18, 1974): 4.

74. [V. Kharazov], "Uluchshat' rukovodstvo pervichnymi partiinymi organizatsiiami, povyshat' ikh rol' vypolnenii reshenii XXIV S"ezda KPSS. Doklad Vtorogo Sekretaria TsKKP Litvy V. Kharazova," Sovetskaia Litva (November 24, 1973), p. 2, cited in Current Digest of the Soviet Press 25, no. 49 (January 2, 1974): 3.

75. Ibid., p. 3.

CHAPTER

6

SOVIETIZATION, CULTURE, AND RELIGION

Christopher Doersam

An aspect of Soviet principle and ideological belief considered important by the Communist Party's elite is the achievement of "ideological modernization" by a nationality. This includes the acceptance of Marxist-Leninist atheistic viewpoints with the doctrine of Sovietization. That doctrine concerns the development of nationalities into one, all-embracing, socialist Soviet people with an internationalist socialist secularized culture. Each nationality's culture is expected to aid in the formation of this new identity and the single international socialist culture by enriching itself with what are termed "internationalist and socialist qualities" from the other cultures among the ethnic groups of the USSR. Contributions to the common socialist Soviet culture originate, supposedly, from all nationalities. Through generalization of this common socialist culture, it is expected that nationality isolation and distinctiveness will gradually disappear.[1] The doctrine of Sovietization also includes propagandizing the atheistic viewpoint, for religion is considered an obstacle hindering the "rapprochement" of various nationalities. The net effect of such a doctrine and effectively implemented policy would be to neutralize nationality identity, causing a type of denationalization. Nevertheless, given the dominant position occupied by the Russians in Soviet society, adoption of such a principle may work to force Russification among the nationalities of the USSR, especially those of the Soviet West (the region comprising Belorussia, Moldavia, Ukraine, and the three Baltic union republics). The eponymous nationalities in these union republics along the western region of the USSR are European in culture and, in that sense, considerably more akin to the Russians and Russian culture than to the Muslim cultures of the Iranian and Turkic nationalities (nationality refers here only to non-Russian ethnic groups) of Central Asia or the highly distinct and Christian nationalities of Transcaucasus, the Georgians and Armenians. A Baltic samizdat author has remarked:

> The theoreticians of Marxism clearly state that upon reaching communism, nations will disappear, and there will be only one language. Uneasy feel the teachers of Marxism in our land when they are queried, "Which language will that one be?"[2]

Important distinctions exist between Russification and Sovietization. Unqualified Russification implies the adoption of Russian language and culture by a nationality and the entire replacement of the nationality's culture and identity by a Russian one. Sovietization, theoretically, does not necessarily signify Russification but, rather, the mere eradication of nationality differences and animosities and the creation of a common Soviet culture. Russification presupposes the virtual annihilation of the nationalities' cultures, whereas Sovietization does not assume the entire substitution of one culture for the culture of another particular ethnic group. It, rather, suggests a synthesis to which the nationality culture may contribute a part of its original culture, thereby preserving certain of its own features in the newly formed general socialist Soviet culture. However, an important tenet of Sovietization is that Russian has to be considered the language of communication among the ethnic groups in the single newly fused Soviet culture and society.[3] The emphasis placed upon this choice of language gives rise to the fear that Sovietization in practice (stated above) will engulf the nationalities' cultures and languages with Russification, owing to the advantageous position due the Russian language in the new projected Soviet society.

The eponymous nationalities of the Baltic region today enjoy a relatively high level of economic and cultural development.[4] Although these three nationalities continue to be underrepresented in the USSR's political establishment, the Communist Party of the Soviet Union, both the proportion and numbers of their membership have substantially increased since the mid-1950s. The 1973 membership of Lithuanians stood at 97,000, with 62,000 Latvians and 46,000 Estonians in the entire CPSU.[5] Under this centralized USSR political system, policies of Sovietization are intended to affect the nationality support systems of the nationalities. A nationality support may be considered an instrument, institution, belief, or tradition with which the members who feel they belong to a particular ethnic group tend to associate and which is thought symbolic of, or essential to, their nationality. The combination of supports may vary with the passage of time. This combination seems to offer a concrete self-identity for each individual vis-a-vis the mass of humanity. Nationality identity, itself a psychological entity attained by an individual's conscious predilictions, receives visible form through operation of the various nationality supports. The present study investigates mainly the impact of the doctrine of Sovietization upon nationality culture and identity among the USSR's Estonians, Latvians, and Lithuanians in the 1970s and the consequent reaction to Sovietization expressed in the rising level of group dissatisfaction among such nationalities.

The utilization of religion and religious institutions as nationality supports will be examined. Most noneponymous nationalities (those whose group names are not applied to local administrative units) residing in the three Baltic union republics will not be considered here, because they do not possess the same administrative status accorded Estonians, Latvians, and Lithuanians. The sole exception will be the Baltic Poles. They have important religious and cultural ties with the Lithuanians and are representatives of an ethnic group whose traditional homeland, Poland, is a Communist state in which the relationship between church and state varies considerably from the situation existing in the Soviet Union. The parameters for measuring the degree of impact Sovietization makes upon the Baltic union republics are the following: the attitude of the Party elites and press of the union republics toward the doctrine and adoption of Russian as one's native tongue (linguistic Russification) by persons of the eponymous nationalities; the creation of institutional forms in order to facilitate cultural exchanges and contacts among the nationalities of the USSR intended to help form a common Soviet culture; publishing in each nationality's language and the use of the eponymous language in the schools of the union republics; basic attitudes of the eponymous nationalities toward traditional group supports, such as folklore, or supports like religion, which itself is antithetical to the principle of one Soviet culture; and the degree of political and cultural dissatisfaction a nationality manifests toward the Soviet system and its ideological doctrine of Sovietization. It is proposed here that despite the increased political mobilization of the eponymous nationalities of the Baltic region, the status of nationality supports incompatible with Soviet Marxist ideology and under continuous attack—religion and nationalistic attitudes and prejudicies for example—and other less provocative nationality supports, seems to indicate that this increased political mobilization and accompanying high socioeconomic level does not evidence a significant degree of Sovietization of the nationality culture and identity. Nor does there appear to be, even if Sovietization occurs to a degree through the adoption of certain practices, a net weakening of nationality support systems in toto and nationality identity among the eponymous nationalities of the Baltic region. This may be attributed to the durable nature and flexibility of nationality as such. Religion, one such cultural support factor, has played an important role for certain nationalities in the area but not for all in crystalizing and expanding nationality dissatisfaction in the 1970s.

This thesis supports the general hypothesis of this book that the level of group dissatisfaction (Baltic in this case), among nationalities tends to rise rather than fall with increasingly high material and cultural achievement. The onset of Soviet modernization, which encompasses besides material gains an attempt to transform these three eponymous nationalities into Soviet variants and adherents to Soviet ideology, also spurs unrest and discontent. The chapter will examine areas of impact of Sovietization and the actual state of various nationality supports in order to determine whether the real condition of nationality identity and cultural vitality warrants the sharply defensive intensity of group dissatisfaction expressed in recent years. The use and shift of nationality support factors will be demonstrated in analyzing the status of religion as such a factor in the cultural sphere for both the eponymous nationalities of the Baltic region and the Baltic Poles. The religions that primarily will be examined are Protestantism, chiefly Lutheranism and Russian Orthodoxy in Latvia and Estonia, and Roman Catholicism in Lithuania. (Judaism in the Baltic region is studied in Chapter 7.)

Religion through the centuries has played a critical role in ethnic group self-identification.[6] Perhaps the reason may be that it functions through beliefs and practices somewhat like nationality identity, granting equality and group identification to its adherents against outsiders. It has been affirmed that proclamation of one's religion in the Soviet state still carries important nationalist implications:

> Even now this sometimes has the curious result that an unbaptized Russian going to work in Turkestan will get himself baptized to show that he is fully Russian. In the same way to be a Catholic is to proclaim oneself a Pole or a Lithuanian. A Lutheran is a German, Latvian or an Estonian.
>
> In Western Europe the only parallel is Ireland, another country where the community you belong to is all important and community is determined by religious inheritance. As in Ireland religious community in the Soviet Union has political overtones. It is a disadvantage to the Catholics, Lutherans and Moslems that they represent a definitely non-Russian focus of feeling. It is always considered possible that they want a political separation.[7]

SOVIETIZATION AND CULTURAL VITALITY

Evidence for official attitudes about the impact of Sovietization upon Baltic cultural supports and identities was sought in the following journals: Kommunist Estonii, Kommunist Sovetskoi Latvii, and Kommunist (Vilnius) in the year 1975.* Unofficial viewpoints regarding governmental policies enacted in the region were surveyed in the Lithuanian samizdat journals, Aušra [Dawn] and Lietuvos Katalikų Bažnycios Kronika [Chronicle of the Catholic Church in Lithuania].

In Estonia, perhaps the most authoritative endorsement and interpretation for the doctrine of Sovietization found in a recent survey of Estonian Party journals may be the statement of Johannes (Ivan) Käbin, First Secretary, Communist Party of Estonia:

> Estonian culture, through spirit and principal content, is a component of an indivisible, socialist culture of the Soviet Union which includes in itself the most worthy traces and traditions of cultures and mode of life of every people of our Homeland. Like any of the Soviet nationality cultures, the Estonian culture nourishes itself not only from its own springs, but also from the spiritual wealth of the fraternal peoples.[8]

Special emphasis is given by Käbin to the role the Russian language plays in a process, which is termed "rapprochement" among the diverse Soviet ethnic groups, as a medium of communication and tool for cultural enrichment that can draw them all into closer contact with each other.[9] Party journals assert further that this rapprochement, or sblizhenie, which is perceived as a drawing together of the many ethnic groups in the USSR, is an objective process. Therefore, it is every Communists's duty to oppose any inducement meant to promote that rapprochement artificially, or any nationalistic manifestation that might deliberately hinder rapprochement and the policies of Sovietization among Soviet ethnic groups.[10]

Organizational structures and institutions have proliferated that foster the idea of mixing cultures and generating a common Soviet patriotism and culture. These institutions provide opportunities on a regular basis for cultural contacts among the nationalities. Since 1967, in Estonia, Days of Culture of the Fraternal Republics and since 1966, the inter-raion Days of Culture were held.[11] In Estonia, cultural festivals that are entitled "days," "weeks," or

---

*Journal numbers 1-10.

"ten-day periods of literature and art" were staged by artists, writers, and performers of the following autonomous and union republics: RSFSR (1960 and 1966), Moldavian SSR (1963), Armenia (1964), Uzbekistan (1968), Georgia (1971), Ukraine (1974), and the Mari Autonomous Soviet Socialist Republic. Prominent Estonian cultural figures and groups have made reciprocal visits to open exhibitions and festivals of Estonian culture, literature, and art, thereby, ostensibly, exchanging cultural values and forms and thus aiding the synthesis of a common Soviet culture. From September 26 to October 5, 1975, the festival, Days of Literature and Art of the Estonian SSR, was held in the Ukraine.[12] The scope of one such event is illustrated by the Ukraine's Days of Culture held in Estonia during 1974. Over a ten-day period, 500 cultural and artistic figures from the Ukraine visited Estonia, giving 88 concerts. Twenty-five films, plus 13 documentaries produced in the Ukrainian SSR, were shown. Attendance at these performances exceeded 200,000 according to reports.[13]

This method of cultural exchange has been extended to the raion level of public administration in Estonia. Each raion cultural establishment maintains cultural connections with five or six Soviet union republics, arranging for Days of Culture representing the raion and exchanging amateur and cultural groups that represent the raion.[14] Penetration of these exchanges goes very deep, for the raion level is a low step in Soviet administration. In the USSR, besides the 15 union republics, 20 autonomous republics, 8 autonomous oblasts, and 10 nationality okrugs, there are 126 krais and oblasts and 3,096 raions. Estonia is divided into 15 raions. In Latvia, there are 26 raions, and Lithuania has 44 raions. Like Estonia, neither Latvia nor Lithuania has an oblast level of administration.[15]

Other means of promoting rapprochement among different ethnic groups are evidenced at places of employment where Russian becomes the language utilized for communication among a multi-ethnic work force. The existence of a multi-ethnic work force, itself, is seen by party leaders as a positive indication of further internationalization of the Soviet population. Amateur performing groups and choirs are exchanged regularly between different factories. In summer 1973, for example, the amateur group from a factory located in Kaunas gave a concert for the workers at its competitor plant in Tartu. The group from Tartu planned a return recital that would include a Lithuanian song, for the Kaunas troupe had sung one Estonian song at Tartu. Such visits are felt to be a method to dispel any ethnic bias. Lectures delivered regularly at the plants and factories concern friendly cooperation among nationalities and the spirit of internationalism. In Tartu, during the first ten months of 1974, the Znanie Society offered more than 400 public lectures about the "friendship of peoples." Emphasis is placed upon there being representatives of the many ethnic groups among the outstanding workers and leadership of the Communist Party cells at factories in Estonia. For example, in a leather-shoe combine in Tartu, among the 22 best workers, there are represented 8 different nationalities (in all, 12 nationalities work there). However, the authorities have determined that the internationalist ideological education and consciousness of the workers must be improved. At a Tartu Party conference in 1974 it emerged that Party ideological work needs some improvement, especially in the inculcation of an internationalist spirit among workers.[16] Thus, the actual institutional framework for internationalist indoctrination has many levels, yet its effectiveness is questioned by a Party elite whose assigned task it is to effectuate this principle, "friendship of peoples."

A particular facet of the ostensible drawing together among the various ethnic groups, or rapprochement between the cultures of different people of the USSR, is emphasized by the Estonians, with poorly concealed national pride. This is the exchange of literary works and their translations into the various languages of the USSR. Party First Secretary Käbin notes that over 800 Estonian works have been translated into the different languages of the Soviet Union and published in 30 million copies within the 30 years following Estonia's incorporation into the USSR.[17] In the period 1940-74, some 1,000 Estonian originals had been translated into the diverse languages of the ethnic groups of the USSR. Among them, Estonian originals were translated into the following languages: 556 into Russian, 88 books into Latvian, 52 works into Lithuanian, and 37 original literary pieces into Ukrainian, and 267 publications into the other languages of the USSR. Correspondingly, in the period 1940-75, 1,291 works of Russian literature, 71 volumes by Latvian authors, 59 works from Ukrainian writers, and 32 books by Lithuanian authors, along with 338 original titles by persons of other Soviet ethnic groups were translated into Estonian.[18] Although the journals refer to the creation of a common Soviet literary typology, great stress seems to be placed in the Party journals in Tallinn upon the high caliber of Estonian input into the formation and resulting content of that Soviet typology in the literary field.[19]

The doctrine promoting rapprochement among ethnic groups and their cultures under socialism mandates an exchange of cultures with socialist nations outside, as well as inside, the USSR. Responding to this opportunity, Estonia appears to maintain particularly close relations with its linguistic kin in socialist central Europe, the Hungarians. The governments of Estonia and Hungary arrange frequent cultural exchanges and contacts between Estonia and Hungary. A special cultural exchange relationship exists between the cities of

Tartu and Vespred. In a Solnok, Hungary, newspaper, Neplap, events in Estonia are regularly reported in some detail.[20] The selective application of this principle of cultural rapprochement and "friendship of peoples" to Hungary by the Estonian SSR's leaders demonstrates a nationality linguistic preference on the part of the Estonian cultural elites and Party authorities. Another manifestation of this selectivity by Baltic authorities appears in the press surveyed: the Mari ASSR with its Uralic eponymous nationality was the sole autonomous SSR reported to have staged a cultural festival in Estonia within the last 15 years.

The press reveals that Sovietization is endorsed by the authorities in Latvia. The "international" quality of Soviet culture is deferentially emphasized, but this feature of Sovietization, Latvia's Party elite stresses, does not encompass the annihilation of what can be considered particular to the nationality.

> From the multifaceted rapprochement of Soviet nations and nationalities they did not become less national. On the contrary, indeed, during the years of Soviet rule national values really received unlimited possibilities for development, the national color became enriched with bright hues, national languages, national literature and art flourished.
>
> The international in a society of mature socialism is developed in mutual connection with national factors. It does not exist solely by itself, but only on the basis of what is national, in unity with it, and it synthesizes in the national genuine wealth and diversity. What is national develops itself on an international base. In the course of this dialectic process new common values are born.[21]

Here again, the exchange of translations and literature between the eponymous nationality and other ethnic groups is focused upon as a method of cultivating rapprochement among the groups by enriching mutually the diverse nationalities and creating a common base. Between 1948 and 1973, Latvian literature was translated and published in 27 languages. More than 650 works by Latvian authors were translated and published in Russian in that period. In the interval, January 1970-December 1971, the following quantities of books from other ethnic groups were published in Latvia; 159 books by Russian authors; 9 works of Ukrainian writers; 5 production of Georgian and Moldavian writers, and 4 volumes of Belorussians and Kazakhs and other ethnic groups of the USSR.[22] In Latvia, translated literature of all types has accounted for 15 percent to 18 percent of all titles, exceeding 40 percent of the copies.[23] Although the Russian role and input into this literary interaction dominates once again, like Estonian publishing and translating, Latvian literature makes a very good proportional contribution to this mixture of literary culture, which is supposedly leading to the creation of a new, all-embracing socialist Soviet literature.

The importance of inculcating the approved themes of internationalization and friendship between people through the system of Party education has been highlighted in the press surveyed. During 1975, some 525,000 persons (20 percent of the total population) were enrolled in the network of Party schools dealing with economic and social questions. Currently, in Latvia, there are 25,000 trained propagandists and 20,000 political information specialists, along with 18,000 assigned agitators, who are stressing the development of socialist consciousness and internationalization among the populace.[24] Also in journals surveyed, there is much emphasis upon the increased educational levels and skills of workers during the Soviet period. Unlike the past, present circumstances offer the opportunity, it is said, for all workers to be fully educated in the "correct" principles of Communist morality and ideology.[25]

DISTINCTIONS BETWEEN VARIOUS CONCEPTIONS OF HOMELAND

Distinctions between the conception of one's homeland and the native land in the Soviet instance become more complex with the presence of the doctrine of internationalism and Sovietization. A synthesis occurs between a narrower concept of the homeland, based upon residence or ethnic identity, and a broader definition that embraces the entire Soviet Union, based itself upon a moral-political criterion that can unite all the different people under the rule of socialism in the USSR. Particularly for the eponymous ethnic groups, a narrower conception of homeland, encompassing each individual union republic, still persists. This is illustrated in the conception of homeland used in lyric poetry of Latvia that personifies and expresses attachment to the nature—the forests and groves—of Latvia. Another related manifestation revealed by Latvian poets utilizes the concept of homeland to refer to their own native town or raion. Riga has been increasingly used in this manner by poets. Perhaps that may be interpreted as a nationalist reaction to the large numbers of Russians, a plurality of Riga's population, residing in the administrative and cultural center of the Latvian SSR.[26] Therefore, the flexible definition of homeland may be employed simultaneously to express Soviet patriotism and love for what is Latvian and the region of Latvia.

An important event reflecting serious concern with the theme of internationalism and friendship among people by the government was the Inter-Republic Theoretical Conference held in May 1975 in Riga. The issue of "The development of spiritual life among Soviet nations under conditions of mature socialism" was thoroughly discussed. Some 600 participants represented the Baltic union republics, along with Moscow, Leningrad, and Volgograd oblasts.[27] Speakers emphasized the idea of fusing every nationality culture into one socialist, Soviet culture and identity. However, discussants at the conference continually stressed a need for exercising tact and sensitivity among the populace upon the part of instructors of internationalist education. Otherwise, recognized principles of mutual respect for nationalities' rights and culture might be violated. Nevertheless, the phenomenon of nationalism itself was condemned and portrayed as a weapon used by various Baltic emigrant organizations to foment dissent and unrest in the Baltic areas among eponymous nationalities.[28] These statements certainly mirror the strong awareness of the participants concerning the current sensitivity of nationalities toward officially approved policies of internationalization and Sovietization that currently exists in the three Baltic union republics.

Latvian Party journals, like the Estonian ones, emphasized industrial accomplishments under Soviet rule and the close industrial and economic relationship of "fraternal republics" of the USSR as factors contributing to further rapprochement of diverse ethnic groups in the USSR and integration of the Latvian economy into the Soviet system.[29] Exchange of theatrical groups between Latvia and other union republics, particularly was stressed in the journals.[30] Implications of a distinct Latvian pride in their industrial and literary achievements and what are termed "Latvian contributions toward the formation of the new Soviet culture" emerge in numerous articles in the Latvian press.

In Lithuania, the same doctrine of Sovietization (espousing the fusion of different nationality cultures to form one common Soviet culture with a socialist internationalist base, through the creation and advocacy of Soviet patriotism and a Soviet identity) is regularly put forth in the official press. However, the process of Sovietization is viewed as a complicated twofold one. There, pride in nationality must include an element of love for the entire Soviet fatherland, and it must exclude any factor of what is termed "bourgeois nationalism." Advancement of Lithuanian industrial production since 1940 is stressed in the press, like Estonia's and Latvia's, in order to indicate benefits derived from participation in the multinational Communist state, the Soviet Union. Closer economic interdependence is perceived as an integrating force that will assist the formation of a Soviet culture with a Soviet identity and the attainment of higher living standards throughout the USSR.[31]

A recent part of the program for cultural rapprochement and exchange was the staging of Days of Culture of the Lithuanian SSR in Soviet Belorussia and Days of Literature and Art of Lithuania in the Russian SFSR in 1974. In 1974, a Festival of Dramaturgy of the Peoples of the USSR was staged in Kaunas. Also, theatrical groups from Moscow, Baku, and Krasnodar visited Vilnius, while the Russian Theatrical Drama Group of Vilnius visited Krasnodar and Baku, and another theatrical troupe from Panevėžys, in Lithuania, toured Moscow.[32] Interconnecting links and economic and cultural progress of the different union republics receive special attention in party journals in Lithuania. For example, at the time of the fiftieth anniversary of the establishment of many of the administrative nationality units of Soviet Central Asia, special articles reported upon "progress" under Soviet rule. An article appeared in the October 1974 Kommunist (Vilnius) describing achievements of the Turkmen SSR under Soviet rule and as a constituent part of the USSR. In December, a similar article described 50 years of "success" in Tajikistan.[33] In January 1975, economic progress in Uzbekistan was featured in Kommunist (Vilnius) and in February 1975's issue, economic and cultural merits of Kirgizistan were highlighted.[34] Special attention is focused upon friendly socialist competition with the Belorussian SSR, which is seen as more of a rival to Lithuania than Latvia or Estonia in the industrial sphere. This may be the case, because both Lithuania and Belorussia have experienced heavy industrial investment, expansion, and urbanization within the last 15 years. Competitions and cooperation in educational and cultural fields are also arranged for the working people of these two union republics.[35] In 1974, a special friendship pact was enacted between Klaipėda, Lithuania, and Mogilev, Belorussia, for social and cultural exchanges and further expansion of socialist-style competition between residents of the two cities. Such agreements have existed among cities in the three Baltic union republics for several years. There is a long-standing arrangement between the port cities of Klaipėda in Lithuania and Liepaja in Latvia. The institutional administrative structure for these programs of cultural exchange permeates the cultural institutions and departments on the local level, as it does in Estonia. The First Vocational Technical College of Klaipėda is said to maintain constant connections with the colleges of 18 other Soviet union and autonomous republics and oblasts in order to enrich and diversify the cultural and vocational life and curriculum of the institution.[36] Academic cooperation exists on the international level for the creation of "friendship of peoples" among socialist nations. Vilnius's higher educational institutions maintain close relations with several universities and institutes located in Poland and the German Democratic Republic. Once again, selective application of policies regarding cultural exchanges and the principle of "friendship of people" emerges, for particular emphasis seems to be placed in Lithuania upon close cooperation in cultural and economic matters with Poland and the German Democratic Republic, areas historically and culturally connected with Lithuania.[37]

Just as in the other two Baltic union republics, special mention is made in Lithuanian journals concerning the publication and exchange of literature and its translation into the languages of the USSR. Officials say that this will help the synthesis of the multi-ethnic Soviet socialist culture. Once again, the press reviewed displays a certain pride in the quantity and quality of Lithuanian literature published during the years of Soviet rule. It is claimed that prior to the socialist takeover in 1940, only 3 million copies of books were published annually in Lithuania but now some 16 million book and brochure copies are being printed yearly.[38] The editions were small in quantity in independent Lithuania. But, if the number of book titles published yearly is considered, the discrepancy between the periods before and after 1940 is not so large as exists in the numbers of copies. The number of titles published between 1919-39 in Lithuania reached 16,721, with the number of different books being published after 1925 averaging 800 to 900 annually. The number of book titles issued by the main publishing houses in Lithuania in 1938 totaled 1,171. In 1973, the total number of titles published for a population 21 percent higher (January 1939, 2,575,000 people; October 1939, with inclusion of Vilnius area and loss of Klaipėda, 3,025,000; January 1970, 3,128,200) equaled 1,649.[39] Along with this pride expressed in the Lithuanian press, somewhat perfunctorily and rhetorically, the Russians and their culture are thanked for what is called by Lithuanian authorities the great Russian contribution to the formation of a common Soviet socialist culture and the enrichment of culture in the Lithuanian SSR.[40]

Judging from statements frequently expressed in journals surveyed, union republic leaders are responding to pressures and fears about erosion and dilution of the nationalities' culture by hinting that the creation of a new Soviet culture does not necessarily doom the development and flourishing of nationalities' forms of culture. The issue of Sovietization and the status of a nationality's culture must be, therefore, an important, politically sensitive issue. Evincing awareness about nationality sensitivities, the press continually stresses the contributions made by the respective nationalities to the general Soviet culture and economy. The holidays and institutional forms, while promoting cultural interaction between ethnic groups and generating what is termed "an internationalist spirit," do give opportunities for contacts with ethnic kindred. Great ambiguity is evident also in the leaders' discussion in the press concerning the formation of the future international socialist culture. Such ambiguity may be interpreted in several ways: it may obscure a drive for eventual denationalization, even Russification, or the vagueness, combined with assertions regarding the eponymous nationalities' achievements and contributions and selective practice of "friendship of peoples," may signify that the culture of each eponymous nationality will continue to preserve its own identity and endure under Soviet conditions, while continuing to develop within certain ideologically acceptable limits. The eponymous elites may act as powerbrokers in this respect by twisting the interpretation and implementation of Sovietization to their own ends. Simultaneously, with the development of each eponymous culture, the ideological doctrine of a common Soviet culture may be utilized as a platitude to gloss over the great differences in the achievements of economic status and cultural development obvious among the many nationalities of the USSR.

The overall impact of the Sovietization doctrine upon the many nationality support factors seems to vary among the three Baltic union republics; however, there are some similarities in its effect. One group support factor that may be compared among the eponymous nationalities is the status of the eponymous language, its retention and use by the nationalities and the extent of publishing in the nationality language of each eponymous group in its own union republic. However, loss of linguistic unity and identification does not always signify a corresponding reduction in the group's vitality and in other support factors and nationality identity. Jews in the USSR provide one example. Nevertheless, a high degree of linguistic retention and self-identification, combined with great amounts of publishing in the eponymous language, can be considered a favorable sign of a nationality's vitality in most instances. This is especially true in respect to the Latvians and Estonians, because neither nationality possesses a tradition of having been an important imperial power in medieval Europe. Lithuanians have this historical tradition. It gives them access to another important nationality support factor, one that might continue to function effectively in the nationality consciousness even if the group should lose linguistic distinctiveness. However, an important indicator for the impact of Sovietization is supplied by the number of members of an eponymous nationality recorded in the census who identify the Russian language as their native tongue. The Russian language has been regarded in Soviet writings as the most important language used among the ethnic groups of the USSR for the purpose of communication and formation of the single new Soviet culture. Identification with the Russian language also implies a certain susceptibility to further influences and penetration by cultural and ethnic Russification beyond the Sovietizing influences. Table 6.1 shows the degree of linguistic Russification (adoption of Russian as one's native tongue by a person identifying

TABLE 6.1

Linguistic Russification among Eponymous Nationalities of the Soviet West within Their Respective Union Republics, 1970
(percent)

Nationality in Its Own Republic	Command of Russian				
				Within Urban Areas	
	Urban	Linguistic Russification	Fluent Command of Russian	Linguistic Russification	Fluent Command of Russian
Belorussians	37.1	9.84	52.3	24.5	55.9
Estonians	54.7	.75	27.5	1.2	36.5
Latvians	51.7	1.84	45.3	2.5	52.4
Luthuanians	45.9	.13	34.8	0.3	51.1
Moldavians	17.2	2.00	33.9	9.4	62.5
Ukrainians	45.8	8.55	35.8	17.1	48.5

City or Oblast, Urban Region	Urban Ethnic Mixture		
	Eponymous Nationality	Russians	Eponymous Nationality, Linguistic Russification
Kiev	64.76	22.89	22.57
Kishinev	37.18	30.67	11.39
Minsk	65.60	23.36	35.41
Riga	40.87	42.75	3.08
Tallinn	55.67	35.04	1.33
Vilnius	42.77	24.46	1.16
Donetsk Oblast	49.98	43.94	34.54
Grodny Oblast	56.92	19.54	18.50
Kharkov Oblast	59.78	34.15	24.27
Lvov Oblast	76.52	16.81	3.47

Source: Itogi vsesoiuznoi perepisi naseleniia 1970 goda. (Moscow: Statistika, 1973), 4: 152–91, 192–202, 273–75, 276–79, 280–83, 317–20.

himself as a non-Russian) prevalent among the Baltic nationalities and other eponymous nationalities of the Soviet West within their own union republics. Data in Table 6.1 tend to demonstrate that the eponymous Baltic nationalities retain self-identification with their own native eponymous language more than their eponymous neighbors in the USSR in similar modernized urban settings with approximately the same mixtures between the eponymous nationality and Russians. This also applies to cities and urban areas like Lvov and Kishinev, which have been under Soviet control only since World War II. The amount of linguistic Russification occurring among the Baltic nationalities within the process of Sovietization has been quite minimal. The three largest Baltic nationalities also tend to experience fewer losses in their ethnic groups from mixed marriages.[41] Another study has shown that among enrollees in Russian language schools, the number of students of Latvian descent who employ Russian at home reaches only 14.5 percent, whereas the general rate for Latvian families utilizing Russian at home is but 7.4 percent.[42] These facts indicate that one nationality support factor, native language and its use, continues to be very strong in the Baltic union republics among the eponymous nationalities. Further evidence for the stability of language as a nationality support factor for the Baltic nationalities is supplied by the publishing figures for 1973 given in Table 6.2. These figures show that there has been less penetration by Russian in the union republics' publishing industry for the Baltic eponymous nationalities than among the other eponymous nationalities of the Soviet West.

In Latvia, which sometimes has been depicted by emigrants as facing imminent Russification, the number of titles and copies in the field of belles lettres originating from foreign authors in 1973 exceeded the number of titles and copies of such Russian works issued there. This interaction with foreign literature and its translation may give a sign of cosmopolitan vitality and Westernism in Latvian society. Also, language data and publishing figures regularly reaffirm that Latvian is not now succumbing to influences of Russification.[43]

A unique feature of Baltic education that tends to support the vitality of Baltic nationalities is the 11-year school course (longer than regular schooling), which allows for supplementary study of Russian, as well as the nationality language.[44] Current data for the language of instruction used in the Lithuanian SSR's schools are given in Table 6.3. Educational data suggest that conditions leading to the adoption of Russian as the native tongue are being avoided during early childhood years. Schools employing the nationality language in instruction continue to occupy a commanding position in the school system. This practice militates against any real or imagined "wave" of linguistic and cultural Russification or denational-

TABLE 6.2

Book and Brochure Publishing in Union Republics of the Soviet West, 1973

	Belo-russia	Estonia	Latvia	Lithuania	Moldavia	Ukraine
Eponymous nationality of total population[a]	81.0	68.2	56.8	80.1	65.4	74.9
Total number titles of brochures and books	2,636	1,966	2,111	1,649	1,627	7,686
Copies[b]	30,248	13,230	14,200	16,618	12,710	140,406
In eponymous language						
Titles of books and brochures						
Number	463	1,375	1,068	1,267	548	2,981
Percent	18	70	51	77	34	39
Copies[b]						
Number	11,507	10,724	11,678	14,552	7,263	103,050
Percent	38	81	82	88	57	73
In Russian language						
Titles of books and brochures						
Number	2,137	477	979	295	1,054	4,408
Percent	81	24	46	18	65	57
Copies[b]						
Number	18,332	1,779	2,163	1,554	5,055	32,728
Percent	61	13	15	9	40	23

[a]1970.
[b]Thousands.
Source: Pechat' SSSR v 1973 godu (Moscow: Statistika, 1974), pp. 94-96.

ization. Also, Table 6.3 reflects the special treatment accorded a noneponym, the Poles, in Lithuania. In the Baltic area, no other noneponymous ethnic group, except the Russian, is provided with schools that employ an noneponymous language as the language of instruction. Such arrangements enhance the special relationship between Lithuania and Poland, and they may contribute to the feeling of solidarity already derived from a common historical and cultural heritage that has many elements antithetical to Russification.

Institutions of higher learning regularly utilize the nationality languages in the Baltic union republics. For subjects in the humanities, classes are conducted in Latvian, Lithuanian, or Estonian in the respective union republic, and Russian may be employed in another section for the particular subject. At Latvia State University, no courses are taught solely in Russian, and courses such as prehistory, library service, philosophy, geography, and biology are taught only in Latvian. However, at some technical institutes in the Baltic area,

TABLE 6.3

Language of Instruction in Primary and Secondary Schools, Lithuanian SSR, 1967-69 (in thousands)

Language of Instruction	Number of Students in Primary and Secondary Schools 1967-68	1968-69
Lithuanian	424	433
Russian	62	65
Polish	22	20

Source: Ekonomika i kultura Litovskoi SSR v 1968 godu (Vilnius: n.p., n.d.), p. 336, reported in Baltic Events 39, no. 4 (August 1973), p. 3.

subjects can be taught only in Russian. Nevertheless, comparatively, the higher educational establishments seem to be in a stronger position for opposing Russification than the higher educational establishments of several other union republics in the Soviet West.[45]

Other cultural supports for the eponymous Baltic nationalities have been receiving a renewed and increasing emphasis during the past few years, especially the uses of folklore and its study by young Baltic intellectuals. At the Institute of Lithuanian Language and Literature in Vilnius, Lithuanian folklore has been systematically classified and published. Its archives are the largest on the subject of folklore in the USSR, containing over 800,000 folklore items. Several recent publications about folklore are Tautosakos savitumas ir verte [The values and originality of folklore], by D. Sauka, and Lietuvos tautosakos stilius ir žanrai [Genres of Lithuanian folklore], by A. Jonynas et al. Poets like Judita Vaičiūnaitė, Janina Degutytė, and Marcelius Martinaitis often utilize folkloric themes and devices in their compositions. Such a concentration upon the traditional has drawn repeated criticism from the more ideological writers. This interest in ethnic folklore persists and is becoming contagious among the new writers of the Baltic region who have matured during the period of Soviet rule.[46] Great interest in folklore and dainas (folksongs) has been manifested by the contemporary Latvian poets Imants Auzinš and Janis Peters.[47] Themes from Baltic folklore have appeared in the dramatic works by Latvian playwrights, Paul Putninš, Peteris Petersons, and Gunars Pride.[48] Thus, it does not seem that overwhelming interest in new Soviet customs and internationalist themes is replacing the traditional supports. Over 10 percent of the population of both Lithuania and Estonia currently participate in amateur groups and choirs that tend to preserve the nationality culture among the populace at the grass roots level.[49] Because many amateur troups are choral societies, folk song festivals are particularly popular. They often reflect pride in the nationality heritage. By popular demand, the Latvian Song Festival Centennial, held in Riga in 1973, ended not with the Soviet "Hymn of the Fatherland" but rather an unscheduled rendition of several traditional Latvian folksongs. Throughout the festival, customary Latvian songs tended to receive a more enthusiastic response than those selections that expressed Soviet internationalist themes.[50] This occurrence again suggests some degree of ineffectiveness in governmental efforts to instill a Soviet identity and internationalist spirit among the eponymous nationalities of the Baltic region.

Despite this relatively high level of Baltic cultural vitality, cultural and political dissent has mushroomed in the three union republics. Particular emphasis has been placed by Baltic dissenters upon the possibility of denationalization via Russification because of the increasing proportion of Russians settling in the three union republics. This is heavily stressed by the Estonian Democratic Movement and Estonian National Front, two underground organizations in Estonia that jointly publish a samizdat journal, Estonian Democrat, in their petition to the United Nations (dated October 24, 1972, but received in the West in 1974). This same idea is emphasized by Latvian and Estonian democrats forming another dissident group in their appeal concerning the Helsinki Conference held in 1975. Cultural and linguistic Russification are depicted as potential villains that will rob the nationalities of their identities and heritage within a short period.[51] The "Letter of Seventeen Latvian Communists" of 1972 further demonstrates how much members of the political elite are concerned about "threatening denationalization."[52] It is alleged by the 17 Latvian Communists that there is no effective leadership countering the forces and drift toward eventual cultural and linguistic Russification, occasioned by the in-migration of many Russians and other Slavs to Latvia. Nevertheless, the three eponymous nationalities appear very strong, when compared with the other eponymous nationalities of the Soviet West, in their respective nationality support systems. The Baltic groups do not seem to show signs of severe deterioration nor do they manifest tendencies toward becoming more culturally and linguistically Russified.

A weakness frequently cited in the samizdat literature is the small population of each Baltic nationality; however, these minipopulations, with their high cultural attainment and strong status of the various nationality support factors, tend to make the cultural elites somewhat more alert than usual to any slight deviation or shift in their high level of nationality supports. Perhaps the smaller populations may, in fact, be more conscious generally of the potential dangers than much larger populations, such as the Ukrainian, who have been experiencing considerable linguistic and cultural Russification in many institutions in the Ukrainian SSR.

It appears that in the Baltic cultural and nationalistic dissent, the future possibility of Russification has been telescoped into the immediate present in order to guard each nationality's interests. Evidence for this emerges in behavior of Lithuanian dissenters (Lithuania has the smallest proportion of Russians in the union republic's population, and its eponymous ethnic group has the highest birth rate among the three eponymous nationalities of the Baltic region). They increasingly anticipate the demise of their nationality as a result of losing its language and culture to the influences of Russification. These assertions appeared in the declaration of the Lithuanian National People's Front and the defense speech of Simas Kudirka, tried May 18-19, 1971, for attempting to defect to the United States on November 27, 1970. Similar viewpoints may be inferred from statements and reports in the _Chronicle of the Catholic Church in Lithuania_, which appeared as an underground journal in 1972 in Lithuania. Other statements regarding denationalization are contained in _Aušra_, another samizdat journal in Lithuania, which first surfaced in October 1975, and whose third issue reached the West in December 1976. Writers in _Aušra_ and _Chronicle of the Catholic Church in Lithuania_ have depicted the Catholic church as an important guardian of Lithuanian culture and nationality identity.[53] _Aušra_, by its title and designated issues, numbers 1 (40)(sic.) and 2 (42), links itself to the nationalistic Lithuanian monthly _Aušra_, which originated from Lithuania Minor in East Prussia (in 1883-86) and opposed Czarist efforts to Russify and denationalize Lithuanians in the nineteenth century. After the 40 issues of _Aušra_ in Czarist times, the new _Aušra_ still views its mission in the same manner: to arouse Lithuanian national consciousness and oppose all forms of denationalization. Its editors, for example, equate the current Soviet attack upon the Catholic Church in Lithuania to similar efforts by the former Russian government, which earlier sought to undermine Catholicism and introduce Russian Orthodoxy into Lithuania openly as a means of promoting Russification.[54]

Further manifestation of cultural dissent not directly connected with religious protests, include petitions concerning the Russification of Lithuanians residing in Belorussia; a protest statement by the dramatist Jonas Jurašas, and his subsequent emigration; and an appeal by Lithuanian artists in August 1972 about the duty for Soviet authorities to preserve better the works of Mikalojus Čiurlionis (the great Lithuanian abstract painter, 1876-1911).[55] The circulation of such statements and petitions creates an atmosphere of rising demands for more attention to the culture of each nationality. Any encroachment by Russian culture, whether actually beneficial or not, may be regarded by dissidents as a potential threat. Paradoxically, this comes not from a weakening cultural position. Rather, such a sustained nationality protest originates from a strong, secured system of nationality supports. Along with the cultural dissent, there has been greater public expression of political dissent and dissatisfaction with Soviet rule. In the city of Kaunas, a major demonstration of students and riot occurred in May 1972, following the funeral of Romas Kalanta on May 18, 1972, who had committed self-immolation in a protest against Soviet rule and restrictions upon religious freedom. On May 18, 1972, V. Stonis in Varena, and, on June 3, 1972, K. Andriuškevičius in Šiauliai, both committed self-immolation as acts of protest against Soviet rule. This was followed by serious student disturbances in Vilnius in June 1972 protesting Soviet rule. Reportedly, Soviet authorities have made special efforts to abort any staged gatherings commemorating these protests and riots.[56] Elsewhere in the Baltics, the same Latvian and Estonian samizdat petitions to the United Nations that decry the prospect of Russification ask for political independence or autonomy.[57]

Thus, measures taken to advance Sovietization and inculcate a firmer spirit of internationalism among the Baltic nationalities within the last few years have elicited a bitter reaction. This is not due to actual significant erosion of nationality supports or identity entirely. Instead, it results from the hypersensitivity of culturally advanced people who consciously desire to rally support in order to block any projected penetration by Russification and denationalization in the long run. Some eponymous nationalities of the Soviet West seem to lack the degree of group vitality exhibited by the Baltic nationalities. Only the Ukrainians among the non-Baltic eponymous nationalities of the Soviet West evidently exhibit a sustained nationality dissent against efforts for Russification and denationalization. Baltic dissatisfaction, expressed in the samizdat, tends to support the nationality identity in itself, because the circulation of such reports may at least make more members of the eponymous groups conscious of those aspects of Sovietization that might threaten the nationalities' existence. However, the real condition of nationality supports does not match the disproportional Baltic share of nationality dissent in the USSR against Sovietization and possible denationalization. The weight of evidence suggests that this high level of dissatisfaction actually emerges from favorable socioeconomic and cultural conditions among Baltic nationalities. Intense dissatisfaction stems from the extreme sensitivity of these nationalities, owing in good part to their more advanced economic and cultural levels and nationality support systems, toward any threat to nationality support factors or identities. Dissent, plus an ambiguous interpretation of Sovietization by Party leaders in journals surveyed and the selective use of cultural exchanges, reveals the pattern. They demonstrate that Sovietization and its institutions have not appreciably lessened the intensity of nationality identity among the eponymous nationalities of the Baltic area. In fact, evidence indicates that the measures used to promote Sovietization have elicited a response heightening the very nationality consciousness that it is the aim of Sovietization to neutralize by internationalist indoctrination and rapprochement between the approved cultures of different ethnic groups.

SOVIETIZATION AND BALTIC RELIGIOUS IDENTITY*

Religion, now largely an aspect of culture disapproved by Soviet authorities, historically played the most significant role in the crystallization of nationality identity and consciousness in nineteenth-century Lithuania.[58] Although the Protestant Herrnhut movement, in the eighteenth and nineteenth centuries, was associated especially with the peasantry of Estonia, the Lutheran church establishments tended to be closely identified with the dominant German nobility.[59] Nevertheless, Soviet ideologists regard all religions and religious institutions as key forces in the generation of "undesired nationalism" and ethnic animosity. This also has political implications, for the several religions of the Baltic region, except Russian Orthodoxy, seem to focus nationalist aspirations and identification away from the Russian core (the traditional controlling ethnic group) of the Soviet Union.[60]

Religious congregations registered by the state in Estonia on January 1, 1969, totaled 366: 144 were Lutheran, with 15 branch congregations; 87 were Orthodox; 82 were Baptist; 13 were Adventist; 14 were Methodist; 11 were Old Believer congregations, and two were Roman Catholic parishes. The number of believers in Estonia at that time was estimated to be 450,000. Reportedly, around 125 pastors in 1969 served Lutheran congregations, which claimed a total membership of 300,000 in 1972. The Russian Orthodox believers of Estonia in 1968 had only 55 priests and 6 deacons, who served the 98 churches then existing. However, the Russian Orthodox church in Estonia does

---

*I wish to thank Walter Jaskievicz for his advice and assistance in verifying Lithuanian materials. Thanks also to Peteris Norvilis and the Reverend Casimir Pugevičius, and the Office of Lithuanian Catholic Religious Aid, Maspeth, L.I., N.Y., for providing certain materials used in the following sections of this chapter.

occupy a favored position in some respects. It is served by an Orthodox convent in Pohtitsa. In Lithuania, by contrast, convents have been banned, and former Catholic nuns are persecuted regularly in administrative actions and job discrimination.[61]

The impact of antireligious campaigns and persecution, along with some territorial changes, may be in part evidenced by the fact that prior to World War II, there had been 157 Orthodox and 185 Lutheran congregations in Estonia. Reportedly, 70 Lutheran pastors, from among the 209 serving in 1939, emigrated from Estonia in 1944. About 60 were deported (1940-45).[62] In 1972, 40 theological students preparing to be pastors were said to be enrolled in courses in the Lutheran academy in Tallinn. Many, in contrast to decades earlier, are young persons. Five Estonian Lutheran pastors in 1972 served German-speaking congregations, notwithstanding the deportations of Baltic Germans carried out after World War II.[63] Unique in the religious situation of Estonia is the fact that the only Methodist churches active in the USSR are found there. This multiplicity of active religious denominations in some ways reflects Estonia's resemblance to Western rather than Eastern Europe. Participation in religious ceremonies has reportedly drastically declined since the late 1950s. According to one Soviet source, in 1969, 11.8 percent of newborn babies were baptized, 2.5 percent of all marriages, and 45.5 percent of funerals were held in church. Archbishop Tooming disclosed that, in 1969, there were 2,000 Lutheran confirmations. The Soviet government has initiated civil ceremonies corresponding to religious ones of the Lutheran church in order to attract youths away from such ceremonies as confirmation. However, the Soviet funeral service has not become very popular, mainly because at the time of bereavement, it does not offer the living the consolation that their deceased relative has an eternal life. Moreover, in 1972, dignitaries of the Lutheran World Federation on an official visit to Lutheran churches in the Baltic region reported slight increases in confirmations, religious weddings, and baptisms within the past few years.[64]

Despite the considerable decline in reported church membership, in religious practices, and numbers of congregations (see Table 6.4) since the Soviet takeover, the high number of believers (450,000) still disturbs the Communist Party of Estonia very much.

The Soviet government continually publishes material in great quantity espousing atheism. In Tallinn, during 1974-75, the Party organization recommended that more effective atheistic education and propaganda be conducted among students, workers at the factories and in their residence, and especially among women (women constitute a large proportion of Estonian believers). More attention was to be devoted to the inculcation of Soviet rites, whose practice and

TABLE 6.4

Lutheran Church in Estonia and Latvia Prior to Soviet Annexation

	Estonia	Latvia
Congregations	185	280
Pastors	191	270
Membership	874,026[a]	1,200,000[b]

[a]1934.

[b]1935.

Sources: Leonas Cuibe, The Lutheran Church of Latvia in Chains (Stockholm: Vasteras, 1963), p. 28; Vello Salo, "The Party and the Church," Tõnu Parming and Elmar Järvesoo, eds., A Case Study of a Soviet Republic: The Estonian SSR: A Study in Depth of a Soviet Republic (Boulder, Colo.: Westview Press, forthcoming).

observance had considerably lapsed since the late 1960s.[65] During the 1974-75 period in Tartu, among school children, a more intensive atheist indoctrination program was initiated. In April 1975, in Tartu, the Party's Commission on Atheism conducted a conference on the topic "Religion in the Service of Anticommunism."[66] According to the press, Lutheranism, once detached, is becoming more involved in contemporary social problems as a means of attracting younger supporters and surviving under the conditions of Soviet society. In the Soviet Estonian press, the final victory of Soviet socialism over religion is still expected to be a long and difficult process.[67] In Estonia, a ban remained in effect from 1944 to 1973 against allowing Lutherans to publish any religious material. The sole publication authorized since the Twentieth CPSU Congress (1956) during this ban had been the Eesti Evangeeliumi Luteriusu aastarammat (Yearbook of the Evangelical Lutheran church). The book was not really made available until 1967 within Estonia.

In the period 1954-71, 91 officially sanctioned atheist publications (332,315 copies) appeared in Estonia. However, Baptists, Methodists, and Lutherans in Estonia, with a promise of future publication, in the early 1970s initiated a project for preparing a new Estonian translation of the Bible.[68] The persistent survival of organized religious institutions in Estonia under these adverse conditions surely testifies to a failure to achieve desired results on the part of the government's well-organized atheistic campaign.

Two protest memoranda released by the clandestine Estonian National Front give little emphasis to religious persecution.[69] This contrasts sharply with the situation existing in much Lithuanian samizdat.[70] In the "Joint Memorandum of Baltic Democrats to the Participants of the Helsinki Conference," circulated in 1975, the need for general religious freedom and freedom of conscious is stressed. However, no historical connection is made between the suppression of religion and attempts by central authorities to achieve denationalization or Russification of Estonians and Latvians by undermining and suppressing a religious institution considered symbolic of the cultural heritage of the two nationalities. In this way, the "Joint Memorandum of Baltic Democrats" (actively opposing denationalization) differs from numerous Lithuanian protest documents and samizdat publication emerging in the 1970s.[71] This disparity suggests that in the 1970s, religion does not have such a high degree of importance in the synthesis of nationality dissatisfaction in Estonia as it does elsewhere in the Baltic area. However, the potentiality exists. Since World War II, the Lutheran church in Estonia has become more Estonian in its ethnic composition, with the deportation of Baltic Germans, and maintains links through the Lutheran World Federation with Lutheran Scandinavia, the German Democratic Republic, and countries of the West. Finland supplies an important model for Estonia. Lutheranism, a religion distinct from Russian Orthodoxy, could logically become a rallying point for anti-Russifiers. The Baptist faith and church may not necessarily serve as a nationality focus, because prominent Soviet sociologists, experts on religion in the USSR, and Western scholars have judged the proliferation of the Baptist faith in the USSR within recent years to be a transnationality phenomenon.[72]

After much destruction during World War II and numerous church closings by the Soviet government, Latvia's Lutheran church has declined considerably in its membership and institutional structure. (See Table 6.4.) The number of pastors active in 1972, reportedly, at the time of a visit of a delegation from the Lutheran World Federation had dwindled to approximately 100, serving 350,000 members. There were 39 student candidates in the theological academy at Riga in 1972 (three candidates were from the Lutheran church in Lithuania).[73] Much of the decline just at the end of World War II in number of pastors had been due to their emigration in 1944. At that time, it is said that 130 from among 224 Lutheran pastors had emigrated from Latvia. About 20, also, were deported or jailed at about that time.[74] According to Latvian Archbishop Lusis of Toronto, there were 70 active Lutheran churches in 1974 in Latvia, with about 300,000 members. This represents approximately a 36 percent decline in churches within the past decade.[75] Lutherans in Latvia are allowed only to issue church calendars, although in 1969, Latvian Catholics were granted permission to publish a prayer book (Catholics and Lutherans constituted, respectively, 24.5 percent and 56 percent of the prewar World War II population).[76] However, the Lutheran Church calendar has maintained its publication rate and has significantly increased each edition's quantity since the era of CPSU Secretary Khrushchev's antireligious campaigns in the late 1950s and despite the reported decline in numbers of churches and congregations within the past decade. Data in Table 6.5 show that this compares favorably to the publication record of Old Believers in Latvia. It has also been reported that participation in religious ceremonies has increased in Latvia within the past few years.[77]

Religious dissent exists in Latvia. Recently, illegal publishing houses have been particularly active. On October 24, 1974, in the Cesis District, Latvian SSR, several young Baptists were seized and charged with the illegal printing of religious books. The illegal publishing house, Khristianin, had operated on a relatively large scale, producing some 15,000 completed copies of The New Testament. This activity seems to be linked with the general Baptist movement in the USSR, not to any purely ethnic Latvian religious movement. In fact, most are of Slavic origin. (See Table 6.6.) The trial in Cesis was held March 12-14, 1975. Although the men arrested, V. I. Pidchenko, V. A. Pikalov, and Y. Gauer, received sentences of four years each, the other five, all women, were released, after serving eight months of their sentences, in observance of International Women's Year. This relative leniency contrasted with the harsh treatment generally accorded religious dissenters in Lithuania in

TABLE 6.5

Religious Publications in Latvia—Religious Calendars, 1958, 1972, and 1973

Calendars	Lutheran (in Latvian)	Old Believer (in Russian)
1958		
Copies	7,000	4,000
Pages	49	104
1972		
Copies	13,000	2,200
Pages	146	81
1973		
Copies	15,000	2,200
Pages	174	80

Source: Latvia P. S. R. Preses Hronika, reported in Baltic Events 47, no. 6 (December 1974), p. 3.

TABLE 6.6

Persons Arrested in Latvia on October 24, 1974, for Involvement with The Khristian Printing Agency: Birthdate, Residence, and Sentence[a]

Name	Year Born	Residence	Sentence
Ekaterina Gritsenko	1943	Kiev Oblast	3 years
E. Gauer	n.a.[b]	Cesis District Latvia	4 years
Ida Korotun	1938	Voroshilov	3 years
Tatiana Kozhemakina	1937	Zhdanov	3 years
Nadezha Lvova	1946	Krasnodar Kray	2½ years
Vitalii Pidchenko	1941	Kharkov	4 years
Viktor Pikalov	1950	Fergana	4 years
Zinaida Tarasova	1942	Kursk Oblast	2½ years

[a]Trial: March 12-14, 1975.
[b]Not available.
Source: "This Is How It Happened," Bulletin of the Council of ECB Prisoners' Relatives, no. 18 (1974), reported in Religion in Communist Dominated Areas 14, nos. 1-3 (January-March 1975): 43-45; "Printers of the Gospels Arrested," Religion in Communist Dominated Areas 14, Nos. 4-6 (April-June 1975): 74-75.

the 1974-75 period (see Table 6.7).[78] In 1970, a Latvian Adventist was tried for operating an illegal press, and recently (in May 1974) two apparently pious Latvians, Olafs and Pavils Bruvers, were arrested for circulating a public opinion questionnaire whose results and format were deemed hostile to Soviet authorities.[79] Further indication of an escalation in religious-oriented dissent, with possible ground for additional expansion, is the appearance, in spring 1976, of a petition by Catholics in Daugavpils, Latvia, protesting religious persecution and a proposal to shut the Catholic church in Daugavpils. This renewal of dissent may be a spinoff from the sustained religious dissent among Lithuanian Catholics since the early 1970s.[80] Although religious dissent reflected in illegal publishing and petitions seems to be expanding in Latvia within recent years, religious dissent for the present seems not to be related directly to Latvian nationality dissatisfaction. In general, Latvian dissident documents that express concern about possible threats to nationality survival give little emphasis to religious persecution as a factor in this perceived denationalizing process.[81]

TABLE 6.7

Persons Arrested in Lithuania for Religious Dissent, Involving Distribution and Illegal Manufacture of *Chronicle of the Catholic Church in Lithuania* and Other Religious Material, Case 345, December 2-23, 1974

Name	Born	Sentence
P. Plumpa	1939	8 years hard labor
P. Petronis	1911	4 years hard labor
J. Strašaitis	1921	1 year confinement
A. Patribavičius	1935	13 months confinement
V. Jaugelis	1948	2 years confinement

Sources: *Lietuvos Kataliku̧ Bažnyčios Kronika 2* (Chicago: L. K. Religinės Šalpos Rėmėjai, 1975), no. 13, pp. 303-04; *No Greater Love: The Trial of a Christian in Soviet Occupied Lithuania* (Brooklyn, N.Y.: Lithuanian R.C. Priests' League of America, 1975), pp. 2-16; "Juozo Gražo ir Kitu Teismas, Iš Lietuvos Kataliku̧ Bažnyčios Kronikos Nr 16," *Darbininkas* 60, no. 35 (August 29, 1975): 1.

Nevertheless, Communist Party authorities in Latvia still regard the existence of the Lutheran church and religion (a competing ideology) in Latvia as a danger to Soviet society. In October 1972, the Central Committee of the Communist Party of Latvia called for perfection and improvement of atheistic education through utilizing more effective means of indoctrination and training at factories, offices, residences, and schools. A network for spreading atheist propaganda is based upon the Znanie Society of Latvia, whose members, in 1974, delivered 7,200 lectures. There are 2,800 atheist propagandists who work in the sovkhozes and kolkhozes and at plants and construction sites. In 1974, 112 persons graduated from the two-year school of Latvia's Znanie Society. There were, in 1975, 3,500 students enrolled in the 36 "universities" of scientific atheism throughout the union republic. In the period 1971-75, 22 atheist books in 238,000 copies were published in Latvia.[82] This great activity directed against religion has not yet accomplished its ultimate aims. The persistence of the Lutheran religion in Latvia, although it has not succeeded in identifying itself with Latvian nationality identity to the same extent as Roman Catholicism with Lithuanian nationality identity and heritage, testifies further to the partial inefficacy of the sustained antireligious campaign conducted for 35 years by the Soviet government. Such failure in this field also mirrors a certain lack of success by Soviet officials to impress the Soviet identity and to neutralize nationality self-consciousness and distinctiveness among the people of the USSR. Individuality seems to be the key element that denies success to Soviet propaganda efforts. Religious belief apparently offers a philosophical individuality with immortality, whereas nationality distinctiveness and strong nationality supports provide an ethnic and cultural individuality. When both are interwoven, the two provide formidable nationality support factors.

The leaders of Lithuania's major religion, Roman Catholicism, were deeply associated with the renaissance of Lithuania in the nineteenth century.[83] This point has been conceded by the Soviet press.[84] Consequently, Roman Catholicism has become closely identified with Lithuanian nationality identity and heritage since the Czarist period.[85]

The current situation of the Catholic church in Lithuania is represented statistically in Table 6.8. In 1940, in Lithuania, there were 1,450 priests; 4 seminaries, with 425 seminarians; 380 monks; 950 nuns; 717 churches; and 320 chapels.[86] The impact of the government's antireligious measures, an aspect of the official doctrine and policies espousing Sovietization and "ideological modernization," is revealed by the fact that since 1945, only two churches have been built, and upon completion, one was taken over by the government in Klaipėda.[87] Since the Soviet occupation in Vilnius alone, 23 Catholic churches and all the chapels except one have been closed (they were converted into different state buildings). Reportedly, no Orthodox churches were so closed in Vilnius or Kaunas.[88]

In Soviet publications, it has been asserted that many Catholic priests participated in the anti-Soviet guerrilla movement.[89] Numerous clergy were arrested (150, it is said, in 1940-41), executed, or deported to Siberia (the number of those deported has been given as at least 180 by two sources and over 300 by another in post-World War II years). During the postwar period, reportedly 257 priests and 3 bishops became refugees in the West. The number of clergy permitted to function actively in 1948 sank to about 400, with 1 bishop, according to one underground source.[90] However, with de-Stalinization, the number of priests allowed to serve congregations increased after 130 returned from exile. Despite a 48 percent reduction in clergy and the closing of all monasteries and convents, compared to 1940, the 1975 figure of 759 Catholic priests and 628 church buildings dwarfs the institutional network of the Lutheran church in Lithuania—the second largest church in Lithuania, with about 20,000 members in 1972 and, it is said, in 1955, 24 congregations, of which 21 were Lithuanian. However, the majority of Lutherans in pre-World War II had been Germans or Latvians.[91] By comparison, approximately two-thirds of Lithuanians in Lithuania

TABLE 6.8

Persons Arrested in Lithuania for Religious Dissent, Involving Possession or Distribution of Chronicle of the Catholic Church in Lithuania or Illegal Manufacture of Religious Materials, Other Cases, 1974-75

Name	Date of Trial	Sentence
Nijolė Sadūnaitė	June 16-17, 1975	3 years hard labor
Juozas Gražys	March 11-17, 1975	3 years confinement
Boleslavas Kulikauskas	September 18, 1974	3½ years hard labor
Jonas Ivanuskas	September 18, 1974	2 years confinement

Sources: Lietuvos Katalikų Bažnyčios Kronika 2 (Chicago: L. K. Religinės Šalpos Rėmėjai, 1975), no. 13, pp. 303-04; No Greater Love: The Trial of a Christian in Soviet Occupied Lithuania (Brooklyn, N.Y.: Lithuanian R.C. Priests' League of America, 1975), pp. 2-16; "Juozo Gražo ir Kitu Teismas, Iš Lietuvos Katalikų Bažnyčios Kronikos Nr 16," Darbininkas 60, no. 35 (August 29, 1975): 1.

(1.6 million to 1.7 million), reportedly, now maintain connections with the Catholic church.[92] In Lithuania, it was said that the commissioner of the Council for Religious Affairs, Kazimieras Tumenas, in a speech at the Polytechnic Institute of Kaunas, publicly admitted that at least half of the population of Lithuania were practicing Catholics. It is further stated by Lithuanian samizdat sources that official documents show that 45 percent of newborn infants are baptized and 25 percent of marriages are performed in churches, with religious burials constituting 51 percent of all funerals.[93] In this way, dissenters show that the Soviet government perforce must admit that the Catholic church still exerts an influence upon a considerable portion of the population in Lithuania. The strength of the Catholic church in Lithuania shows also in reports that unlike the situation existing in Latvia and Estonia among Lutherans, the sacrament of confirmation continues to be administered to many. In 1974, it is said, confirmation was received by 17,844 persons in the Catholic church in Lithuania, despite the more oppressive policies recently adopted by the government regarding the operations of religious institutions in Lithuania and a campaign against Catholic activists and dissenters.[94]

There is intense dissatisfaction and apprehension among Catholics in Lithuania regarding the future needs of the church. The median age of priests in 1974 was near 60, increasing from 55 in 1971.[95]

Only ten candidates are permitted to register annually by the government in the sole interdiocesan seminary at Kaunas, though there are many more qualified applicants. Total enrollment is limited to 50 students. Relative to the difference in institutional size (numbers of churches) between the Lutheran church in Latvia and Lithuania and the Catholic church in Lithuania, total enrollment allowed in 1972 at the theological academy in Riga for the Lutheran churches of Latvia and Lithuania proportionately is five to six times greater than the numbers allowed to register in the Catholic seminary at Kaunas. Thus, the Soviet government seems to be exerting special pressure upon the Catholic church in Lithuania in order to reduce its institutional structure and clergy.[96] In 1975 approximately one-sixth of the 759 living priests were retired.[97] Clergy and churches are highly concentrated in rural areas. In the five cities of Kaunas, Vilnius, Klaipėda, Šiauliai, and Panevėžys reside about 11 percent of the total number of Catholic priests, while around 26 percent of the Poles and Lithuanians (traditionally Catholic) of the union republic live there.[98] The restrictive admission policy instituted by the Soviet government has effectively reduced the number of clergy, as data in Table 6.10 show, and poses a genuine threat. Despite this loss, the church's influence has continued to remain strong in the 1970s, even generating considerable nationality dissatisfaction. In Panevėžys raion, for example, the party leadership has complained, not only is the celebration of religious holidays among the rural population widely prevalent but the urban populace participates in religious holidays by taking the occasion to visit their rural relatives for family reunions.[99]

Another source of Baltic dissatisfaction arises from the presence of a sizable Polish minority in Lithuania and the existence of strong historical and religious connections between Poland and Lithuania. These induce comparisons between the status of the Catholic church in the two Communist-dominated countries by the Catholic faithful in Lithuania. Large numbers of existing churches, priests and seminaries illustrate the superior position enjoyed by the Catholic church in Poland. It is highly unlikely that the Soviet government would permit anything comparable to the situation existing in Poland. The Catholic church earlier achieved great prestige as a national symbol by opposing Czarist Russification and supporting Lithuanian independence. Soviet authorities, whose central leadership is heavily Slavic, would hardly allow a rejuvenation of the institutional framework of an organization (the Catholic church) that would pose a nationalist threat against Soviet authority. The Catholic church would probably offer an even greater nationalistic counterfocus to the Soviet government than to the Communist Polish government, because Communist leadership in Poland is essentially Polish in the almost ethnically homogeneous state of present-day Poland.

TABLE 6.9

Catholic Churches in Lithuania, 1974

Diocese	With Residing Pastor	With Neighboring Pastor	Total
Kaunas Archdiocese	108	14	122
Vilnius Archdiocese	74	11	85
Kašiadorys	60	5	65
Panevėžys	110	10	120
Telšiai	114	28	142
Vilkaviškis	88	6	94
Total	554	74	628

Sources: C. Pugevičius, ed., World Lithuanian Roman Catholic Directory (Brooklyn, N.Y.: Lithuanian R.C. Priests' League of America, 1975), pp. 55-88, 95-96, 100-03; "Vyskupijų Kunigų Sarašai 1974 IX 1-15;" Mirusieji 1974 m iki gruodzio 14 d.; "Okupuotoj Lietuvoje 1975 Mire Kunigai," Darbininkas (New York) 61, no. 4 (January 23, 1976): 1; also, copies of the original lists of priests of dioceses for 1974 were consulted.

Special treatment afforded Poles in Lithuania by the Soviet government goes so far as to allow most Catholic churches in Vilnius to conduct services in Lithuanian and Polish.[100] Simultaneously, the Soviet government regularly publishes atheistic educational material and propaganda in Polish and Lithuanian editions in the Lithuanian SSR.[101]

Measures designed to accomplish Sovietization and to impede activities of the Catholic church among young people in order to diminish its influence with the population were initiated in the mid-1960s. Article 143 of the Penal Code of Lithuania stipulates that violation of the constitutional separation of church and state is punishable by imprisonment of a term up to one year, or by a fine of 100 rubles.[102] On May 12, 1966, the Presidium of the Lithuanian SSR issued a new instruction regarding application of Article 143 and what constituted a violation. Among the listed violations was "the organization and regular holding of classes for teaching religion to minors in violation of established rules."[103] Another decree of the Presidium of the Lithuanian SSR Supreme Soviet stated that implementation of Article 143 provides administrative penalties of up to 50 rubles for clergy organizing any labor or literary circles for children and adolescents that have no relation to religious duties and rituals. By this decree, the government sought to prohibit any formal or informal activity of cultural or recreational church organizations among children. In 1969, the prohibition was extended to the organizing and holding of excursions with children by priests, and all special retreat services were forbidden.[104] In short, these official actions constituted a coordinated attempt by the government through laws and decrees to reduce the operation, influence, and contact by Catholic church figures among the populace. The prohibition against holding instructional classes for young people made preparation for receiving the sacraments of confirmation and holy eucharist very difficult.

The response of Catholics in Lithuania to these measures was initiated by the clergy, who conducted a systematic campaign of petitions, beginning in 1968, in the Telšiau diocese and spreading throughout all dioceses of Lithuania. They protested these new restrictions and the enforced limit upon new admissions into the seminary. Both, they felt, violated the Soviet constitution and Soviet law.[105] Between 1968 and mid-1972, 15 more such protest petitions came from the clergy. In the five dioceses, 362 (nearly 47 percent) of the 773 priests living in September 1974 had signed at least one of the petitions. In the dioceses of Panevėžys and Vilkaviškis, which are in a less modernized and ethnically more homogenous area than Kaunas and Vilnius, the share of participating clergy climbed to 83 percent and 56 percent, respectively.[106] Dissent expanded after the arrests of the Reverend Šeškevičius in 1970 and the Reverend Zdebskis in 1971 for instructing children in preparation for the sacrament of holy eucharist. Each received a prison sentence of one year. At Zdebskis's trial in November 1971, a physical confrontation occurred between a crowd consisting of 500 to 600 Catholics and the police. Reports concerning Zdebskis's alleged ill-treatment by the police and the closed trial had inflamed the hostility of militant Catholics toward the government.[107] At this time, a widespread petition campaign was initiated to protest both the imprisonment of clergy for instructing children in religion and for other infringements against religious practices. In the period 1971-73, 12 such mass petitions appeared in Lithuania, bearing 59,769 signatures.[108] The largest petition, with 17,054 signatures, appeared in January 1972. It was directed to CPSU General Secretary Brezhnev and called for cessation of religious persecution in Lithuania.[109] The demonstrations and riots by students in Kaunas and Vilnius in spring 1972 further mirrored a growing amount of religious and nationalistic dissatisfaction with the regime's policies. Clandestine nationalistic groups of intellectuals and students had been formed during the 1960s. Such a group was the Lithuanian Catholic Association.[110] In March 1972, a major underground journal appeared in Lithuania, which seemingly sought to fuse religious and nationality dissent effectively.

TABLE 6.10

Catholic Priests in Lithuania, 1965-74

Diocese	1965	1967	1969	1974	1975
Kaunas Archdiocese	199	202	190	171	168
Vilnius Archdiocese	107	109	103	97	96
Kašiadorys	83	81	78	73	71
Panevėžys	173	168	162	159	156
Telšiai	171	173	164	155	151
Vilkaviškis	137	128	125	118	117
Total	870	861	822	773	759

Sources: C. Pugevičius, ed., World Lithuanian Roman Catholic Directory (Brooklyn, N.Y.: Lithuanian R.C. Priests' League of America, 1975), pp 55-88, 95-96, 100-03; "Vyskupijų Kunigų Sarašai 1974 IX 1-15;" Mirusieji 1974 m iki gruodzio 14 d.; "Okupuotoj Lietuvoje 1975 Mire Kunigai," Darbininkas (New York) 61, no. 4 (January 23, 1976): 1; also, copies of the original lists of priests of dioceses for 1974 were consulted.

On March 19, 1972, the first issue of the Chronicle of the Catholic Church in Lithuania appeared. Twenty-four issues had reached the West by February 1977, despite a special KGB campaign conducted against the journal since November 1973 and numerous arrests for those printing or circulating it (see Table 6.7).[111] In this period, the subject matter of this journal has undergone considerable evolution. Initially a periodical reporting incidents of religious persecution, it has transformed itself into a journal increasingly reflecting all the nationality's discontents. Issues numbers 1 and 2 focused upon religious persecutions, arrests of clergy, and various petitions submitted by Catholics complaining against infringement of rights.[112] With issue number 3, (1972) considerable attention is given to describing the manipulation of seminary candidates by Party and government officials.[113] The interference by governmental authorities in ecclesiastical administration and assignment of priests is emphasized further in issue number 4 (1972).[114] The attitudes expressed suggest that the originators of the journal are somewhat "anti-establishment" in their viewpoint toward a Church hierarchy that must cooperate to a certain extent with the government.[115] In issue number 3, the editors also began to widen the scope from which they seek legal precedents against Soviet actions and even to expand their demands upon the USSR government. In this issue appeared a petition by believers that asked the same treatment for Lithuanians accorded Catholics in

Poland and East Germany.[116] In the Chronicle of the Catholic Church in Lithuania, nationality motifs first appear with statements protesting the suppression of the wearing of folk dress in religious processions and a prayer for the fatherland at the close of issue number 4.[117] Issue number 5 (1973) concentrates mainly upon the dilemma posed by persecution and denial of educational opportunities to believers and their children (this is a theme stressed throughout the publication of the journal). However, it is issue number 6 (1973) that highlights charges that Lithuanian history is accorded poor treatment in the union republic's schools. Perhaps the growing nationality dissatisfaction is expressed in issue number 6 by the editors' partial endorsement of an anticlerical film, Herkus Mantas. The film, about repelling the Teutonic knights in the thirteenth century, aroused nationalist feeling.[118]

This evolution toward a greater focus upon nationality matters is evidenced by the reporting about a trial of several ethnographers in issue number 10 in 1974.[119] Reports about the government's harassing those who are considered to be exhibiting an excessive interest in Lithuanian ethnography and the cultural and artistic heritage of the Catholic church in Lithuania continued in later issues.[120] However, overtones of ethnic discontent are present in complaints made by the journal's editors about the dismissal of Povilas Kulevecas from his position as a member of Lithuanian SSR's Council of Ministers. The editors allege that his discharge was prompted not so much by the charge that he obtained a doctorate in economics illegally but, rather, because he tended to favor Lithuanians, although he only learned Lithuanian after he had come to Lithuania, having been born in Georgia. The editor further points out that Kulevecas's ministerial post was then taken by a Russian.[121] Also, the non-Baltic ethnic makeup of athletic groups competing in the Baltic games in 1972 in Vilnius has been scorned by the editors. Nationalistic outbursts have occurred during athletic competitions. Issue number 23 reported that in November 1975 a victory celebration for a soccer team in Vilnius escalated into a confrontation between 2,000 young people and the KGB. Singing Lithuanian songs, the youths reached the KGB building, where they jeered the security police. Numerous arrests ensued while the crowd was dispersed by army and militia units.[122] Issue number 17 (1975) outlines economic and cultural methods allegedly used by Soviet authorities to promote denationalization among Lithuanians. Issue number 20 (1975) reports measures taken to encourage the use and study of Russian in schools.[123] These and other statements seem to suggest that the editors suspect that a policy of denationalization continues in effect. Although the journal has focused more upon nationality dissatisfaction than previously, it consistently reports incidents of religious persecution in employment and in schools.[124] Issue number 13 (1975) was devoted entirely to reporting the trial of those apprehended during 1973-74 in Case 345 for distributing and producing this journal and other religious literature. At the trial, the prosecutor emphatically charged that the journal was trying to turn people against the state by using misrepresented facts and attempting to spread nationalistic and anti-Soviet ideas among the populace.[125]

Since this dissident material began appearing, several administrative changes in Lithuania have been made, including the replacement of the deputy minister of the Council of Religious Affairs, Justas Rugienis, by Kazimieras Tumėnas.[126] The USSR government, apparently both through diplomatic channels and allowing visits abroad by clergy of Lithuania considered reliable, has been attempting to press the Vatican to withhold significant recognition from Catholic dissidents and to counter unfavorable publicity generated by the activities of Catholic militants. The anti-establishment mood of the journal is fueled further by a fear of betrayal, resulting from the Vatican's seeking an accommodation with the Communist governments. This has been expressed in numerous issues.[127] This feeling of being ignored and isolated grew throughout 1973-75. There have been numerous arrests and searches conducted by the KGB, as it tries to crush the publication of this underground journal.[128] All these pressures and a feeling of isolation from the Vatican's policies may account for the growing militancy exhibited in the journal. For example, in 1975, the journal published addresses and names of persons who aided in searches by the KGB, and nationality dissatisfaction is increasingly revealed.[129] One method is also to elicit a wider base of support. The ever-expanding focus of the journal is further demonstrated by its increased reporting about events in the general Russian and Soviet human rights movement. The compilers of the Chronicle of the Catholic Church in Lithuania express sympathy with the movement and openly seek additional support for their cause from it, while they champion such Russian dissidents as Alexander Solzhenitsyn.[130] In issue no. 21 (1976), the trial of Sergius Kovalëv, a founder of the Human Rights Committee in Moscow, was reported. Among the charges was his possession and use in the underground Chronicle of Current Events of three issues of the Chronicle of the Catholic Church in Lithuania. Thus, a connecting link between the nationality and religious dissatisfaction in Lithuania and the general Soviet human rights movement seems to have been established.[131] Emphasis is also placed, in the secular Lithuanian samizdat journal Aušra, upon ties and sympathy among all protesters, including Russian Orthodox and secular Soviet human rights dissenters.[132] These ethnic themes and civil rights goals, which are more secular than religious in nature, may define the nationality supports and aims toward which those associated with the Catholic church in the Chronicle will shift their concern if the Catholic church cannot maintain its physical establishment in Lithuania. However, the more secular, ethnically oriented editors of Aušra give great significance to the role that the Catholic church has played in the preservation of Lithuanian nationality identity. Lithuanians who assist the drive for atheistic indoctrination have been labeled traitors, as were those who aided the programs of Czarist Russification in the nineteenth century directed against the Catholic church and Lithuanian language. The tireless devotion of a Bishop Valančius (1801-75), is said by Aušra's editors to be needed for times during which the spiritual treasures of the Lithuanian nationality is threatened by Soviet indoctrination.[133] The editors of the Chronicle of the Catholic Church in Lithuania may be trying to broaden the scope of their support by emphasizing nationality themes. Yet religion, notably Catholicism, still plays a very important part in nationality consciousness among more nonsectarian dissenters. Aušra's editors, perceiving themselves to be secular protectors of Lithuanian ethnic solidarity, consider the nationality's spiritual culture a bulwark blocking denationalization and a contemporary battleground in the struggle for group survival. In Aušra No. 3, moral support was expressed by a former "Gulag" prisoner for Nijolė Sadūnaitė, the Roman Catholic dissident imprisoned in Lithuania in 1975.[134] However, the timely appearance of Aušra does suggest that if the institutional framework of the Catholic church should lose power to rally Lithuanians, other nationality supports, not directly associated with the church, would be readily available to replace the church and its structure.

In the spread of Catholic dissatisfaction during the early 1970s may be seen the failure to impose an effective policy of Sovietization for eradicating the influence of religion in Lithuania. Atheistic indoctrination may be considered a facet of Sovietization and Soviet "ideological modernization" of a nationality. The imposition of new restrictions has tended to provoke more and more nationality awareness. It has strengthened more secular elites, who perceive it as a denationalizing device. Despite growing persecution, the Catholic church remains the religious institution in the Baltic union republics with the strongest physical establishment and nationality identification. That position tends to thwart efforts to discredit or attack the Catholic church in Lithuania. Religious institutions so far seem not to play a similar role in the crystalization and expansion of nationality dissatisfaction in Latvia and Estonia in the 1970s.

Evidence validates the hypothesis that the current doctrine of Sovietization, in ethnic terms, through its policies has neither destroyed nor significantly undermined the nationality support systems, for it has not neutralized the group identities of the three Baltic eponymous nationalities. The tremendous alertness of these groups to real or imagined dangers has resulted in a disproportional outpouring of nationality dissatisfaction when measures of Sovietization, implying a type of denationalization, are implemented in the area. Nationality identity, here as elsewhere, seems to fill a fundamental need for self-assertion and differentiation for everyone in the contemporary world.[135] Nationality, like religion, confers both an individual and group identity in some respects. Essentially, nationality identity must be an adult's personal choice, and, therefore, the nationality's identifying features may also originate from collective opinions concerning the particular nationality. Such conscious choices and conceptions possess an intangible quality, which gives them a great flexibility under the changing circumstances surrounding the human group's condition. This adaptibility is the very quality that proves most intractable in the face of policies advocating denationalization or the neutralization of nationality identities.

Because nationality identity and religious affiliation possess certain similar attributes, when religion is used by an ethnic group as a nationality support, the group acquires a double cohesiveness and protection against penetration, absorption, or assimilation by outsiders. Unlike religion, the present institutional legitimacy granted administratively to the eponymous nationalities supports the persistence of the concept of nationality differentiation. The failure of the campaign, so far, to achieve effective neutralization of the nationality identities among these groups may bolster their continued separate survival, because these Baltic eponymous groups will not be subjected again, probably, to pressures and demographic catastrophes like World War II and Soviet occupation. In the long run, the increasing proportion of non-Russians populating the USSR may tend to offset further those policies pressing nationalities, under the guise of Sovietization, to succumb to Russification. The three eponymous Baltic nationalities are—through increased political and educational mobilization and proper adjustment of their nationality support systems to contemporary Soviet condition—stymying denationalization and loss of their group identities. Obviously, such shifting and adjustment demonstrates the range of choices kept open by these highly self-aware groups. Given this flexibility, efforts threatening such denationalization among nationalities already possessing relatively strong support systems will only increase nationality dissatisfaction and unrest in the Baltic area for the foreseeable future.

NOTES

1. Leonid Brezhnev, The Fiftieth Anniversary of the Union of Soviet Socialist Republics (Moscow: Progress, 1972), pp. 16-38.

2. P. Rimgaudas, "Vysk M. Valančiaus 100 m. mirties," Aušra 40, no. 1 (October 1975): 41-42.

3. Brezhnev, p. 32.

4. Yaroslav Bilinsky, "The Background of Contemporary Politics in the Baltic Republics and the Ukraine," Problems of Mininations: Baltic Perspectives, ed. Arvids Ziedonis, Jr., Rein Taagepera, and Mardi Valgamae (San Jose, Calif.: Association for the Advancement of Baltic Studies, 1973), pp. 89-114.

5. "KPSS v tsifrakh," Partinaia zhizn, no. 14 (July 1973), p. 18.

6. Salo Baron, Modern Nationalism and Religion (New York: Harper & Brothers, 1947), pp. 21-22.

7. John Lawrence, "Observations on Religion and Atheism in Soviet Society," Religion in Communist Lands 1, nos. 4-5 (July-October 1973): 20-21.

8. I. Käbin, "V edinoi sem'e sovetskikh narodov," Kommunist Estonii, no. 7 (1975), p. 22.

9. Ibid., p. 24.

10. I. Obram, "Zhivotvornaia sila leninskoi natsional'noi politiki," Kommunist Estonii, no. 8 (1975), p. 28.

11. A. Laanemäe, "Rastsvet kul'tury i khudozhestvennogo tvorchestva mass," Kommunist Estonii, no. 5 (1975), p. 71.

12. N. Bassel', "Ob internatsional'nykh sviaziakh estonskoi sovetskoi literatury," Kommunist Estonii, no. 7 (1975), p. 51; Iu. K. Iurna, "Vzaimoobogashchaiushchie, uglubliaiushchie druzhbu sovetskikh narodov," Kommunist Estonii, no. 9 (1975), p. 52; Käbin, p. 22.

13. Iurna, p. 58.

14. Laanemäe, p. 71.

15. Narodnoe khoziaistvo SSSR v 1973 godu (Moscow: Statistika, 1974), p. 48.

16. I. Kalits and I. Pott, "Internatsionalistskoe vospitanie v trudovom kollektive," Kommunist Estonii, no. 2 (1975), pp. 57-65.

17. Käbin, p. 23.

18. Bassel', p. 48.

19. Ibid., pp. 52-56.

20. "Prazdnik vengerskogo naroda," Kommunist Estonii, no. 4 (1975), p. 107.

21. Dz. Shmidre, "Natsional'nye otnosheniia na etape zrelogo sotsializma," Kommunist Sovetskoi Latvii, no. 9 (1975), p. 42.

22. Ibid., p. 41.

23. A. Drizul, "Razvitie dukhovnoi zhizni," Kommunist Sovetskoi Latvii, no. 7 (1975), p. 16.

24. Ibid., p. 13.

25. Ibid., pp. 12-16.

26. V. Labrentse, "Obraz rodiny v latyshskoi sovetskoi poezii," Kommunist Sovetskoi Latvii, no. 2 (1975), pp. 65-70.

27. "Razvitie dukhovnoi zhizni sovetskikh natsii v usloviiakh zrelogo sotsializma," Kommunist Sovetskoi Latvii, no. 7 (1975), p. 84.

28. Ibid., pp. 85-90.

29. Drizul, pp. 12-16.

30. Ibid., p. 17.

31. Genrikas Zimanas, "Obshchenatsional'naia gordost' Sovetskikh liudei," Kommunist (Vilnius), no. 8 (1975), pp. 37-46.

32. A. Barkauskas, "Lietuvos KP Centro Komiteto sekretoriaus A. Barkausko kalba," Literatura ir Menas, no. 1 (January 4, 1975): 2.

33. Ch. Ataev, "V edinom stroiu," Kommunist (Vilnius), no. 10 (1974), pp. 37-43; I. Rakhimova, "Segodniashnii den' Tadzhikistana," Kommunist (Vilnius), no. 12 (1974), pp. 31-34.

34. K. Kulmatov, "Rastsvet sovetskogo Kirgizistana," Kommunist (Vilnius), no. 2 (1975), pp. 43-47; A. Salimov, "Plody leninskoĭ natsional'noi politiki," Kommunist (Vilnius), no. 1 (1975), pp. 33-37.

35. V. Khotianovskii, "Nauchno-issledovatel'skii institut i zavod," Kommunist (Vilnius), no. 2 (1975), pp. 69-72; Yu. Pozhela, "Sovrevnovanie uchenykh," Kommunist (Vilnius), no. 8 (1975), pp. 18-20.

36. A. Zhalis, "Velikaia sila druzhby narodov," Kommunist (Vilnius), no. 1 (1975), p. 15.

37. I. Maniushis, Ekonomika i kul'tura sovetskoi Litvy (Vilnius: Mintis, 1973), p. 124.

38. "35 let druzhby i pobed," Kommunist (Vilnius), no. 6 (1975), p. 17.

39. P. Gaučys, "Knyga," in Lietuvių Enciklopedija, ed. Juozas Kapočius et al. (Boston: Lietuvių Enciklopedijos Leidykla, 1957), 12: 157; Antanas Mažiulis, "Spaustuvė," in ibid. (1963), 28: 345; Simas Sužiedėlis, "Book" and "Population," in Encyclopedia Lituanica, ed. Simas Sužiedėlis et al. (Boston: Juozas Kapočius, 1970, 1975), 1, 4: 382-86, 322-23;

40. A. Sniečkus, Soviet Lithuania on the Road of Prosperity (Moscow: Progress Publishers, 1974), pp. 109-12.

41. Bilinsky, p. 106; J. Newth, "The 1970 Soviet Census," Soviet Studies 24, no. 2 (October 1972): 220.

42. A. I. Kholmogorov, Internatsional'ye cherty sovetskikh natsii (Moscow: "Mysl," 1970), trans. as "International Traits of Soviet Nations," Soviet Sociology 11, nos. 3-4 (Winter-Spring 1972-73): 311, 322.

43. Pechat' SSSR v 1973 godu (Moscow: Statistika, 1974), p. 98; "Latvian Seaman Risks Life To Gain Freedom—Interview with the Latest Defector—[Peteris Reimis]," From FCI/LNA, London, January 30, 1974, reported in Religion in Communist Dominated Areas 13, nos. 1-2 (January-February 1974): 26.

44. Jaan Pennar, Ivan I. Bakalo, and George Z. F. Bereday, Modernization and Diversity in Soviet Education (New York: Praeger, 1971), p. 241.

45. Bilinsky, p. 100.

46. Bronius Vaskelis, "The Assertion of Ethnic Identity Via Myth and Folklore in Soviet Lithuania," Lituanus 19, no. 2 (Summer 1973): 16-27.

47. Vaira Vikis-Freibergs, "Echoes of Dainas and the Search for Identity in Contemporary Latvian Poetry," Journal of Baltic Studies 6, no. 1 (Spring 1975): 17-29.

48. Alfred Straumanis, "Folklorist Embellishments in Soviet Latvian Drama," Journal of Baltic Studies 6, nos. 2-3 (Summer and Fall 1975): 153-61.

49. A. Laanemäe, p. 65, and Sniečkus, p. 107.

50. Valda Melngailė, "The Sense of History in Recent Soviet Latvian Poetry," Journal of Baltic Studies 6, nos. 2-3 (Summer and Fall 1975): 130-39.

51. Estonian Democratic Movement and the Estonian National Front, "Memorandum to the UN on Independence for the Baltic States," as reported in The Violations of Human Rights in Soviet Occupied Lithuania: A Report for 1974, ed. Lithuanian American Community (Glenside, Pa.: Lithuanian American Community, 1975), pp. 18-26; "A Memorandum of Baltic Democrats to the Participants of the Helsinki Conference," UBA Information Service News Release, August 23, 1975; Lithuanian American Community, ed., The Violations of Human Rights in Soviet Occupied Lithuania: A Report for 1975 (Glenside, Pa.: Lithuanian American Community, 1976), pp. 31-38.

52. "Letter of Seventeen Latvian Communists," Congressional Record, 92nd Cong., February 15-22, 1972, 118, pt. 4: 4820-22.

53. Lietuvos Katalikų Bažnyčios Kronika (Chicago: L. K. Religinės Šalpos Rėmėjai, 1974), no. 4, pp. 203-04, no. 7, pp. 285-88; "Sovietineje Lietuvos Mokykloje Iš Lietuvos Katalikų Bažnyčios Kronikas Nr. 16," Darbininkas 60, no. 31 (August 1, 1975): 1; "A Declaration of the Lithuanian National Peoples' Front," Lithuanian American Community, ed., The Violations of Human Rights in Soviet Occupied Lithuania: A Report for 1975, pp. 39-49; "The Case of Simas 'Kudirka'," in Lithuanian American Community, ed., The Violations of Human Rights in Soviet Occupied Lithuania: A Report for 1971 (Delran, N.J.: Lithuanian American Community, 1972), pp. 18-24; Rimgaudas, pp. 42-45; "Nejaugi Musu Dalis Bus Kaip Prusu? Iš Nr. 17," Darbininkas 60, no. 44 (October 31, 1975): 1-2; Ibid., 61, no. 49 (December 3, 1976), p. 1.

54. Jonas Grinius, "Aušra," Encyclopedia Lituanica, ed. Simas Sužiedėlis et al. (Boston: Juozas Kapočius, 1970), 1: pp. 216-18; "Aušros Gadynė Iš Aušros 2/42," excerpt from Aušra, vol. 42,

(February 16, 1976), reported in Darbininkas 61, no. 29 (July 16, 1976): 1; Aušra 40, no. 1 (October 1975): 1-4; Rimgaudas, pp. 31-34.

55. Jonas Jurašas, "Personal Interview," Draugas (Chicago) (January 25, 1975), reported in "Censorship in the Theatre," Lithuanian American Community, ed., The Violations of Human Rights in Soviet Occupied Lithuania: A Report for 1975, pp. 93-96; "Appeal of Lithuanian Intellectuals on Preservation of Paintings of M. K. Čiurlionis," Lituanus 19, no. 2 (Summer 1973): 71-72; "Discrimination of Lithuanians in the Belorussian SSR," ibid., 21 (Spring 1975): 70-74.

56. Emmett George, "Party Response to Lithuanian Unrest," The Soviet West: Interplay between Nationality and Social Organization, ed. Ralph Clem (New York: Praeger, 1975), p. 93; "Self Immolation and National Protest in Lithuania," Lituanus 18, no. 4 (Winter 1972): 58-68; Lietuvos Katalikų Bažnyčios Kronika, no. 7, pp. 298-99, 304-05.

57. Estonian Democratic Movement and the Estonian National Front, pp. 19-23.

58. Rimgaudas, pp. 31-41.

59. Stephen P. Dunn, Cultural Processes in the Baltic Area Under Soviet Rule (Berkeley, Calif.: Institute of International Studies, 1966), pp. 7-12; Max Saar, "The Herrnhut Movement, Its Expansion and Fate," and Arthur Voobus, "Christianization or War of Conquest," in Johanni Kopp eximio domino, Estonia Christiana (Uppsala, Sweden: Estonian Theological Society in Exile, 1965), pp. 162-72 and 45-78.

60. Y. Minkiavichus, "Some Aspects of Relationship Between Nationalism and Religion," Politicheskoe samoobrazovanie (Moscow), no. 2 (1973), pp. 106-12, reported in Religion in Communist Dominated Areas 13, nos. 10-12 (October-December 1974): 166-68; O. Sergizhaev and M. Suzhikov, "Religion and Nationalities," Partiinaia zhizn' Kazakhstana, no. 1 (1970), pp. 75-76, reported in "A New Anti-Religious Book Praised," Religion in Communist Dominated Areas 9, nos. 17-18 (September 1970): 46-47.

61. Vello Salo, "Anti-Religious Rites in Estonia," Religion in Communist Dominated Lands 1, nos. 4-5 (July-October 1973): 28-33; V. Salo, "The Party and the Church in Soviet Estonia," in A Case Study of a Soviet Republic: The Estonian SSR, ed. Tõnu Parming and Elmar Järvesoo (Boulder, Colo.: Westview Press, forthcoming), pp. 376-453; Latvian Evangelical Lutheran Church of New York, Memorandum in Support of Proposed Resolution Regarding Christians in Estonia Latvia and Lithuania, December 1973 (New York: Latvian Evangelical Lutheran Church of New York, 1973), pp. 9-10.

62. Vello Salo, "The Party and the Church in Soviet Estonia," p. 380; Assembly of Captive European Nations," Principal Aspects of the Religious Persecutions by the Communists in the Baltic Coun-

tries," mimeographed (New York: Assembly of Captive European Nations, n.d.), p. 1; Latvian Evangelical Lutheran Church of New York, p. 10.

63. "Lutheran World Federation President Visits Lutherans in the USSR," Lutheran World Federation, Geneva, Switzerland, reported in *Religion in Communist Dominated Areas* 11, nos. 7-9 (July-September 1972): 131.

64. Salo, "Anti-Religious Rites in Estonia," pp. 28-31, app., p. 32; Salo, "The Party and the Church in Soviet Estonia," pp. 429-30; Jennifer McDowell, "Soviet Civil Ceremonies," *Journal for the Scientific Study of Religion* 13, no. 3 (1974), pp. 278-79; "Lutheran World Federation President Visits Lutherans in the USSR," p. 130.

65. "Zadachi ateisticheskoi raboty," *Kommunist Estonii*, no. 1 (1975), p. 90; "Usilit ateisticheskuiu propagandu," *Kommunist Estonii*, no. 8 (1975), p. 91.

66. "Usilit ateisticheskuiu propagandu," p. 91.

67. A. Soidla, "Krizis sovremennogo Liuteranstva," *Kommunist Estonii*, no. 6 (1975), pp. 43-51.

68. Salo, "The Party and the Church in Soviet Estonia," pp. 416, 419, 431-32.

69. Estonian Democratic Movement and Estonian National Front, pp. 18-26.

70. Rimgaudas, pp. 34-42.

71. Memorandum of Baltic Democrats to the Participants of the Helsinki Conference," pp. 31-38.

72. A. I. Klibanov and L. N. Mitrokhin, "The Schism of Contemporary Baptism," *Social Compass* 21, no. 2 (1974): 133-51, and Ethel Dunn, "Introduction," ibid., p. 117.

73. "Lutheran World President Visits Lutherans in the USSR," pp. 130-31; Latvian Evangelical Lutheran Church of New York, pp. 9-10.

74. Assembly of Captive European Nations, p. 1. Latvian Evangelical Lutheran Church of New York, pp. 9-10.

75. *Baltic Events* 47, no. 6 (December 1974): 3.

76. Fyodor Savin, "Religious Publication in the Soviet Union," Novosti Press Agency (Moscow), as reported in *Religion in Communist Dominated Areas* 11, nos. 4-6 (April-June 1972): 72.

77. "Lutheran World President Visits Lutherans in the USSR," p. 130.

78. "This Is How it Happened," *Bulletin of the Council of ECB Prisoners' Relatives* (Moscow), no. 18 (1974), pp. 2-3, reported in *Religion in Communist Dominated Areas* 14, nos. 1-3 (January-March 1975): 43-44; "Printers of Gospels Arrested," ibid. 14, nos. 4-6 (April-June 1975): 74-75.

79. Kathleen Matchett, "Some Other Minorities," *Religious Minorities in the Soviet Union*, ed. Michael Bourdeaux (London: Minority Rights Group, 1973), p. 20; (letter to editor) "A Latvian Appeals for Help for Two Brothers Imprisoned in the USSR," reported in *Religion in Communist Dominated Areas* 13, nos. 5-6 (May-June 1974): 94-96.

80. "Roman Catholics in Latvia Petition USSR Government," *UBA Information Service News Release*, no. 312 (April 27, 1976), pp. 1-2.

81. "A Memorandum of Baltic Democrats to the Participants at the Helsinki Conference," pp. 31-38.

82. L. Freiberg, "Aktual'nye voprosy nauchno-ateisticheskogo vospitaniia," *Kommunist Sovetskoi Latvii*, no. 6 (1975), pp. 33-39.

83. Rimgaudas, pp. 34-41.

84. Motiejus Valančius, "Kare pas Salantų pilį," *Gimtasis Krastus* (Vilnius) 471, no. 7 (February 12, 1976): 6.

85. Rimgaudas, pp. 41-45.

86. Lithuanian American Community, ed., "Struggle for Survival," *The Violations of Human Rights in Soviet Occupied Lithuania: A Report for 1974* (Glenside, Pa.: Lithuanian American Community, 1975), p. 45.

87. Bohdan R. Bociurkiw, "Religious Dissent in the USSR: Lithuanian Catholics" (Paper presented at the Banff 1974 International Conference of the American Association of Slavic Studies, the British National Association for Soviet and East European Studies, and the Canadian Association of Slavists, Banff, Alberta, Canada, September 4, 1974), p. 2.

88. "Vilniaus ir Kauno Uždarytos Bažnyčios Iš Lietuvos Kat. Bažnyčios Kronikos Nr. 18," *Darbininkas* (New York) 60, no. 50 (December 12, 1975): 1-2.

89. J. Rimaitis, *Religion in Lithuania* (Vilnius: Gintaras, 1971), p. 16.

90. V. Brizgys, *Religious Conditions in Lithuania under Soviet Russian Occupation* (Chicago: Lithuanian Catholic Press, 1975), pp. 18-19; A. Kalme, *Total Terror* (New York: Appleton-Century-Crofts, 1951), p. 183; Assembly of Captive European Nations, op. cit., p. 2; Simas Sužiedėlis, "Refugees," and "Roman Catholics," Sužiedėlis et al., eds., 4: 459, 525; M. Raišupis, *Dabarties Kankiniai* (Chicago: Krikščionis Gyvenime, 1972), pp. 15, 393, 429.

91. "Lutheran World Federation President Visits Lutherans in the USSR," p. 131; Kristupas Gudaitis, "Protestants—Evangelical Lutheran Church," and Paulius Dylys, "Protestants—The Evangelical Reformed Church," in Sužiedėlis et al. eds., 4: 356-59, 359-62.

92. Bociurkiw, p. 3.

93. "Sovietineje Lietuvos Mokykloje Iš Lietuvos Katalikų Kronikos Nr. 16," Darbininkas (New York) 60, no. 31 (August 1, 1975): 2.

94. Lietuvos Katalikų Bažnyčios Kronika 2 (Chicago: L. K. Religinės Šalpos Rėmėjai, 1975), no. 12, pp. 242-43.

95. Lithuanian American Community, ed., The Violations of Human Rights in Soviet Occupied Lithuania: A Report for 1971, p. 36; Lithuanian American Community, ed., "Struggle for Survival," p. 45.

96. Lithuanian American Community, ed., "Struggle for Survival," p. 45.

97. C. Pugevičius, ed., World Lithuanian Roman Catholic Directory (Brooklyn, N.Y.: Lithuanian Roman Catholic Priests' League of America, 1975), p. 100.

98. P. Adlys and A. Stanaitis, Lietuvos TSR Gyventojai (Vilnius: Mintis, 1973), pp. 103-12; C. Pugevičius, ed., pp. 73-88; pp. 94-96, p. 102; "Okupuotoj Lietuvoje 1975 Mirę Kunigai," Darbininkas (New York) 60, no. 4 (January 23, 1976): 1.

99. N. Liutkiavichiute, "Zabota o cheloveke, ego soznanii," Kommunist (Vilnius), no. 10 (1975), pp. 36-38.

100. Rimaitis, p. 28; Lucian Blit, "The Insoluble Problem: Church and State in Poland," Religion in Communist Lands 1, no. 3 (May-June 1973): 8-11.

101. Adomas Shernas, Predsmertnoe pis-mo (Kaunas: Shvieca, 1973) (300 copies printed in Polish language).

102. Lithuanian American Community, ed., The Violations of Human Rights in Soviet Occupied Lithuania: A Report for 1972 (Delran, N.J.: Lithuanian American Community, 1973), p. 45.

103. Ibid., pp. 45-46.

104. Ibid., pp. 46, 48-50.

105. Bociurkiw, pp. 3-4.

106. Ibid., p. 4.

107. Ibid., pp. 7-10.

108. Ibid., p. 4.

109. "Self-Immolations and National Protest in Lithuania," Lituanus 18, no. 4 (Winter 1972): 70-72.

110. Lithuanian American Community, ed., "The Lithuanian National Movement During the 1960s," in The Violations of Human Rights in Soviet Occupied Lithuania: A Report for 1975, pp. 46-50.

111. "Nijolės Kelionė Į Lagerį iš Lietuvos Katalikų Bažnyčios Kronikos Nr. 24;" Darbininkas (New York) 62, No. 6 (February 11, 1977): 1; Lietuvos Katalikų Bažnyčios Kronika 2, no. 8, pp. 11-22.

112. Lietuvos Katalikų Bažnyčios Kronika, nos. 1-2, pp. 27-117.

113. Ibid., no. 3 (1972), pp. 121-27.

114. Ibid., no. 4 (1972), p. 167.

115. Ibid., pp. 166, 168-70.

116. Ibid., no. 3, p. 142.

117. Ibid., no. 4, pp. 202-04.

118. Ibid., no. 5 (1973), pp. 217, 221-22; ibid., no. 6, p. 251-52, 255-59, 269-77 (measures used to discriminate against and persecute believing school children); ibid., pp. 249-51, 252-54, 265.

119. Ibid., no. 6, pp. 261-64; ibid. 2, no. 10, pp. 127-37.

120. "Sovietinėje Lietuvos Mokykloje Iš Lietuvos Katalikų Bažnyčios Kronikos Nr. 16," Darbininkas (New York) 60, no. 31 (August 1, 1975): 1-2; "Psychiatric Mistreatment and Death of Mindaugas Tamonis from Kronika No. 10 and No. 20," reported in Lithuanian American Community, ed., The Violations of Human Rights in Soviet Occupied Lithuania: A Report for 1975, pp. 109-14.

121. "Iš Lietuvos Katalikų Bažnyčios Kronikos No. 17," Darbininkas (New York) 60, no. 49 (December 5, 1975): 2.

122. Ibid., p. 2; "Demonstracijos Vilniaus Stadijone Iš Lietuvos K. Bažnyčios Kronikos Nr. 23," Darbininkas (New York) 62, no. 2 (January 14, 1977): 1.

123. "Nejaugi Mūsų Dalis Bus Kaip Prūsu, Iš Lietuvos Katalikų Bažnyčios Kronikos Nr. 17," Darbininkas (New York), 60, no. 44 (October 31, 1975): 1-2; "Nutautinima Jau ir Mokukloje Iš Lictuvis Katalikų Bažnyčios Kronika No. 20," Darbininkas (New York), 61, no. 10 (March 5, 1976): 1.

124. Lietuvos Katalikų Bažnyčios Kronika, no. 3; pp. 127-41; "Iš Lietuvos Kronikos No. 17," Darbininkas (New York), 60, no. 47 (November 21, 1975): 1 (The first reference is to report of Ona Brilienė and the second one to persecution of Aldona Kezytė).

125. Lietuvos Katalikų Bažnyčios Kronika 2, no. 13, pp. 249-304.

126. Lietuvos Katalikų Bažnyčios Kronika, no. 6, p. 261; Bociurkiw, p. 19.

127. Ibid., no. 4, pp. 172-74; "The Status of the Catholic Church in Lithuania: An Open Letter to the Archbishop of Berlin from the Chronicle of the Catholic Church in Lithuania No. 19," reported in Lithuanian American Community, ed., The Violations of Human Rights in Soviet Occupied Lithuania: A Report for 1975, p. 70.

128. Lietuvos Katalikų Bažnyčios Kronika 2, no. 8, pp. 10-22.

129. "Iš Liet. Kat. Bažnyčios Kronikos No. 18," Darbininkas (New York) 61, no. 1 (January 2, 1976): 1.

130. Lieutovos Katalikų Bažnyčios Kronika 2, no. 15, pp. 357-59.

131. "Sergiejaus Kovailiov Teismas, Iš LKB Kronikos No. 21," Darbininkas (New York) 61, no. 30 (July 23, 1976): 1-2.

132. "Solidarizuojamės su rusų disidentais!," Aušra, no. 2 (42) (February 16, 1976): 40-41; Aleksandras Solženicynas, "Gyventi Be melo," ibid., no. 1 (40) (October 1975): 45-52.

133. Rimgaudas, op. cit., p. 42, 43-44, 44-45; *Darbininkas* 61, no. 49 (December 3, 1976): 1.

134. Ibid., p. 42, 44-45.

135. Cynthia Enloe, *Ethnic Conflict and Political Development* (Boston: Little, Brown, 1973), p. 268.

CHAPTER

7

RESOURCES OF THE ETHNICALLY DISENFRANCHISED

Eli M. Lederhendler

Some Western and Soviet scholars have argued that modernization brings with it a weakening of nationality group attachments. Modernity has been depicted by these scholars as a "universal solvent" that undermines traditional societies. Insofar as ethnic identity is linked to tradition (ancestral language, dress, customs, kinship communities, religion), it, too, is undermined and dissolved. The mobile, nuclear family, living in a cosmopolitan, urban setting, finds less and less need for a kinship community and its cultural appurtenances.[1] The Soviet version of this theory differs from its Western counterpart in that it emphasizes the subordination of nationality to class interests as capitalism develops, as well as the growing together of those nationalities that share a common socialist economic base.

On the other hand, there are abundant examples of nations and nationalities that have expressed their ethnic self-awareness increasingly with the development of modern conditions. One possible resolution for this debate is that for nationalities, modernization may prove a double-edged sword. It promotes assimilation under certain conditions, and collective self-awareness under others.[2]

> Development does not automatically herald the demise of ethnicity. It does introduce a period of flux, cultural and social. . . . The uncertainties of transitional society provoke a self-consciousness about identity that was superfluous in the past. One of the ironies of modernization is that it combats ethnic loyalty while it stimulates ethnic awareness.[3]

The confrontation between various nationality groups in a cosmopolitan urban setting may intensify ethnic self-awareness by throwing the differences into relief. Modernization may heighten the expectations of nationalities, create new aspirations and needs that go beyond the realm of material satisfaction, and cause groups to draw closer together in reaction to the atomizing and alienating tendencies of modernity. Improved communications put geographically separated groups in contact with each other. As information about conditions abroad spreads more rapidly, new standards for evaluating conditions at home are established.

The basic question raised here is not whether nationality distinctiveness and modernization are compatible but, under what conditions they are so. What combination of social, cultural, economic, and political factors promotes the assimilation of nationalities, and what combination can promote opposite tendencies? Can nationality identity and modernization be not only compatible but even mutually reinforcing?

The assimilating thrust of modernization has been given official ideological sanction in the Soviet Union. The development of the urbanized, industrial, and multinational Soviet society in recent decades may properly be seen as an example of modernization. If the nationality question persists in such a society, then the study of a Soviet nationality can be especially helpful in revealing factors that support ethnicity amid modernity.

In dealing with the factors operating in the Soviet nationality question, some observers stress the primary significance of economics. Others view state and Party policies as the major determinant. Still others point out the importance of demographic trends. This chapter will be based on the assumption that the configuration of the Soviet nationality question is determined by a range of factors whose relative weight will vary according to the particular situation. The range of factors can be divided into three categories: objective physical and identity factors, relativity factors (actual or perceived comparative status), and regulatory factors (catalyzing or pacifying social or political conditions).

By studying the growth of expressed dissatisfaction among Baltic Jews during the late 1960s and early 1970s, the operation of one factor in particular—that of cultural identity—may be explored. Certainly, other forces were at work in promoting the growth of Jewish dissatisfaction: chiefly catalyzing political factors, such as Soviet policy on Jewish cultural facilities; events in the Middle East; and the anti-Zionist press campaign in the USSR. These political catalysts, however, affected Jews elsewhere in the Soviet Union and yet did not produce the same quantitative or qualitative effect as they did among Baltic Jews. Political factors may be treated here as a constant, while focus is put on those conditions that are exceptional in the Baltic Jewish situation. These exceptional characteristics center around these Jews' national-cultural identity.*

Others have already speculated on the significance of Jewish cultural identity in the Baltic region for the overrepresentation of Baltic Jews in the emigration movement.[4] The present inquiry will, however, go beyond the salient fact of Baltic Jewish cultural identity and examine its relationship to the modernization process. This chapter will attempt to prove that the especially rapid growth of publicly articulated Jewish nationality dissatisfaction in the Baltic republics was largely facilitated by the unusual interplay of modernization and Jewish cultural identity occurring in that region. What may be learned about the interaction of these two factors can hopefully shed some light on the Soviet nationality question, as such, and help to answer the question: Under what conditions will ethnic identity flourish amid modernization?

The original source material employed here includes statistical data from Soviet censuses and sociological studies; samizdat materials, petitions and appeals written by Baltic Jews; and personal interviews conducted with Jewish emigrants from Riga and Vilnius now living in New York. The interviewees were not sufficiently numerous or representative to supply valid quantitative findings, but their observations were invaluable in contributing the human factor to the story told by statistics and printed matter.

JEWS AND JEWISHNESS IN THE BALTIC REPUBLICS

As of 1970, there were 36,700 Jews living in Latvia, and an additional 24,000 in Lithuania. For the purposes of this chapter, "Baltic Jews" will denote Latvian and Lithuanian Jews only. This is due to the small size of the Jewish community in Estonia (5,000) and to the extreme paucity of information about this community in the Soviet period. The accuracy of Soviet Jewish population statistics had been questioned by some observers. Estimates of the combined Baltic Jewish population have ranged up to 80,000.[5]

These Jews represent a small remnant of what were once large and creative Jewish communities, in the years before the Nazi

---

*The author is indebted for this insight to Mordecai Altschuler of the Hebrew University of Jerusalem.

holocaust. For part of the period between the two world wars, Baltic Jews were protected by nationality rights legislation. They created agencies of self-administration in religious, social, and educational affairs, as well as a spectrum of political parties, a vast array of press and publications, and a thriving cultural life, expressed through literature, the arts, and scholarship. Jews of the Soviet heartland had been deprived of most of these outlets and facilities since the Bolshevik revolution.[6] The relatively late incorporation of Baltic Jewry into the Soviet Union contributed many of the factors that helped to preserve its nationality and cultural identity.

While a considerable proportion of Jews residing in the Baltic republics in 1970 were immigrants from other parts of the Soviet Union,[7] a nucleus remained that had (or whose parents had) experienced a full Jewish life in pre-Soviet times. This nucleus was reinforced in the years following 1956 through the return of large numbers of Baltic Jews who had been deported during the period of annexation.[8] Their nationality distinctiveness was profound and deep-rooted, and could not be erased in only one generation.

One of the most visible manifestations of this identity is the comparatively high proportion of Baltic Jews who claimed to speak a Jewish language (either Hebrew or Yiddish in European parts of the USSR) in the 1959 and 1970 Soviet censuses (see Table 7.1). In addition, a study of pre-1971 Soviet immigrants in Israel found that of the 23 percent who had at least partial knowledge of Hebrew upon their arrival, 70 percent were "western" Jews (from the annexed territories).[9] Caution ought to be maintained, however, concerning language statistics. A low rate of language retention does not in and of itself indicate a low level of nationality consciousness. Linguistic acculturation may take place without the disappearance of other ethnic traits and identity support factors. Such a view, separating ethnic identity from language maintenance, has been expressed by Western scholars, and recently by several Soviet scholars as well.[10] However, the high proportion of Jewish-language knowledge among Baltic Jews does suggest several things. Baltic Jews have retained sufficiently close bonds to make knowledge of a Jewish language useful or satisfying. These Jews also have a greater potential for organizing activities, such as Jewish theater and choir groups. They have greater access to whatever Jewish culture still exists in the Soviet Union.

Language is only one of the cultural supports that have preserved Jewish identity in the Baltic republics. Riga and Vilnius are among the few Soviet cities that still have synagogues. This is all the more remarkable in view of the small size of the Jewish communities there. The synagogues are attended chiefly on Jewish holidays. In Vilnius, for example, the synagogue also serves as the community's source

TABLE 7.1

Jewish Language Usage, by Soviet Union Republic, 1959 and 1970 (in percent)

Republic	As Native Language 1959	As Native Language 1970	As Native or Second Language 1970	Native Speakers as Percent of Total Speakers
Georgia	72.3	80.9	–	–
Lithuania	69.0	61.9	63.0	98.0
Latvia	47.9	46.2	49.4	93.5
Moldavia	50.0	44.7	52.1	85.7
Azerbaijan	35.2	41.3	46.6	88.6
Uzbekistan	49.6	37.5	42.3	88.6
Turkmenia	n.a.*	30.2	36.7	82.3
Kirgizia	30.3	26.7	33.5	79.7
Kazakhstan	22.7	22.8	27.6	82.6
Estonia	24.8	21.5	24.8	86.7
Armenia	7.0	21.1	23.9	88.4
Tajikstan	23.2	19.9	21.9	90.8
Belorussia	n.a.	17.8	28.3	63.0
Ukraine	16.9	13.1	20.2	65.0
RSFSR	13.4	11.8	21.3	55.0

*Not available.

Sources: Itogi vsesoiuznoi perepisi naseleniia SSSR 1970 goda. Natsional'nyi sostav naseleniia SSSR, vol. 4 (Moscow: "Statistika," 1973), pp. 9, 20, 43, 152, 192, 202, 223, 253, 263, 273, 280, 284, 295, 303, 306, 317; Itogi vsesoiuznoi perepisi naseleniia 1959 goda, 16 vols. (Moscow: "Gosstatizdat," 1962-63), vol. 1, (1963), p. 300; vol. 2, (1963), p. 168; vol. 3, (1963), p. 124; vol. 4 (1962), p. 138; vol. 5, (1962), p. 162; vol. 6, (1963), p. 134; vol. 7, (1963), p. 134; vol. 8, (1963), p. 160; vol. 9, (1962), p. 90; vol. 10, (1962), p. 92; vol. 11, (1963), p. 128; vol. 12 (1963), p. 116; vol. 13, (1963), p. 102; vol. 14, (1963), p. 128; vol. 15, (1962), p. 94; vol. 16, (1962), p. 184; Mordecai Altschuler, "Hayehudim bamifkad ha'ochlosin hasoveti," Behinot, no. 2/3 (1972): 22; Zev Katz, "The Jews in the Soviet Union," in Handbook of Major Soviet Nationalities, Zev Katz, et al., eds. (New York: The Free Press, 1975), p. 372.

for matzos (unleavened Passover bread). Not only pious Jews but also families who do not regard themselves as religious partake of this service. The synagogues, however, are very small, and many Jews are fearful of being seen there by KGB informers.[11]

Until 1956, Baltic Jews relied mainly on activities that could be engaged in at home, among individuals or in small family groups. Such activities included the celebration of Jewish holidays and weddings. A recent emigrant from Riga reported the almost universal celebration there of the Hanukkah holiday:

> In Moscow, almost nobody really knows how to celebrate Jewish holidays. And if they do celebrate, then they do it very symbolically in a Zionist way. But in Latvia all the rituals are carefully observed, and young people of our age know them as well as their parents. The whole of Jewish Riga will celebrate Hanukkah in families or in groups.[12]

Other Jewish emigrants have concurred with this assessment of the relative strength of Jewish cultural identification in the Baltic republics and the Soviet "heartland."[13]

Beginning in the late 1950s, nationality conscious elements of Latvian and Lithuanian Jewry began to shift the emphasis from family-based cultural supports toward broader collective forms of activity. A theater and choir ensemble were organized in Vilnius in 1956, and similar groups began to develop in Kaunas and Riga in 1957. The Vilnius group included one member who had received professional training in the State Yiddish Theater in Moscow (before it was closed in 1949). Another of the organizers, a member of the Communist Party of the Soviet Union and former partisan, printed up a Yiddish alphabet in order to be able to train youngsters for the ensemble. This, however, was suppressed by the authorities, and the "guilty" member was expelled from the Party.[14] The theater ensemble and chorus continued to perform in Vilnius until most of the members emigrated to Israel.

In Riga, the group encountered strong opposition. Priority in rehearsal space was given to Latvian and Russian amateur groups. When the Jewish group began to organize a folk orchestra as well, the leaders were called before the town Party committee. The cultural secretary told them that the party would not tolerate Jewish cultural development outside Birobijan (the USSR's Jewish Autonomous Oblast).[15] The drama group was liquidated, but despite similar pressure on the choir, it was continued in a semilegal fashion. After it had performed once, it was "too late" for it to be abolished. Instead, the group was forced to limit Jewish songs to 50 percent of its program, to begin and end with non-Jewish songs, and to drop the name "Jewish choir."[16] In February 1963, the choir was also liquidated.[17]

A spokesman for the Riga group, as well as a member of the Vilnius group, later attributed the survival of the ensemble in Lithuania to the presence in the republic of Poles. The fact that the Poles, another numerous extraterritorial nationality, enjoyed cultural rights in the fields of language, publishing, and the arts made it difficult for the authorities to forbid all but Russian- or Lithuanian-language culture, and drew attention away from the Jewish group.[18] Concurrently, attempts to organize Jewish theaters in Kiev, Kishinev, Moscow, and Leningrad met with failure.[19]

Another group identity support that began to be used during the 1960s as a basis for collective activity was the shared memory of the Nazi slaughter of Jews. Semilegal outings and commemorative meetings, sometimes involving hundreds of young Jews, took place at Rumbuli, a mass gravesite outside Riga. Similar meetings were held at Ponar, outside Vilnius, and at the Ninth Fort in Kaunas. These gatherings would later play an important role in the development of a more militant Jewish nationalism and an active struggle for emigration.[20] Complementing these examples of active identification with aspects of Jewish culture and history has been a relatively low level of acceptance among Baltic Jews of the new Soviet cultural rituals and traditions (see Table 7.2).

The maintenance of strong social ties among Baltic Jews has remained a significant support for their group identity. The smallness of the communities has undoubtedly helped a great deal in this regard. One former resident of Riga reported that although he had never taken part in Jewish activist circles, he lived in the same building as one of the better-known leaders, and was acquainted with several others. It is logical that the activist nucleus would have greater weight in these communities than did similar groups in the larger communities of Moscow, Leningrad, or Kiev.[21]

Yet another factor, which may be a cause as well as a result of Baltic Jews' strong social bonds, is the great propensity they show for endogamy. While comprehensive data about Jewish marriage patterns are not available, scattered findings show that Jewish males in Vilnius and Riga tend to be endogamous by a ratio of two to one; Jewish women in Vilnius show a much higher ratio (see Tables 7.3, 7.4, and 7.5). But in this regard, Baltic Jews differ only slightly from other Soviet Jews for whom statistics are available.[22]

Antisemitism also plays a role in maintaining Jewish social closeness. Popular antisemitism was reported to be quite high in Lithuania, having allegedly inspired a pogrom in Plunge as late as 1958. Bitter memories still remain of the role of some Lithuanians and Latvians who collaborated with the German occupiers in the extermination of Jews.[23] A Vilnius woman has verified that her son was able to play only with Jewish children, for the others ostracized him.[24]

TABLE 7.2

Attitude toward and Dissemination of New Soviet Life-Style Rituals among Nationalities in the Latvian SSR, 1964-69 (in percent)

	Attitude			
Nationality	Approve	Reject	Will Not State	Dissemination*
Latvians	88.0	6.3	5.7	71.0
Russians	84.4	5.9	9.7	51.0
Belorussians	89.5	6.6	3.8	68.0
Poles	86.6	4.3	9.1	58.0
Lithuanians	87.0	1.8	11.2	63.0
Ukrainians	90.6	4.2	5.2	57.0
Jews	63.8	11.0	20.2	34.0
Estonians	70.0	10.0	20.0	60.0
Average	–	–	–	57.0
Total	86.8	5.9	7.3	–

*"Dissemination" refers to active adoption or participation as distinct from the attitudinal question of the rest of this table.

Source: A. I. Kholmogorov, Internatsional'nye cherty sovetskikh natsii (Moscow: "Mysl'" Izdatel'stvo, 1970), trans. in Soviet Sociology 11, nos. 3/4 (1972-73): 211-327; ibid., 12, nos. 1, 2 (1973): 3-33, 27-68, see also, table on p. 274 and charts on pp. 266-69 of vol. 11, no. 3/4.

An emigrant from Riga minimized the level of popular antisemitism there and attributed whatever did exist to government-inspired propaganda. He admitted, however, that although he had had many non-Jewish friends during his school years, in the adult world, there existed a "five o'clock shadow," which tended to separate Jews socially. He also related an incident that took place at his factory. His foreman, a member of the Party, began to insult the Jews and, in particular, expressed his disappointment that more Jews had not been killed by the Nazis. This Jew made a formal complaint to the local Party committee, but the foreman was only given a slight reprimand. The wife of this emigrant claimed not to have experienced any antisemitism but suggested that this might have been due to her "non-Jewish" appearance and her fluent command of Latvian.[25]

Another Riga Jew described an incident that happened to him in Daugavpils, Latvia, on January 9, 1972:

> On that day my comrade and I were beaten up by a group of hooligans. Such things happen from time to time, but when the beatings were accompanied with insults such as "Yids and swine, Hitler didn't kill enough of you? We'll hang you all!" then it is clearly similar to antisemitism. . . . Only one of the antisemitic assailants has been arrested. . . . The court session itself was postponed at the last minute. When an incident like this is treated so casually, how can I be certain that a similar incident will not occur involving me or some other Jew tomorrow?[26]

TABLE 7.3

Jewish Endogamy and Exogamy in Novaia Vilnia District, Lithuania, 1945-64
(in percent)

	1945-49	1950-54	1955-59	1960-64
Jewish husbands with Jewish wives*	71	52	77	65
Jewish husbands with non-Jewish wives*	29	48	23	35
Jewish wives with Jewish husbands*	76	68	92	93
Jewish wives with non-Jewish husbands*	24	32	8	7

*Because the actual number of marriages was not noted in the original study, for each five-year period, the total number of husbands and the total number of wives are each taken to be equal to 100. Here, 100 percent represents the entire share of Jewish husbands and Jewish wives in their respective groups within the population covered by the original study. It does not (necessarily) represent equal numbers of Jewish husbands and Jewish wives in actual numerical terms. See J. A. Newth, "A Statistical Study of Intermarriage Among Jews in Part of Vilnius," pp. 65-66.

Source: J. A. Newth, "A Statistical Study of Intermarriage Among Jews in Part of Vilnius," Bulletin on Soviet and East European Jewish Affairs, no. 1 (1968), p. 68, based on O. A. Gantskaia and G. F. Debets, "On the Graphical Representation of the Results of a Statistical Enquiry into Inter-National Marriages," Sovetskaia etnografiia, no. 3 (1966), pp. 109-18.

TABLE 7.4

Expected (Random) Frequency and Actual Frequency of Jewish Males Selecting Jewish Females from Total Females, 1945-49, 1950-54, 1955-59, and 1960-64

Years	Expected (Random) Frequency	Actual Frequency
1945-49	0.06	1.7
1950-54	0.02	0.9
1955-59	0.08	2.3
1960-64	0.03	1.3

Source: J. A. Newth, "A Statistical Study of Intermarriage Among Jews in Part of Vilnius," Bulletin on Soviet and East European Jewish Affairs, no. 1 (1968), p. 69 (see source, Table 7.3).

TABLE 7.5

Mixed Marriages, by Nationality and Sex, in the Latvian SSR, 1964-69 (in percent)

Nationality and Sex	In a Mixed Marriage
Latvian	
Male	11.8
Female	11.3
Russian	
Male	29.8
Female	31.8
Belorussian	
Male	57.5
Female	65.6
Polish	
Male	67.6
Female	71.6
Ukrainian	
Male	77.2
Female	60.0
Jewish	
Male	36.0
Female	34.8
Lithuanian	
Male	55.5
Female	35.0

Source: A. I. Kholmogorov, Internatsional'nye cherty sovetskikh natsii (Moscow, "Mysl'" Izdatel'stvo, 1970), trans. in Soviet Sociology 11, nos. 3/4 (1972-73): 283.

To sum up, then, it seems clear that Jewish cultural identity, while circumscribed, has been preserved in the Baltic republics to a greater extent than in core Soviet areas. This has occurred because of the late entry of these Jewish communities into the Soviet Union, as well as a variety of internal and external support factors operating in the area.

A MODERNIZED NATIONALITY IN A DEVELOPED NATIONAL ENVIRONMENT

The Baltic Jews comprise a highly urbanized, educated group in a social context that is itself very modern. This is evident from figures given in Tables 7.6 and 7.7. The rapid growth in urbanization and industrialization has had profound effects in the Baltic republics.

Approximately 99 percent of Latvia's and Lithuania's Jews live in cities.[27] In addition to being highly urbanized, Baltic Jews comprise a highly educated group, relative to their weight in the republics' population (see Table 7.6).

The Baltic social context is itself quite modern and developed, having experienced rapid growth in urbanization and industrialization (see Table 7.7), and boasts a high standard of living. In 1970, average per capita income in the Baltic republics (1,499 rubles) far exceeded the USSR average (1,194 rubles).[28] Partly because of this growth, the Baltic area has been the recipient of a large flow of migration from neighboring Soviet republics.[29] This influx is apparently not entirely welcome. The concern of the eponymous Baltic nationalities over the growing Russian share in their population is evident, for example, in the letter sent by Latvian Communist dissidents to Western Communist leaders in 1972.[30] Here is a clear case of rising ethnic tension, rather than assimilation, resulting from the mixing of nationalities in a modern setting. Some successes of modernization have, thus, produced new problems. The rise of new economic, intellectual, and political elites as the Baltic nationalities continue to develop has led to increased competition with, and resentment of, the elite groups of immigrant nationalities and Russians. Modernization has not muted Baltic nationality consciousness but, rather, has provided new supports for it, through the development of greater resources and aspirations.[31]

The tensions arising out of Baltic modernization have had a direct impact on the status of the Jews in those republics. Jews are undoubtedly perceived by the eponymous groups as agents of linguistic and cultural Russification, and may be treated locally as proxies for the Russians in the venting of popular frustrations. Only 2 percent of Latvian Jews regard Latvian as their native tongue, placing them

TABLE 7.6

Jewish Students at Higher Educational Institutions, by Republic, 1960-61*

Republic	Number of Jewish Students	Jews as Percentage of Total Students	Percent Jewish Share in Total Population	Percent Jewish Share in Urban Population
RSFSR	46,555	3.1	0.7	1.3
Ukraine	18,673	4.4	2.0	4.2
Belorussia	3,020	5.1	1.9	5.8
Moldavia	1,225	6.4	3.3	13.8
Georgia	910	1.6	1.3	2.6
Latvia	800	3.7	1.7	3.1
Lithuania	413	1.6	0.9	2.3
Estonia	126	0.9	0.5	0.8

*Includes correspondence students.

Source: Viacheslav Gliutin, Vysshee obrazovanie v SSSR, (Moscow: Novosti, 1965), cited in Alec Nove and J. A. Newth, "The Jewish Population: Demographic Trends and Occupational Patterns," The Jews in Soviet Russia Since 1917, ed. Lionel Kochan, 2d. ed. (London and New York: Oxford University Press, 1972), p. 154.

TABLE 7.7

Indicators of Modernization in the Baltic Republics, 1913, 1940, and 1973

Republic	Growth of Industrial Production[a]			Urban Population as Percentage of Total			Number of Students in Higher Education (per 10,000 population)	
	1913	1940	1973	1913	1940	1974	1940	1973
Estonia	100	130	4,300	19	34	67	45	153
Latvia	100	90	3,100	38	35	65	52	175
Lithuania	100	260	10,200	13	23	55	20	182
USSR[b]	100	770	11,300	18	33	60	41	186

[a]1913 = 100.

[b]Average.

Source: V. Stanley Vardys, "Modernization and Baltic Nationalism," Problems of Communism 24, no. 5 (1975): 36.

slightly above the Russians, among whom the figure is 1.3 percent. Aside from the Russians themselves, Ukrainians and Jews in Latvia rate highest in regarding Russian as their native tongue: 46 percent and 45 percent, respectively. In their knowledge of Latvian, Jews stand higher than Russians and Ukrainians, however. Among Ukrainians, 24 percent claimed such knowledge; among Russians, 31.5 percent; among Jews, 43 percent.[32] In their social relations, Jews also seem closer to the Russians than to the eponymous nationalities: Baltic Jews who do intermarry with non-Jews tend to choose Russian mates.[33]

Jews, along with Ukrainians and Russians, are highly visible elements in the Baltic urban population and are a competing group in the field of specialized secondary and higher education. Under conditions of urban housing shortage, Baltic families moving to the cities see the urbanized Jews and other immigrants as obstacles to the satisfaction of their own needs and desires. Even Jewish Communists may be moved aside from their positions in the Party by aspiring Communists of eponymic Baltic nationality, as the case of the Jewish Communist leader Ziman(as) recently showed in Lithuania.[34]

Baltic Jews, in their turn, perceive an increasing deprivation, especially in their access to Communist Party positions, governmental posts, and higher education.[35] A Jewish instructor at the Pedagogical Institute in Vilnius was reportedly told by the head of the Institute, "It matters little that today you excel others in German or English languages, in physics or mathematics, chemistry or music. We will develop our own cadres so that tomorrow Lithuanians will be more qualified than you."[36] The central Communist Party press in mid-1971 found it necessary to condemn discrimination based on nationality in hiring practices, singling out the Latvian, Lithuanian, and Georgian republics as areas where resentment of outsiders was high.[37] If this is the case, then resentment is certainly felt by Jews, as well as other "outsiders," living there.

Modernization in the Baltic union republics has undoubtedly had other effects on the Jews there, effects not arising from ethnic tensions but rather from more positive influences. The Western orientation, which is present in these union republics, and the contacts maintained with Finland, Poland, and Western churches are significant in this regard. While such contacts are not new in Baltic history, modernization has improved the capability for communication and exchange of information. Standards for evaluation of conditions in these republics may, thus, be more "Western" than in other parts of the Soviet Union. This creates an atmosphere that is different from that prevailing in "heartland" areas. In such an atmosphere, maintaining contacts with Israel or Western Jewish communities may not be such radical or conspicuous acts as they would be for Jews in other Soviet areas.

Finally, Baltic Jews are aware that Baltic eponymous nationalities have themselves produced dissident elements. In contrast to the democratic dissidents whom the Jews have encountered in the Russian republic, the Baltic groups' grievances stem precisely from the nationality question. (The Baltic eponymous nationalities, having attained independent statehood following World War I, are, of course, highly developed in a political and national sense.) While there seems to be little if any direct connection between Jewish and Baltic nationality dissidents, they all share certain common experiences, concepts, and categories of thought. The existence of several such groups in a relatively small population probably has a mutually reinforcing effect on all of them. A former Jewish activist from Vilnius reported that discussions did indeed take place between Jewish and Lithuanian nationalists. He himself admitted to a certain ambivalence toward the Lithuanians. On the one hand, he admired their intense nationalism. On the other, he hated them for the role that some had played in World War II. The Jewish activists realized that whatever would weaken Soviet totalitarianism would also help the Jews who wished to emigrate. Their strategy was to support the cause of Lithuanian nationalists, without participating in their activities.[38] There are some obvious parallels among the various nationality dissent groups and their "constituencies": The collective memories of annexation and occupation, the rapid social changes introduced by Sovietization and modernization, the ties they have preserved with their dispersed conationals, the perceived threats to their linguistic and cultural identity, and the like. There are, of course, significant differences as well, the most important being the fact that the eponymous Baltic nationalities have a fairly high legal standing due to the union republic status of their homeland. Jews, as a group in the Soviet Union, lack comparable legal protection.

NATIONALITY DISSATISFACTION AMONG BALTIC JEWS

The expression of Jewish dissatisfaction and self-assertion in the Baltic republics has taken five forms: the formation of Zionist circles and the dissemination of samizdat, the promotion of cultural activities and Holocaust memorials, letters and petitions to Soviet and non-Soviet authorities, public demonstrations, and emigration.

Clandestine Zionist (or Jewish nationalist) circles began to form in the 1950s. These small groups expressed an attachment to Jewish nationality and to Israel as the Jewish homeland. Some of them were inspired by older Zionists, who had been active in the pre-Soviet period and who were returning from Siberian deportation. Others were started by members of the younger generation, who had experienced war and/or deportation in their childhood.[39] These groups focused on the need to educate postwar Jewish youth about Zionism and Jewish history. In 1957, a group in Riga issued its first samizdat publication, which related the story of the Warsaw Ghetto uprising of 1943.[40] Other materials circulated included Israeli Prime Minister Ben-Gurion's speeches about the 1956 Sinai Campaign, Jewish poetry, sections of Simon Dubnow's _History of the Jews_, and (later on) Israeli Attorney General Hausner's summation at the trial of Nazi war criminal Adolf Eichmann.[41] An influential piece of samizdat produced in Riga was the translation of Leon Uris's novel about Israel's fight for independence, _Exodus_. At least two groups worked separately on the translation, apparently with no awareness of each other, during 1962-64.[42] By the late 1960s, one Riga group had circulated, besides a version of _Exodus_, two works by the prewar Zionist leader and theoretician Vladimir Zeev Jabotinsky; a book by the Slovak Communist Yaroslav Mniachko, entitled _Aggressors_, which condemned the Soviet view of the Arab-Israeli conflict; and a press bulletin, with material extracted from the Israeli Communist newspaper _Kol Ha'am_.[43] The character of this early samizdat activity is revealed in descriptions given by two former participants from Riga: "The nature of the way it was organized was such that no one knows more than his small piece of the truth. . . . I knew of five to ten people in those days. Someone else knew five or so. Everyone really believes that it began in his kitchen. . . . This is because the movement was so diffused—so spontaneous."[44] (See Appendix C for full quotations.)

After the Israeli-Arab war of 1967, the demand for samizdat increased; it was felt that material ought to be sent from the Baltic into central Russian regions as well, where Jewish samizdat was not yet available. The various Riga groups organized a samizdat committee in 1969, and contact was established with similar groups that were forming in other cities. In addition to translations and reproductions of materials received from abroad, the Riga committee now began to produce original material as well.[45] The goal of the samizdat, by that time, was seen as the creation of a reserve of people willing to undertake the effort of application for exit permits. The leader of the Riga committee felt that application for visas was highest in cities where samizdat was circulated.[46]

Other activities of the Zionist circles included the establishment of a series of "open-door" houses, where Jews could meet to discuss Jewish topics, sing Jewish songs, and receive information.[47] Slides were made from Israeli picture postcards, and by 1969-70, three men were conducting several illustrated lectures a week. At times, they traveled outside Riga as "guest lecturers."[48] Hebrew-language study groups existed sporadically throughout the 1960s, and these blossomed especially after 1969, encouraged by similar successes in Leningrad.[49] In the Soviet context, in which facilities for Jewish cultural and educational activities have been all but liquidated, these clandestine publications, lectures, open houses, and Hebrew classes are indeed expressions of nationality dissatisfaction and defiance.

A certain degree of controversy exists, however, with regard to the significance of legal or semilegal Jewish cultural activities. To what extent, for example, can it be said that the amateur theater and choir groups were an expression of the Jewish nationality's dissatisfaction? They may more properly be considered an expression of Jewish cultural consciousness as such and an adjustment to new conditions, rather than an expression of militant activism. Among the participants themselves there emerged ambivalent feelings. Some of them expressed the view that by forming a Jewish troupe, they were furnishing the Soviet government with excellent propaganda: It would now be able to point to the "flourishing" of Jewish culture in the USSR. Thus, a dissident stance might well have dictated the abstention from such cultural activity. Others, however, felt that the preservation of at least some Jewish cultural activity was worth the risk of being considered unwitting collaborators.[50] Besides their cultural content, the performances of the amateur groups served as a social focus for the Baltic Jews qua Jews, something that they had lacked, outside the synagogue, since the Soviet annexation. This heightened the Baltic Jews' collective consciousness and made them aware that it was possible, after all, to wring certain nationality rights from the Soviet government. The same could be said for the rare, officially sponsored concerts, such as the 1966 tour of Israeli singer Geula Gil. After her concert in Riga, the enthusiastic audience took to the streets and turned the event into a spontaneous demonstration.[51]

Holocaust memorial activities may be said to fall somewhere between legal cultural events and clandestine expressions of dissatisfaction. The events that developed around the Rumbuli mass gravesite outside Riga are a case in point. Memory of the "Great Fatherland War" runs deep in the Baltic republics, and memorials to the dead are legitimate, officially sponsored activities. In the fall of 1962, a group of young Jews decided to visit the site where thousands of Riga's Jews were massacred in 1951. They were reacting to the impact of the Eichmann trial, to Yevgeny Yevtushenko's Russian peom "Babi Yar," and to the fact that the fate of the Jews as such was never mentioned at any of the official "antifascist" gatherings.[52] The location of the Jewish massacre was ascertained with the help of a returned deportee and local farmers. A homemade memorial plaque was nailed to a tree when a small group of Jews assembled for the first open air meeting. As a participant later recalled, "This was done in defiance of the Soviet law which forbids the display of public signs by private persons without official authorization."[53]

Another inscribed memorial was set up in 1963, on the occasion of the twentieth anniversary of the Warsaw Ghetto uprising. Fifty people attended that meeting, following which it was decided to undertake the preservation and landscaping of the site. This was accomplished with the help of hundreds of Jews who came with shovels, rakes, pails, turf, and stones on Sunday afternoons. It was obvious that activities of this scale would not go unnoticed by the authorities, and petitions were then sent asking for official recognition of the project and an official announcement of forthcoming meetings.[54] This step was opposed by the more radical Zionists among the organizers, who did not want to collaborate with the government in any way. The authorities at first refused permission for a separate Jewish memorial, but then granted authorization for the landscaping and restoration of mass gravesites. While thus opposing the Jewish gatherings, the authorities made the Rumbuli activities quasilegal. Barred from press announcements, the Jews used the synagogue to publicize the gatherings, and continued to hold memorial meetings, despite official harassment through 1973. On December 9, 1973, the militia prevented 150 Riga Jews from meeting at Rumbuli and arrested three participants. Soviet President Podgorny later laid a wreath at the site of a Nazi concentration camp in Salaspils, Latvia, evidently reflecting a return to a policy of allowing only multi-ethnic "antifascist" commemorations.[55]

The expression of Jewish nationality dissatisfaction had, in the meantime, become more public, with the start of a campaign of letters and petitions in 1968. On February 15 of that year, 26 Lithuanian Jews (some of whom were Party members) wrote a collective letter to Antanas Sniečkus, then first secretary of the Communist Party in Lithuania. The letter protested against discrimination against Jews in Party cadres and in higher education, against the suppression of Jewish cultural identity, and against antisemitic incidents: "We are not wanted here, we are being completely oppressed, forcibly denationalized, and even publicly insulted in the press—while at the same time we are forcibly kept here."[56]

There followed a growing number of letters and petitions, both individual and collective, addressed to Soviet, as well as to non-Soviet, authorities.[57] A study of these documents has revealed the high proportion of Baltic Jews involved in this campaign, and the particularly high concentration of the effort in the Baltic republics (the proportion of participants per Jewish population). (See Table 7.8.)

TABLE 7.8

Petitions Addressed to Soviet and Non-Soviet Authorities: Percentage by Jews and Collective and Individual Petitions by Geographic Distribution, 1968-70

Petition Signatories by Republic					
Republic	Size of Jewish Population*	Percentage of Total USSR Population	Number of Signers	Percentage of Total Signers	Number of Signers per 10,000 Jews
Lithuania	24,000	1.1	44	4.5	18.3
Vilnius	16,491		44		27.5
Latvia	36,700	1.7	244	25.3	66.0
Riga	30,581		240		80.0
Georgia	55,000	2.6	349	36.2	63.5
RSFSR	808,000	37.6	267	27.7	3.3

Collective and Individual Petitions by Geographical Distribution

Location	Number of Petitions: Collective	Number of Petitions: Individual	Total
Moscow	25	56	81
Riga	24	86	110
Vilnius	10	10	20
Georgia	9	13	22
Leningrad	6	6	12
Minsk	3	5	8
Kiev	2	4	6
Kharkov	—	17	17
Others	5	21	26
Total	84	218	302

*1970.

Note: Share of Vilnius and Riga in total number of petitions equals 43 percent.

Source: Shimon Redlich, "Ha'atzumot shel yehudei brit ha'moatsot k'bitul l'hitorrut leumit (1968-1970)," Behinot 5, no. 5 (1974): 23.

The majority of the petitions focus on the desire of Jews to emigrate, and on the motivations of the signatories.

Among the motivations for emigration most frequently mentioned are the following: family suffering and dispersal during World War II, and the desire to be reunited with relatives abroad; antisemitism or alienation felt in the USSR; and attachment to Israel, the Jewish people, and Jewish traditions and the lack of opportunity to express this in the USSR.[58] While these themes are present in petitions from various Soviet cities, the theme of cultural attachment is most frequently, and understandably, cited in letters from Baltic Jews (see Appendix C).[59] A further indication of the attitudes that prompted these petitions is contained in a study of Soviet Jewish immigrants in Israel, undertaken in 1972. The study distinguishes between zapadniki ("Westerners," those from the Soviet-annexed territories) and "heartlanders" (see Table 7.9). The study states that "Soviet immigrants who did not feel at home in the USSR tend to have a stronger Jewish background than the others, report feeling antisemitism more often (though the correlation is only 20), and do not feel themselves "Russian" in Israel."[60]

Public displays of dissatisfaction may be said to have begun with the holocaust commemorations and the riotous finales of such concerts as the one in 1966 already mentioned. After 1970, however, organized protest demonstrations were added to other methods used in the campaign for emigration. A very dramatic demonstration (or series of demonstrations), initiated largely by Baltic Jews, took place in February and March of 1971. On February 26, a group of Jews went to the offices of the Latvian Ministry of Internal Affairs and the Lat-

TABLE 7.9

Feelings of Alienation and Integration in the USSR:
Soviet Jewish Emigrants in Israel, 1972
(in percent of informants)

Feelings	USSR	Zapadniki*	Heartlanders
Always felt at home	2.8	1.4	4.1
Most of the time felt at home	20.1	15.7	24.3
Felt at home up to a certain event or period	13.2	10.0	16.2
Felt at home in some respects and not in others	2.8	1.4	4.1
Infrequently felt at home	25.0	27.1	23.0
Never felt at home	36.1	44.3	28.4

*"Westerners," those from the Soviet-annexed territories.

Source: Zvi Gitelman, "Values, Opinions, and Attitudes of Soviet Jewish Emigres" (Paper delivered at meeting of the American Association for the Advancement of Slavic Studies, Atlanta, Ga., October 9-11, 1975), p. 18.

vian Council of Ministers to demand exit visas; they were refused. On March 10, 56 of the Riga activists traveled to Moscow, to the reception room of the Presidium of the USSR Supreme Soviet. They were joined by approximately 100 others from Vilnius, Kaunas, Daugavpils, Tallinn, and from Lvov and Berdichev in the Ukraine. They proceeded to stage a sit-in and hunger strike that lasted 26 hours, during the course of which they submitted a written protest and were interviewed by Western correspondents. After the militia was called in, the protesters were forced to leave. The next day, however, they marched en masse to the Ministry of Internal Affairs.[61]

The event that brought the Soviet Jewish underground into the international spotlight was the 1970 trial in Leningrad of a group of Jews accused of attempting to hijack a Soviet plane. All but one of the defendants were residents of Riga. This may simply have been due to the fact that the group had to be drawn from a small, intimate circle of people because of security precautions. It has been suggested, however, that such an act was typical of the Riga activists, with their highly emotional nationality feelings. The Moscow activists, by contrast, had learned the more sophisticated techniques and adherence to Soviet legality practiced by the Democratic Movement dissidents.

As in other forms of dissident behavior, Baltic Jews have taken a numerically disproportionate share in the emigration from the Soviet Union (see Table 7.10). It may be asked, however, To what extent is emigration a true specific indicator of nationality dissatisfaction? Three major objections have been expressed in this regard. One is that Baltic Jews may emigrate for the same basic reasons as (it is assumed) people everywhere do: to achieve greater social and economic security. The second is that the Baltic Jews may have emigrated in larger numbers because many of their friends and relatives did and not necessarily because their nationality experience or attitudes were any more acute than those of other Soviet Jews. The third is that it may very well be Soviet governmental policy, and not higher Baltic Jewish dissatisfaction, which is responsible for the greater rate of emigration among these apparently nonassimilable and geographically peripheral groups.

All three arguments have some merit. There can be no doubt that general social and economic improvement are among the goals pursued by Jewish emigrants. In the 1972 study of Soviet Jews in Israel, a majority reported that their standard of living in Israel was similar to or higher than that which they had experienced in the USSR, especially with regard to housing conditions.[62] (See Tables 7.11 and 7.12.)

The growing trend of Soviet Jews to emigrate to the United States and other Western countries rather than Israel (now estimated at 40

TABLE 7.10

Jewish Emigration from the USSR, by Geographic Community, through June 1974

Community	Total Number Emigrated	Percent of Total Emigrants	Percent of Each Community That Has Emigrated
Georgia	27,400	27	47
Central Asia	7,100	7	4
Baltics	25,400	25	33
Ukraine	15,300	15	2
Moldavia	10,100	10	8
RSFSR	10,100	10	1

Note: In 1971, Latvian and Lithuanian Jews made up over one-third of the Jewish emigrants. Over the longer period of 1967-75, however, the greater flow of emigrants from other Soviet areas is reflected in the following proportional shift: Ukraine: 29 percent; Georgia: 27 percent; Baltics: 18 percent; Moldavia: 10 percent; Central Asia: 8 percent; RSFSR: 7 percent; Caucasus: 1 percent. (Source: Zvi Gitelman, "Values, Opinions and Attitudes of Soviet Jewish Emigres" [Paper delivered at meeting of the American Association for the Advancement of Slavic Studies, Atlanta, Ga., October 9-11, 1975], pp. 9-10.)

Source: Zev Katz, "The Jews in the Soviet Union," Handbook of Major Soviet Nationalities, ed. Zev Katz et al. (New York: The Free Press, 1975), p. 385.

percent of the total emigrants) may also reflect the importance of economic and social considerations to many of the emigrants. In 1972, 540 Soviet Jews were reported by the Hebrew Immigrant Aid Society (HIAS) to have entered the United States; in 1973, the figure climbed to 1,773; in 1974, the number was 4,150.[63] It may be significant that Baltic Jews, who have been so overrepresented in the overall Jewish emigration, do not occupy a similar position among those arriving in the United States, as Table 7.13 shows.

With regard to the second reservation relating to the motivations for leaving the USSR, an emigrant from Riga reported that it was not until after many acquaintances had left that he and his family began to think seriously of emigrating.[64] Thus, there is some validity to this argument, too. Finally, it seems entirely plausible that governmental policy is at work in producing more exit visas from peripheral areas than from "core" Soviet cities. This may have the dual function of reducing troublemaking elements in sensitive areas, while retaining the brainpower of the highly educated and technically trained Jews of the Russian SFSR.

Nevertheless, while these factors must certainly contribute to the emigration of Soviet Jews, they do not adequately explain the dominant role played by Baltic Jews in the Jewish movement. Baltic Jews, it was noticed, have not figured prominently in the emigration to the United States, producing a more "Zionist" emigration. The fact that many friends and relatives have been leaving from the Baltic republics may owe something to social ties; but surely if more Baltic Jews had acquaintances who emigrated than other Soviet Jews had, a greater impulse to emigrate must have existed among Baltic Jews in the first place. While outsiders have no way of gauging the quanti-

TABLE 7.11

Difference in Income and Standard of Living after Move to Israel by Soviet Jews, 1972 (percent of informants)

Factor	Loss	Similar	Gain
Standard of living	22	27	51
Income	50	25	25

Source: Zvi Gitelman, "Values, Opinions, and Attitudes of Soviet Jewish Emigres" (Paper delivered at meeting of the American Association for the Advancement of Slavic Studies, Atlanta, Ga., October 9-11, 1975), p. 39.

TABLE 7.12

Density of Living and Satisfaction with Housing after Move to Israel by Soviet Jews, 1972 (percent of informants)

Factor	Loss	Similar	Gain
Density of living	22	16	62
Satisfaction with housing	30	29	41

Source: Zvi Gitelman, "Values, Opinions, and Attitudes of Soviet Jewish Emigres" (Paper delivered at meeting of the American Association for the Advancement of Slavic Studies, Atlanta, Ga., October 9-11, 1975), p. 40; see also, Table 7.11.

TABLE 7.13

Immigration to the United States during the First Half of 1975, by Union Republic of Origin[a]

Republic (SSR)	Number of Arrivals
Belorussia	62
Estonia	3
Georgia	42
Latvia	59
Lithuania	30
Moldavia	132
Russia	600[b]
Ukraine	1,568[c]
Total	2,954

[a]Partial list.
[b]Twenty percent.
[c]Fifty-three percent.
Source: Hebrew Immigrant Aid Society, Statistical Abstract, Midyear Report 1975, vol. 16, no. 2 (1976), p. 15.

tative effects of Soviet policy on Jewish exit visas, emigration statistics can be put side by side with spontaneous expressions of Jewish dissatisfaction, like petitions, which are patently not governed by central Soviet policy. There is a direct correlation between the high number of petitions from the Baltic republics and the high level of emigration from that area. This reinforces the view that the desire for emigration has still found its greatest expression in the Baltic republics and Georgia, regardless of policy (see Tables 7.8 and 7.10). Emigration is therefore another legitimate gauge of Jewish nationality dissatisfaction, and is linked in the Baltic republics to cultural identity.

A significant question remains concerning the differing degrees of activism shown by Jews in Latvia and Lithuania. If the Jews in Lithuania shared a similar cultural background with Latvian Jews, and scored even higher on such indicators as Jewish-language knowledge than Latvian Jews, why have they also not been as vocal as the Latvian Jews in demonstrating their dissatisfaction (see Tables 7.1 and 7.8)? Most available estimates of Soviet Jewish emigration presently group Latvian and Lithuanian Jews together in one category. More specific information would probably reveal more about this situation. One estimate of Soviet Jewish emigration for the year 1972 did list Latvian Jews and Lithuanian Jews separately: those from

Latvia made up 7 percent of the emigrants, while those from Lithuania made up 11 percent.[65] Thus, while Lithuanian Jews may not be as vocal or conspicuous in the Jewish protest movement, the possibility exists that they are "voting with their feet." Still, the question remains: Why are Lithuanian Jews apparently less vocal?

Several suggestions have been made concerning the lack of parity between these two communities. One observer has suggested that because Lithuanian Jews managed to retain at least some representation in the Communist Party and were able to maintain their amateur ensembles, their grievances were not as sharply defined as those of the Latvian Jews.[66] Another possible factor, he suggests, is the more visceral fear that exists among Lithuanian Jews of general antisemitism, making them more reluctant to be conspicuous.[67] While there is probably much merit in these suggestions, it is certainly relevant that among the Baltic republics, Lithuania stands on the lowest rung with regard to such indicators of modernization as urbanization and per capita income. The social environment of Lithuanian Jews may, therefore, prompt a response that is somewhat different from that of the Latvian community.

MODERNIZATION, NATIONALITY CULTURE, AND EXPRESSED DISSATISFACTION

The link between cultural identity, cultural activities, and nationality dissatisfaction is made implicit through the coincidence of statistics on language retention, emigration, attitudes toward Soviet and Jewish culture, and petitions. This correlation was made explicit in the petitions of many Baltic Jews, as well as in testimony given by Soviet Jewish activists (see Appendix C). This does not diminish the importance of political events and social conditions, which actually triggered the large-scale public expression of Jewish dissatisfaction. Several of the more important of these catalyzing factors were the following: the abatement of Stalinist terror, the Middle East war of 1967, the growth of an anti-Zionist campaign in the Soviet press, and the signing by the Soviet Union of the Universal Declaration of Human Rights (which includes the right of free emigration). Nevertheless, while these factors were operative in all Soviet areas, the greatest reaction to them came from the numerically weak, but culturally strong, communities of the Baltic union republics and Georgia. These communities possessed a core of cultural identity that prepared them to react to the events of the 1960s. These events did not create dissatisfaction out of a void; they served rather to escalate and intensify processes and attitudes already present.

It was the fight to maintain the cultural ensembles and memorial meetings that gave experience to Jewish nationalists in dealing with the authorities, and it raised the collective consciousness of the Jewish population. Most of those involved in the cultural sphere also actively circulated samizdat and participated in the emigration struggle.[68] Samizdat, which began as a tool of cultural and historical education, was easily turned into a medium for the emigration movement. The same applies to the clandestine Zionist circles, Hebrew study groups, and open houses that operated for years in the Baltic republics. Far from being a miracle, the emergence of a Soviet Jewish underground there was the result of very real cultural, social, and historical processes.

What of the alleged homogenizing tendencies of the modernizing process? From the case of the Baltic Jews, it is evident that modernization's assimilating thrust can be deflected by a strong cultural identity factor when it is accompanied by catalyzing political or social factors. The same process is observable among the eponymous Baltic nationalities, among whom nationality consciousness has been anything but diminished through their rapid modernization. The modernizing process itself has aided the growth of nationality dissatisfaction. Rising expectations and aspirations, when confronted with perceived limitations or deprivation, often result in frustration and dissatisfaction. "Modern developments have equipped ethnic communities . . . with new political resources and aspirations. . . . Ethnic groups are proving that nations do not have a monopoly on political development."[69] Thus it should not be surprising that the Soviet Jewish experience of rapid assimilation in the 1920s and 1930s, the beginning stages of that group's modernization and Sovietization, were not repeated with the newly Sovietized, but already modernized, Baltic Jewry.[70] Moldavian Jews, whose cultural history, linguistic adherence, and recent incorporation into the Soviet Union most resemble that of the Baltic Jews, live in a less highly developed social environment than do the Baltic Jews and are not as active in their expression of nationality dissatisfaction. (The Georgian Jews, with their premodern social structure and religious attachment, are a wholly different case: problems of modernization, assimilation, and dissatisfaction do not apply to them at the same level as among the Soviet West's Jews.) On the other hand, Jews of the Russian SFSR, who live in modern, urban areas, lack the strong cultural identity that is present in the Baltic community, and are proportionately less involved in the Jewish dissident movement. The greater numbers of the Moscow Jews and the status of Moscow as the most "public" Soviet city raise that Jewish community to its position of importance in the Jewish movement. When judged in proportion to their respective populations, Baltic Jewish activists have formed a much larger group than have those of Moscow or Leningrad.

In the context of recent Soviet Jewish history, Baltic Jews have experienced an unusual interplay of strong cultural identity with a high level of modernization, evidently a highly volatile mixture (this interplay is illustrated in Figures 7.1 and 7.2). While maintaining a relatively high level of nationality consciousness, the Baltic Jews have developed sophisticated techniques of communication and informational exchange and have responded to pressures and tensions generated by the very successes of modernization in their social environment.

Although the Baltic Jewish experience is applicable as well to the eponymous Baltic nationalities, other factors are operating in the latters' group dissatisfaction. Because of the history and present status of the three Baltic nationalities, political factors are much more important than they are in the Jewish case. There is present in Baltic nationality dissent an element of territorial loyalty and a desire for a greater measure than presently attainable of administrative autonomy. This can play no part in the Jewish nationality question at this time. Consequently, cultural factors play a greater role in the avenues presented for the Baltic Jews' development than for the eponymous Baltic nationalities.

The comparison of the Jews to nationalities with union republic status can therefore be only partial. Nevertheless, it is significant that eponymous groups, too, seem to turn to cultural identity as a nationality support when political or territorial outlets for their group identity are limited. Evidence of such tendencies may be found, for example, in the importance attached to nationality literature in Estonia, song festivals in Latvia, and linguistic purity in Lithuania. The "possession" of a territory by a Soviet nationality may not greatly alter the basic process of its search for viable support factors. It is impossible to say, for example, whether or not an eponymous group, such as the Belorussians, has an ultimate advantage over a noneponymous group, such as the Jews, in the struggle for group maintenance. At most, the possession of a territory may shift the focus of that group's nationality question toward the institutional and bureaucratic structures for which territory serves as a base. There seems to be a certain degree of similarity in the development of nationality consciousness among Soviet Jews, eponymous nationalities, and dispersed, noneponymous nationalities, despite the vast differences in their respective legal status. How much difference is there between the behavior of nationality conscious Lithuanians, Crimean Tatars, and Jews? In the final analysis, each group faces similar dilemmas of maintaining its collective existence, defining its relationship with the Soviet state, and making timely shifts in its reliance on the various nationality support factors.

Other comparisons may perhaps be made with the mobile Soviet Armenians, Georgians, or Soviet Germans. Even a superficial glance at their development tends to confirm the thesis of this chapter. The

FIGURE 7.1

Modernization

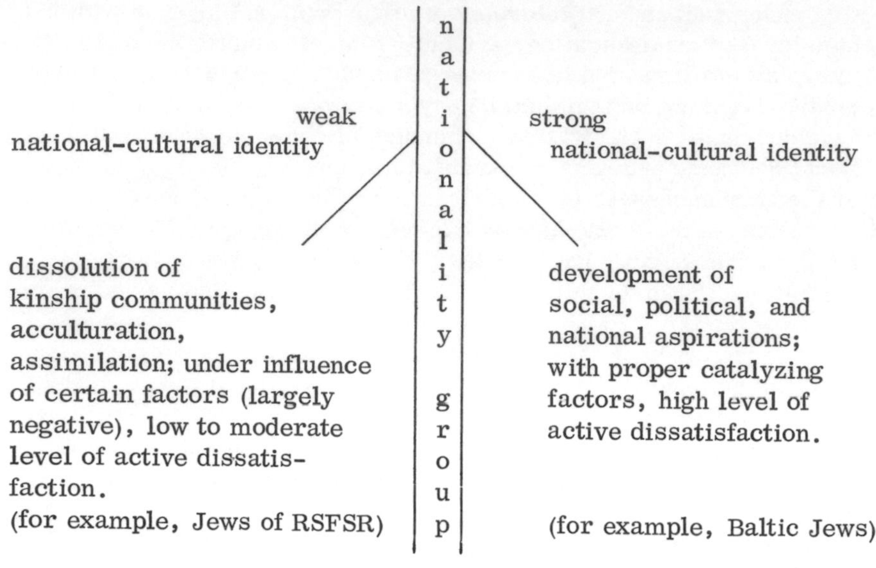

Source: Compiled by the author.

FIGURE 7.2

Strong National-Cultural Identity

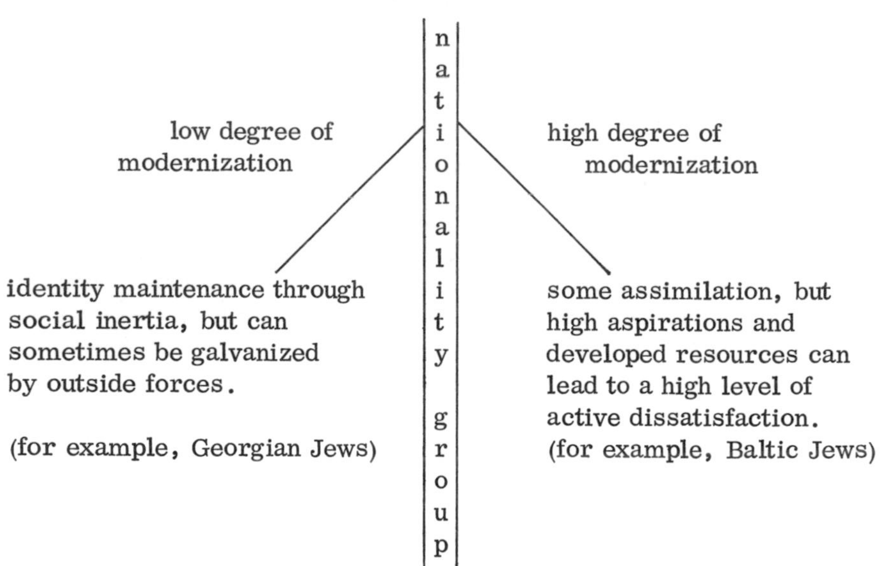

Source: Compiled by the author.

Armenians, for example, possess a standard of living that approaches that of the western union republics and have experienced a growth in industrial production at the second highest rate in the Soviet Union. Their specialized production of electronic devices is well-known, and it is significant that they have retained a dominant role in the local scientific establishment. In 1969, 94 percent of scientific personnel in Armenia were Armenians. Armenians also have the second highest ratio of scientific personnel to population among 17 major nationalities, placing them right after the Jews. With all of these manifestations of modernization, Armenians have retained a strong sense of nationality and cultural identity, exhibited in their high level of native language maintenance and in open expressions of sentiment against the Turks.[71] Similarly, the Georgians, while remaining largely agricultural, have also exhibited a large industrial growth rate, and rank high in such indicators as savings per capita, living space, doctor to population ratio, and metallurgical production. They, too, have manifested a strong attachment to their nationality language, being the lowest in their knowledge of Russian except for the Azerbaijanians. Nationality consciousness appears to be high in Party and academic circles.[72] The recent emigration of Soviet and Polish Germans suggests several parallels with the Jewish case, and deserves an in-depth comparative study.

The main thing that can be extrapolated from the experience of the Baltic Jews is this: social and economic modernization do not in themselves necessarily promote political stability and may, under certain conditions, give rise to serious disaffection among ethnic segments of a population. These conditions may be political in nature, arising from tensions related to governmental control. They may be economic, deriving from competition, use of natural resources, variations in standard of living, and so on. Social acceptance or discrimination also destabilizes a multi-ethnic situation.

Economic problems can cause individual or interest group dissatisfaction. Adverse political and social conditions may create a more collective sense of grievance, but they do not, at the same time, affect all members of a nationality to an equal degree; nor are all political opinions alike. When, however, a nationality possesses a relatively strong sense of cultural identity, this can serve as a conduit through which dissatisfactions that are triggered by political, economic, or social conditions may spread rapidly among members of the group. Dissatisfaction may then become focused on the greatest common denominator of such a nationality: its language and culture. The medium can thus become the object of primary concern. The nationality group is led to reevaluate the potentials of its existence as a nationality, and it will then shift to support factors that it views as more likely to ensure its survival. Among Baltic Jews, this process has led to a shift from the pre-Soviet identity supports of communal autonomy and religion, to an attempted accommodation to such accepted Soviet cultural forms as folk ensembles and war commemorations, and finally to emigration.

As modernization ensures the economic base of more and more Soviet nationalities, they may also be inspired to reevaluate their positions. If the Baltic and Baltic Jewish examples are trustworthy guides, the emphasis in the Soviet nationality question could shift dramatically in the direction of increased self-assertion on the part of the nationalities. Activated by political catalysts, by the tempo of modernization, and by the new perceptions of relative status that modernization brings, nationalities will find a firm base of self-assertiveness in their historic and cultural identities.

The "question" would then take on a more radical significance. For if the Soviet regime can deal with the Jewish, German, and (to an extent) the Baltic nationalities by using the safety valve of emigration, the same will not be true of nationalities that lack a base outside the Soviet Union. The "question" will at that point have to be faced squarely, for it will challenge the very foundations of Soviet society.

NOTES

1. For a full discussion of this issue, see Peter Berger et al., The Homeless Mind (New York: Random House, 1973), pp. 64, 77-80, 92; Karl Deutsch, Nationalism and Social Communication, 2d ed. (Cambridge, Mass.: MIT Press, 1966); Cynthia Enloe, Ethnic Conflict and Political Development (Boston: Little, Brown, 1973); Zvi Gitelman, "Modernizatsia, z'chuyot adam, v'haleumiut hayehudit bivrit hamoatsot," Shvut, no. 2, book 8 (1974): 9-14; Marion J. Levy, Jr., Modernization and the Structure of Societies (Princeton, N.J.: Princeton University Press, 1969), pp. 90, 128, 171, 742, 752; V. Stanley Vardys, "Modernization and Baltic Nationalism," Problems of Communism 24, no. 5 (1975): 32-48.

2. Gitelman, p. 14.

3. Enloe, pp. 27-28, 34.

4. Zvi Gitelman, "Assimilation, Acculturation, and National Consciousness Among Soviet Jews" (New York: Synagogue Council of America, 1973), pp. 36-43; Zev Katz, "The Jews in the Soviet Union," Handbook of Major Soviet Nationalities, ed. Zev Katz et al. (New York: The Free Press, 1975), pp. 385-86.

5. Itogi vsesoiuznoi perepisi naseleniia 1970 goda. Natsional'nyi sostav naseleniia SSR (Moscow: Statistika, 1973), 4: 263, 273, 280; see also, Katz et al., eds., pp. 356, 364-65; Mordecai Altschuler,

"Hayehudim bamifkad ha'ochlosin hasovieti," Behinot, no. 2/3, (1972): 12-16.

6. For a description of these communities, see Yahadut latvia (Tel Aviv: Association of Latvian and Estonian Jews in Israel, 1963); Yahadut lita (Tel Aviv: Association of Lithuanian Jews in Israel, 1972), vol. 2; Yosef Gar, "Baltische Lender," Algemeyne entsiklopedye in Yidish, vol. 11, Yidn VI (New York: Jewish Encyclopedic Handbooks, 1964), pp. 321-401; for English articles, see "Latvia" and "Lithuania," Encyclopedia Judaica (Jerusalem: Keter Publishing House, 1971), 10: 1462-69, 11: 361-90; see also, The Jews in Latvia, ed. Mendel Bobe et al. (Tel Aviv: Association of Latvian and Estonian Jews in Israel, Ben-nun Press, 1971); David Ebner, "A Demographic Study of the Latvian Jewish Population Between the Two World Wars" (Typescript, written under a research grant from the YIVO Institute for Jewish Research, New York, 1970).

7. A. I. Kholmogorov, Internatsional'nye cherty sovetskikh natsii (Moscow: Izdatel'stvo "Mysl'," 1970), trans. in Soviet Sociology 11, nos. 3/4 (1972-73): 249.

8. Leonard Schroeter, The Last Exodus (New York: Universe Books, 1974), pp. 61-63; see also, Yosef Gar, Azoi is es geshen in lite: tsu der geschichte fun der sovietisher memshole, 1940-1941 (Tel Aviv: "Hamenora" Publishing House, 1965), pp. 1-33; David Grodner, "In Soviet Poland and Lithuania," Contemporary Jewish Record 4 (1941): 143-47; Dov Levin, "The Jews and the Sovietization of Latvia," Soviet Jewish Affairs, no. 1 (1971): 46-48; Shimon Redlich, "The Jews in the Soviet Annexed Territories 1939-41," ibid., pp. 83-84; Ben-zion Pinchuk, "Haglayat yehudim min hashtachim she'tsurfu l'vrit hamoatsot bashanim 1939-1940," Shvut no. 2, book 8 (1974): 48-54.

9. Zvi Gitelman, "Values, Opinions, and Attitudes of Soviet Jewish Emigres," (Paper delivered at meeting of the American Association for the Advancement of Slavic Studies, Atlanta, Ga., October 9-11, 1975), p. 15.

10. Enloe, pp. 18-19; see also, Gitelman, "Assimilation, Acculturation and National Consciousness Among Soviet Jews," pp. 33-36; Milton Gordon, Assimilation in American Life (New York: Oxford University Press, 1964), pp. 60-83; I. Kon, "Dialektika razvitiia natsii," Novyi Mir, no. 3 (1970), cited by Maurice Friedberg, "The Plight of Soviet Jews," Problems of Communism 19, no. 6 (November-December 1970): 18; I. S. Gurvich, "Nekotorye problemy etnicheskogo razvitiia narodov SSSR," Sovetskaia etnografiia, no. 5 (1967), cited in Gitelman, "Assimilation, Acculturation and National Consciousness Among Jews," p. 35.

11. Interview with emigrants from Vilnius, December 18, 1975, Brooklyn, N.Y.; see also, A. A. Gershuni, Yehudim v'yahadut bivrit hamoatsot (Jerusalem: Feldheim Publishers, 1970), pp. 252-53.

12. Alla Rusinek, Like A Song, Like A Dream (New York, Charles Scribner's Sons, 1973), p. 79.

13. Interviews with emigrants, October 27, 1975, New York, N.Y.; December 6-7, 1975, New York, N.Y.; December 9, 1975, Brooklyn, N.Y.; December 18, 1975, Brooklyn, N.Y.

14. Interview with former member of Jewish theater group of Vilnius, December 18, 1975, Brooklyn, N.Y.

15. David Garber, "Choir and Drama in Riga," Soviet Jewish Affairs, no. 1 (1974): 40.

16. Ibid., p. 41.

17. Ibid., pp. 42-43.

18. Ibid., p. 44; interview with emigrants, December 18, 1975, Brooklyn, N.Y.

19. Garber, p. 44; see also, Schroeter, p. 39.

20. Schroeter, pp. 68-70; Mordecai (Perakh) Lapid, "The Memorial at Rumbuli," Jewish Frontier 38 (June 1971): 11-19.

21. Interview with emigrants, December 9, 1975, Brooklyn, N.Y.

22. Mordecai Altschuler, "Some Statistics on Mixed Marriages Among Soviet Jews," Bulletin of Soviet and East European Jewish Affairs, no. 6 (December 1970), pp. 30-32; Gitelman, "Assimilation, Acculturation and National Consciousness Among Soviet Jews," pp. 22-30; Katz, et al., eds., p. 380; Alec Nove and J. A. Newth, "The Jewish Population: Demographic Trends and Occupational Patterns," The Jews in Soviet Russia Since 1917, ed. Lionel Kochan, 2d ed. (London and New York: Oxford University Press, 1972), pp. 143-45; Kholmogorov, pp. 278-83; Ludmila Terentjeva, "How Do Youths From Bi-National Families Determine Their Nationality?" trans. in Bulletin of Baltic Studies, no. 4 (December 1970), pp. 5-11.

23. "Letter of Twenty-Six Lithuanian Jewish Intellectuals to Comrade A. Sniečkus" (February 15, 1968), Redemption! Jewish Freedom Letters From Russia, ed. Moshe Decter (New York: American Conference on Soviet Jewry, 1970), p. 13; Chasya Pincus, "Adolescent Russian Immigrants in Israel," Israel and the Diaspora: An Indivisible Entity (Jerusalem: 1974 Annual of the Office for Economic and Social Research, the Jewish Agency), pp. 102-03; Yosef Gar, "Jews in the Baltic Countries Under German Occupation," Russian Jewry, 1917-1967, ed. Jacob Frumkin, et al. (New York: Thomas Yoseloff, 1969), pp. 123-56; Samuel Gringauz, "The Death of Jewish Kaunas," in ibid., pp. 157-70; Raul Hilberg, The Destruction of the European Jews (Chicago: Quadrangle, 1961), pp. 203-05; Raul Hilberg, Documents of Destruction (Chicago: Quadrangle, 1971), pp. 47-55, 56-57.

24. Interview with emigrants from Vilnius, December 18, 1975, Brooklyn, N.Y.

25. Interview with emigrants from Riga, December 9, 1975, Brooklyn, N.Y.

26. "An Unofficial Press Conference, Questions and Answers by Latvian Jews," *Jews in Eastern Europe* 5, no. 1 (August 1972): 56.

27. *Itogi vsesoiuznoi perepisi 1970 goda. Natsional'nyi sostav naseleniia SSSR* (Moscow: Statistika, 1973) 4: 274-75, 280-81, 317-18.

28. Vardys, p. 38; "Narodnoe khoziaistvo latviiskoi SSR v 1972 goda" (Riga: Statistika, 1973), p. 56.

29. Vardys, p. 39.

30. "Letter to Communist Party Leaders," *Congressional Record*, 92nd Cong., 2nd sess., February 21, 1972, 118, pt. 4: 4820-23.

31. Yaroslav Bilinsky, "The Background of Contemporary Politics in the Baltic Republics and the Ukraine: Comparisons and Contrasts," *Problems of Mininations: Baltic Perspectives*, ed. Arvids Ziedonis, Jr., et al. (San Jose, Calif.: Association for the Advancement of Baltic Studies, 1973), pp. 99-101; "Letter to Communist Party Leaders," pp. 4820-23; Vardys, pp. 40-41, 45-46.

32. Kholmogorov, p. 275, and in *Soviet Sociology* 12, no. 1 (1973): 10.

33. Kholmogorov, vol. 11, no. 3/4, p. 283; Terentjeva, pp. 9-11.

34. Dov Levin, "Ziman(as): derech-chaim shel manhig komunisti yehudi b'lita," *Shvut* 1, book 4 (1973): 95-100.

35. "Letter of Twenty-Six Lithuanian Jewish Intellectuals to Comrade A. Sniečkus," pp. 11-12; William Korey, *The Soviet Cage* (New York: Viking Press, 1973), p. 55.

36. Korey, p. 55.

37. E. Bagramov, "The Development and Drawing Together of Socialist Nations," *Pravda*, July 16, 1971, pp. 3-4; condensed text in *Current Digest of the Soviet Press* 23, no. 28 (1971): 8, 12; Korey, p. 62; New York *Times*, July 19, 1971, p. 13.

38. Deposition of Meir Bareli, February 12, 1973 (Hebrew, typescript, The Centre for Contemporary Jewry, Oral Documentation Section, Hebrew University of Jerusalem), pp. 14-16; Rein Taagepera, "Dissimilarities Between the Northwest Soviet Republics," Ziedonis et al. eds., p. 81; Jacob Dreyer, "Dissent in the USSR and the Jewish Question," *Midstream* 17, pt. 1 (March 1971): 7-20; Zev Katz, "The New Nationalism in the USSR," *Midstream* 19, pt. 2 (February 1973): 3-13; William Parente, "The Nationalities Revival in the Soviet Union," *Midstream* 17, pt. 2 (August-September 1971): 59-65; Roman Rutman, "Jews and Dissenters: Connections and Divergences," *Soviet Jewish Affairs* 3, no. 2 (1973): 26-37; Schroeter, p. 378.

39. Schroeter, pp. 63-64; deposition of Meir Bareli, pp. 13-14.

40. Schroeter, p. 64.

41. Ibid.

42. Ibid., pp. 64-68.

43. Ibid., p. 77.

44. Ibid., pp. 75-76.

45. Ibid., p. 78.

46. Ibid.; Evrei i evreiskii narod: evreiskii samizdat (Jerusalem: Centre for Documentation of East European Jewry, Hebrew University, 1974), vol. 1.

47. Schroeter, p. 78.

48. Ibid., p. 79.

49. Ibid., pp. 79-80.

50. Interview with former member of Vilnius theater group, December 18, 1975, Brooklyn, N.Y.; deposition of Meir Bareli, pt. 2, p. 1.

51. Schroeter, pp. 72-73; interview with Riga emigrants, December 9, 1975, Brooklyn, N.Y.

52. Lapid, p. 12.

53. Ibid., p. 12.

54. Ibid., p. 14.

55. Ibid., pp. 14-18; Schroeter, pp. 69-70; "Chronicle of Events," Soviet Jewish Affairs 4, no. 1 (1974), p. 124.

56. "Letter of Twenty-Six Lithuanian Jewish Intellectuals to Comrade A. Sniečkus," p. 14.

57. Evrei i evreiskii narod: petitsii, pis'ma, i obrashcheniia evreiev SSSR (Jerusalem: Centre for Documentation of Eastern European Jewry, Hebrew University, 1973, 1974), vols. 1-2 (1973); vols. 3-4 (1974).

58. Evrei i evreiskii narod: petitsii, pis'ma, i obrashcheniia evreiv SSSR, vols. 1-4; Shimon Redlich, "Ha'atsumot shel yehudei brit hamoatsot k'bitui l'hitorrut leumit (1968-1970)," Behinot, no. 5 (1974): 7-24.

59. Redlich, "Ha'atzumot shel yehudei brit hamoatsot k'bitui l'hitorrut leumit, 1968-1970," Behinot no. 5 (1974): 11-20; "Exodus," 2 (1971), trans. and reproduced in Bulletin of Soviet and East European Jewish Affairs, no. 6 (1970): 51-70; letters of Soviet Jews, reproduced in Bulletin of Soviet and East European Jewish Affairs, pp. 58, 75-76.

60. Gitelman, "Values, Opinions and Attitudes of Soviet Jewish Emigres," p. 19.

61. Korey, pp. 180-81; all the participants were in Israel by June.

62. Gitelman, "Values, Opinions and Attitudes of Soviet Jewish Emigres," pp. 39-40.

63. United Hebrew Immigrant Aid Society Service, "Interpretative Statement," mimeographed (New York: United HIAS, 1975), p. 5.

64. Interview with Riga emigrant, December 9, 1975, Brooklyn, N.Y.

65. L. Berger, "A Sociogram of the Jewish Diaspora," *Israel and the Diaspora: An Indivisible Entity*, p. 73.

66. Korey, p. 174.

67. Ibid.

68. Garber, p. 44.

69. Enloe, pp. 13-14.

70. Gitelman, "Modernizatsia z'chuyot adam, v'haleumiut hayehudit bivrit hamoastot," pp. 10-14; Zvi Gitelman, *Jewish Nationality and Soviet Politics* (Princeton, N.J.: Princeton University Press, 1972), pp. 498-503.

71. Mary Matossian, "Armenia and the Armenians," in Katz et al., eds., pp. 144, 147, 154, 158-59.

72. Richard Dobson, "Georgia and Georgians," in Katz et al., eds., pp. 162-63, 166, 172, 174, 184-86.

CHAPTER

8

SOCIAL DISTANCE AMONG ETHNIC GROUPS

Juozas A. Kazlas

For over a century, social theoreticians have predicted that modernization would cause the merger of ethnic groups existing together within multinational states. It was thought that industrialization, urbanization, education, and social mobility would bring the members of the various ethnic groups into contact with one another, and that the resulting interaction would lead to mutual understanding and the withering away of social distinctions based on ethnic background. The passage of time has exposed weaknesses in this "simplistic view that geographical and social isolation have been the critical factors in sustaining cultural diversity."[1] Human beings and social groups do not merge at random with anyone they happen to bump into: assimilation can be speeded or retarded, perhaps even stopped, by (1) memories of happy or unfortunate contacts in the past; (2) the way in which the present interaction was initiated (for example, voluntarily or by force); (3) the political, economic, and social structure of the relationship; and (4) whether the cultural values of the parties involved are similar, complementary, or antagonistic.

All of the above factors help to create patterns of acceptance and rejection, of empathy and misunderstanding, of miniscule alli-

---

The author expresses his gratitude to the Program on Soviet Nationality Problems, Columbia University, and especially to its director, Edward Allworth, for the encouragement and financial aid that made this Baltic research effort possible. Thanks also go to Maarit Poom, Liivi Joe, and Elmar Järvesoo, Dagmar Vallens and Biruta Surmanis, and Egle Juodvalkyte and Skirma Kondratas for translating or helping to distribute the questionnaire. Tom Lourie contributed insights and the new emigrants patiently and courageously answered the questions.

ances and banal clashes in daily life, which are the substance of relations among ethnic groups. These relations, in turn, help to define ethnic identities in a society and increase or decrease their importance for group members, raise or lower the boundaries between ethnic groups, and thereby assist the survival or gradual dissolution of ethnic communities. The Soviet Union is one place where these processes constitute an important factor in the political and social evolution of the country, and nowhere are they more salient than in the Baltic region.

This chapter examines patterns of interaction among ethnic groups in the Baltic republics. This approach to the Soviet nationality question will be unusual in several ways. It will deal primarily with popular ethnic stereotypes and attitudes rather than Soviet governmental policy or population patterns. It will also try to illuminate the reality behind statistical configurations in the Soviet census by using microdata gathered during interviews with recent emigrants from the Soviet Baltic, and gleaned from Soviet sociological studies and samizdat literature. It will present evidence that attitudes of acceptance or rejection toward individual ethnic groups are much more differentiated than commonly supposed, varying significantly according to the social context in which the interaction takes place. Finally, the inquiry will focus primarily not on cultural assimilation but rather on relations among ethnic groups, relations that form the framework within which assimilation does or does not take place. In doing so, it will attempt to create a systematic typology, however tentative, of ethnic social distance in the Soviet Union and will argue that the phenomenon is surprisingly complex, involving multiple distinctions among ethnic groups and cultural regions.

USSR officials and Western specialists have put their major emphasis on relations between the Russians and other Soviet ethnic groups. Soviet leaders point to statistics about the increasing use of Russian as a native tongue and extol Soviet patriotism and proletarian internationalism, while Westerners (and many members of the Soviet nationalities) complain about assimilation and Russification; Soviet officials thunder against bourgeois nationalism and nationalistic remnants of the past, while emigrants speak gleefully of anti-Russian national resistance. Both sides think in terms of a Russian versus non-Russian, center versus periphery, dichotomy.

In many ways, this is a realistic perspective: the Soviet Union has inherited a burdensome legacy from the Russian empire, that "prison house of nations." The internationalist ideals of communism have been frustrated by a tradition of ethnic antagonisms going back to Czarist times, by the fact that the Bolsheviks had to use large numbers of Russian troops to establish Soviet power in the nationality republics, and by the Russian political and economic dominance in the Soviet state today. Furthermore, the blatant Russian nationalism evokes a corresponding defensive nationalism from many of the Soviet nationalities, who perceive threats to their own survival both in deliberate governmental policy and in natural sociological phenomena, such as migration and rates of birth and intermarriage. The Russians are the single largest group in the Soviet state, possessing a rich and powerful modern culture, whose expansion is helped by Russian dominance in the educational system and the mass media. Moreover, the top leadership embraces a policy of gradual assimilation, whether out of commitment to a particular interpretation of Marxist ideology, calculations about securing political stability by homogenizing the ethnic foundations of the state, or simple surrender to Russian chauvinism.

Given this situation, it is not surprising that observers of the Soviet nationality question have often failed to distinguish several interrelated but nevertheless distinct phenomena: commitment to the modernization of one's society according to Marxist principles (as interpreted by the Soviet establishment or, perhaps, by Marxist dissenters); loyalty to the Soviet state, which makes such modernization possible; affection for the Russian nation as the principal ethnic group within the Soviet state; desire to interact with Russians in various social contexts (one can, for example, like Russians but not want to intermarry with them), willingness to introduce elements of the Russian language and culture into one's own culture; acceptance of the Russian language as a substitute for one's own language (in certain spheres of social life or in all spheres); and abandonment of one's ethnic identity for assimilation into the Russian nation.

In discussing these phenomena, some analysts began to make theoretical distinctions. For example, the concept of Sovietization was introduced to distinguish the present regime's nationality policies from those of Czarist Russia, and Soviet Russification was divided into objective and subjective categories. Objective Russification entailed acquiring elements of the Russian culture, whereas subjective Russification involved emotional identification with the Russians.[2] A tripartite categorization was also created in which Sovietization is the process of modernization and industrialization within the Marxist-Leninist norms; Russianization is the process of internalizing the Russian language and cultural standards; and Russification is the process whereby non-Russians are transformed objectively and psychologically into Russians.[3] Thus, one can conceive of a Soviet nationality that welcomes industrialization and the erection of a socialist economy, and adheres loyally to the Soviet state and its symbols, without adopting the Russian language and customs. One can also imagine a nationality that becomes bilingual, or even ceases using its native language entirely, without necessarily losing consciousness of a separate ethnic identity.

Both these frameworks mark an advance in theoretical sophistication. However, they deal with stages in cultural development and, except in the case of (subjective) Russification, do not address themselves specifically to relations among ethnic groups. A Russianized person or nationality may tend to be more friendly toward Russians than one who is not Russianized, but this is not inevitably true. Russianization may be a prelude to Russification, or it may be a terminal stage, depending on the nature of the relationship between the two ethnic groups. Furthermore, Soviet specialists have been urged to go beyond the study of Russian relations with other ethnic groups to an examination of relations among the nationalities themselves.[4] The Soviet Union consists of more than 100 different nationalities, and the interaction between any two Soviet ethnic groups may well be influenced to some degree by the state of the other nationalities in the area and the nature of their relationships with one another.

The Soviet government proclaims friendship among all the Soviet ethnic groups. It sponsors cultural exchanges, "friendship festivals," academic conferences, and athletic competitions among the nationality republics. There are Russian translations of books written in the nationality languages, and films made in the various republics are distributed throughout the Soviet Union. The newer Soviet history books minimize differences among nationalities within single regions and try to construct an image of historical solidarity against non-Russian external foes (while giving Russians much of the credit for developing good relations among neighboring nationalities). Nevertheless, conversations with recent emigrants suggest persuasively that the average Soviet citizen has only a superficial acquaintance with the history and literature, not to mention the languages, of the different Soviet nationalities.[5] Furthermore, the priority given to the study of Russian language, literature, and history and the special emphasis put on friendly relations with the Russian people give the impression that the Soviet government identifies "internationalism" with pro-Russian attitudes and "bourgeois nationalism" with anti-Russian feelings. Official criticism of "Great Russian chauvinism" is rare. Many (although not all) Soviet sociological studies regarding "internationalism" in particular areas give data about knowledge of the Russian language by the nationalities but ignore the extent to which the Russians or the other ethnic groups speak the language of the eponymous nationality. This one-way concept of internationalism has prompted a Ukrainian dissident to entitle his book *Internationalism or Russification?*[6] The identification of internationalism with Russification not only puts a disproportionate burden on the nationalities in maintaining good relations between them and the Russians (thus tilting the balance further toward inequality) but it, also, has obvious negative implications for the survival of the various group identities.

Attitudes toward other ethnic groups, along with pride and self-awareness, play significant roles in each nationality's collective support system. These regulatory support factors, especially in the defensive manifestations—group intolerance, mistrust, indifference, and prejudice—often greatly strain relations between ethnic groups. Simultaneously, such factors may nevertheless work to reinforce and sustain the separate identity of each group involved with others in the same multi-ethnic state. Responding to concerns about fruitful approaches to the nationality question and the related matter of group maintenance through action of internal group support systems, a theoretical framework is proposed here for the USSR that takes into account attitudes both toward Russians and toward nationalities.

		Attitudes Toward Russians: Positive	Attitudes Toward Russians: Negative
Attitudes Toward Nationalities	Positive	internationalist	Russophobe
	Negative	Russophile	narrow nationalist

This classification is an improvement over the conventional Russian versus non-Russian dichotomy, but it ignores differences and possible conflicts among the nationalities themselves.

A more complex framework would divide Soviet nationalities into European/Soviet Western (primarily Baltic and Slavic) and Asian (primarily Caucasus and Central Asian) categories:

	Like Russians	Dislike Russians
Like European, Asian Nationalities	internationalist	Russophobe
Like European, Dislike Asian Nationalities	Europhile	anti-Russian Europhile
Like Asian, Dislike European Nationalities	pro-Russian Europhobe	Europhobe
Dislike All Nationalities	Russophile	narrow nationalist

Other variations are possible. For example, someone might consider the differences between Belorussians, Ukrainians, and Russians to be insignificant and lump the three groups together into one category. Russophiles and Russophobes would then become Slavophiles and Slavophobes, and anti-Russian Europhiles would be basically Baltophiles. It may also be necessary to separate the Asian nationalities into Caucasus and Central Asian categories. Finally, it is possible that the nationalities cannot be classified into regional categories at all, that attitudes toward one nationality are independent of attitudes toward other nationalities in the same cultural group or region.

MEASURING GROUP ANTIPATHIES

One of the techniques most widely used by social scientists to measure acceptance or rejection between ethnic groups is the social distance scale. Initiated in 1925, social distance research has generated approximately one new scientific report a month since 1926.[7] The technique involves asking respondents to state whether they would be willing to admit members of diverse ethnic groups: (1) to close kinship by marriage; (2) to private clubs as personal friends; (3) to their streets as neighbors; (4) to employment in their occupation in their country; (5) to citizenship in their country; and (6) as visitors to their country. Theoretically, the answers should form a Guttman scale. That is, a person who answers one of the questions positively will probably answer all successive questions positively (for example, if a person is willing to accept members of a group as friends, he will probably have no objection to admitting them into his street as neighbors or into his country as visitors). A person who answers one question negatively is likely to answer all preceding questions negatively as well (for example, if he does not want to allow a certain nationality into his country as visitors, he is unlikely to want them as friends or relatives either). The scale is used to assign scores to various ethnic groups, who can then be compared as to how far they are accepted by the group from which the test sample was drawn.

Until recently, it was impossible to draw such a systematic typology for ethnic relations in the Soviet Union. The Soviet government was unwilling to permit foreigners to enter the country and conduct sociological research on such a politically sensitive topic, while Soviet sociologists worked under constraints in approach and subject matter. Any study that found widespread ethnic hostility could potentially further exacerbate tensions and, even more important, would document the regime's failure to solve the nationality problem. Thus, one Soviet sociologist claimed that the social distance scale was inapplicable to research in the USSR, since racial prejudice is practically absent in a socialist society, and almost all respondents would appear on one side of the scale—the unprejudiced side.[8]

A Western reader would be wrong if he dismissed such an assertion out of hand. Most Soviet citizens would indeed score very low on the scale in its present form. Few of them would want to expel a Soviet nationality or ethnic group from the country or exclude it from their yacht clubs. The social distance scale has to be revised so that it will be sensitive to points of ethnic tension in Soviet society. In interviews with recent emigrants from the USSR, a questionnaire was used which contained five questions:

1. Would you be pleased if a close relative of yours (son, daughter, brother, or sister) wanted to marry a person of this ethnic group?
2. Would you choose a person of this ethnic group as a close personal friend?
3. Would you like to work together with a person of this ethnic group?
4. If you could choose your immediate superior, would you be willing to work under a person of this ethnic group?
5. If you had to go to a Soviet government or Party office on official business, would an official of this ethnic group treat you favorably, if he knew that you were (person's ethnic group)?

Furthermore, an attempt was made to measure strength of attitude by providing five possible answers for each ethnic group: (1) Yes—almost always, (2) Yes—sometimes, (3) no—rarely, (4) No—almost never, and (5) ?—I don't know. By assigning a numerical value to each answer, it was possible to construct average scores for each ethnic group, measuring the degree to which it was accepted or rejected in various spheres of social life and comparing it to other Soviet ethnic groups. Another section of the questionnaire tested to what extent there was a polarization between Russians and non-Russians: respondents were asked to indicate whether they preferred Russians or members of other ethnic groups as relatives, friends, colleagues, supervisors, and government officials.

In order to explore the attitudes of the Baltic nationalities toward other Soviet ethnic groups, a search was conducted for recent Estonian, Latvian, and Lithuanian emigrants from the USSR. About 30 adults were found who had come to the West within the past three years. Lithuanians constituted the largest group, and 14 of them agreed to fill out the questionnaire, as did 6 Latvians and 1 Estonian. Because it was impossible to interview personally a substantial number of Estonian and Latvian emigrants, more emphasis will be placed in this chapter upon Lithuanian attitudes than on those of the other two Baltic nationalities.

Two objections may be raised: that emigrants are probably not typical of the total population and that in any case, the sample is too small to yield meaningful results. The assumption of this chapter is that ethnic attitudes tend to be more pervasive in a society than political attitudes and, hence, that emigrant opinions about various Soviet ethnic groups may be representative rather than idiosyncratic, in direction if not in intensity. Of course, as in all small samples, only the most striking variations in the statistical pattern can be attributed much significance,[9] and there is the further problem that feelings toward certain ethnic groups may be strongly colored by political considerations (for example, attitudes toward Russians may be influenced to some degree by opinions about the Soviet political system). Confirmation of the data was sought from outside sources (conversations with Soviet experts and travelers to the Baltic region, samizdat material, and official Soviet census figures and sociological studies) and by asking the emigrants themselves about the attitudes of the Baltic nationalities. Thus, even if a respondent denied feeling personal antagonism toward any ethnic group, he or she could still report which ethnic groups were popular or unpopular among the general population. Finally, the results of this Baltic project were compared with those of a study conducted by the author among recent emigrants who were members of the German nationality in the Soviet Union.[10] (See Table 8.1.) The remarkable similarity of the basic patterns in both the Baltic and the German samples gives increased confidence in the significance of the results. Nevertheless, the statistics in this chapter are used for illustration rather than for strict mathematical proof. The entire work has a simple heuristic goal: to introduce new perspectives and approaches in the analysis of the Soviet nationality question and to serve as an admittedly modest empirical starting point for future comparative studies.

POSITIVE BALTIC SELF-ASSESSMENT

The first set of statistics compares the attitudes of the Lithuanian sample with those of 66 Soviet Germans who filled out a similar questionnaire in 1975. Lithuanians, Latvians, and Soviet Germans all evaluated the Baltic nationalities very positively (the Germans gave them the highest scores after their own nationality), perceiving them as the most Western in culture of all Soviet nationalities. Germans who had moved to the Baltic area from Central Asia were struck by how polite the people were in public. A woman, who came to West Germany from Kirgizia, upon first meeting the author at a gathering of recent Soviet German emigrants remarked that he must be from the Baltic region. Asked why, she pointedly looked at his Ivy League

TABLE 8.1

Attitudes of Recent Lithuanian and Soviet German Emigrants about Relations with Baltic Nationalities Compared*

Ethnic Group	As Relative	As Friend	As Worker	As Supervisor	As Official
Lithuanian sample					
Estonian	0.4	1.7	1.6	1.6	1.4
Latvian	0.1	1.7	1.6	1.4	1.2
Lithuanian	2.0	2.0	2.0	1.9	1.3
Soviet German sample					
Estonian	0.2	1.2	1.2	1.1	1.3
Latvian	0.1	1.1	1.3	1.0	0.9
Lithuanian	0.1	1.0	1.2	1.0	0.8

*See also, Appendix D.

Note: Scores range from 2 (which signifies total acceptance to -2 (total rejection); 0 indicates indifference or neutrality.

Source: Data derived from written questionnaires completed by Baltic respondents in the United States and Europe (1976-77) and by Soviet Germans interviewed in Federal Republic of Germany (Spring-Fall 1975).

coat and tie and said that people in the Baltic republics were different from other people in the Soviet Union—they were better dressed and obviously more cultured. Several Soviet Germans mentioned that remnants of German culture could be found in Estonia and Latvia, where members of the older generation still speak the German language. One man had seen his first German Bible when he came to Estonia: it had been saved by its owner from the prewar period.

Both Lithuanians and Germans stated that the Baltic nationalities considered themselves occupied by the Russians, and emphasized the high degree of solidarity among the three nationalities. They applaud each other's athletic teams and dance groups or choirs with particular exuberance at international events, especially if they are in competition with some Russian unit. One German speculated that the Soviet authorities would like to break this solidarity. He described a dance that he attended that was organized by some Estonian workers for a visiting Lithuanian work brigade. Some outsiders entered unnoticed, mingled in the crowd, and tried to start fights. They were expelled, and the general consensus was that they were sent in by the secret police to create enmity between the two nationalities.

Most Soviet Germans gave the three Baltic nationalities identical scores in the questionnaire. Some Germans gave a marginally higher score to the Estonians because they had lived in Estonia for several years, and a few scattered individuals thought that the Lithuanians were not as friendly to the Germans as the Latvians and Estonians were (the traditional links with German culture of the latter two nationalities may explain why most of the Soviet Germans who moved to the Baltic region settled in Estonia and Latvia). About one-third of the Lithuanian Soviet German respondents were opposed to marriages with members of any ethnic groups other than their own, which lowered the social distance scores for the Baltic nationalities as relatives. In general, the Lithuanians gave systematic preference only to their own nationality, usually treating the other two nationalities as equally attractive. However, a few of the Lithuanians did mention that there was slightly less enthusiasm among some Lithuanians for Latvians than for Estonians. (One of the six Latvians also gave Lithuanians somewhat lower scores than the other two Baltic nationalities. The remaining five rated all Balts equally or gave preference only to Latvians). Latvians were pictured as more urban, educated, and sophisticated but rather cool, and at times a bit snobbish toward Lithuanians, who tend to have peasant backgrounds. One man said that there was a muted dispute between the two nationalities over which one possessed the oldest living Indo-European language, while another observed that a certain degree of wariness is to be expected between neighboring ethnic groups. This may be especially true if the two groups are related by their common origins, but took different paths in religion (the Latvians are predominantly Lutheran, the Lithuanians Catholic) and culture (German influence is strong in Latvian culture, and Polish influence in Lithuanian culture). One Latvian remembered that Lithuanian youths, including young intellectuals, sought employment on Latvian farms during the economic depression of the 1930s. The resulting frictions may have had some influence on present-day attitudes. Perhaps there is also a subconscious mixture of fear, anger, and frustration at the thought that Lithuania's northern flank is threatened by Russification in Latvia, which occasionally finds expression in dark hints that Latvians are more prone to collaborate with Russians than other Balts. Of 11 Lithuanian respondents who answered a question asking whether the Baltic nationalities would assimilate with the Russians, none thought Estonians would, one thought that Lithuanians would, and five thought that Latvians would (in contrast, all the Latvian respondents thought that none of the Baltic nationalities would be assimilated). One of the recurring themes heard during the interviews was Lithuanian admiration for the Estonian refusal to learn or use the Russian language (the Germans also characterized Lithuanians and Estonians as

TABLE 8.2

Spoken Language of Baltic Eponymous Nationalities, 1970

Nationality	Percentage of Own Republic's Population	Percentage Who Speak Russian
Lithuanians	80.1	35.0
Latvians	56.8	47.1
Estonians	68.2	28.2

Source: Itogi vsesoiuznoi perepisi naseleniia 1970 goda. Natsional'nyi sostav naseleniia SSSR. (Moscow: Statistika, 1973), 4: 273, 280, 317.

particularly nationalistic in this respect). The 1970 Soviet census confirms the emigrants' personal experiences on this point (see Table 8.2).

Any differences among the Baltic nationalities are minor compared to the similarities of culture and outlook that bind them together. The common nature of their problems gives rise to feelings of sympathy and a desire to help one another when possible. One visitor to the Baltic region, for example, met groups of young Latvians and Lithuanians who visited each other over weekends in order to exchange information and advice about topics of mutual interest. A Latvian mentioned the influence that Lithuanian writers and nationalist intellectuals had exerted on Latvian literature and politics. Another Latvian said that Latvians are happy to see collective farms in southern Latvia increasingly worked by Lithuanian immigrants, because they lessened the Russian presence.

It is always dangerous to infer ethnic affection or hostility from linguistic data, which are influenced by variables such as the ethnic composition of the area and the length of time that various subgroups lived there. Nevertheless, it is tempting to speculate about the reasons why Latvians in Lithuania, Estonians and Lithuanians in Latvia, and Latvians in Estonia tend to speak the languages of the eponymous nationalities at significantly higher rates than the non-Baltic nationalities (for example, Belorussians, Poles, and Ukrainians) in these republics. A Soviet sociologist, in analyzing his sample of the population in Latvia, found that Lithuanians were more likely to speak Latvian than other non-Latvian ethnic groups in the republic.[11] He attributed this fact to the similarity of the two languages, but there may be a more sociological explanation as well: positive attitudes toward an ethnic group promote friendly interaction and the willingness to learn the group's language. Conversely, the apparent reluctance of the non-Baltic nationalities to learn the Baltic languages may be partially explained by the existence of social attitudes that tend to inhibit interaction with the Balts and further social intercourse with Russians and other non-Baltic ethnic groups.

There is a great deal of quasi-ideological hostility among the Baltic nationalities toward the Russians. Both the Baltic emigrants and Soviet Germans told remarkably similar stories about times that they (or their friends or relatives) had asked for directions in Russian in one of the Baltic republics and had received no cooperation until it was made clear that they were not Russian. Apparently, the Russian man on the street is aware of this antagonism. (Some Russian inhabitants of Lithuania left the republic during the Cuban missile crisis in 1962. One of them explained to a Lithuanian friend that if war started, the Lithuanians would try to slaughter the Russians in Lithuania.) Two of the Soviet Germans (who were unacquainted with each other) had overheard conversations among Russians in Leningrad expressing puzzlement and anger at the hostility of the Balts. The Russians could not understand what more they wanted, because the Russians had helped to industrialize their republics and because they (Baltic nationalities) had the best standards of living in the country.

A young Lithuanian who was traveling by motorcycle near Leningrad ran out of gas. A Russian truck driver finally stopped to help, but told him that few other Russians would have done so because the motorcycle had Lithuanian license plates and the Lithuanian hostility toward Russians was well known. He himself would sell some gasoline only because he needed the money for vodka. Another Lithuanian met many people during his travels in Russia who said that the Baltic nationalities had collaborated with German invaders during World War II and were stockpiling weapons for the next war. When they asked the Lithuanian for confirmation, the young man replied, perhaps somewhat imprudently, with fictitious stories about disassembled tanks that were stored in the forests by Baltic nationalists and could be put together at the initiation of hostilities. A third Lithuanian had become embittered during his Soviet army service when he was frequently called a "fascist" because "Lithuanians are all fascists."

One of the causes of antagonism toward Russians is resentment at what many believe is their privileged status in Soviet society. When asked whether Russians received better jobs and apartments than other nationalities, 71 percent of the Soviet Germans, twelve out of fourteen Lithuanians, and four out of five Latvians answered in the affirmative (one Lithuanian said that Russians had been favored in earlier times but that people are more willing to protest inequities now, and the authorities want to avoid disturbances). Yet, nine of the Lithuanians stated that Lithuanians in their own republic have the same chances to receive good jobs and official honors as members of other ethnic groups, two said that they have better chances, and only three said that they have worse chances (three out of five Latvians also answered this question positively). Furthermore, the respondents seem to have been generally satisfied with their chosen professions in the Soviet Union, with their ability to influence decisions at their place of work, and their opportunities for promotion. This apparent contradiction between a Lithuanian perception of Russian occupational privilege, on the one hand, and optimism about personal career prospects, on the other, can be explained by the nature of the relationship between the center and the periphery in the Soviet system.

Conversations with the Soviet Germans, who had been scattered throughout the Soviet Union, revealed a conviction that each ethnic group has a predominant influence in its own republic. In answering a query about whether Russians receive better jobs and apartments than others, two of the Germans wrote "not in Estonia"; others wrote "not always," "only in their own republic," and "better than the Germans." Many Soviet Germans believed that the eponymous nationalities had definite advantages in finding attractive jobs and obtaining admission into republic institutions of higher education. German sensitivity to the advantages of having one's own ethnic-territorial unit was partially responsible for the fact that 95.3 percent of them did not think Germans enjoyed the same opportunities to receive good jobs and official honors as members of other nationalities. The Lithuanians, in fact, agreed that Baltic supervisors at work and officials in government offices tend to favor their own nationality. However, Lithuanians simultaneously related incidents showing that ultimate power belongs to the center, which is, in turn, dominated by the Russians. For example, workers (particularly Russians) arriving from other republics often get priority over local residents waiting for new housing. Some influential positions are assigned to Russians who act as "watchdogs" for the central authorities. One former official said that Russian officials, with blatant disregard for Baltic interests, often rid themselves of unpopular or incompetent subordinates by having them transferred to the Baltic republics. Finally, Russian dominance of the center gives Russians a competitive advantage at the Union-wide level (in military and diplomatic careers, for example) and permits them to have a decisive voice in formulating the general policies that nationalities have to follow. The most bitterly resented policies involve the growing use of the Russian language in governmental and educational institutions (for example, doctoral dissertations are now accepted only if they are written in Russian), the reinterpretation or suppression of Baltic history, and the continual influx of new Russian settlers. Furthermore, Moscow's censorship of drama and literature awakens specifically nationalistic hostilities, for many people believe this outside control stifles Baltic culture. However, the implementation of many policies is left to local officials. They have a great deal of leeway in the distribution of various benefits, and indeed in setting the whole tone of life in their area, subject of course to occasional vetoes by the central authorities.

Much of the hostility of Baltic nationalities toward Russians has a rather abstract quality: they dislike Russians as a group and will vent their antagonism on strangers, but they often find individual Russians attractive on a personal level. It is significant that Lithuanian respondents gave Russians more favorable social distance ratings as friends than as coworkers, reversing the usual order of acceptability. One Lithuanian emigrant remembered making a comment about "those damn Russians" and then realizing that two of her friends in the room were themselves Russian. Exactly 43 out of 66 Germans, 9 out of 14 Lithuanians, and 4 out of 6 Latvians had Russians questioned for this study as close personal friends, more than any ethnic group other than their own nationality (see Table D.4). Both the Lithuanians and Soviet Germans found Russians warm, open, and unpretentious in their personal relations, although often narrow, chauvinistic, and boorish, especially in their public roles (this is particularly true of Russians who come from other republics on "shopping expeditions" in search of consumer goods). One dissident Baltic intellectual found Russians more sensitive to social justice than Balts, who tended to be preoccupied with nationality rights.

All the Baltic emigrants distinguished between those Russians who had lived in their republics a long time and those who had arrived recently. One Estonian said that "old" Russian settlers in Estonia were embarrassed by "new" settlers and complained about their "uncultured" behavior. Several Lithuanians described Russian friends of theirs who spoke Lithuanian, associated mostly with Lithuanians, and were often biting in their descriptions of Russians in other parts of the Soviet Union. The "Balticization" of Russian settlers, especially in the rural areas, is mentioned by Soviet sociologists,[12] and reflected in the Soviet census (see Table E.2), which shows that substantial numbers of Russians have a command of the eponymous Baltic languages. In addition, a Soviet study of mixed marriages in the three Baltic capitals reveals that slightly over half of the children of Baltic-Russian marriages choose to be identified as Balts in their official documents.[13] This can be interpreted as an indication not only of the high level of ethnic consciousness on the part of the Baltic parents (and grandparents!), which is transmitted to the children, but also of a certain degree of tolerance and sympathy on the part of some Russian husbands and wives. It may also suggest that the status of the Russian population in the Baltic republics does not offer enough advantages to tempt a disproportionate number of youths to assume a Russian ethnic identity.

OUTSIDERS RATED LOWER

The non-Russian, noneponymous ethnic groups constitute 7.1 percent of the population in Estonia, 11.3 percent in Lithuania, and 13.4 percent in Latvia. Both the Lithuanian and the Soviet German samples tended to rate them less favorably than they did the Baltic eponymous nationalities, although the Germans were less negative on the whole than the Lithuanians (see Table 8.3). Unlike the data regarding Baltic nationalities, the social distance ratings of non-Baltic European nationalities are hard to fit into a Russian versus non-Russian conceptual framework. In the section of the questionnaire that asked the respondents to choose between Russians and members of other ethnic groups, the Lithuanians were generally reluctant to favor Russians and tended to manifest negative feelings toward nationalities by claiming no preference between the two groups (see Table D.3). The Soviet Germans, however, were much less reticent in showing approval of Russians, and preferred them by wide margins not only to the Caucasus and Central Asian nationalities but even to some of the non-Baltic Soviet Western nationalities. About one-half of the Latvian sample followed this pattern, whereas the one Estonian respondent preferred the Western nationalities to Russians, and Russians to Asian nationalities. Many Germans who showed Russophobe tendencies had lived substantial amounts of time in one or more of the Baltic republics.

The Slavic nationalities—Belorussians, Ukrainians, and Poles—are the most numerous of the noneponymous nationalities in the Baltic republics. Both the Baltic and Soviet German emigrants agreed that it is often impossible to distinguish Belorussians and Ukrainians from Russians, since the two nationalities tend to associate with Russians, speak their language, and intermarry with them. Belorussians are perhaps the most unpopular of all the Soviet Western nationalities. They were described by both groups of emigrants as uneducated and primitive. Lithuanians were especially appalled by the fact that Belorussians often seemed not only indifferent to, but actually ashamed of, their nationality. Respondents who had visited the Belorussian republic described a dull countryside, with poor roads, shabby buildings, and backward people. However, these stereotypes seem to contradict both the 1959 and the 1970 Soviet censuses, which show that more Belorussians than Lithuanians per 1,000 received a secondary and/or higher education.[14] Assuming

TABLE 8.3

Lithuanian and Soviet German Attitudes toward Soviet Western Ethnic Groups throughout the USSR*

Noneponymous Ethnic Group	As Relative	As Friend	As Worker	As Supervisor	As Official
Lithuanian sample					
Russian	-1.6	-0.1	-0.4	-1.8	-1.0
Belorussian	-1.7	-0.8	-0.1	-0.3	-0.5
Ukrainian	-1.1	0.5	0.6	-0.1	0.4
Moldavian	-1.1	0.0	0.1	0.3	0.1
Jewish	-1.1	0.1	0.2	0.0	0.3
Soviet Polish	-1.2	-0.3	-0.1	-0.9	-0.5
Soviet German	-0.3	1.2	1.2	1.2	0.5
Soviet German sample					
Russian	-1.4	0.8	1.1	0.7	-0.2
Belorussian	-1.4	0.3	0.5	0.2	-0.5
Ukrainian	-1.2	0.7	0.7	0.2	-0.4
Moldavian	-1.3	0.2	0.7	0.0	-0.1
Jewish	-1.1	0.2	0.4	0.2	0.3
Soviet German	2.0	1.9	1.9	1.7	1.7

*See also, Appendix D.

Note: Scores range from 2 (total acceptance) to -2 (total rejection); 0 indicates neutrality or indifference.

Source: Data derived from written questionnaires completed by Baltic respondents in the United States and Europe (1976-77) and by Soviet Germans in Federal Republic of Germany (Spring-Fall 1975).

the censuses are accurate, there are several possible explanations for the negative perceptions of the Belorussians: (1) they are simply false, based on nationalistic prejudices or historical conditions that are no longer true; (2) Belorussians get more years of education, but it is inferior in quality (this would be hard to argue for the Belorussians residing in the Lithuanian republic); (3) cultural traditions are more important than formal education (this was the response of some emigrants who were confronted with the official statistics); (4) manifestations of Belorussian backwardness are more visible, in the same way that black poverty is more visible than white poverty in the United States; and (5) educated Belorussians pass for Russians, and only uneducated Belorussians are correctly identified according to their nationality.

Ukrainians were better liked than Belorussians—several Lithuanian respondents called them the most popular non-Baltic nationality—and were described as having both the positive and negative characteristics of the Russians. Some respondents considered Ukrainians, perhaps because they have no pretensions to ruling an empire, more friendly and less arrogant than Russians, while others mentioned that they were more likely to be "just off the farm." A few Germans considered Ukrainians sly and somewhat untrustworthy. Both Lithuanians and Soviet Germans believed that Ukrainians who remained in their own republic had a higher level of ethnic consciousness than those who settled in other republics. One German woman who had moved to Kharkov, in the more Russianized eastern part of the Ukraine, was hospitalized soon after her arrival. The other women in her ward told her to speak Ukrainian, not Russian, "because you're in the Ukraine now."

The questionnaires distributed to Soviet Germans did not ask them to evaluate the Polish minority in the USSR. The relatively low Lithuanian scores for Soviet Poles as friends and coworkers resulted from an almost even split in the sample, with the negative answers being as numerous as positive ones, but slightly more intense. It was felt that many Poles, especially of the older generation, were somewhat arrogant because they had formerly constituted the dominant elite in the region and because of the high prestige of Polish culture. Significantly more Lithuanian respondents were reluctant to deal with Poles as authority figures (supervisors and government officials) than as friends or coworkers. There were also complaints that Poles who remained in Lithuania after the war tended to merge with the Russians rather than Lithuanians (linguistic data in the 1970 census seem to support this contention).[15] All respondents agreed that despite the remaining Polish schools in Lithuania, the Polish community had lost its vitality after the war, when most of its members left for Poland. The remaining Poles are said to be of a low cultural level, to drink to excess, to be uninterested in education, and to be gradually undergoing assimilation. The lack of solidarity between Poles and Lithuanians in the USSR is illustrated by an incident which occurred shortly after the 1968 invasion of Czechoslovakia by Russian and Warsaw Pact troops. A Czech visitor to Vilnius was beaten up by two Lithuanians who, when arrested, became very apologetic, explaining that they had mistaken him for a Pole. The Lithuanians who evaluated Soviet Poles positively stressed the cultural and religious ties. All respondents expressed admiration and envy for the relative freedom and vitality of culture in Poland, and a few had studied the Polish language or repeatedly visited Poland in order to become acquainted with cultural trends in the West.

Neither Soviet Germans nor Lithuanians had very strong feelings about Moldavians. A few of the Germans pictured Moldavians as a not very industrious, somewhat backward, and Russophile peasant nationality. Two Lithuanians who had visited Moldavia mentioned the Latin warmth of the people, whose easy conviviality was reinforced by the presence of excellent varieties of wine.

A very different image was evoked by the Jews in the USSR. Both the Soviet Germans and Lithuanians portrayed Jews as intelligent, clever, hard working, and "most likely to succeed." Respondents believed that a disproportionate number of Soviet professionals, as well as black-marketeers, factory supervisors, and local government officials (in some republics), were Jewish. Half of the Lithuanians and 17.2 percent of the Soviet Germans remembered Jews as supervisors, and three-fourths of the Lithuanians and 25.4 percent of the Soviet Germans had met Jewish government officials (the differences between the two nationalities reflect the fact that many of the Germans came from Siberia and parts of Central Asia, where Jews are less visible than in the Baltic republics). Such blatant success (perceived or real) creates envy, which was evident in a minority of both samples: comments were made that the Jews were "damned clever" and "stuck together and helped one another advance," and it was noted that even Jews who were in trouble had resources (such as influential friends abroad) that were unavailable to the other nationalities. In addition, some Germans reported unpleasant experiences with Jews, who associated them with the wartime Nazi atrocities ("fascist" is a common derogatory nickname for Soviet Germans, used by members of all nationalities). Some Lithuanians recalled that Jews had been sympathetic to the Russians in the early years of Soviet rule (in 1950, 7 percent of the Communist Party members in Lithuania were Jewish, and 27 Lithuanian; by 1975, the comparable proportions were 1.6 and 68.5 percent respectively).[16] Moreover, those respondents who made negative comments did not seem to be afflicted with the virulent antisemitism of the past, nor did they espouse theories about "Jewish conspiracies." On the positive side, many respondents appreciated Jews as intelligent, cultured companions (almost half of the Lithuanians and 12.1 percent of the Germans had had Jews as close personal friends). The fact that Jews are perceived as a European nationality with high standards of living may explain why a surprising 17.9 percent of the German sample were willing to see their son or daughter marry a Jew. There also seem to be increasingly close ties between Jews and the Baltic nationalities. Lithuanian respondents observed that many more Jews are learning Lithuanian now than in former times (the Soviet census shows that large numbers of Jews speak Russian as a native tongue and Lithuanian as a second language—see

Appendix E), perhaps due to the influx of Lithuanians into the main cities and their growing influence in the local seats of power. There was also an immense outpouring of enthusiasm for Israel after the Six-Day War, which raised the prestige of the Soviet Jews in the eyes of Baltic people. One Latvian dissident wrote that the war was seen as a symbol of a small nation winning against overwhelming odds—a topic which is of great interest to the Baltic nationalities.[17] Finally, the recent Jewish mass exodus from the Soviet Union helped to sharpen public perception of a state of conflict rather than cooperation between Jews and the regime, and this may have increased pro-Jewish sentiments among some segments of the population.

The Lithuanians in this sample reciprocated the high esteem Soviet Germans showed for Baltic nationalities; Soviet Germans received the highest scores of all non-Baltic ethnic groups. Soviet German descriptions of their reception in Estonia and Latvia would suggest that they are at least as popular there as in Lithuania. Lithuanian characterizations of Soviet Germans matched the Soviet German self-image to a remarkable degree: they were considered honest, clean, hard-working, and religious people, who achieve a modest but comfortable standard of living through diligence and "playing according to the rules." There is also sympathy for the tribulations of this nationality: deported during the war from their settlements in the Ukraine, the Caucasus, and the Volga German ASSR, they were not permitted to return to their former homes at the cessation of hostilities. Of the Germans, 41.3 percent now live in the Russian SFSR, primarily in Siberia, and 53.4 percent in Kazakhstan, Kirgizia, and Tajikistan. Every Soviet German knows that when Mikoyan received a delegation of Soviet Germans in Moscow, he told them that Germans would not be permitted to emigrate from Soviet Central Asia, because without them the economy would fall apart in that region. Nevertheless, substantial numbers of Soviet Germans began to move to the Baltic union republics, primarily Estonia and Latvia, in the mid-1960s. The Soviet census lists them under the 98,806 Germans (out of 1.8 million) whose residence is not given.[18]

It is not clear why Soviet Germans were given permission to enter the Baltic region. Local authorities were probably glad to acquire competent, diligent workers, especially when they did not add to the Russian element in the population. One German dissident speculated that the central government consented in the hope that the Germans would assimilate faster with the Baltic nationalities than they would with Asians. Both objectives became problematic when the vagaries of West German-Soviet diplomatic relations created an opportunity for certain Soviet Germans to emigrate to West Germany. The Germans in the Baltic region organized to pressure the Soviet government for permission to leave the country, and confrontations developed. For whatever reason—German unrest in an already volatile region, tardy response by Moscow to the new migration from Central Asia, or simply a desire to minimize German influence in the western border regions—by 1969 no more Soviet Germans were being allowed to migrate to the Baltic republics. The Baltic area was an ideal theater for dissident activities: geographic compactness made communication easy, the closeness of Leningrad and Moscow facilitated contact with the western press, and the attitudes of the local Baltic population were conducive to group consciousness-raising. One Soviet German who had grown up in Siberia observed that he had not realized that there was a nationality question in the Soviet Union until he moved to the Baltic region. Members of the eponymous nationalities were often supportive. One Soviet German activist said that German demonstrators in Moscow were jeered by passersby but applauded in Estonia.

Some Estonians offered to participate in the demonstrations. Many Soviet German emigrants remembered that Estonian local officials had been more sympathetic to their requests than Russian officials in the same departments. Whatever the reasons, Germans in the Baltic republics seem to have been particularly successful in obtaining exit visas: in this sample, 3.1 percent of the Soviet Germans came from Lithuania, 6.3 percent from Latvia, 53.1 percent from Estonia, and 40.6 percent from the remainder of the Soviet Union.

SOVIET TRANSCAUCASUS/ASIAN NATIONALITIES REJECTED BY SOME

The Caucasus nationalities occupy an intermediate position between Soviet Western and Asian culture in the USSR. This fact was reflected in attitudes of Baltic and Soviet German respondents toward Transcaucasus ethnic groups (see Table 8.4). There was a noticeable rise in the number of Latvians and Germans who preferred to associate with Russians rather than with members of the nationalities being rated, and the Lithuanian scores for Transcaucasus nationalities were lower in some social contexts than for the Russians or Belorussians. Both the Balts and Soviet Germans considered Transcaucasus groups to be energetic, passionate, somewhat exotic people who, along with Jews, are the businessmen of the Soviet Union (hence maybe somewhat unscrupulous) and have a fierce sense of family loyalty and pride of nationality. Extensive contacts have taken place between Baltic and Transcaucasus nationalities not only in the city markets, where Transcaucasus entrepreneurs sell their vegetables and flowers, but also through a highly popular official cultural

TABLE 8.4

Lithuanian and Soviet German Attitudes toward Transcaucasus Groups*

Transcaucasus Groups	As Relative	As Friend	As Worker	As Supervisor	As Official
Lithuanian sample					
Armenian	-1.4	0.1	-0.4	-0.1	0.4
Georgian	-1.3	-0.4	-0.3	-0.1	0.5
Azerbaijanian	-1.6	-0.9	-0.8	-0.4	-0.3
Soviet German sample					
Armenian	-1.3	0.0	0.3	0.0	-0.2
Georgian	-1.4	0.0	0.5	0.1	-0.2
Azerbaijanian	-1.4	-0.2	0.3	-0.1	-0.2

*See also, Appendix D.

Note: Possible range of scores is from 2 (total acceptance) to -2 (total rejection); 0 indicates indifference or neutrality.

Source: Data derived from written questionnaires completed by Baltic respondents in the United States and Europe (1976-77) and by Soviet Germans in Federal Republic of Germany (Spring-Fall 1975).

exchange program, which reveals the ancient and modern glories of Armenian and of Georgian culture to the Balts. In addition, several Lithuanians mentioned that large numbers of Georgian troops are stationed in Lithuania. Their contacts with local citizens are rather friendly, sometimes leading to mixed marriages. For these reasons the low social distance ratings given by Baltic respondents to Transcaucasus nationalities are rather surprising. One possible explanation for them is that the Baltic people may admire Armenian or Georgian culture in the abstract, but find the life-style of Transcaucasus people they meet unattractive. Social class may also be a factor. Those respondents who belonged to the intelligentsia seemed to be enthusiastic about the Georgians and Armenians that they had met, and declared them to be the most popular nationalities in Lithuania. On the other hand, surveying the noise, dirt, and chaos of a bazaar operated by peddlers from the Transcaucasus, one Latvian was overheard remarking to another Latvian that "these are our blacks." Another explanation may lie in the distinction between liking a nationality and wanting to engage in social intercourse with it. This may be illustrated by the experience of one Lithuanian respondent who attended a sports congress in Georgia. On the first evening, athletes were told not to leave their dormitories at night because it might be too dangerous. Several Lithuanians decided that the danger existed only for Russians, and left to tour the town. They encountered a group of fierce-looking Georgians who inquired where they were from and, upon learning that they were Lithuanian, invited them for a drink. The Lithuanians accepted, not wanting to test the common stereotype of Georgians as people ready to engage in knife fights upon the slightest insult, real or imagined. They were led to a tavern where their drinking glasses were filled, and the Georgians proposed the first toast of the evening: "To our common enemies—the Russians!" Such passionate people may be admired, but at the same time regarded as too nerve-wracking to be personal friends. Similarly, the solidarity of families and clans in the Transcaucasus can be warmly approved of without creating a desire in outsiders to live by their rules after intermarriage with one of their members.

Both Balts and Germans tended to rate Armenians and Georgians equally, although a few Balts preferred Armenians for their more urbane and less violent image. On the negative side, both Balts and Germans repeat the stereotype that Armenians are cunning and business-oriented "like the Jews," and respondents in both groups whispered of perverse sexual practices. A few Soviet German respondents showed some inclination to accept Armenians as marriage partners. As in the Jewish case, this may relate to the image many Soviet citizens have of Armenians being a nationality that tends to succeed professionally. On the whole, however, one-fourth to one-half of the Germans and one-half to three-fourths of the Latvians preferred Russians to Transcaucasus people in various social contexts. Few of the respondents had met people from the Transcaucasus in their stable, everyday social relations (as friends, colleagues, or officials). Lithuanians gave Armenian and Georgian officials the next highest ratings after Baltic officials. This may indicate a belief in a basic similarity of political outlook, despite Georgian admiration for Stalin (himself a Georgian). No such tendency was detectable in the Soviet German sample. In fact, a few Germans remembered that they or their parents had had Georgians as rather unsympathetic guards during wartime deportations.

There was a tendency in all the sample to rate Azerbaijanians slightly lower than the other two Transcaucasus groups. Some respondents felt that they embodied many of the negative and few of the positive qualities of Transcaucasus nationalities, and grouped them with Central Asians. Both the Balts and the Soviet Germans felt that there was a definite cultural gap between Soviet Western and Central Asian nationalities (the Balts were likely to include Tatars in a general "Asian" category). (See Table 8.5.) Both groups of emigrants had remarkably similar perceptions of the Asians, who

TABLE 8.5

Lithuanian and Soviet German Ratings of Soviet Muslim Nationalities*

Nationality	As Relative	As Friend	As Worker	As Supervisor	As Official
Lithuanian sample					
Kazakh	-1.7	-1.1	-0.7	-0.9	-0.5
Kirgiz	-1.7	-1.0	-0.7	-0.9	-0.5
Turkmen	-1.7	-1.0	-0.7	-0.9	-0.5
Uzbek	-1.5	-0.9	-0.6	-0.8	-0.4
Tajik	-1.5	-0.9	-0.6	-0.9	-0.5
Tatar	-1.7	-1.2	-1.6	-0.8	-0.8
Soviet German sample					
Kazakh	-1.6	-0.1	0.4	-0.2	-0.3
Kirgiz	-1.6	-0.1	0.5	0.1	0.0
Turkmen	-1.7	-0.3	0.2	-0.1	-0.3
Uzbek	-1.7	-0.2	0.2	-0.1	-0.3
Tajik	-1.7	-0.4	0.2	-0.1	-0.3
Tatar	-1.5	0.3	0.8	0.3	-0.1

*See also, Appendix D.

Note: Possible range of scores is from 2 (total acceptance) to -2 (total rejection); 0 indicates indifference or neutrality.

Source: Data derived from questionnaires completed by Baltic respondents in the United States and Europe (1976-77) and by Soviet Germans in Federal Republic of Germany (Spring-Fall 1975).

are popularly called "chërnye" (Russian: "blacks") in the Soviet Union. The common negative stereotypes emerge: they are "savage," dirty, uneducated, lazy, dishonest, occasionally violent, with primitive family customs, in which women are totally subordinated to men. Two-thirds of the Soviet Germans, as well as three-fifths of the Latvians, would prefer to marry Russians rather than members of Central Asian nationalities. Soviet Germans who had lived in Central Asia told stories of Asian antagonism toward all Soviet Westerners. Asians promised such Western Soviet acquaintances believed that when the Chinese came to liberate Soviet Asia, they would slit Westerners' throats (a few Asians acknowledged that Soviet Germans were not there by choice). In some areas it was considered dangerous for a woman to walk alone at night. Complaints were heard that the Asians did not do their fair share of work on collective farms, leaving the burden to the Germans, then stole collective property or spent their time illegally growing and selling watermelons. Although poor students, government quotas insured that they were admitted to good jobs and gained admission to union republic institutions of higher learning. In rural areas, they let their homes go to ruin, then were envious of the clean, prosperous German houses and gardens. But there were also descriptions of villages and collective farms where Asian-Soviet Western relations were basically friendly, especially in Kazakhstan and Kirgizia (Tajiks were considered more chauvinistic by some Germans). Few Baltic people had met enough Central Asians to establish clear preferences among them. Two Lithuanians said that Uzbeks have both a higher culture and more pride in nationality than other Soviet Asian groups. Another was impressed by Tajiks he had met. Most unofficial information about Muslim nationalities came from fellow Balts who returned home from exile in the Soviet East, as well as new Russian settlers from Central Asia. These Russians often boasted that Russia had managed to modernize the Balts, but still had a long way to go with Muslim nationalities. The Soviet Germans were divided in their perceptions of Tatars: some considered them Asian; others thought they were rather Westernized. One Soviet German woman said that they look "like Russians with black hair." Lithuanians distinguished between Asiatic Tatars and the Karaim Tatars, who have lived amicably in Lithuania for over 500 years.

The preceding discussion of ethnic stereotypes and behavioral attitudes makes clear why 86 percent of the Soviet Germans and Lithuanians questioned and 100 percent of the (6 out of 6) Latvians agreed that tensions remain among Soviet ethnic groups in everyday life. It shows also that some Soviet citizens make fairly complex distinctions among ethnic groups. Many but not all of these distinctions are based on the major regional cultures: Baltic, Slavic, Caucasus, and Central Asian. Evidence confirms that the theoretical framework for ethnic acceptance and rejection that was proposed at the beginning of this chapter is more than a collection of empty categories. Some respondents appear to be Russophobes or Slavophobes. Many of the Lithuanians fall into these categories, and the 5 to 20 percent of the Soviet Germans who preferred Central Asians over Russians in various social contexts may be classified there as well. Both samples contained Europhiles (those partial to Soviet Westerners), anti-Russian Europhiles, and Baltophiles, and also significant numbers of internationalists. These last rated all ethnic groups equally and sometimes wrote declarations at the top of a questionnaire that a person's ethnicity is unimportant, or that all ethnic groups include both good and bad people. Finally, reports were also received that parts of certain groups, such as Belorussian and Ukrainian nationalities, were Slavophile or Russophile, and that many Central Asians were Europhobe (anti-Soviet Western). In general, the results of this study demonstrate the cleavages among the Soviet nationalities in daily life. Over one fourth of the emigrants from the Baltic region (notorious for its anti-Russian sentiment) preferred Russians to Soviet Muslims. Only one in twenty showed a preference for Muslims over Russians. Whether or not the Russian elite could manipulate these social divisions in a time of crisis to prevent development of political solidarity among the nationalities is a crucial question, but one that lies outside the scope of this chapter.

While some respondents accepted or rejected certain ethnic groups in all social contexts, this pattern was by no means universal, and even those who did so often varied the intensity if not the direction of their evaluations. Yet others shifted their evaluations from positive to negative, or vice versa, according to the social context, but maintained the relative standings of the ethnic groups by making the acceptance or rejection more or less intense. Many respondents also belonged to several different acceptance/rejection categories, depending on the social context. For example, it was not unusual to find one individual a narrow nationalist when evaluating possible marriage partners, a Europhile in his choice of friends, and an internationalist when considering possible co-workers. In general, respondents were most willing to accept other ethnic groups as equals (for instance, as coworkers and, to a lesser extent, as friends), less willing to meet them in positions of authority (as supervisors at work or as government officials), and least willing to accept them in intimate relationships, especially in marriage.

Differences in the acceptability of an ethnic group according to social context can be explained by the varying degrees of intimacy and subordination required by different types of social interaction. In some instances, they can also be explained by the "inconsistency" of an ethnic group's image: its members may be perceived as pleasant drinking companions but harsh or demanding superiors, lazy coworkers but sympathetic officials. This "image inconsistency" may arise both from unclear stereotypes held by the respondents, and from the fact that different types of personalities within the same ethnic group are drawn to different occupations.

The social differentiation of response to other ethnic groups helps to preserve the cohesion and viability of the Baltic nationalities. The internationalization of the demographic environment is met by insulating the various aspects of social life from one another. Respondents mentioned that students at universities and families living in large apartment buildings frequently seek out members of their own nationality for close friendships, despite the existence of opportunities to interact with members of other ethnic groups. Various clubs and restaurants become social islands where Baltic people gather to enjoy themselves in a setting free of other ethnic groups. The same effect is also obtained by visits to rural areas that are largely populated by the eponymous nationalities.

Social barriers almost never involve total rejection of another ethnic group, but their permeability varies with the social context involved, and also with the cultural compatibility of the ethnic group or person in question. For this reason the Russians' ability to assimilate a particular nationality may vary not only with Russian institutional power and demographic strength, but also with the attractiveness and acceptability of Russian culture and values to the eponymous nationality. In effect, social distance becomes a screening mechanism that tends to block the penetration of a culture by those elements that are most incompatible with its values, and that acts with increasing rigorousness as it defends those social structures most vital to the culture's survival. In this way, the mechanism functions actively as an important regulatory factor in each nationality's internal group support system, while intervening and mediating in the relations among ethnic groups that comprise such a crucial part of the nationality question in the USSR and other multi-ethnic states.

NOTES

1. Fredrik Barth, Ethnic Groups and Boundaries (Boston: Little, Brown, 1969), p. 9.

2. Frederick C. Barghoorn, Soviet Russian Nationalism (New York: Oxford University Press, 1956), p. 68.

3. Vernon V. Aspaturian, "The Non-Russian Nationalities," Prospects for Soviet Society, ed. Allen Kassof (New York: Praeger, 1968), pp. 159-60.

4. Edward Allworth, "Restating the Soviet Nationality Question," Soviet Nationality Problems, ed. Edward Allworth (New York: Columbia University Press, 1971), p. 11.

5. Lowell Tillett, The Great Friendship: Soviet Historians on the Non-Russian Nationalities (Chapel Hill: University of North Carolina Press, 1969), pp. 403-04.

6. Ivan Dzyuba, Internationalism or Russification? A Study in the Soviet Nationalities Problem, 2d ed. (London: Weidenfeld and Nicolson, 1970).

7. Howard J. Ehrlich, The Social Psychology of Prejudice (New York: John Wiley & Sons, 1973), p. 61.

8. A. A. Susokolov, "Neposredstvennoe mezhetnicheskoe obshchenie i ustanovki na mezhlichnostnye kontakty," Sovetskaia

etnografiia no. 5 (1973): 73-78, trans. in Soviet Sociology 13, no. 1/2 (Summer-Fall 1974): 148.

9. Hubert M. Blalock, Jr., Social Statistics (New York: McGraw-Hill, 1972), pp. 162-63.

10. Juozas A. Kazlas, "The German Minority in the USSR and Its Relations with Other Soviet Nationalities" (Ph.D. diss., Yale University, 1977).

11. A. I. Kholmogorov, Internatsional'nye cherty sovetskikh natsii (na materialakh konkretno-sotsiologicheskikh issledovanii v Pribaltike) (Moscow: Izdatel'stvo "Mysl'," 1970), pp. 3-138, trans. in Soviet Sociology 11, no. 3/4 (Winter-Spring 1972-73): 317.

12. Ibid., p. 291.

13. L. N. Terent'eva, "Opredelenie svoei natsional'noi prinadlezhnosti podrostkami v natsional'no-smeshannykh sem'iakh," Sovetskaia etnografiia no. 3 (1969): 20-30, trans. in Bulletin of Baltic Studies (December 1970): 11.

14. Itogi vsesoiuznoi perepisi naseleniia 1970 goda. Natsional'nyi sostav naseleniia SSSR (Moscow: Statistika, 1972-73) (hereafter cited as Itogi . . . 1970 goda), pp. 480, 509, 511.

15. Itogi . . . 1970 goda, vol. 4, p. 273.

16. Lietuvos Kominist̄u Partija Skaičiais (Vilnius: Mintis Publishing House, 1976), p. 120.

17. Alberts Sābris, Lokanums un Spīts ([Brooklyn], N.Y.: Grāmatu Draugs, 1974), p. 21.

18. Itogi . . . 1970 goda, vol. 4, pp. 12-15.

APPENDIX A
WHAT AGITATES THE HISTORY TEACHER?

I have been teaching history for many years. During that period I have attended hundreds of history lessons given by the teachers of our school. I have observed and compared. A picture of the qualitative growth of history lessons is formed before my eyes. . . .

Iu. Orginis and V. Merkis' history book for the 7th-9th grades published several years ago was to have become the teacher's basic aid in teaching the history of our native land. In part it has facilitated our work. However, the teachers have claims to lodge against the writers. In the textbook the class view of historical phenomena gets lost in secondary things. The authors, as though they wished to justify themselves, wrote the following in the preface: "The authors have tried to present as much knowledge as possible on a relatively few pages; knowledge that would impel the student to think historically. The teacher will have to explain more complex things."

There are too many "complex things," I regret to say. Not every teacher finds it easy to understand the abundant material. In the "Growth of Culture" section, nearly nine pages are devoted to an attempt to list all the cultural phenomena of the 13th to the 15th centuries. Hundreds of facts are presented. Yet there is no Marxist assessment of the phenomena of that culture. But for us, as I have pointed out, it is especially important for a textbook to point out ideological problems, so that they [the students] are not overwhelmed by the abundant figures and facts. . . .

The approach to writing [in historical textbooks] should also be exacting and principled, because we have literary works that paint Lithuania's distant past in bright colors only. Princes defend the people, and there is no difference between the average individual and the feudal lord. There is no class struggle, no antagonism. I do not want to belittle the significance of these works, for they instill love of the native land and hate for its enemies. However, it is necessary to teach the students to distinguish profound historical

---

Selected excerpts from the article "Chto volnuet uchitelia istorii" [What disturbs a history teacher], appearing in Sovetskaia Litva (March 14, 1973), p. 2. The author, Ch. Mantauskas, was director of, and history teacher in, a secondary school in Lithuania.

Appendix A was compiled by Kenneth E. Nyirady.

truth from the secondary window-dressing, which the schools partly inherited from the bourgeois system, when the main task of history teaching was to shape a so-called national consciousness. . . .

Every teacher's holy civic duty is to treat Lithuania's remote past correctly, see it with the eyes of a communist, and reveal the manifestations of the class struggle. Only then will this past cease to be perceived as a beautiful tale about princes and appear as genuine historical truth.

In publishing historical works, it would obviously be advisable to take into account the importance of this or that historical stage. Recent years have witnessed the appearance of many books on the past. They are needed, but it must not be forgotten that works dealing with the socialist period are no less important.

Some books lack a [social] class [and communist], party approach to the assessment of historical events. The recently published book The Castles of Lithuania (Zamki litvy) fails to tackle adequately the social aspect and has no scientific depth. In other publications the class position is not always clearly revealed or is sometimes oversimplified.

Publications concerning local lore carry much historical material. However, some volumes contain unnecessary sighs over the disappearance of straw roofs and the appearance of electric transmission lines in what once were wide-open fields. Reading that stuff, young people may get an incorrect idea about our reality.

APPENDIX B
USSR MINISTERIAL ORGANIZATION AND BALTIC INCUMBENTS

TABLE B.1

USSR Ministerial Organization: List of Union-Wide Ministries

Automotive industry
Aviation industry
Chemical industry
Chemical and petroleum machine building
Civil aviation
Communications equipment industry
Construction of petroleum and gas industry enterprises
Construction, road and municipal machine building
Defense industry
Electrical equipment industry
Electronics industry
Foreign trade
Gas industry
General machine building
Heavy and transport machine building
Instrument making, automation equipment, and control systems
Machine building
Machine building for animal husbandry and fodder production
Machine building for light and food industry and household appliances
Machine tools and tool building industry
Maritime fleet
Medical industry
Medium machine building
Petroleum industry
Power machine building
Pulp and paper industry
Radio industry
Railways
Shipbuilding industry
Tractor and agricultural machine building
Transport construction

Source: Directory of Soviet Officials, vol. 1, National Organizations (n.p.: Central Intelligence Agency, December 1975), p. 63.

TABLE B.2

USSR Ministerial Organization: List of Union-Republic (Dual-Control) Ministries

Agriculture
Coal industry
Communications
Construction
Construction of heavy industry enterprises
Construction materials industry
Culture
Defense
Education
Ferrous metallurgy
Finance
Fish industry
Food industry
Foreign affairs
Geology
Health
Higher and secondary specialized education
Industrial construction
Installation and special construction work
Internal affairs
Justice
Land reclamation and water resources
Light industry
Meat and dairy industry
Nonferrous metallurgy
Petroleum refining and petrochemical industry
Power and electrification
Procurement
Rural construction
Timber and wood processing industry
Trade

Source: Directory of Soviet Officials, vol. 1, National Organizations (n.p.: Central Intelligence Agency, December 1975), p. 63.

Appendix B was compiled by Richard Shryock.

TABLE B.3

Baltic Republic Ministerial Organization: Estonian SSR
(as of January 1, 1975)

Ministries	Ministers	Date Appointment
Union-Republic		
Agriculture	H. Männik	*
Communications	A. Kaldma	*
Construction	Uno Jürisoo	June 1968
Construction materials industry	L. Vikhvelin	October 1965
Culture	J.-K. Jürna	June 1973
Education	Ferdinand Eisen	April 1960
Finance	Albert Norak	February 1967
Food industry	Jaan Tepandi	October 1965
Foreign affairs	Arnold Green	February 1962
Health	V. Rätsep	*
Higher and secondary specialized education	Aare Purga	August 1972
Internal affairs	Valter Ani	June 1961
Justice	Walter Raudsalu	December 1970
Light industry	Y. Vladychin	October 1965
Meat and dairy industry	A. Essenson	December 1971
Procurement	August Pedajas	January 1970
Timber and wood processing industry	V. Chernyshav	October 1965
Trade	K. Todeson	December 1963
Republic		
Consumer services	V. Hallamägi	*
Forestry and conservation of natural resources	Heino Teder	June 1966
Motor transport and highways	Richard Sibul	November 1958
Municipal services	Arseni Blum	March 1969
Social security	G. Sarri	March 1974

*Date of change, as of July 4, 1975.

Source: Directory of Soviet Officials, vol. 3, Union Republics (n.p.: Central Intelligence Agency, May 1975), pp. 71-72; Eesti Nõukogude Entsuklopeedia, 8 vols. (Tallinn: n.p., 1968-74).

Tõnu Parming gave valuable advice and supplemental information for Table B.3.

TABLE B.4

Baltic Republic Ministerial Organization: Latvian SSR
(as of July 4, 1975)

Ministries	Ministers	Date of Appointment
Union-Republic		
Agriculture	Kazimirs Anspoks	November 1973
Communications	Osvalds Stungrovics	June 1973
Construction	Ivars Ulmanis	1970
Construction materials industry	Kārlis Jēgers	1965
Culture	Vladimirs Kaupužs	January 1962
Education	Mirdza Kārkliņa	May 1969
Finance	K. Tolmadzhev	March 1961
Food industry	Irina Kuznetsova	October 1965
Foreign affairs	Viktors Krūmiņš	April 1967
Health	Vilhelms Kaņeps	December 1962
Higher and secondary specialized education	Edgars Linde	June 1975
Internal affairs	Jānis Brolišs	July 1972
Justice	Jānis Dzenītis	October 1970
Land reclamation and water resources	Viktor Samolevskii	March 1966
Light industry	Eduards Jablonskis	July 1972
Meat and dairy industry	Sviatoslav Vannakh	May 1973
Procurement	Zigfrīds Girgensons	December 1969
Trade	Roberts Praude	February 1963
Republic		
Consumer services	Ivan Bastin	August 1966
Forestry and the timber industry	Leons Vītols	December 1971
Local industry	Nikolai Altukhov	July 1973
Motor transport and highways	Egons Slēde	August 1969
Municipal services	Ivans Bērziņš	February 1969
Social security	Valentīna Pihele	September 1961
Woodworking industry	Vsevolods Birkenfelds	1972

Source: Directory of Soviet Officials, vol. 3, Union Republics (n.p.: Central Intelligence Agency, May 1975), pp. 151-52; "Latvijas PSR augstākās padomes Lēmums par Latvijas PSR valdibas–Latvijas PSR Ministru Padomes sastādīšanu," Padomju jaunatne (July 5, 1975, April 6 and May 17, 1976): 2; this source combines Union Republic and Republic ministries.

Jānis Kresliņš gave valuable advice and supplemental information for Table B.4.

TABLE B.5

Baltic Republic Ministerial Organization:
Lithuanian SSR

Ministries	Ministers	Date of Appointment
Union-Republic		
Agriculture	Grigaliunas	April 1965
Communications	Onaitis	December 1968
Construction	Sakalauskas	January 1962
Construction materials industry	Jasiunas	December 1966
Culture	Sepetys	July 1967
Education	Rimkus	July 1973
Finance	Sikorskis	August 1957
Food industry	Dulskas	October 1970
Foreign affairs	Dirzinskaite-Piliusenko	February 1966
Health	Kleiza	June 1960
Higher and secondary specialized education	Zabulis	March 1966
Internal affairs	Mikalauskas	September 1968
Justice	Randakevicius	November 1970
Land reclamation and water resources	Velicka	October 1965
Light industry	Adomaitis	October 1965
Meat and dairy industry	Vuklis	September 1962
Procurement	Kareckas	March 1966
Rural construction	Bagdonas	September 1967
Trade	Mikutis	November 1953
Republic		
Consumer services	Plekavicius	June 1966
Forestry and timber industry	Matulenis	December 1949
Furniture and wood-working industry	Kuris	October 1965
Local industry	Kuskov	May 1973
Motor transport and highways	Martinaitis	September 1955
Municipal services	Seris	July 1971
Social security	Paceviciene	December 1973

Source: Directory of Soviet Officials, vol. 3, Union Republics (n.p.: Central Intelligence Agency, May 1975), pp. 171-72.

Walter Jaskievicz gave valuable advice and supplemental information for Table B.5.

APPENDIX C
JEWISH DISSATISFACTION

RIGA ACTIVISM

The following are full quotations from two Riga activists, Mendel Gordin and Viktor Fedoseyev. Gordin was in a key position at the Central Bacteriological Research Center, after having served as a staff physician at a regional Latvian hospital. He was not active in Jewish causes until the Six-Day War of 1967. By 1968, he was openly celebrating Jewish holidays and practicing certain religious rituals. He applied for an exit visa in February 1969. Fedoseyev lived in Riga from the early 1960s until 1968, when he and his wife moved to Moscow. Fedoseyev became the editor of Iskhod [Exodus], a Jewish samizdat newsletter. This information, as well as the following quotations are in The Last Exodus, by Leonard Schroeter (New York: Universe Books, 1974).

Gordin:

> It is difficult to say when and for how long there has been a Zionist underground in Riga. In my opinion, there was always a very lively Jewish life in Riga, but for a long time it was deeply underground. Given Soviet society and its characteristics, that is the only place it could be. By the late 1950's, there was a small group of people who were already publishing Jewish samizdat in Riga. But you cannot find out the facts by asking only one person, or even a number. The nature of the way it was organized was such that no one knows more than his small piece of the truth. I don't know exactly. I knew of five to ten people in those days. Someone else knew five or so. I don't know what they were doing exactly. We learned not to ask. We didn't want to know too much. People were close to their own activity in a very narrow circle. By 1969 and 1970, when we began collective demonstrations—then the movement is easier to understand.

Fedoseyev:

Appendix C was compiled by Eli M. Lederhendler.

> In Riga, there was a real feeling that there were Jews who constantly affirmed their Jewishness. This was in startling contrast to most Soviet cities. But I never became aware of a movement, that is a real movement in a well-organized sense, during the years we lived there. Of course, now that the Jewish movement is open and dramatic in the Soviet Union, everyone really believes that it began in his kitchen, and that he was "the" or at least "a" leader of it. This is not braggadocio. This is because the movement was so diffused—so spontaneous. It arose out of deep needs and deeper frustration. Of course, it differed from place to place. But everywhere in the Soviet Union, the ground was plowed and the seeds were planted.

PETITIONS

(The following petitions of Baltic Jews express most directly the link between Jewish cultural identity and nationality dissatisfaction. They are to be found in Exodus [no. 2], a Soviet Jewish samizdat journal and are translated in Bulletin of Soviet and East European Jewish Affairs, no. 6 [December 1970], pp. 58, 75-76. The pertinent sections have been excerpted.)

An Open Letter
To the United Nations Secretary-General U Thant
To the President of the UN Human Rights Commission
To the Prime Minister of the State of Israel Mrs. Golda Meir

Every signatory of this letter appeals to you for help, as you are public and state figures, capable of helping us through your authority and influence to be repatriated to Israel and reunited with our relatives. . . .

Before the Second World War there was a large Jewish community in Lithuania with great Jewish cultural traditions. Jewish schools, theatres, publishers, etc., raised Jewish culture to great heights in this region of the world and honoured the world culture of our people. Many great Jewish writers were born in this region and it is not for nothing that the town of Vilnius was called by Jews in the whole world "the Lithuanian Jerusalem."

Thanks to its high Jewish culture, Lithuanian Jewry was closely linked with Palestine before the Second World War. Many Jews left Lithuania to settle in Palestine in spite of the close restrictions on immigration imposed by the then English authorities. Apart from this, as a result of the war, many Jews who survived the Hitler death-machine also found themselves in Israel. Thus we are linked to Israel by close ties of family and spirit and this is proven by our constant exchange of letters with our relatives.

At the present moment there is no trace of the former Jewish culture in our area. There are no Jewish schools, no professional theatres, no publishing houses; there are even no Jewish newspapers and there are no reasons to expect all these to be reborn.

We are cut off from our long history, from our traditions, and from the spiritual heritage of our ancestors.

We have absorbed Lithuanian and Russian culture but we have not become Lithuanians or Russians. We remain Jewish, although we are deprived of everything that the other peoples of USSR have.

This is why we link all our future with our departure from here and our settling in the State of Israel with our relatives; we want to live together with them in an atmosphere of Jewish culture and traditions. . . .

Vilnius, May 1970
(nine signatories)

To the Central Committee of the Communist
Party of the USSR
To the Council of Ministers of the USSR
To the Presidium of the Supreme Soviet of the USSR

We, Jews of Riga, apply to the supreme governmental bodies of the USSR to allow us to leave for our national motherland, the State of Israel. . . .

We state that our desire to leave for the State of Israel is in no way linked with the material conditions of our existence. It is due entirely to moral factors. . . .

Two to three hundred years are not a long period in history of the Jewish people, but during this time a full-blooded Jewish community was born on Latvian territory and it had all the special qualities of a way of life and culture. A vast network of Jewish schools and secondary schools, of theatres, clubs, libraries, organizations for sport and for young people, were developed. A Jewish teachers' training college was functioning, etc.

Latvian Jewry was characterized by its close links with the Jewish movement for national liberation in Palestine in the 1920's and 30's, the movement that was directed against British colonialism. Thousands of our relatives and friends under the influence of their national feeling surmounted all the difficulties created by the English authorities and went to Palestine, . . . in order to recreate a Jewish national state. . . .

Thus the Jews of Latvia are even to this day linked with Israel (former Palestine) by a whole complex of family, national and cultural ties and traditions. . . .

Twenty-five years have gone by since the war ended. A new generation has grown up and it has been artificially cut off from the spiritual values of its people. In Latvia there are absolutely no elements of Jewish national culture: no school, no newspaper, no theatre for Jews, etc. We are therefore condemned to the unenviable prospect of a forced assimilation, which we refuse absolutely. . . .

Riga, July 1970
(About 36 signatures)

To the UN Secretary-General, U Thant
To the Chairman of the Human Rights Commission
To the President of the State of Israel, Mr. Z. Shazar

. . . We, all the undersigned, have received a Jewish education and have been brought up as Jews in the days when there still were Jewish schools, Jewish theatres and other national institutions in Lithuania. We have been brought up in the spirit of the Bible, of Jewish history and of national consciousness. Under any conditions, wherever we found ourselves to be, we have always dreamt of our historic motherland Israel, and immediately after the denunciation of the cult of personality we started our attempts to join our relatives in Israel. But this is constantly refused to us, in spite of the fact that the USSR has also signed the Declaration of Human Rights.

We have no claims on the USSR and we bear no grudge against it. All we are asking for is to be allowed to go to OUR OWN COUNTRY. . . .

Vilnius (n.d.)
(13 signatories)

TESTIMONY OF IOSIF MENDELEVICH AND DAVID GARBER

The importance of the cultural element in Jewish nationality dissatisfaction is evident in the testimony of these two former Riga activists. Iosif Mendelevich, currently serving a 12-year sentence in a Soviet prison camp, was one of the defendants in the Leningrad hijacking trial of 1970. According to a prisoner's profile distributed by the Greater New York Conference on Soviet Jewry, Mendelevich was "born into a family close to the Jewish tradition. Iosif Mendelevich studied Hebrew on his own as an adolescent and read whatever he could find on Jewish history and culture."

The samizdat transcript of the Leningrad trial states the following:

> Session of 15 December: Examination of Witnesses—
>
> Examination of Iosif Mendelevich (age 23). He said that he had grown up in a family where Jewish traditions were valued. He had always had a profound interest in the history and destiny of the Jewish people and that for him and his family the question had long before been decided to regard Israel as their spiritual and historical homeland [Exodus, no. 4 (1971), trans. in Soviet Jewish Affairs (1971)].

David Garber, active in the Riga theater ensemble and Rumbuli memorial meetings, as well as in Jewish samizdat, also tied cultural activity to the emigration movement:

> The existence and abolition of the drama group and choir played an important role in the growth of national consciousness among Latvian Jews. The groups aroused new interest in and love for Jewish culture and encouraged Jews to overcome the fear which Stalinism had implanted in all peoples and to demand the rights guaranteed them by Soviet law. They also created a basis on which Jews could meet each other legally, after many years of keeping apart, to talk about matters of Jewish national interest.
>
> The members of the drama group and choir did not join other collectives, as the authorities had hoped, but became active in other fields. Thus, from 1963 Riga Jews started to organize the building of a monument in memory of Jews killed in the Holocaust, in a wood outside Riga, at Rumbuli, and most of the members took part in this work. In the past four years most of the members have arrived in Israel [David Garber, "Choir and Drama in Riga," Soviet Jewish Affairs 4, no. 1 (1974): 44].

APPENDIX D
HOW BALTIC NATIONALITIES AND SOVIET GERMANS SEE THEMSELVES AND OTHERS

TABLE D.1

Intensity of Ethnic Preferences
(average scores)

Nationality	Relative	Friend	Worker	Supervisor	Official
Lithuanian Sample					
Estonian	0.4	1.7	1.6	1.6	1.4
Latvian	0.1	1.6	1.6	1.4	1.2
Lithuanian	2.0	2.0	2.0	1.9	1.3
Russian	-1.6	-0.1	-0.4	-0.8	-1.0
Belorussian	-1.7	-0.8	-0.1	-0.3	-0.5
Ukrainian	-1.1	0.5	0.6	0.1	0.4
Moldavian	-1.1	0.0	0.1	0.3	0.1
Armenian	-1.4	0.1	-0.4	-0.1	0.4
Georgian	-1.3	-0.4	-0.3	-0.1	0.5
Azerbaijanian	-1.6	-0.9	-0.8	-0.4	-0.3
Kazakh	-1.7	-1.1	-0.7	-0.9	-0.5
Kirgiz	-1.7	-1.0	-0.7	-0.9	-0.5
Turkmen	-1.7	-1.0	-0.7	-0.9	-0.5
Uzbek	-1.5	-0.9	-0.6	-0.8	-0.4
Tajik	-1.5	-0.9	-0.6	-0.9	-0.5
Tatar	-1.7	-1.2	-0.6	-0.8	-0.8
Jewish	-1.1	0.1	0.2	0.0	0.3
Soviet Polish	-1.2	-0.3	-0.1	-0.9	-0.5
Soviet German	-0.3	1.2	1.2	1.2	0.5
Soviet German Sample					
Estonian	0.2	1.2	1.2	1.1	1.3
Latvian	0.1	1.1	1.3	1.0	0.9
Lithuanian	0.1	1.0	1.2	1.0	0.8
Russian	-1.4	0.8	1.1	0.7	-0.2
Belorussian	-1.4	0.3	0.5	0.2	-0.5

Ukrainian	-1.2	0.7	0.7	0.2	-0.4
Moldavian	-1.3	0.2	0.7	0.0	-0.1
Armenian	-1.3	0.0	0.3	0.0	-0.2
Georgian	-1.4	0.0	0.5	0.1	-0.2
Azerbaijanian	-1.4	-0.2	0.3	-0.1	-0.2
Kazakh	-1.6	-0.1	0.4	-0.2	-0.3
Kirgiz	-1.6	-0.1	0.5	0.1	0.0
Turkmen	-1.7	-0.3	0.2	-0.1	-0.3
Uzbek	-1.7	-0.2	0.2	-0.1	-0.3
Tajik	-1.7	-0.4	0.2	-0.1	-0.3
Jewish	-1.1	0.2	0.4	0.2	0.3
Tatar	-1.5	0.3	0.8	0.3	-0.1
Soviet German	2.0	1.9	1.9	1.7	1.7
Accept all nationalities[a]	n = 1	n = 2	n = 4	n = 2	–
Reject all nationalities[b]	–	–	–	n = 3	–

Appendix D was compiled by Jouzas A. Kazlas.

[a]Several respondents stated that they were willing to accept members of every ethnic group in various social contexts.

[b]Three individuals wrote that they found supervisors of any nationality disagreeable.

Note: Possible range of scores is from 2 (total acceptance) to -2 (total rejection); 0 indicates indifference or neutrality. Three of the twelve respondents stated that it is impossible to judge individuals by their nationality. If they had been assigned arbitrary scores and included in this chart, the scores for all nationalities would have been raised somewhat, and the differences among nationalities would have been diminished. However, the basic trends and relative standings would have remained the same.

Sources: Data derived from written questionnaires completed by Baltic respondents in the United States and Europe (1976-77) and by Soviet Germans (Spring-Fall 1975) in Federal Republic of Germany; both supplemented by selected personal interviews.

TABLE D.2

Ethnic Acceptance or Rejection
(answers grouped into a yes/no dichotomy)

	Relative		Friend		Worker		Supervisor		Official	
	Yes	No	Yes	No	Yes	No	Yes	No	Yes	No
Lithuanian sample (n)*										
Estonian	10	4	14	–	13	1	12	–	10	2
Latvian	8	5	12	–	11	1	9	1	8	3
Lithuanian	14	–	14	–	14	–	12	–	9	3
Russian	3	10	8	5	7	5	4	6	2	10
Belorussian	3	9	5	7	7	5	5	5	2	7
Ukrainian	5	8	11	3	11	3	7	4	6	5
Moldavian	5	8	7	5	9	6	7	3	4	5
Armenian	3	9	8	5	7	6	5	4	5	4
Georgian	4	9	6	7	7	6	5	5	6	4
Azerbaijanian	3	9	5	7	5	6	4	5	3	6
Kazakh	3	9	4	8	5	5	3	6	2	6
Kirgiz	3	9	4	7	5	5	3	6	2	6
Turkmen	3	9	4	7	5	5	3	6	2	6
Uzbek	3	9	4	7	5	5	3	6	2	6
Tajik	3	9	4	7	5	5	3	6	2	6
Tatar	3	9	4	8	5	4	3	5	1	7
Jewish	5	7	9	5	10	4	6	5	7	6
Soviet Polish	5	8	7	5	7	5	3	8	4	7
Soviet German	7	6	13	1	13	1	11	1	6	3

Soviet German sample (in percent)										
Estonian	59.5	32.4	89.1	4.3	86.0	10.0	86.4	9.1	90.9	4.6
Latvian	52.9	35.3	88.2	8.8	86.8	2.6	32.4	5.9	65.8	7.7
Lithuanian	48.6	31.4	79.4	14.7	81.1	5.4	75.0	6.3	64.9	13.5
Russian	9.4	90.6	80.5	19.5	87.2	12.8	76.7	23.3	40.4	53.2
Belorussian	3.7	88.9	60.0	32.0	63.3	30.0	51.9	33.3	25.0	50.0
Ukrainian	14.3	82.1	70.4	25.9	70.6	26.5	54.3	37.1	31.6	52.6
Moldavian	10.7	78.6	40.7	29.6	69.0	17.2	39.9	32.1	28.1	31.3
Armenian	11.1	74.1	37.0	37.0	53.3	23.3	40.7	25.9	22.6	35.5
Georgian	3.5	75.9	34.6	38.5	55.2	17.2	42.9	21.4	25.0	37.5
Azerbaijanian	3.7	74.1	30.8	46.2	50.0	25.0	29.6	33.3	22.6	35.5
Kazakh	6.9	89.7	43.3	46.7	57.1	25.7	38.9	44.4	25.0	47.5
Kirgiz	3.6	89.3	46.2	46.2	61.3	25.8	46.4	32.1	32.3	35.5
Turkmen	3.6	89.3	30.8	50.0	44.8	27.6	33.3	33.3	22.6	35.5
Uzbek	3.6	89.3	34.6	50.0	46.7	26.7	33.3	33.3	19.4	38.7
Tajik	3.6	89.3	33.3	63.0	46.7	26.7	33.3	33.3	18.8	40.6
Jewish	17.9	78.6	48.3	34.5	61.3	19.4	48.4	29.0	25.0	40.6
Tatar	7.1	85.7	53.9	34.6	65.5	13.8	51.9	29.6	32.3	38.7
Soviet German	100.0	–	98.3	–	100.0	–	98.1	1.9	93.8	2.1

*The symbol (n) designates absolute numbers.

Note: Three respondents who stated that they were willing to accept members of every ethnic group were included in the "yes" columns. Respondents who left blanks or marked "don't know" for particular ethnic groups were excluded from the totals.

Sources: Data derived from written questionnaires completed by Baltic respondents in the United States and Europe (1976–77) and by Soviet Germans (Spring-Fall 1975) in Federal Republic of Germany; both supplemented by selected personal interviews.

TABLE D.3

Choosing between Russians and Members of Nationalities

Nationality	Relative			Friend			Worker			Supervisor			Official		
	Prefer Russian	Both Same	Prefer Nation-ality	Prefer Russian	Both Same	Prefer Nation-ality	Prefer Russian	Both Same	Prefer Nation-ality	Prefer Russian	Both Same	Prefer Nation-ality	Prefer Russian	Both Same	Prefer Nation-ality
Lithuanian sample (n)*															
Estonian	–	3	11	–	4	10	–	4	10	–	4	10	–	4	10
Latvian	–	5	9	–	6	8	–	7	7	–	7	7	–	6	8
Lithuanian	–	3	11	–	3	11	–	3	11	–	3	11	–	4	10
Belorussian	3	10	1	4	9	1	4	9	1	4	8	2	3	9	2
Ukrainian	1	4	9	1	5	8	1	7	6	–	8	6	–	7	7
Moldavian	–	8	6	–	9	5	–	10	4	1	8	5	1	7	6
Armenian	–	10	4	–	9	5	1	11	2	–	12	2	–	7	7
Georgian	–	9	5	–	10	4	2	8	4	–	10	4	–	7	7
Azerbaijan-ian	1	11	2	1	12	1	3	10	1	2	11	1	1	10	3
Kazakh	2	11	1	2	11	1	2	11	1	3	10	1	2	11	1
Kirgiz	2	11	1	2	11	1	2	11	1	3	10	1	2	11	1
Turkmen	2	11	1	2	11	1	2	11	1	2	11	1	1	12	1
Uzbek	2	10	2	2	10	2	2	11	1	2	11	1	1	12	1
Tajik	2	10	2	2	10	2	2	10	2	2	11	1	1	12	1
Tatar	1	10	3	–	12	2	1	10	3	1	10	3	2	10	2
Jewish	2	7	5	2	6	6	2	7	5	2	8	4	2	8	4
Soviet Polish	2	8	4	3	8	3	2	8	4	1	9	4	1	8	5
Soviet German	1	5	8	1	4	9	1	4	9	–	5	9	–	6	8

Soviet German sample (in percent)															
Estonian	–	17.6	82.4	4.3	26.1	69.6	2.0	26.5	71.4	7.3	26.8	65.9	–	36.8	63.2
Latvian	3.3	30.0	66.7	8.3	27.8	63.9	2.5	35.0	62.5	8.6	40.0	51.4	–	51.6	48.4
Lithuanian	–	36.7	63.3	5.4	32.4	62.2	2.5	40.0	57.5	5.6	41.7	52.8	–	53.1	46.9
Belorussian	34.6	61.5	3.8	25.8	71.0	3.2	30.3	60.6	9.1	21.9	75.0	3.1	16.1	80.6	3.2
Ukrainian	30.8	53.8	15.4	21.2	57.6	21.2	14.7	52.9	32.4	9.4	75.0	15.6	13.3	76.7	10.0
Moldavian	34.6	50.0	15.4	25.8	48.4	25.8	20.0	54.3	25.7	31.3	56.3	12.5	16.1	64.5	19.4
Armenian	41.7	45.8	12.5	36.4	42.4	21.2	28.6	51.4	20.0	36.4	60.6	3.0	29.0	61.3	9.7
Georgian	52.2	43.5	4.3	38.2	41.2	20.6	27.8	52.8	19.4	36.4	54.5	9.1	33.3	60.0	6.7
Azerbaijan-ian	54.5	40.9	4.5	41.9	45.2	12.9	32.4	47.1	20.6	34.4	62.5	3.1	30.0	63.3	6.7
Kazakh	63.6	36.4	4.5	38.7	41.9	19.4	27.8	50.0	22.2	32.4	52.9	14.7	32.3	54.8	12.9
Kirgiz	63.6	36.4	4.5	38.7	41.9	19.4	29.4	50.0	20.6	31.3	59.4	9.4	30.0	60.0	10.0
Turkmen	63.6	36.4	4.5	41.9	38.7	19.4	33.3	48.5	18.2	37.5	56.3	6.3	33.3	56.7	10.0
Uzbek	63.6	36.4	4.5	38.7	41.9	19.4	30.3	51.5	18.2	37.5	50.0	12.5	33.3	56.7	10.0
Tajik	63.6	36.4	4.5	41.9	41.9	16.1	30.3	51.5	18.2	34.4	53.1	12.5	33.3	56.7	10.0
Jewish	40.9	40.9	18.2	29.0	48.4	22.6	32.4	44.1	23.5	34.4	53.1	12.5	26.7	60.0	13.3
Tatar	54.5	36.4	9.1	29.0	41.9	29.0	23.5	50.0	26.5	29.0	58.1	12.9	26.7	63.3	10.0
Soviet German	–	3.2	96.8	–	14.5	85.5	1.6	26.2	72.1	6.8	23.7	69.5	8.2	36.7	55.1

*The symbol (n) designates absolute numbers.

Source: Data derived from written questionnaires completed by Baltic respondents in the United States and Europe (1976–77) and by Soviet Germans in Federal Republic of Germany (Spring–Fall 1975); both supplemented by selected personal interviews.

TABLE D.4

Individuals Met by Respondents in the USSR

Nationality	Worker	Neighbor	Supervisor	Official	Friend	Relative
Lithuanian sample (n)*						
Estonian	5	2	–	–	6	–
Latvian	5	1	–	–	3	1
Lithuanian	14	14	13	14	14	14
Russian	14	12	6	14	9	2
Belorussian	6	3	–	2	1	–
Ukrainian	7	5	1	6	5	2
Moldavian	2	–	–	–	–	–
Armenian	2	–	–	2	–	–
Georgian	1	–	–	–	–	–
Azerbaijanian	1	–	–	–	–	–
Kazakh	2	–	1	1	–	–
Kirgiz	2	–	–	–	–	–
Turkmen	1	–	–	–	–	–
Uzbek	2	–	–	–	–	–
Tajik	1	–	–	–	–	–
Tatar	4	2	1	–	1	–
Jewish	11	6	6	10	5	1
Soviet Polish	8	9	1	3	3	1
Soviet German	2	–	–	–	–	1
Soviet German sample (in percent)						
Estonian	54.7	48.5	46.9	50.8	45.5	–
Latvian	25.0	10.6	9.4	14.3	12.3	3.0

Lithuanian	18.8	7.6	7.8	7.9	4.6	1.5
Russian	93.8	89.4	89.1	98.4	65.2	28.8
Belorussian	29.7	7.6	3.1	14.3	6.1	–
Ukrainian	56.3	39.4	21.9	42.9	15.2	4.6
Moldavian	10.9	3.0	–	7.9	1.5	–
Armenian	9.4	6.1	–	7.9	1.5	–
Georgian	12.5	4.6	3.1	7.9	4.5	–
Azerbaijanian	17.2	3.0	–	11.1	3.0	1.5
Kazakh	42.2	27.3	21.9	41.3	13.6	1.5
Kirgiz	20.3	16.7	9.4	20.6	6.1	1.5
Turkmen	4.7	–	–	7.9	–	–
Uzbek	14.1	9.1	4.7	14.3	7.6	–
Tajik	15.6	12.1	6.3	22.2	4.6	–
Jewish	26.6	7.6	17.2	25.4	12.1	3.0
Tatar	32.8	24.2	4.7	12.7	13.6	1.5
Soviet German	81.3	80.3	14.1	15.9	87.9	100.0

*The symbol (n) designates absolute numbers.

Note: This section shows which nationalities the respondents interacted with in the Soviet Union. To be more precise, it shows which nationalities the respondents perceived in the Soviet Union and remembered at the time of these interviews. For example, several respondents mentioned that it was often difficult to know whether one was dealing with a Russian, Belorussian, or Ukrainian. The latter two nationalities may therefore, be under-represented in these charts. Some "slippage" may have occurred among nationalities within a region: the author overheard discussions about which of the Transcaucasus (or Muslim) nationalities particular individuals belonged to. In general, the least reliable columns are probably those dealing with social contexts. A personal knowledge of the people one is interacting with (such as workers or officials) may be lacking whereas the most reliable columns are those dealing with more intimate relationships (friends and relatives).

Source: Data derived from written questionnaires completed by Baltic respondents in the United States and Europe (1976–77) and by Soviet Germans in Federal Republic of Germany (Spring–Fall 1975); both supplemented by selected personal interviews.

APPENDIX E
ETHNIC AND LINGUISTIC DIFFERENCES

TABLE E.1

Ethnic Composition of Baltic Republics

Nationality	Number	Percent of Republic's Population	Percent of Urban Population	Percent of Rural Population
Estonia				
Estonians	925,157	68.2	57.5	88.2
Russians	334,620	24.7	33.9	7.5
Ukrainians	28,086	2.1	2.8	0.7
Belorussians	18,732	1.4	1.9	0.4
Finns	18,537	1.4	1.3	1.6
Jews	5,288	0.4	0.6	—
Latvians	3,286	0.2	0.3	0.2
Poles	2,651	0.2	0.3	0.1
Lithuanians	2,356	0.2	0.2	0.1
Tatars	2,205	0.2	0.2	—
Others	15,161	1.1	1.1	1.2
Total	1,356,079			
Latvia				
Latvians	1,341,805	56.8	47.0	73.0
Russians	704,599	29.8	38.0	16.1
Belorussians	94,898	4.0	4.0	4.0

Poles	63,045	2.7	2.9	2.3
Ukrainians	53,461	2.3	3.0	1.1
Lithuanians	40,589	1.7	1.2	2.6
Jews	36,680	1.6	2.5	–
Gypsies	5,427	0.2	0.3	0.2
Estonians	4,334	0.2	0.2	0.2
Tatars	2,688	0.1	0.2	–
Others	16,601	0.7	0.8	0.5
Total	2,364,127			
Lithuania				
Lithuanians	2,506,751	80.1	73.2	87.1
Russians	267,989	8.6	14.5	2.6
Poles	240,203	7.7	6.1	9.3
Belorussians	45,412	1.5	2.4	0.5
Ukrainians	25,099	0.8	1.5	0.1
Jews	23,564	0.8	1.5	–
Latvians	5,063	0.2	0.2	–
Tatars	3,460	0.1	0.1	–
Gypsies	1,880	0.1	0.1	–
Others	8,815	0.3	0.4	0.1
Total	3,128,236			

Appendix E was compiled by Juozas A. Kazlas.

Source: Itogi vsesoiuznoi perepisi naseleniia 1970 goda. Natsional'nyi sostav naseleniia SSSR (Moscow: Statistika, 1973) 4: 273, 280, 317.

TABLE E.2

Linguistic Composition of Baltic Republics
(in percent)

Nationality	Own Language			Russian			Estonian			Other
	Native	Second	Total	Native	Second	Total	Native	Second	Total	Total
Estonia										
Estonian	99.2	0.5	99.7	0.7	27.5	28.2	–	–	–	0.1
Russian	98.4	1.2	99.6	–	–	–	1.5	12.6	14.1	1.2
Ukrainian	51.9	18.1	70.0	47.0	47.7	94.7	1.0	4.1	5.1	0.4
Belorussian	43.4	14.6	58.0	55.7	39.7	95.4	0.6	2.7	3.3	1.1
Finnish	51.5	–	51.5	20.4	43.7	64.1	27.8	32.1	59.9	0.5
Jewish	21.5	3.3	24.8	70.0	19.3	89.3	7.7	24.8	32.5	9.3
Latvian	67.2	11.5	78.7	19.1	49.1	68.2	13.4	20.7	34.1	0.5
Polish	30.2	–	30.2	50.4	39.9	90.3	11.5	11.6	23.1	17.4
Lithuanian	73.9	6.7	80.6	21.1	67.2	88.3	4.2	5.5	9.7	1.4
Tatar	69.3	9.6	78.9	29.3	61.8	91.1	1.3	5.3	6.6	0.8
Other	71.0	4.0	75.0	23.4	60.6	84.0	4.7	5.3	10.0	2.0
Latvia										
Latvian	98.1	0.9	99.0	1.8	45.3	47.1	–	–	–	0.4
Russian	98.7	0.9	99.6	–	–	–	1.2	17.1	18.3	1.4
Belorussian	43.6	7.2	50.8	53.3	34.5	87.8	2.5	11.8	14.3	0.9
Polish	44.4	–	44.4	39.1	42.6	81.7	13.1	23.5	36.6	5.7
Ukrainian	53.9	13.7	67.6	45.2	47.2	92.4	0.7	5.1	5.8	0.4
Lithuanian	79.3	4.5	83.8	5.8	29.8	35.6	14.3	40.7	55.0	0.6
Jewish	46.2	3.2	49.4	52.3	36.0	88.3	1.2	20.3	21.5	5.7
Gypsy	72.5	1.6	74.1	3.7	24.5	28.2	23.5	41.1	64.6	0.7
Estonian	65.4	9.9	75.3	15.4	34.6	50.0	19.1	34.0	53.1	0.6
Tatar	59.0	9.8	68.8	40.2	54.5	94.7	0.4	3.8	4.2	2.1
Other	62.6	4.8	67.4	31.8	55.4	87.2	4.4	6.8	11.2	3.2
Lithuania										
Lithuanian	99.5	0.2	99.7	0.2	34.8	35.0	–	–	–	0.8
Russian	97.8	1.5	99.3	–	–	–	2.0	30.8	32.8	1.7
Polish	92.4	–	92.4	3.8	55.2	59.0	3.2	10.6	13.8	1.8
Belorussian	52.3	7.7	60.0	40.7	46.6	87.3	1.3	9.6	10.9	6.0
Ukrainian	52.4	11.4	63.8	45.3	44.8	90.1	1.9	12.1	14.0	1.0
Jewish	61.9	1.1	63.0	35.0	37.7	72.7	2.8	33.4	36.2	3.5
Latvian	81.7	5.8	87.5	6.5	24.3	30.8	11.6	54.9	66.5	0.4
Tatar	24.0	3.0	27.0	35.2	43.4	78.6	21.2	16.7	37.9	21.7
Gypsy	89.9	0.9	90.8	2.6	30.2	32.8	6.7	37.8	44.5	1.3
Other	66.3	3.3	69.6	24.0	45.3	69.3	7.9	17.8	25.7	3.3

Source: Itogi vsesoiuznoi perepisi naseleniia 1970 goda. Natsional'nyi sostav naseleniia SSSR (Moscow: Statistika, 1973) 4: 273, 280, 317.

TABLE E.3

Urban-Rural Ethnic Differences in Baltic Republics
(in percent)

Nationality	Urban	Rural
Estonia		
Estonians	54.7	45.3
Russians	89.3	10.7
Ukrainians	87.5	12.5
Belorussians	90.8	9.2
Finns	59.8	40.2
Jews	97.7	2.3
Latvians	77.3	22.7
Poles	85.9	14.1
Lithuanians	81.6	18.4
Tatars	91.9	8.1
Others	61.9	38.1
Total	65.0	35.0
Latvia		
Latvians	51.7	48.3
Russians	79.7	20.3
Belorussians	62.8	37.2
Poles	68.0	32.0
Ukrainians	82.4	17.6
Lithuanians	42.1	57.9
Jews	99.1	0.9
Gypsies	71.2	28.8
Estonians	68.3	31.7
Tatars	89.4	10.6
Others	73.9	26.1
Total	62.5	37.5
Lithuania		
Lithuanians	45.9	54.1
Russians	84.9	15.1
Poles	39.8	60.2
Belorussians	83.7	16.3
Ukrainians	92.4	7.6
Jews	99.1	0.9
Latvians	50.6	49.4
Tatars	67.1	32.9
Gypsies	80.5	19.5
Others	76.7	23.3
Total	50.2	49.8

Source: Itogi vsesoiuznoi perepisi naseleniia 1970 goda. Natsional'nyi sostav naseleniia SSSR (Moscow: Statistika, 1974) 4: 273-75, 280-83, 317-20.

BIBLIOGRAPHY

MATERIALS IN ENGLISH FOR THE STUDY OF NATIONALITY GROUP SUPPORTS IN THE USSR

The writings listed in this bibliography have been selected by the authors of the present study from among many available in English concerning ethnic survival in the Soviet scene and, especially, the Baltic region of the Soviet West. The emphasis here is given to the most recent times and developments. Some titles pertain to earlier periods of modern life. These works support the entire inquiry, but especially relate to the retrospective investigation carried on in Chapter 2. Because the whole book is narrow in focus and unified in methodology, a subject category breakdown has been replaced in the organization of this list of titles by several classes of publications: (1) bibliographies, directories, and reference works; (2) documents and statistics; (3) methodological studies; (4) journals, newspapers, and serials; (5) other books; and (6) other articles and separate conference papers. A large quantity of additional material can be located by use of the footnotes and bibliographies abundant in the following entries.

BIBLIOGRAPHIES, DIRECTORIES, REFERENCE WORKS

"Bibliography of Bibliographies about General Soviet Nationality Problems. Recent Soviet Writings about Soviet Nationality Problems. Selected Readings," Soviet Nationality Problems. Edited by Edward Allworth. New York: Columbia University Press, 1971, pp. 257-81.

Braham, R. Jews in the Communist World, A Bibliography 1945-60. New York: Twayne, 1961.

Crowley, Edward L., et al., eds. Prominent Personalities in the U.S.S.R. Metuchen, N.J.: Scarecrow Press, 1968.

Directory of Soviet Officials. Union Republics, vol. 3. Central Intelligence Agency, May 1975.

Fluk, L. Jews in the Soviet Union: An Annotated Bibliography. New York: American Jewish Committee, Institute of Human Relations, 1975.

Hodnett, Grey, and Ogareff, Val. Leaders of the Soviet Republics 1955-1972. Canberra: Department of Political Science Research School of Social Sciences, Australian National University, 1973.

Jegers, Benjamins. Bibliography of Latvian Publications Published Outside Latvia 1940-1960. 2 vols. Stockholm: Daugava, 1968, 1972.

Kantautas, Adam, and Kantautas, Filomena. A Lithuanian Bibliography. Edmonton: University of Alberta Press, 1975.

Katz, Zev, et al., eds. Handbook of Major Soviet Nationalities. New York: Free Press, 1975.

Keefe, Eugene K., et al. Area Handbook for the Soviet Union. Washington, D.C.: U.S. Government Printing Office, 1971.

Kinder, Hermann, and Hilgemann, Werner. The Anchor Atlas of World History. Garden City, N.Y.: Anchor Books, Anchor Press/Doubleday, 1971.

Parming, Marju Rink, and Parming, Tõnu. A Bibliography of English-Language Sources on Estonia. New York: Estonian Learned Society in America, 1974.

Pugevicius, C., ed. World Lithuanian Roman Catholic Directory. New York: Lithuanian Roman Catholic Priests' League of America, 1975.

Suziedeles, Simas, et al., eds. Encyclopedia Lituanica. Vols. 1-4. Boston: Juozas Kapocius, 1970-75.

DOCUMENTS, STATISTICS

Altschuler, Mordecai. "Some Statistical Data on the Jews Among the Scientific Elite of the Soviet Union." Jewish Journal of Sociology 15, no. 1 (1973): 45-55.

____. "Some Statistics on Mixed Marriages Among Soviet Jews." Bulletin of Soviet and East European Jewish Affairs, no. 6 (1970): 30-32.

Brezhnev, Leonid. The Fiftieth Anniversary of the Union of the Soviet Socialist Republics. Moscow: Progress Publishers, 1972.

Chronicle of the Catholic Church in Lithuania (trans. from Lithuanian), nos. 4-13 in pamphlets. Maspeth, N.Y.: Lithuanian Roman Catholic Priests' League of America, 1973-77.

"The Chronicles of the Lithanian Catholic Church Continue Publication." Lituanus 21, no. 3 (1975): 64.

"A Declaration of the Lithuanian National People's Front." Lituanus 22, no. 1 (1976): 65-71.

"Declaration by the Priests of the Catholic Church in Lithuania Dated August 1969," Lituanus 19, no. 3 (1973): 46-53.

Decter, Moshe, ed. Redemption! Jewish Freedom Letters from Russia. New York: American Jewish Conference on Soviet Jewry, and the Conference on the Status of Soviet Jews, May 1970.

"Estonian and Latvian Memorandum to the Conference on Security and Cooperation—1975," Lituanus 21, no. 3 (1975): 65-73.

Käbin, Johannes (Ivan). Estonia Yesterday and Today. Moscow: Progress Publishers, 1971.

"Letter to Seventeen Latvian Communist Party Leaders." Congressional Record. 92d Cong., 2nd sess. February 15-22, 1972, 118, pt. 4: 4820-23.

Lithuanian American Community, Inc., ed. The Violations of Human Rights in Soviet Occupied Lithuania: A Report for 1971. Delran, N.J.: Lithuanian American Community, 1972.

____. The Violations of Human Rights in Soviet Occupied Lithuania: A Report for 1972. Delran, N.J.: Lithuanian American Community, 1973.

____. The Violations of Human Rights in Soviet Occupied Lithuania: A Report for 1973. Glenside, Pa.: Lithuanian American Community, 1974.

____. The Violations of Human Rights in Soviet Occupied Lithuania: A Report for 1974. Glenside, Pa.: Lithuanian American Community, 1975.

____. The Violations of Human Rights in Soviet Occupied Lithuania: A Report for 1975. Glenside, Pa.: Lithuanian American Community, 1976.

Mickiewicz, Ellen, ed. Handbook of Soviet Social Science Data. New York: Free Press, 1973.

"National and Religious Protests in Lithuania. From the Underground Chronicle of the Catholic Church in Lithuania," Lituanus 20, no. 2 (1974): 68-75; Litaunus 20, no. 3 (1974): 73-75; Litaunus 20, no. 4 (1974): 62-68.

No Greater Love and the Trial of a Christian in Soviet Occupied Lithuania. New York: Lithuanian Roman Catholic Priests' League of America, 1975.

"Roman Catholics in Latvia Petition USSR Government," UBA Information Service News Release no. 312, April 27, 1976.

Saunders, George, ed. Samizdat: Voices of the Soviet Opposition. New York: Monad Press (distributed by Pathfinder Press), 1974.

Sniečkus, A. Soviet Lithuania on the Road of Prosperity. Moscow: Progress Publishers, 1974.

"Two Memoranda to the United Nations from Soviet Occupied Estonia," Lituanus 21, no. 2 (1975): 64-75.

Two Memoranda to UNO from Estonia. Stockholm: Estonian Information Centre, 1974.

United Hebrew Immigrant Aid Society Service. "Interpretive Statement, 1975." Mimeographed. New York: United HIAS Service, 1975.

____. "Statistical Abstract, 1975." Mimeographed. New York: United HIAS Service, 1975.

Voss, A. Lenin's Behests and the Making of Soviet Latvia. Moscow: Progress Publishers, 1970.

METHODOLOGICAL STUDIES

Allworth, Edward. "Foreword." The Soviet West: Interplay between Nationality and Social Organization. Edited by Ralph S. Clem, pp. 5-8. New York: Praeger, 1975.

____. "Restating the Soviet Nationality Question," Soviet Nationality Problems. Edited by Edward Allworth, pp. 1-21. New York: Columbia University Press, 1971.

____, ed. Soviet Nationality Problems. New York: Columbia University Press, 1971.

Barth, Fredrick, ed. Ethnic Groups and Boundaries: The Social Organization of Culture Difference. Bergen-Oslo: Universitets Forlaget, 1969.

Berger, Peter, et al. The Homeless Mind: Modernization and Consciousness. New York: Random House, 1973.

Black, C. E. The Dynamics of Modernization. New York: Harper and Row, 1966.

Claude, Innis L. National Minorities: An International Problem. Cambridge, Mass.: Harvard University Press, 1955.

De Vos, George, and Romanucci-Ross, Lola, eds. Ethnic Identity: Cultural Continuities and Change. Palo Alto, Calif.: Mayfield, 1975.

Deutsch, Karl. Nationalism and Social Communication. 2d ed. Cambridge, Mass.: MIT Press, 1966.

Enloe, Cynthia H. Ethnic Conflict and Political Development. Boston: Little, Brown, 1973.

Francis, E. K. Interethnic Relations. An Essay in Sociological Theory. New York: Elsevier, 1976.

Glazer, Nathan, and Moynihan, Daniel P., eds. Ethnicity: Theory and Experience. Cambridge, Mass.: Harvard University Press, 1975.

Levy, Marion J., Jr. Modernization and the Structure of Societies. Princeton, N.J.: Princeton University Press, 1969.

Lewis, Robert A.; Rowland, Richard H.; and Clem, Ralph S. Nationality and Population Change in Russia and the USSR: An Evaluation of Census Data, 1897-1970. New York: Praeger, 1976.

Schermerhorn, R. A. Comparative Ethnic Relations: A Framework for Theory and Research. New York: Random House, 1970.

Shibutani, Tamotsu, and Kwan, Kian M. Ethnic Stratification: A Comparative Approach. New York: Macmillan, 1965.

Skotheim, Robert Allen. The Historian and the Climate of Opinion. Reading, Mass.: Addison-Wesley Publishing Company, 1969.

Zimmern, Alfred, ed. Modern Political Doctrines. London: Oxford University Press, 1939.

JOURNALS, NEWSPAPERS, SERIALS

Baltic Events. Published by Rein Taagepera (University of California-Irvine) and Juris Dreifelds (Brock University, Canada), a bi-monthly, 1973-76. (See also, Estonian Events.)

The Baltic Review. Stockholm: Baltic Humanitarian Association, 1946-49.

The Baltic Review. New York: Committees for a Free Estonia, Latvia and Lithuania, 1953-71.

Books Abroad. Norman: University of Oklahoma, 1927-76. (The Autumn 1973 issue was devoted to Baltic literature and contains an index of earlier articles.)

Bulletin of Baltic Studies. Nos. 1-8. New York: Association for the Advancement of Baltic Studies, 1970-71.

Bulletin of Soviet and East European Jewish Affairs. London: Institute of Jewish Affairs, World Jewish Congress, 1968-70. After 1970, called Soviet Jewish Affairs.

A Chronicle of Current Events. London: Amnesty International Publications, 1968-72.

A Chronicle of Human Rights in the USSR. New York: Khronika Press, 1972-77.

The Current Digest of the Soviet Press. 1970-76.

Dispersion and Unity. Jerusalem: World Zionist Organization, 1960-76.

Estonian Events. Published by Rein Taagepera (University of California–Irvine), 1967-72.

Jewish Frontier. New York: Labor Zionist Alliance, 1933-76.

Jewish Journal of Sociology. London: World Jewish Congress, 1959-76.

Jews in Eastern Europe. London: European Jewish Publications, 1959-76.

Journal of Baltic Studies. New York: Association for the Advancement of Baltic Studies, 1970-76.

Lituanus. Published primarily by the Lituanus Foundation, 1954-76.

Midstream. New York: Herzl Institute, 1955-76.

Newsletter From Behind the Iron Curtain. Stockholm: Estonian Information Centre, May 1947-76.

Problems of Communism. Washington, D.C.: U.S. Information Agency, 1952-76.

Soviet Jewish Affairs. London: Institute of Jewish Affairs, World Jewish Congress, 1971-76.

Soviet Sociology. White Plains, N.Y.: International Arts and Sciences Press, 1962-76.

Translations on USSR Economic Affairs. Washington, D.C.: U.S. Joint Publications Research Service, 1971-75.

UBA Information Service News Release series. New York: United Baltic Appeal/Baltic Appeal to the United Nations, 1966-76.

OTHER BOOKS

Anderson, Edgar. Latvia–Past and Present 1918-1968. Compiled and edited by E. Dobelis. Waverly, Ia.: Latvju grāmata, 1968.

Anderson, E. N. Nationalism and the Cultural Crisis in Prussia, 1806-1815. New York: Octagon Books, 1966.

Andrups, Janis, and Vitauts, Kalve. Latvian Literature. Stockholm: M. Goppers, 1954.

Babris, Peter J. Baltic Youth under Communism. Arlington Heights, Ill.: Research Publishers, 1967.

Baron, Salo. Modern Nationalism and Religion. New York: Harper and Bros., 1947.

Bilmanis, Alfred. A History of Latvia. Princeton, N.J.: Princeton University Press, 1951.

____. Latvia as an Independent State. Washington, D.C.: Latvian Legation, 1947.

Black, Cyril E. Rewriting Russian History. New York: Praeger, 1956.

Bobe, Mendel, et al. The Jews in Latvia. Tel Aviv: Association of Latvian and Estonia Jews in Israel, Ben-nun Press, 1971.

Bourdeaux, Michael, et al., eds. Religious Minorities in the Soviet Union. London: Minority Rights Group, 1973.

Brizgys, V. Religious Conditions in Lithuania under Soviet Russian Occupation. Chicago: Lithuanian Catholic Press, 1975.

Carr, E. H. The Bolshevik Revolution (1917-1923), vol. I. Middlesex, England, and Victoria, Australia: Penguin Books, 1971.

Chase, Thomas G. The Story of Lithuania. New York: Stratford House, 1946.

Clem, Ralph S., ed. The Soviet West: Interplay between Nationality and Social Organization. New York: Praeger, 1975.

Cuibe, Leonas. The Lutheran Church of Latvia in Chains. Stockholm: Vasteras, 1963.

Daumantas, Juozas. Fighters for Freedom. New York: Manyland Books, 1975.

Dunn, Stephen P. Cultural Processes in the Baltic Area Under Soviet Rule. Berkeley, Calif.: Institute of International Studies, 1966.

Estonian Theological Society in Exile—eximio Dominio (to the most Respected) Iohanni Kapp. Estonia Christiana. Uppsala, Sweden: Estonian Theological Society in Exile, 1965.

Frumkin, Jacob, et al. Russian Jewry 1917-1967. New York: Thomas Yoseloff, 1969.

Gilboa, Yehoshua. The Black Years of Soviet Jewry. Boston: Little, Brown, 1971.

Gitelman, Zvi. Jewish Nationality and Soviet Politics. Princeton, N.J.: Princeton University Press, 1972.

Graham, Malbone W., Jr. New Governments of Eastern Europe. New York: Henry Holt, 1927.

Halecki, Oscar. Borderlands of Western Civilization. New York: Ronald Press, 1952.

Hayward, Max, and Fletcher, William. Religion and the Soviet State. New York: Praeger, 1969.

Heer, Nancy Whittier. Politics and History in the Soviet Union. Cambridge, Mass.: MIT Press, 1971.

Horm, Arvo. Phases of the Baltic Political Activities. Stockholm: Baltic Humanitarian Association, 1973.

Jackson, J. Hampden. Estonia. 2d ed. London: George Allen & Unwin, 1948.

Kalme, A. Total Terror. New York: Appleton-Century-Crofts, 1948.

Keylor, William R. Academy and Community: The Foundation of the French Historical Profession. Cambridge, Mass.: Harvard University Press, 1975.

Kochan, Lionel, ed. The Jews in Soviet Russia Since 1917. 2d ed. London: Oxford University Press, 1972.

Koressaar, V., and Rannit, A., eds. Estonian Poetry and Language. Stockholm: Kirjastus Vaba Eesti [for] Estonian Learned Society in America, 1965.

Korey, William. The Soviet Cage. New York: Viking Press, 1973.

Künnapas, Teodor; Järvesoo, Elmar; and Susi, Heino. "Higher Education and Scientific Research in Soviet Estonia." In A Case Study of a Soviet Republic: The Estonian SSR. Edited by Tõnu Parming and Elmar Järvesoo. Boulder, Colo.: Westview Press, forthcoming.

Nirk, Endel. Estonian Literature. Tallinn: Eesti Raamat, 1970.

Page, Stanley W. The Formation of the Baltic States. Cambridge, Mass.: Harvard University Press, 1959.

Reshetar, John S., Jr. The Soviet Polity: Government and Politics in the U.S.S.R. New York: Dodd Mead & Co., 1971.

Rigby, T. H. Communist Party Membership in the U.S.S.R. 1917-1967. Princeton, N.J.: Princeton University Press, 1968.

Rimaitis, J. Religion in Lithuania. Vilnius: Gintaras, 1971.

Royal Institute of International Affairs. The Baltic States. London: Oxford University Press, 1938.

Rusinek, Alla. Like a Song, Like a Dream. New York: Charles Scribner's Sons, 1973.

Schroeter, Leonard. The Last Exodus. New York: Universe Books, 1974.

Senn, Alfred. The Emergence of Modern Lithuania. New York: Columbia University Press, 1959.

Silde, Adolfs. Resistance Movement in Latvia. Stockholm: Latvian National Foundation, 1972.

Smolar, B. Soviet Jewry Today and Tomorrow. New York: Macmillan, 1971.

Spekke, Arnolds. History of Latvia. Stockholm: M. Goppers, 1957.

Szporluk, Roman, ed. The Influence of East Europe and the Soviet West on the USSR. New York: Praeger, 1975.

Tillett, Lowell. The Great Friendship: Soviet Historians on the Non-Russian Nationalities. Chapel Hill: University of North Carolina Press, 1969.

Uustalu, Evald. The History of Estonian People. London: Boreas, 1952.

Vardys, V. Stanley, ed. Lithuania Under the Soviets. New York: Praeger, 1965.

Von Rauch, Georg. The Baltic States. Berkeley: University of California Press, 1974.

Vööbus, Arthur. Studies in the History of the Estonian People. 3 vols. Stockholm: Estonian Theological Society in Exile, 1969-74. Issued as papers of the Estonian Theological Society in Exile, nos. 18, 19, 26.

Widmer, Michael J. "Nationalism and Communism in Latvia: The Latvian Communist Party Under Soviet Rule." Ph.D. dissertation, Harvard University, 1969.

Ziedonis, Arvids, Jr., et al., eds. Baltic History. Columbus: Association for the Advancement of Baltic Studies, Ohio State University, 1974.

____. Baltic Literature and Linguistics. Columbus: Association for the Advancement of Baltic Studies, Ohio State University, 1973.

____. Problems of Mininations: Baltic Perspectives. San Jose, Calif.: Association for the Advancement of Baltic Studies, 1973.

OTHER ARTICLES, SEPARATE CONFERENCE PAPERS

Allworth, Edward. "Nationality Group Rights in the Soviet Union." In U.S., Congress, House, Subcommittee on Europe, Committee on Foreign Affairs. Détente: Hearings. 93rd Cong., 2d sess. Washington, D.C.: Government Printing Office, 1974, pp. 327-38.

Armstrong, John. "The Jewish Predicament in the Soviet Union." Midstream 17, pt. 1, no. 1 (1971): 27-31.

Antanaitis, Algirdas. "New Trends in the Soviet-Lithuanian Novel." Lituanus 16, no. 2 (1970): 13-19.

Bilinsky, Yaroslav. "The Background of Contemporary Politics in the Baltic Republics and the Ukraine: Comparisons and Contrasts." Problems of Mininations: Baltic Perspectives. Edited by Arvids Ziedonis, Jr., et al., pp. 89-122. San Jose, Calif.: Association for the Advancement of Baltic Studies, 1973.

Blit, Lucian. "The Insoluble Problem: Church and State in Poland." Religion in Communist Lands 1, no. 3 (May-June 1973): 8-11.

Bociurkiw, Bohdan. "Religious Dissent in the USSR: Lithuanian Catholics." Paper presented at the Banff 1974 International Conference of the American Association of Slavic Studies, the British Universities' Association of Slavists, the British National Association for Soviet and East European Studies, and the Canadian Association of Slavists, September 4, 1974, at Banff, Alberta, Canada.

____. "The Shaping of Soviet Religious Policy." Problems of Communism 23, no. 3 (May-June 1973): 37-51.

____. "Soviet Religious Policy and the Status of Judaism in the USSR." Bulletin of Soviet and East European Jewish Affairs, no. 6 (1970): 13-19.

____. "Soviet Research on Religion and Atheism Since 1945." Religion in Communist Lands 2, no. 1 (January-February 1974): 11-16.

Budreckis, Algirdas. "Liberation Attempts from Abroad." Lithuania 700 Years. Edited by Albertas Gerutis. 3rd rev. ed. New York: Manyland Books, 1969.

____. "Lithuanian Resistance 1940-52." Lithuania 700 Years. Edited by Albertas Gerutis. 3rd rev. ed. New York: Manyland Books, 1969.

Checinski, Michael. "Soviet Jews and Higher Education." Soviet Jewish Affairs 3, no. 2 (1973): 3-16.

Dreifelds, Juris. "Characteristics and Trends of Two Demographic Variables in the Latvian S.S.R." Bulletin of Baltic Studies, no. 8 (Winter 1971): 10-17.

_____. "Trends in Nationalism in Soviet Latvia Since 1964." Paper presented at the Symposium on Nationalism in the USSR and Eastern Europe under Brezhnev and Kosygin, October 1975, at University of Detroit.

Dreyer, Jacob. "Dissent in the USSR and the Jewish Question." Midstream 17, pt. 1 (March 1971): 7-20.

Ebner, David. "A Demographic Study of the Latvian Jewish Population Between the Two World Wars." New York. Typescript.

Ekmanis, Rolfs. "Soviet Attitudes Towards Pre-Soviet Latvian Writers." Journal of Baltic Studies no. 3 (Spring 1972): 44-70.

Ettinger, Shmuel. "Prospects for Jewish Culture in the USSR." Dispersion and Unity 17/18 (1973): 139-48.

Fletcher, William C. "Religious Dissent in the USSR in the 1960s." Slavic Review 30, no. 2 (June 1971): 298-316.

Friedberg, Maurice. "Jewish Ethnicity in the Soviet Union." Midstream 18, no. 7 (1972): 54-62.

_____. "The Plight of Soviet Jews." Problems of Communism 19, no. 6 (December 1970): 17-26.

Gantskaia, O. A., and Debets, G. F. "O graficheskom izobrazhenii rezul'tatov statisticheskogo obsledovaniia mezhnatsional'nikh brakov." Trans. as "On the Graphic Representation of a Statistical Survey of Inter-ethnic Marriages." Sovetskaia etnografiia, no. 3 (1966): 110-18. Trans. in Soviet Sociology 6, no. 4 (1968): 45-55.

Garber, David. "Choir and Drama in Riga." Soviet Jewish Affairs 4, no. 1 (1974): 39-44.

George, Emmett. "Party Response to Lithuanian Unrest." The Soviet West. Edited by Ralph S. Clem, pp. 90-105. New York: Praeger, 1975.

Gerutis, Albertas. "Independent Lithuania." Lithuania 700 Years. Edited by Albertas Gerutis. 3rd rev. ed. New York: Manyland Books, 1969.

_____. "Occupied Lithuania." Lithuania 700 Years. Edited by Albertas Gerutis. 3rd rev. ed. New York: Manyland Books, 1969.

Gitelman, Zvi. "Assimilation, Acculturation, and National Consciousness Among Soviet Jews." New York: Synagogue Council of America, 1973.

____. "The Jews," Problems of Communism 16, no. 5 (1967): 92-101.

____. "Values, Opinions, and Attitudes of Soviet Jewish Emigres." Paper prepared for delivery at the meeting of the American Association for the Advancement of Slavic Studies, October 9-11, 1975, Atlanta, Ga.

Greenbaum, Alfred. "Soviet Nationality Policy and the Problem of the 'Fluid' Nationalities." Jews and Non-Jews in Eastern Europe. Edited by Bela Vago and George Mosse, pp. 257-69. Jerusalem: Israel Universities Press, 1974.

Grinius, Jonas. "Literature and the Arts in Captive Lithuania." Lithuania under the Soviets. Edited by V. Stanley Vardys. New York: Praeger, 1965.

Grodner, David. "In Soviet Poland and Lithuania." Contemporary Jewish Record 4, no. 2 (1941): 136-47.

Grossman, Mary Ann. "Soviet Efforts at the Socioeconomic Integration of Latvians." The Soviet West. Edited by Ralph S. Clem, pp. 71-89. New York: Praeger, 1975.

Harned, Frederic T. "Latvia and the Latvians." Handbook of Major Soviet Nationalities. Edited by Zev Katz et al., pp. 94-117. New York: Free Press, 1975.

____. "Lithuania and the Lithuanians." Handbook of Major Soviet Nationalities. Edited by Zev Katz et al., pp. 118-40. New York: Free Press, 1975.

Ivask, Ivar. "Recent Trends in Estonian Poetry." Books Abroad 42, no. 4 (Autumn 1968): 517-20.

____, ed. First Conference on Baltic Studies: A Summary of Proceedings. Tacoma, Wash.: Pacific Lutheran University, 1970.

Ivinskis, Zenonas. "Lithuania during the War: Resistance against the Soviet and the Nazi Occupants." Lithuania under the Soviets. Edited by V. Stanley Vardys. New York: Praeger, 1965.

Jakstas, Juozas. "Lithuania to World War I," Lithuania 700 Years. Edited by Albertas Gerutis. 3rd rev. ed. New York: Manyland Books, 1969.

Järvesoo, Elmar. "The Economic Transformation of Postwar Estonia." A Case Study of a Soviet Republic: The Estonian SSR. Edited by Tõnu Parming and Elmar Järvesoo. Boulder, Colo.: Westview Press, forthcoming.

Jüriado, Andres. "Nationalism vs. Socialism in Soviet Estonian Drama." Lituanus 19, no. 2 (1973): 23-42.

Kass, Norman. "Youth of the Lithuanian SSR and the Question of Nationality Divisiveness." The Soviet West. Edited by Ralph S. Clem, pp. 134-48. New York: Praeger, 1975.

Katz, Zev. "The New Nationalism in the USSR." Midstream 19, pt. 2 (1973): 3-13.

Kavolis, Vytautas. "Images of Young People in Soviet Lithuanian Literature." Lituanus 16, no. 2 (1970): 38-48.

Kholmogorov, A. I. Internatsional'nye cherty Sovetskikh natsii (na materialakh konkretno-sotsiologicheskikh issledovanii v Pribaltike. Moscow: "Mysl'," Publishers, 1970. Trans. in Soviet Sociology 11, no. 3/4 (Winter-Spring, 1972-73): 211-327; 12, no. 1 (Summer 1973): 3-33; 12, no. 2 (Fall 1973): 27-68.

King, Gundar J., and Dreifelds, Juris. "Demographic Changes in Latvia." Problems of Mininations: Baltic Perspectives. Edited by Arvids Ziedonis, Jr., et al., pp. 131-36. San Jose, Calif.: Association for the Advancement of Baltic Studies, 1973.

Korey, William. "The Soviet Jewish Future: Some Observations on the Recent Census." Midstream 20, no. 9 (1974): 37-50.

Koropeckyi, I. S. "National Income of the Baltic Republics in 1970." Journal of Baltic Studies no. 7 (Spring 1976): 61-73.

Kuperman, Yuri. "'No Places!' The Jewish Outsider in the Soviet Union." Soviet Jewish Affairs 3, no. 2 (1973): 17-25.

Kurman, George. "Estonian Literature in Soviet Estonia Since 1940." A Case Study of a Soviet Republic: The Estonian SSR. Edited by Tõnu Parming and Elmar Järvesoo. Boulder, Colo.: Westview Press, forthcoming.

Lapid (Perakh), Mordecai. "The Memorial at Rumbuli." Jewish Frontier 38, no. 6 (June 1971): 10-19.

Latvian Evangelical Lutheran Church of New York. Memorandum in Support of Proposed Resolution Regarding Christians in Estonia, Latvia and Lithuania." Mimeographed. New York: Latvian Evangelical Lutheran Church of New York, December 1973.

Lawrence, John. "Observations on Religion and Atheism in Soviet Society." Religion in Communist Lands 1, nos. 4-5 (July-October 1973): 18-23.

Leimanis, Eizens. "The Polytechnical Institute of Riga and Its Role in the Development of Science." Journal of Baltic Studies 3 (Summer 1972): 113-23.

Levin, Dov. "Jews in the Soviet Lithuanian Forces in World War II: The Nationality Factor." Soviet Jewish Affairs 3, no. 1 (1973): 57-64.

____. "The Jews and the Sovietization of Latvia." Soviet Jewish Affairs 5, no. 1 (1975): 39-56.

Lipset, Harry. "The Status of National Minority Languages in Soviet Education." Soviet Studies 19, no. 2 (October 1967): 181-89.

Loeber, Dietrich A. "Baltic Authors under Soviet Law: Regular Publishing and Samizdat." Problems of Mininations: Baltic Perspectives. Edited by Arvids Ziedonis, Jr., et al., pp. 175-92. San Jose, Calif.: Association for the Advancement of Baltic Studies, 1973.

Lutheran World Federation. "Lutheran World Federation President Visits Lutherans in USSR." Religion in Communist Dominated Areas 11, nos. 7-9 (July-September 1972): 130-31.

McDowell, Jennifer. "Soviet Civil Ceremonies." Journal for the Scientific Study of Religion 13, no. 3 (1974): 265-81.

Maciuika, Benedict V. "Acculturation and Socialization in the Soviet Baltic Republics." Lituanus 18, no. 4 (1972): 26-34.

____. "The Apparat of Political Socialization in Lithuania: Structure and Performance." Problems of Mininations: Baltic Perspectives.

Edited by Arvids Ziedonis, Jr., et al., pp. 151-60. San Jose, Calif.: Association for the Advancement of Baltic Studies, 1973.

____. "The Role of the Baltic Republics in the Economy of the USSR." Journal of Baltic Studies 3, no. 1 (Spring 1972): 18-25.

Mažeika, Povilas A. "Russian Objectives in the Baltic Countries." Problems of Mininations: Baltic Perspectives. Edited by Arvids Ziedonis, Jr., et al., pp. 123-28. San Jose, Calif.: Association for the Advancement of Baltic Studies, 1973.

Medvedev, Roy A. "Socialist Democracy and Socialist Economics." On Socialist Democracy. New York: Alfred A. Knopf, 1975, pp. 231-73.

Melngaile, Valda. "The Sense of History in Recent Soviet Latvian Poetry." Journal of Baltic Studies 6, nos. 2-3 (Summer-Fall 1975): 130-40.

Minkiavichus, Y. "Some Aspects of Relationship between Nationalism and Religion." Politicheskoe Samoobrazovanie, no. 2 (1973), pp. 106-11. Reported in Religion in Communist Dominated Areas 13, nos. 10-12 (October-December 1974): 166-68.

Newth, J. A. "Jews in the Soviet Intelligentsia—Some Recent Developments." Bulletin of Soviet and East European Jewish Affairs, no. 2 (1968), chapter 7, pp. 1-12.

____. "A Statistical Study of Intermarriage Among Jews in Vilnius." Bulletin of Soviet and East European Jewish Affairs, no. 1 (1968): 64-69.

Parente, William. "The Nationalities Revival in the USSR." Midstream 17, pt. 2, no. 7 (1971): 59-65.

Parming, Tönu. "Developments in Nationalism in Soviet Estonia Since 1964." Paper presented at the Symposium on Nationalism in the USSR and Eastern Europe under Brezhnev and Kosygin, October 1975, at University of Detroit.

____. "The Impact of Demographic Changes on Ethnic Processes in Soviet Estonia." Paper presented at the Conference on Population Change and the Soviet Nationality Question, December 1975, at Columbia University.

____. "Population Changes in Estonia, 1935-1970." Population Studies 26, no. 1 (March 1972): 53-78.

Penikis, Janis J. "Comparisons of Baltic Political Cultures." Paper presented at the Third Conference on Baltic Studies, 1972, at University of Toronto. Abstracted in Problems of Mininations: Baltic Perspectives. Edited by Arvids Ziedonis, Jr., et al., p. 65. San Jose, Calif.: Association for the Advancement of Baltic Studies, 1973.

Pennar, Jaan. "Nationalism in the Soviet Baltics." Ethnic Minorities in the Soviet Union. Edited by Erich Goldhagen, pp. 198-215. New York: Praeger, 1968.

____. "Soviet Nationality Policy and the Estonian Communist Elite," A Case Study of a Soviet Republic: The Estonian SSR. Edited by Tõnu Parming and Elmar Järvesoo. Boulder, Colo.: Westview Press, forthcoming.

Pincus, Chasya. "Adolescent Russian Immigrants in Israel." Israel and the Diaspora an Indivisible Entity. Jerusalem: Annual of the Office for Economic and Social Research, The Jewish Agency.

Pospielovsky, Dimitry. "The Kaunas Riots and the National and Religious Tensions in the USSR." Radio Liberty Research Bulletin (May 31, 1972), pp. 127-72.

"Printers of Gospels Arrested." Religion in Communist Dominated Areas 14, nos. 4-6 (April-June 1975): 74-75.

Puzinas, Jonas. "The Origins of the Lithuanian Nation." Lithuania 700 Years. Edited by Albertas Gerutis. 3rd rev. ed. New York: Manyland Books, 1969.

____. "The Situation in Occupied Lithuania: Administration, Indoctrination and Russianization." Lituanus 19, no. 1 (1973): 55-72.

Rackauskas, J. A. "Education in Lithuania Prior to the Dissolution of the Jesuit Order (1773)." Lituanus 22, no. 1 (1976): 5-41.

____. "The Educational Commission of Poland and Lithuania 1773-1794: 200th Anniversary of Its Establishment." Lituanus 19, no. 4 (1973): 63-70.

Rakowska-Harmstone, Teresa. "The Dialectics of Nationalism in the USSR." Problems of Communism 23, no. 3 (May-June 1974): 1-22.

Ränk, Gustav. "Scholarship in Ethnography in the Estonian SSR." A Case Study of a Soviet Republic: The Estonian SSR. Edited by Tõnu Parming and Elmar Järvesoo. Boulder, Colo.: Westview Press, forthcoming.

Redlich, Shimon. "Jewish Appeals in the USSR: An Expression of National Revival." Soviet Jewish Affairs 4, no. 2 (1974): 24-37.

____. "The Jews in the Soviet Annexed Territories 1939-41." Soviet Jewish Affairs 1, no. 1 (1971): 81-90.

Remeikis, Thomas. "The Administration of Power: The Communist Party and the Soviet Government." Lithuania under the Soviets. Edited by V. Stanley Vardys, pp. 111-40. New York: Praeger, 1965.

____. "Nationalism in Soviet Lithuania Since 1964." Paper presented at the Conference on Nationalism in the USSR and Eastern Europe under Brezhnev and Kosygin, October 1975, at University of Detroit.

Rutman, Roman. "Jews and Dissenters: Connections and Divergences." Soviet Jewish Affairs 3, no. 2 (1973): 26-37.

____. "The Party and the Church in Soviet Estonia." A Case Study of a Soviet Republic: The Estonian SSR. Edited by Tõnu Parming and Elmar Järvesoo. Boulder, Colo.: Westview Press, forthcoming.

Salo, Vello. "Anti-Religious Rites in Estonia." Religion in Communist Lands 1, nos. 4-5 (July-October 1973): 28-33.

Sapiets, Janis. "The Baltic Republics." The Soviet Union and Eastern Europe: A Handbook. Edited by George Schöpflin. New York: Praeger, 1970.

"Self-Immolations and National Protest in Lithuania," Lituanus 18, no. 4 (Winter 1972): 58-72.

Shochat, Azriel. "Jews, Lithuanians, and Russians, 1939-1941." Jews and Non-Jews in Eastern Europe. Edited by Bela Vago and George Mosse, pp. 301-14. Jerusalem: Israel Universities Press, 1974.

Silbajoris, Rimvydas. "Challenge to Arcadia: Notes on Soviet Lithuanian Poetry." Lituanus 19, no. 2 (1973): 5-15.

____; Ziedonis, Arvids, Jr.; and Anderson, Edgar, eds. Second Conference on Baltic Studies: Summary of Proceedings. Norman, Okla.: Association for the Advancement of Slavic Studies, 1971.

Silenieks, Juris. "The Humanization of the Recent Soviet-Latvian Short Story." Lituanus 16, no. 2 (1970): 49-56.

"Sociology of Religion in the USSR." Social Compass 21, no. 2 (1974): 115-206.

"Soviet Cultural Policies in Lithuania," Lituanus 19, no. 2 (1973): 67-72.

Stramanis, Alfred. "Folklorist Embellishment in Soviet Latvian Drama." Journal of Baltic Studies 6, nos. 2-3 (Summer-Fall 1975): 153-61.

Suziedelis, Simas. "Lithuania from Medieval to Modern Times: A Historical Outline." Lithuania under the Soviets. Edited by V. Stanley Vardys, pp. 3-19. New York: Praeger, 1965.

Taagepera, Rein. "Dissimilarities Between the Northwestern Soviet Republics." Problems of Mininations: Baltic Perspectives. Edited by Arvids Ziedonis, Jr., et al., pp. 69-88. San Jose, Calif.: Association for the Advancement of Baltic Studies, 1973.

____. "Estonia and the Estonians." Handbook of Major Soviet Nationalities. Edited by Zev Katz et al., pp. 75-93. New York: Free Press, 1975.

____. "Estonia: Uppity Satellite." Nation, May 7, 1973, pp. 585-88.

____. "The Impact of the New Left on Estonia." East European Quarterly 10, no. 1 (Spring 1976): 43-51.

____. "Nationalism, Collaborationism and New Leftism in Soviet Estonia," A Case Study of a Soviet Republic: The Estonian SSR. Edited by Tõnu Parming and Elmar Järvesoo. Boulder, Colo.: Westview Press, forthcoming.

____. "Nationalism in the Estonian Communist Party." Bulletin of the Institute for the Study of the USSR 17 (January 1970): 3-15.

____. "The Problem of Political Collaboration in Soviet Estonian Literature." Journal of Baltic Studies 6 (Spring 1975): 30-40.

Terentjeva, Ludmila. "Opredelenie sovei natsional'noi prinadlezhnosti podrostkami v natsional'no-smeshannykh sem'iakh." Sovetskaia etnografiia no. 3 (1969): 20-30. Trans. in Bulletin of Baltic Studies 6, no. 8 (December 1970): 5-11.

"This Is How It Happened." Bulletin of the Council of ECB Prisoners' Relatives, no. 18 (1974): 2-3. Reported in Religion in Communist Dominated Areas 14, nos. 1-3 (January-March 1975): 43-45.

Valgemäe, Mardi. "Drama and the Theatre Arts in the Estonian SSR." A Case Study of a Soviet Republic: The Estonian SSR. Edited by Tõnu Parming and Elmar Järvesoo. Boulder, Colo.: Westview Press, forthcoming.

____. "Recent Developments in Soviet Estonian Drama." Bulletin of the Institute for the Study of the USSR 16 (September 1969): 16-24.

Vardys, V. Stanley. "The Baltic Peoples." Problems of Communism 16, no. 5 (September-October 1967): 55-64.

____. "Independent Lithuania: A Profile." Lithuania under the Soviets. Edited by V. Stanley Vardys, pp. 21-46. New York: Praeger, 1965.

____. "Modernization and Baltic Nationalism." Problems of Communism 24, no. 5 (September-October 1975): 32-48.

____. "The Partisan Movement in Postwar Lithuania." Lithuania under the Soviets. Edited by V. Stanley Vardys, pp. 85-108. New York: Praeger, 1965.

____. "Protests in Lithuania Not Isolated." Lituanus 18, no. 2 (1972): 5-7.

____. "The Role of the Baltic States in the Soviet Union." The Influence of East Europe and the Soviet West on the USSR. Edited by Roman Szporluk, pp. 147-79. New York: Praeger, 1975.

____. "Soviet Social Engineering in Lithuania: An Appraisal." Lithuania under the Soviets. Edited by V. Stanley Vardys, pp. 237-59. New York: Praeger, 1965.

Vaškelis, Bronius. "The Assertion of Ethnic Identity via Myth and Folklore in Soviet Lithuania." Lituanus 19, no. 2 (Summer 1973): 16-27.

Vignieri, Vittorio. "Soviet Policy toward Religion in Lithuania: The Case of Roman Catholicism." Lithuania under the Soviets. Edited by V. Stanley Vardys. New York: Praeger, 1965.

Vikis-Freibergs, Vaira. "Echoes of the Dainas and the Search for Identity in Contemporary Latvian Poetry." Journal of Baltic Studies 6, no. 1 (Spring 1975): 17-29.

Weingard, Joan T. "Language and Literature in Estonia: Kulturpolitik or Natural Evolution?" The Soviet West. Edited by Ralph S. Clem, pp. 8-29. New York: Praeger, 1975.

Ziedonis, Arvids, Jr. "Contemporary Themes in the Literature of Soviet Latvia," Lituanus 16, no. 3 (1970): 51-75.

ABOUT THE EDITOR AND CONTRIBUTORS

EDWARD ALLWORTH, Director, Program on Soviet Nationality Problems, Columbia University, Ph.D. Columbia University (1959), is editor and coauthor of Soviet Nationality Problems (1971), The Nationality Question in Soviet Central Asia (1973), author of Soviet Asia: Bibliographies (1975), and other books. The graduate seminar in nationality problems that generated this book was taught by Professor Allworth, whose chapter provides the methodology about nationality support factors and the general proposition uniting the entire volume.

CHRISTOPHER DOERSAM, M.I.A. Columbia University (1975), Certificate of the Russian Institute (1975), Ph.D. candidate in political science, Columbia University, taught History of the USSR, Manhattan College, summer school 1975. He examines the dilemma faced by organized religion in a Soviet Western region under atheistic communism and suggests possible variant support factors for eponymous and other groups in the area.

JUDITH FLEMING, M.A. University of Washington (1975) in Russian studies, Ph.D. candidate in political science, Columbia University, emphasizes the central role of having "one's own" leaders governing their ethnic group and the dissatisfaction stimulated by imposing outsiders or even semicoopted insiders upon a given nationality. She evaluates the importance of ethnic leadership for group support in contemporary conditions.

JUOZAS A. KAZLAS, Ph.D. Yale University (1977) in political science, a teaching assistant in political science, Yale University, 1973-77, and recently a member of foreign policy task force staff, Public Agenda Foundation, has conducted extensive interviews with new arrivals in the Federal Republic of Germany from the USSR, mainly ethnic Germans. His chapter also employs interview data to question the conceptualization of ethnic relations in a dominant/subordinate arrangement, such as that obtaining today in the USSR, and to investigate the function of ethnic stereotypes in nationality group maintenance.

ELI M. LEDERHENDLER, M.A. Jewish Theological Seminary of America (1977) in Jewish history, and participant, Seminar in

Soviet Nationality Problems, Columbia University, 1975-76, has taught Hebrew language and Jewish history in Jewish schools since 1972. Lederhendler's chapter shows how expressed nationality dissatisfaction grows under modernized, comfortable economic conditions when an ethnic group mobilizes its internal cultural-identity support system to redress grievances focused entirely outside material wants.

KENNETH E. NYIRADY, M.A. SUNY at Binghamton (1976) in Russian history, is a Ph.D. candidate in Uralic Studies, Columbia University. Nyirady assesses the historian's contribution to supporting his ethnic group by analyzing the published output of Baltic history writers during two five-year periods, 1960-64 and 1970-74, showing changes over time and comparing different nationalities within the selected region to identify significant variations evident in the authorized printings.

TÖNU PARMING, Ph.D. Yale University (1976), assistant professor of sociology, University of Maryland, is author of The Collapse of Liberal Democracy and the Rise of Authoritarianism in Estonia (1975), "Population Changes in Estonia, 1935-1970," Population Studies, and other studies. Here, he looks at historical variations in nationality support factors, whose often subtle fluctuations provide an explanation for contemporary differences in nationality assertiveness among people of the Soviet Baltic region and, by extension, other modernized ethnic groups.

RICHARD P. SHRYOCK, M.A. Columbia University (1976), Ph.D. candidate in political science, Columbia University. He analyzes the impact of a pre-existing competence in economic management upon the morale and outlook of ethnic group leaders at the top and middle level in a non-Russian Soviet region and he connects selection of economic priorities with nationality discontent in the USSR, using the Baltic microcosm.

RELATED TITLES
Published by
Praeger Special Studies

NATIONALITY AND POPULATION CHANGE IN RUSSIA AND THE USSR: An Evaluation of Census Data, 1897-1970

Robert A. Lewis
Richard H. Rowland
Ralph S. Clem

SOVIET ASIA: BIBLIOGRAPHIES: A Compilation of Social Science and Humanities Sources on the Iranian, Mongolian, and Turkic Nationalities/With an Essay on the Soviet-Asian Controversy

Edward Allworth

DEMOGRAPHIC DEVELOPMENTS IN EASTERN EUROPE

edited by Leszek A. Kosinski

THE SOVIET WEST: Interplay between Nationality and Social Organization

edited by Ralph S. Clem

NONSTATE NATIONS IN INTERNATIONAL POLITICS: Comparative System Analyses

edited by Judy S. Bertelsen

SMALL STATES AND SEGMENTED SOCIETIES: National Political Integration in a Global Environment

edited by Stephanie G. Neuman

THE POLITICS OF DIVISION, PARTITION, AND UNIFICATION

edited by Ray Edward Johnston